fushigi yûgi

The Mysterious Play
VOL. 9: LOVER

Story & Art By
YÛ WATASE

FUSHIGI YÛGI
THE MYSTERIOUS PLAY
VOL. 9: LOVER
SHÔJO EDITION

STORY AND ART BY YUU WATASE

English Adaptation/Yuji Oniki
Translation Assist/Kaori Kawakubo Inoue
Touch-up & Lettering/Andy Ristaino
Cover Design/Hidemi Sahara
Graphics & Design/Hidemi Sahara
Editor/William Flanagan
Shôjo Edition Editor/Elizabeth Kawasaki

Editor in Chief, Books/Alvin Lu
Editor in Chief, Magazines/Marc Weidenbaum
VP, Publishing Licensing/Rika Inouye
VP, Sales & Product Marketing/Gonzalo Ferreyra
VP, Creative/Linda Espinosa
Publisher/Hyoe Narita

Printed in Canada

Published by VIZ Media, LLC
P.O. Box 77010
San Francisco, CA 94107

1st English edition published 1999

Shôjo Edition
10 9 8 7 6 5 4 3
First printing, October 2003
Third printing, October 2008

www.viz.com
store.viz.com

CONTENTS

Chapter Forty-Nine
Valley of Tears.. 5

Chapter Fifty
Ice Guardians.. 32

Chapter Fifty-One
A Hazardous Bargain..................................... 71

Chapter Fifty-Two
Mirage of Hell.. 99

Chapter Fifty-Three
Defiled Love...128

Chapter Fifty-Four
The Depths of Fear..159

Glossary...189

STORY THUS FAR

Chipper middle high-school girl Miaka is physically drawn into the world of a strange book—THE UNIVERSE OF THE FOUR GODS. Miaka is offered the role of the lead character, the Priestess of the god Suzaku, and is charged with a mission to save the nation of Hong-Nan, and in the process have her three wishes granted.

While Miaka makes a short trip back to the real world, her best friend Yui is sucked into the book only to suffer rape and manipulation, which drives her to attempt suicide. Now, Yui has become the Priestess of the god Seiryu, the bitter enemy of Suzaku and Miaka.

The only way for Miaka to gain back the trust of her former friend is to summon the god Suzaku and wish to be reconciled with Yui, so Miaka reenters the world of THE UNIVERSE OF THE FOUR GODS. The Seiryu warriors ruined Miaka's first attempt to summon Suzaku, but oracle Tai Yi-Jun has a new quest for Miaka and her Celestial Warriors of Suzaku—to obtain Shentso-Pao treasures of the other gods, which will allow them to summon the god Suzaku. In the northern country of Bei-Jia, Tamahome finds out where the first treasure is, and on his way back to tell the other Suzaku warriors, he runs into Yui. Bitterly, Yui tells him he's just a character in a book. Suzaku warrior Nuriko goes ahead to Black Mountain to find the treasure, but before the rest of the warriors could get there, Nuriko and Seiryu warrior Ashitare battle at the entrance, a fight that kills them both!

THE UNIVERSE OF THE FOUR GODS *is based on ancient China, but Japanese pronunciation of Chinese names differs slightly from their Chinese equivalents. Here is a short glossary of the Japanese pronunciation of the Chinese names in this graphic novel:*

CHINESE	JAPANESE	PERSON OR PLACE	MEANING
Xong Gui-Siu	Sô kishuku	Tamahome's Name	Demon Constellation
Hong-Nan	Konan	Southern Kingdom	Crimson South
Qu-Dong	Kutô	Eastern Kingdom	Gathered East
Bei-Jia	Hokkan	Northern Kingdom	Armored North
Xi-Lang	Sairô	Western Kingdom	West Tower
Shentso-Pao	Shinzahô	A Treasure	God's Seat Jewel
Tai Yi-Jun	Tai Itsukun	An Oracle	Preeminent Person
Teniao-Lan	Touran	A City	Unique Crow Orchid
Jie-Lian	Yuiren	Youngest Daughter	Connection & Lotus
Diedu	Kodoku	A Potion	Seduction Poison

CHAPTER FORTY-NINE
VALLEY OF TEARS

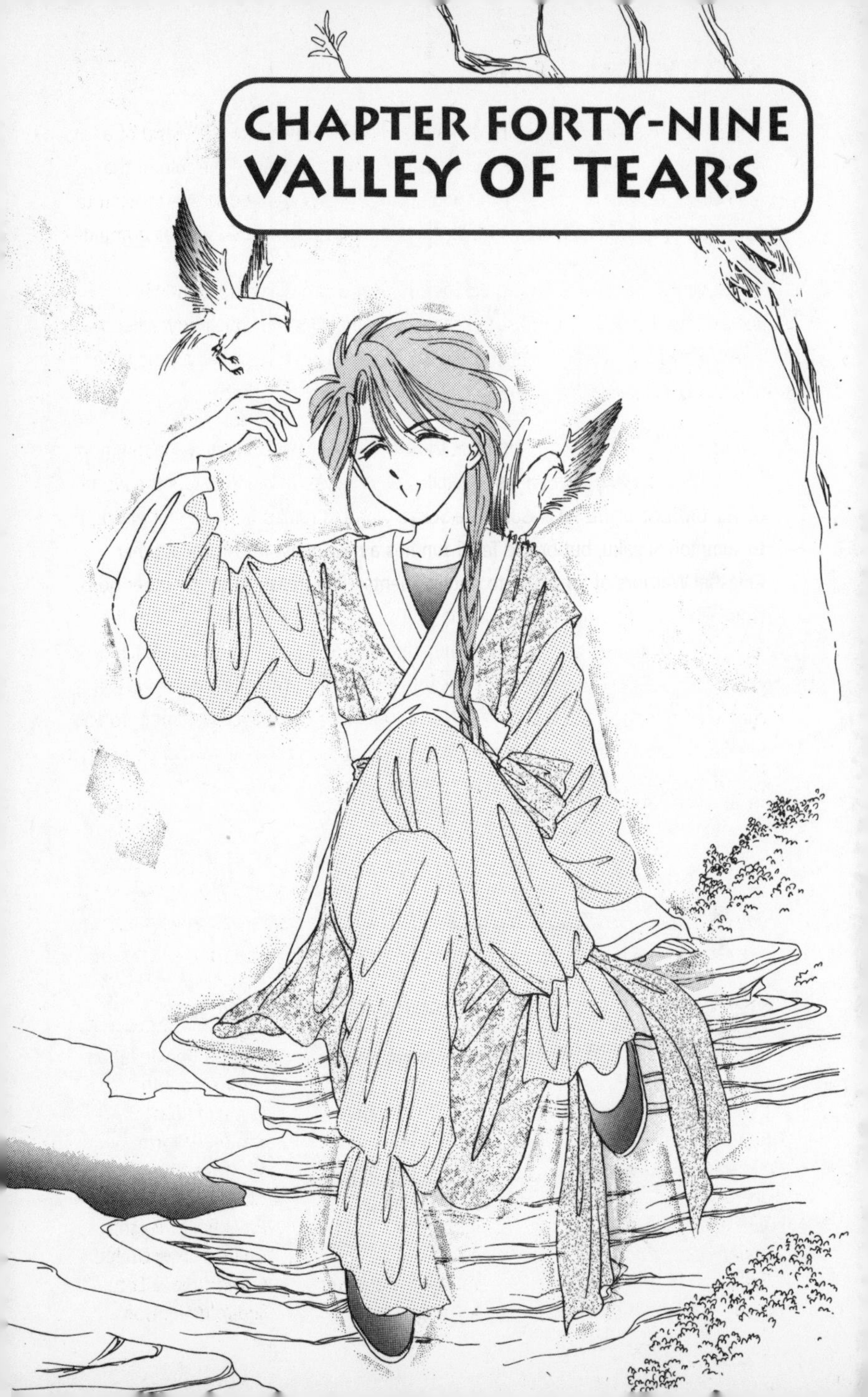

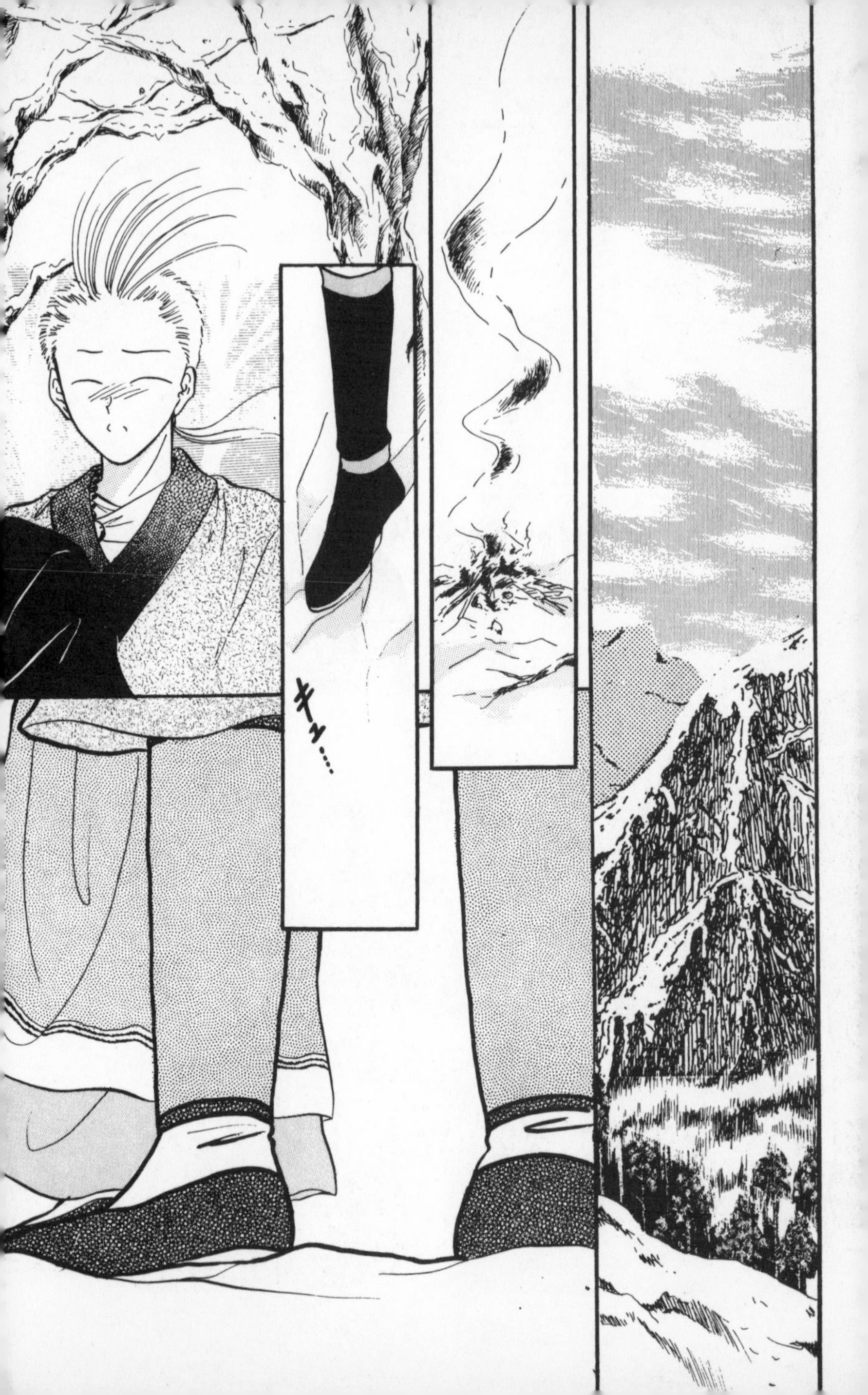
キュ…

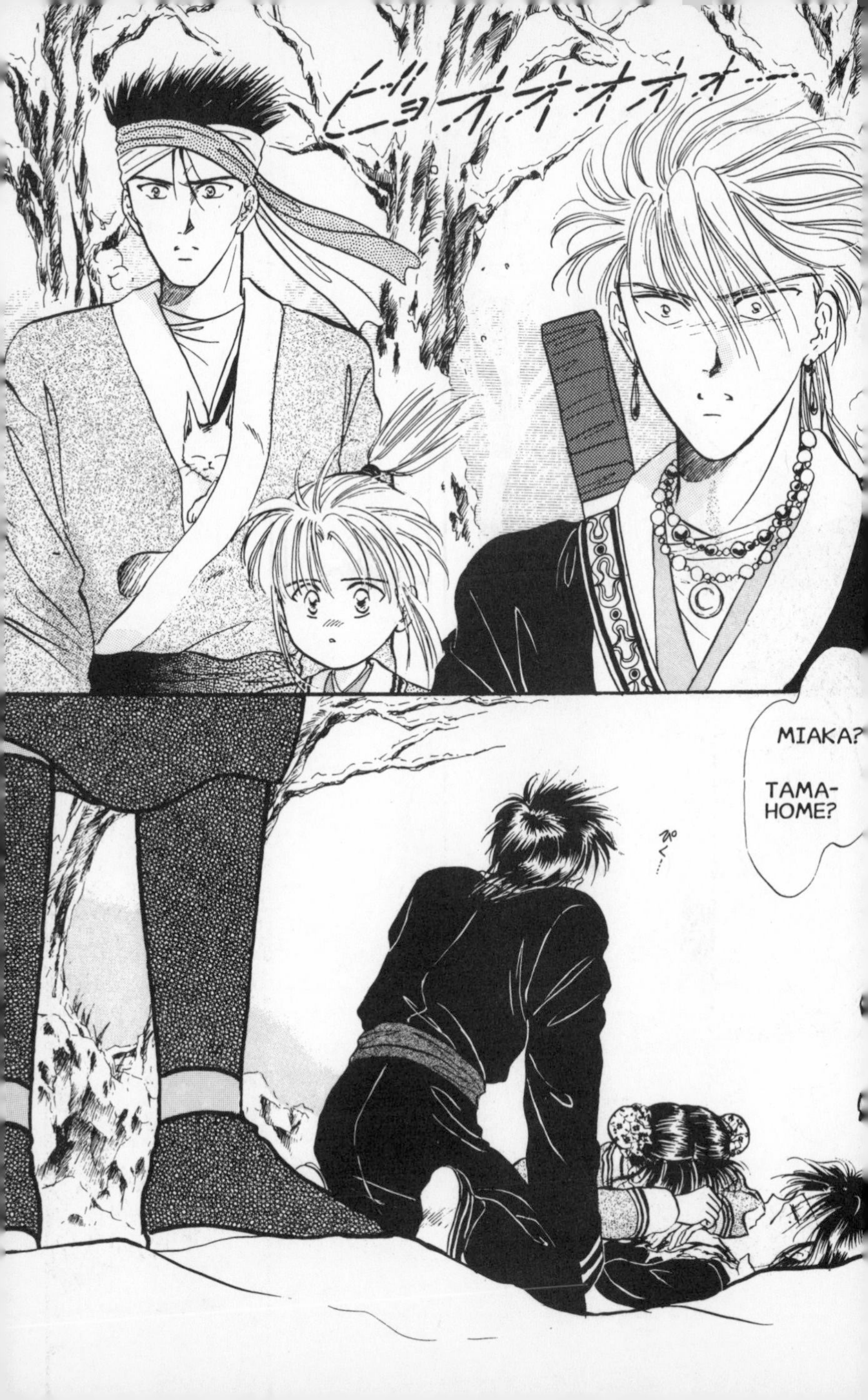
ビョオオオオオ……
MIAKA?
TAMA-HOME?
ぷく……

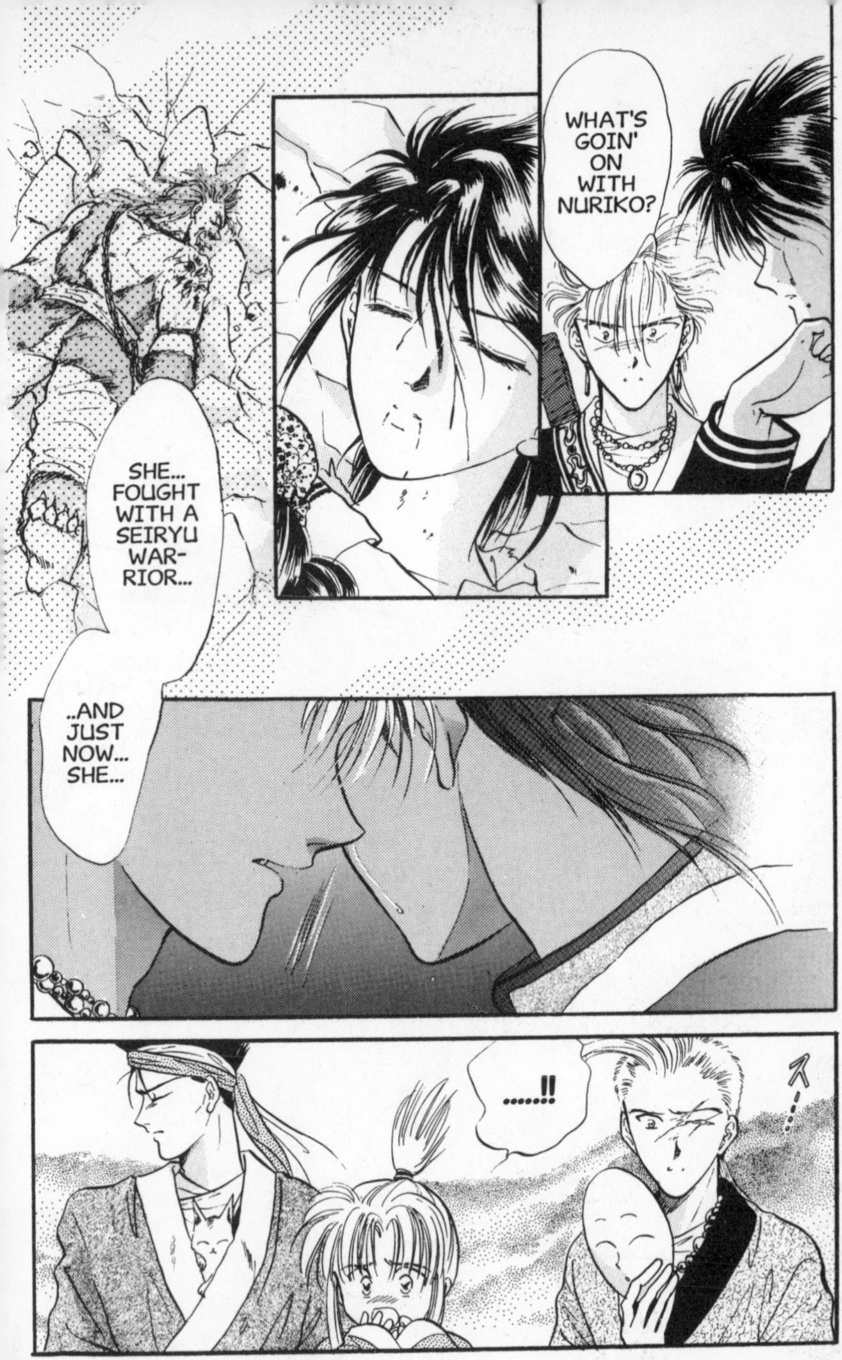
WHAT'S GOIN' ON WITH NURIKO?
SHE... FOUGHT WITH A SEIRYU WAR-RIOR...
..AND JUST NOW... SHE...
......!!
ス

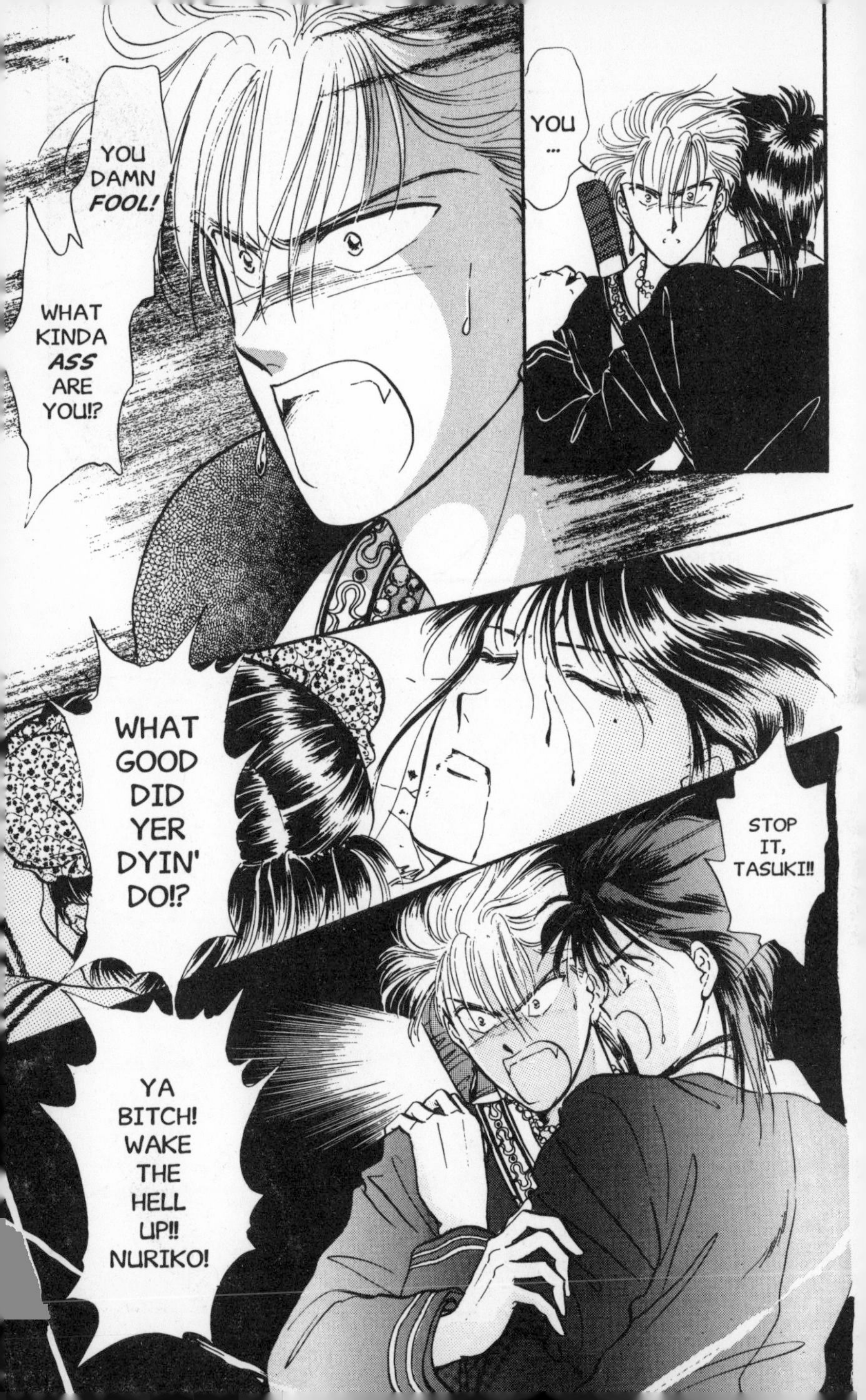
YOU ...
YOU DAMN FOOL!
WHAT KINDA ASS ARE YOU!?
WHAT GOOD DID YER DYIN' DO!?
STOP IT, TASUKI!!
YA BITCH! WAKE THE HELL UP!! NURIKO!

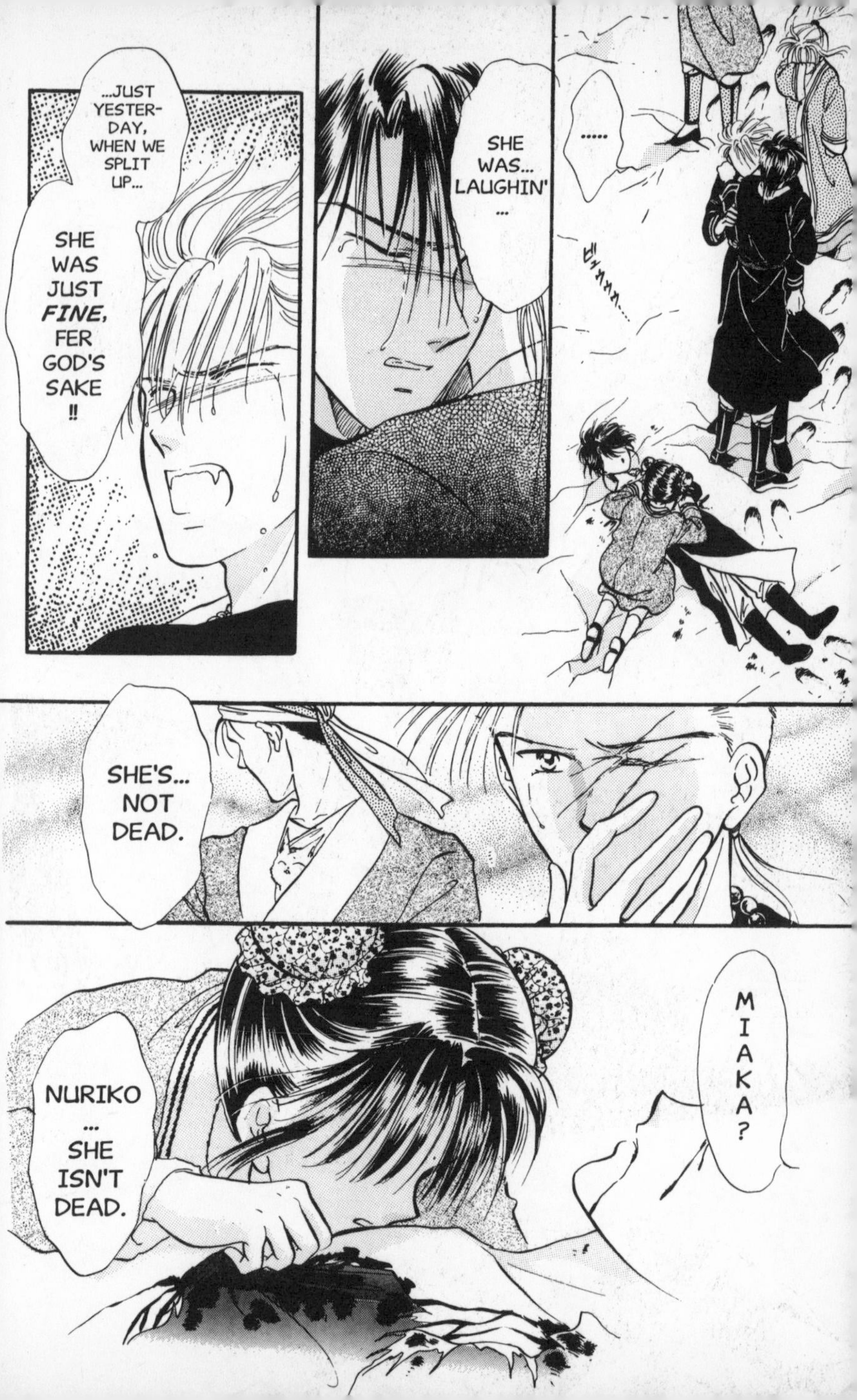
.....
SHE WAS... LAUGHIN'...
...JUST YESTER-DAY, WHEN WE SPLIT UP...
SHE WAS JUST ***FINE***, FER GOD'S SAKE!!
SHE'S... NOT DEAD.
MIAKA?
NURIKO... SHE ISN'T DEAD.

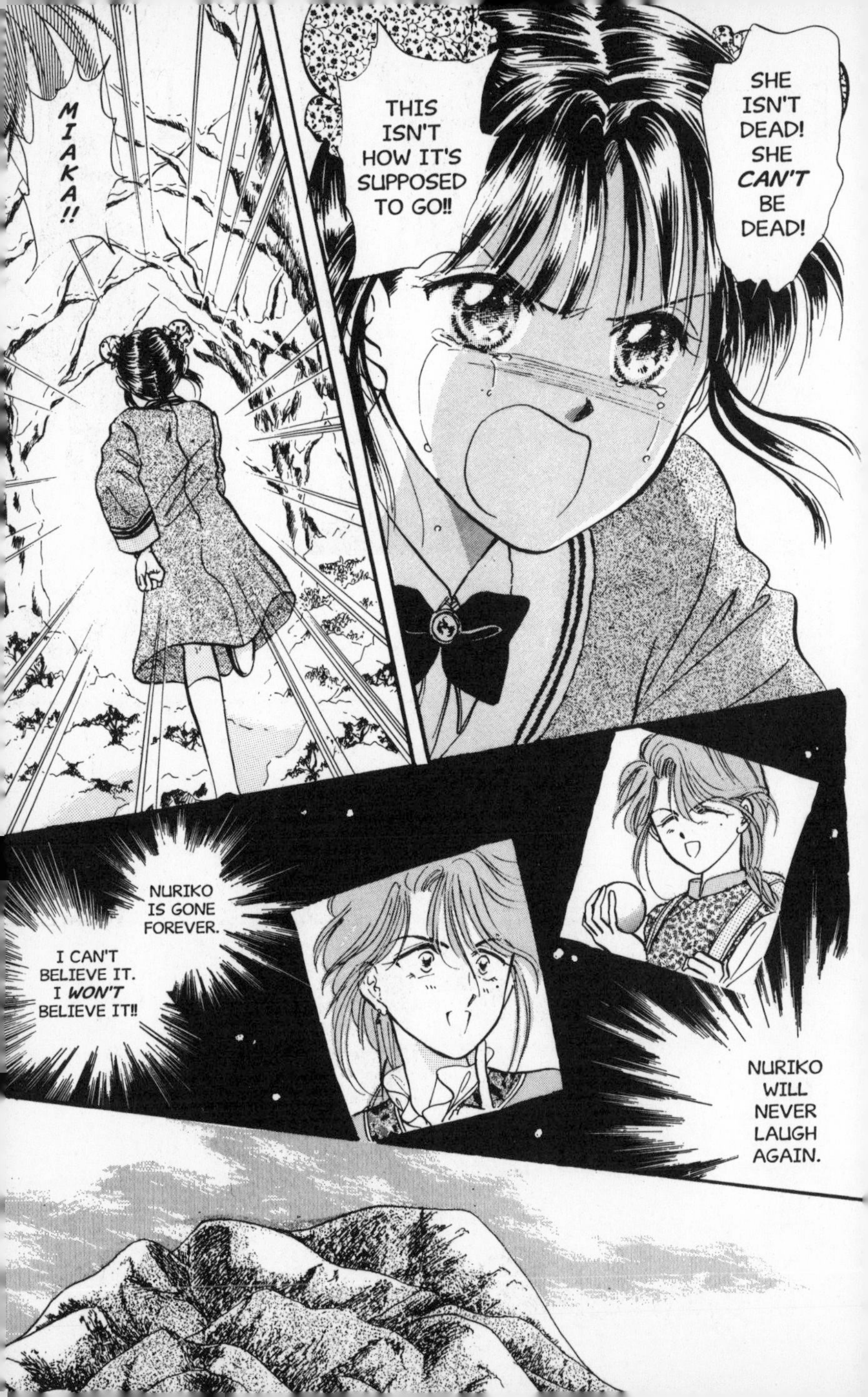

SHE ISN'T DEAD! SHE CAN'T BE DEAD!
THIS ISN'T HOW IT'S SUPPOSED TO GO!!
MIAKA!!
NURIKO IS GONE FOREVER.
I CAN'T BELIEVE IT. I WON'T BELIEVE IT!!
NURIKO WILL NEVER LAUGH AGAIN.

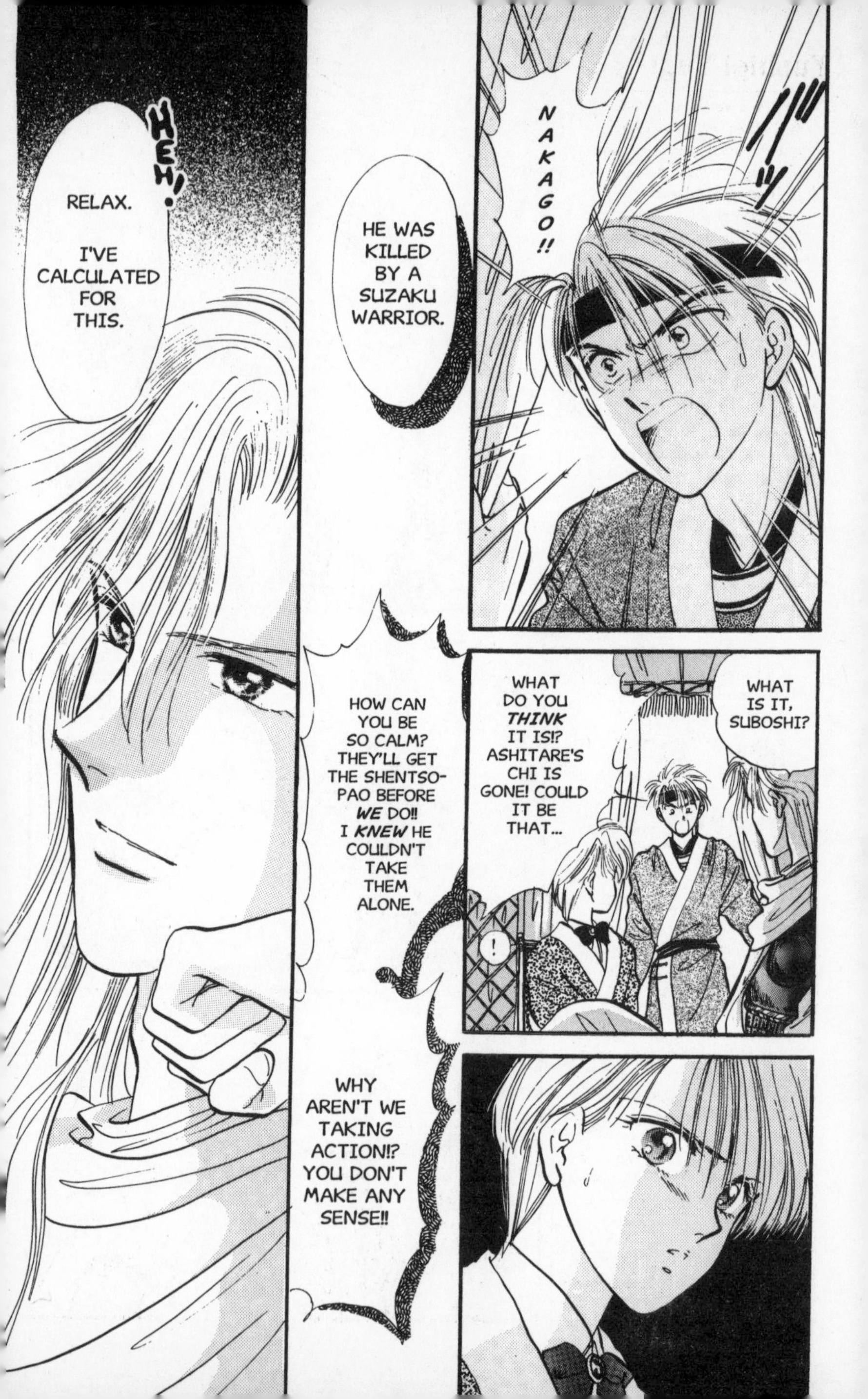
NAKAGO!!
HE WAS KILLED BY A SUZAKU WARRIOR.
WHAT IS IT, SUBOSHI?
WHAT DO YOU *THINK* IT IS!? ASHITARE'S CHI IS GONE! COULD IT BE THAT...
!
HOW CAN YOU BE SO CALM? THEY'LL GET THE SHENTSO-PAO BEFORE *WE* DO!! I *KNEW* HE COULDN'T TAKE THEM ALONE.
WHY AREN'T WE TAKING ACTION!? YOU DON'T MAKE ANY SENSE!!
HEH!
RELAX.
I'VE CALCULATED FOR THIS.

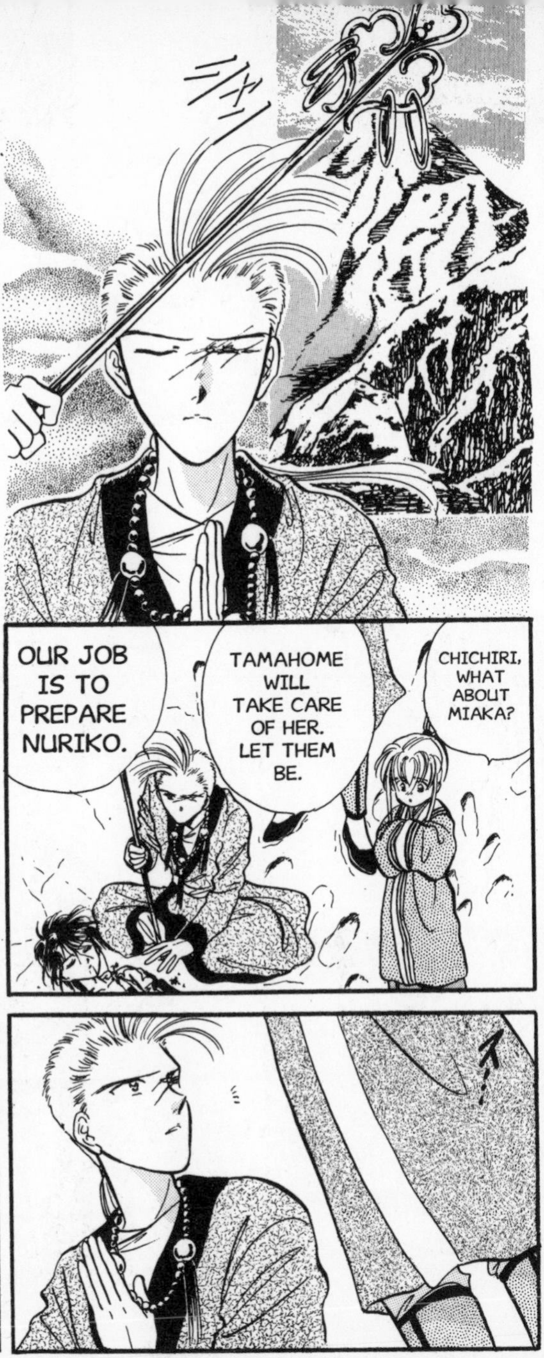
CHICHIRI, WHAT ABOUT MIAKA?
TAMAHOME WILL TAKE CARE OF HER. LET THEM BE.
OUR JOB IS TO PREPARE NURIKO.

Hello, and welcome to Volume 9. In the previous volume, I mentioned the pressure I was under, and I received many kind letters from you all expressing your concern. Thank you!

I can handle the work, but sometimes the psychological stress kicks in. But no matter how low I get, give me a couple of days and I bounce back.

To continue my Chinese travels from the previous volume... What really struck me about the night we had our royal feast in Xian was the number of foreign tourists! (I guess we're foreign in China, too.) I just couldn't help staring at them! The space was wide like a dance hall, and there was a stage in front where they danced and played ethnic music. I kept on taking pictures of all the extravagant ancient Chinese costumes! The food was...well...okay. Pretty princesses like the ones below would serve us food, wine, and other items.

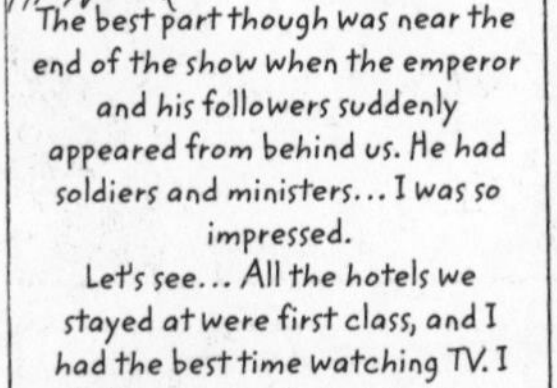
She looks like she's high-school age!

The best part though was near the end of the show when the emperor and his followers suddenly appeared from behind us. He had soldiers and ministers... I was so impressed.

Let's see... All the hotels we stayed at were first class, and I had the best time watching TV. I didn't understand what they were saying, but the comedy programs were funny, and they also had cooking shows! But the one I'd most like to see more of was about this young couple (an actress played the man), and the woman was a ghost or phantom. It had fighting and warriors. The clothes and atmosphere resembled the look I have in Fushigi Yûgi!

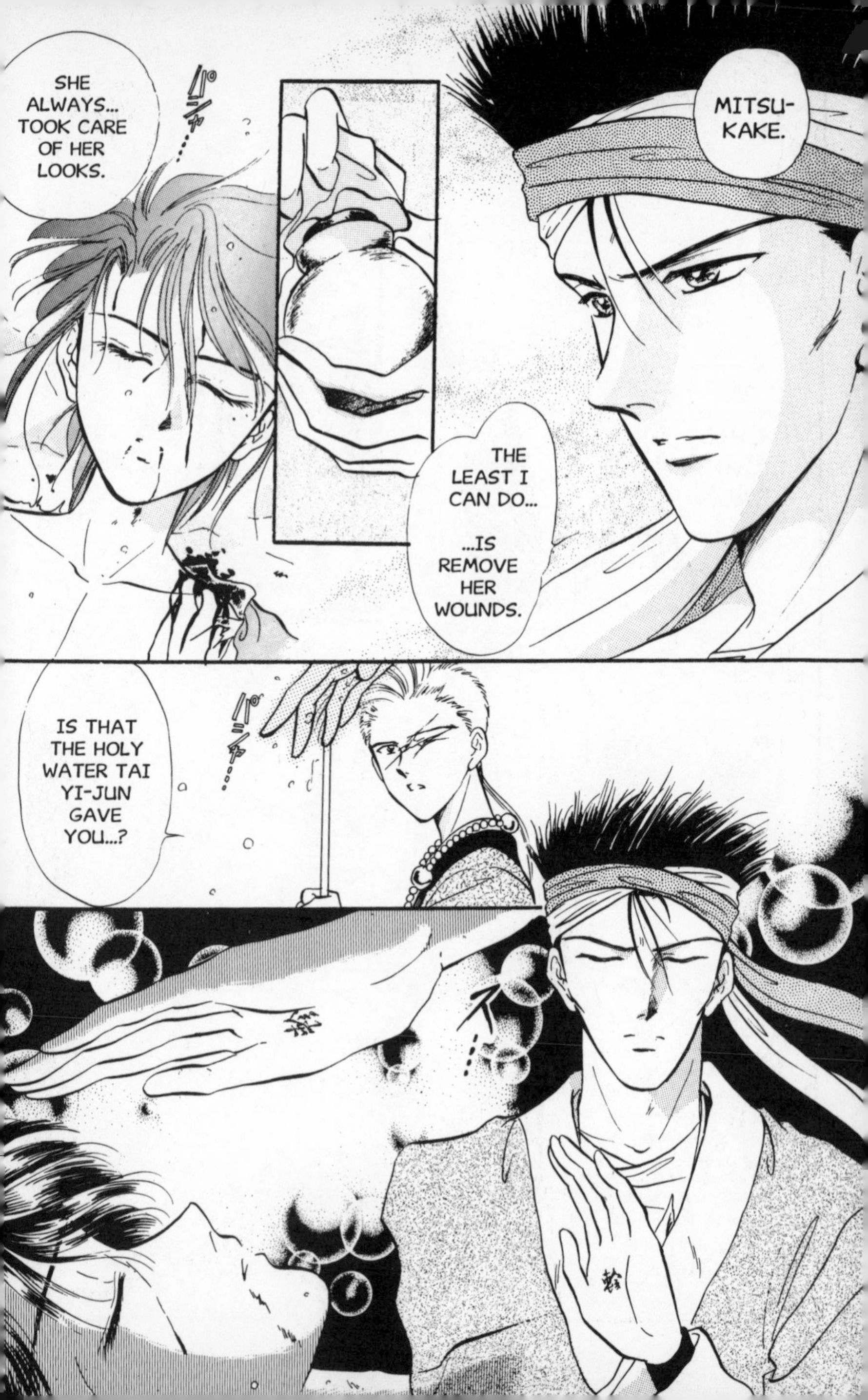
MITSU-KAKE.
SHE ALWAYS... TOOK CARE OF HER LOOKS.
パシャ…
THE LEAST I CAN DO...
...IS REMOVE HER WOUNDS.
パシャ…
IS THAT THE HOLY WATER TAI YI-JUN GAVE YOU...?

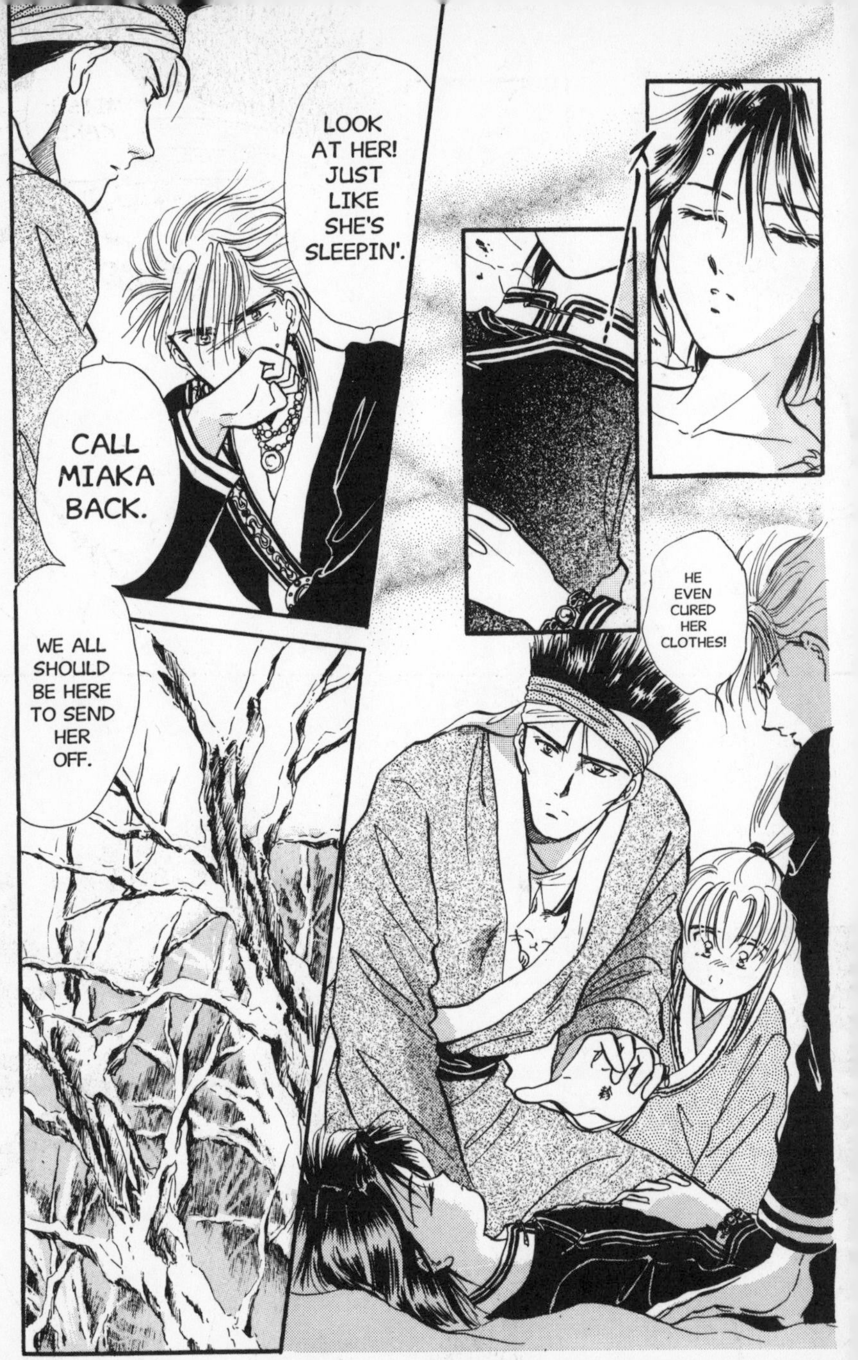
LOOK AT HER! JUST LIKE SHE'S SLEEPIN'.
CALL MIAKA BACK.
HE EVEN CURED HER CLOTHES!
WE ALL SHOULD BE HERE TO SEND HER OFF.

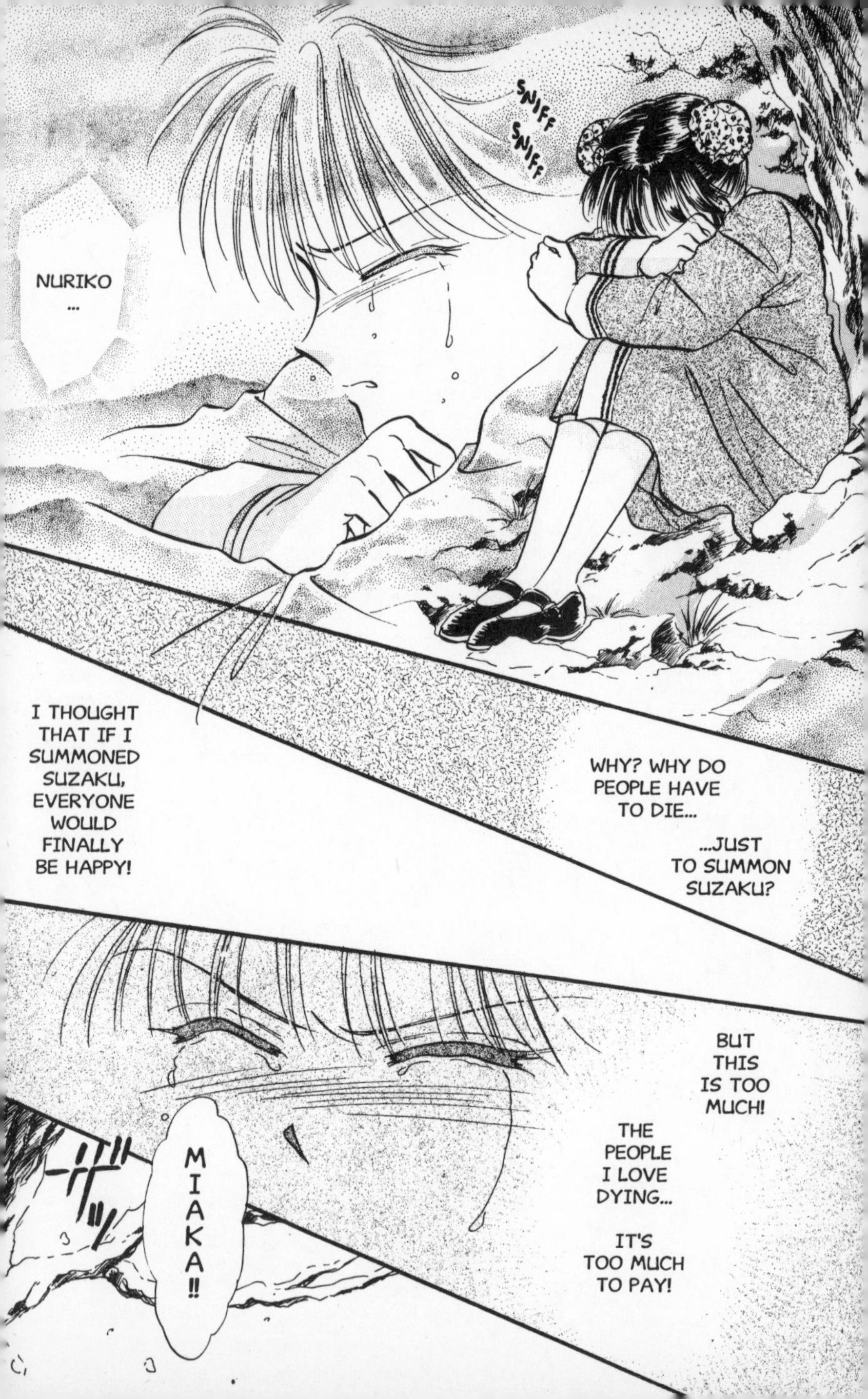
SNIFF SNIFF
NURIKO ...
WHY? WHY DO PEOPLE HAVE TO DIE...
...JUST TO SUMMON SUZAKU?
I THOUGHT THAT IF I SUMMONED SUZAKU, EVERYONE WOULD FINALLY BE HAPPY!
BUT THIS IS TOO MUCH!
THE PEOPLE I LOVE DYING...
IT'S TOO MUCH TO PAY!
MIAKA!!

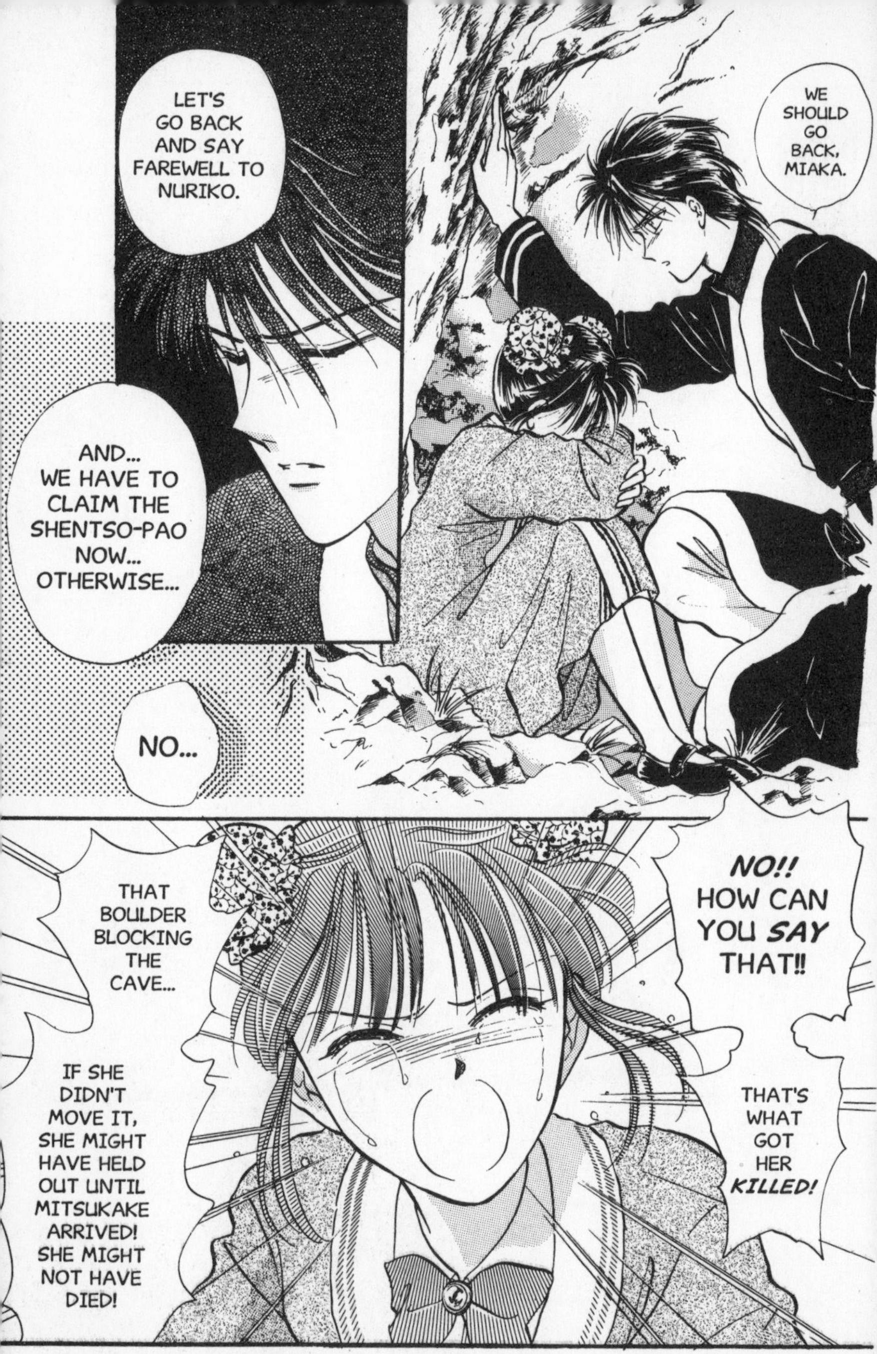
WE SHOULD GO BACK, MIAKA.
LET'S GO BACK AND SAY FAREWELL TO NURIKO.
AND... WE HAVE TO CLAIM THE SHENTSO-PAO NOW... OTHERWISE...
NO...
NO!! HOW CAN YOU ***SAY*** THAT!!
THAT BOULDER BLOCKING THE CAVE...
THAT'S WHAT GOT HER ***KILLED!***
IF SHE DIDN'T MOVE IT, SHE MIGHT HAVE HELD OUT UNTIL MITSUKAKE ARRIVED! SHE MIGHT NOT HAVE DIED!

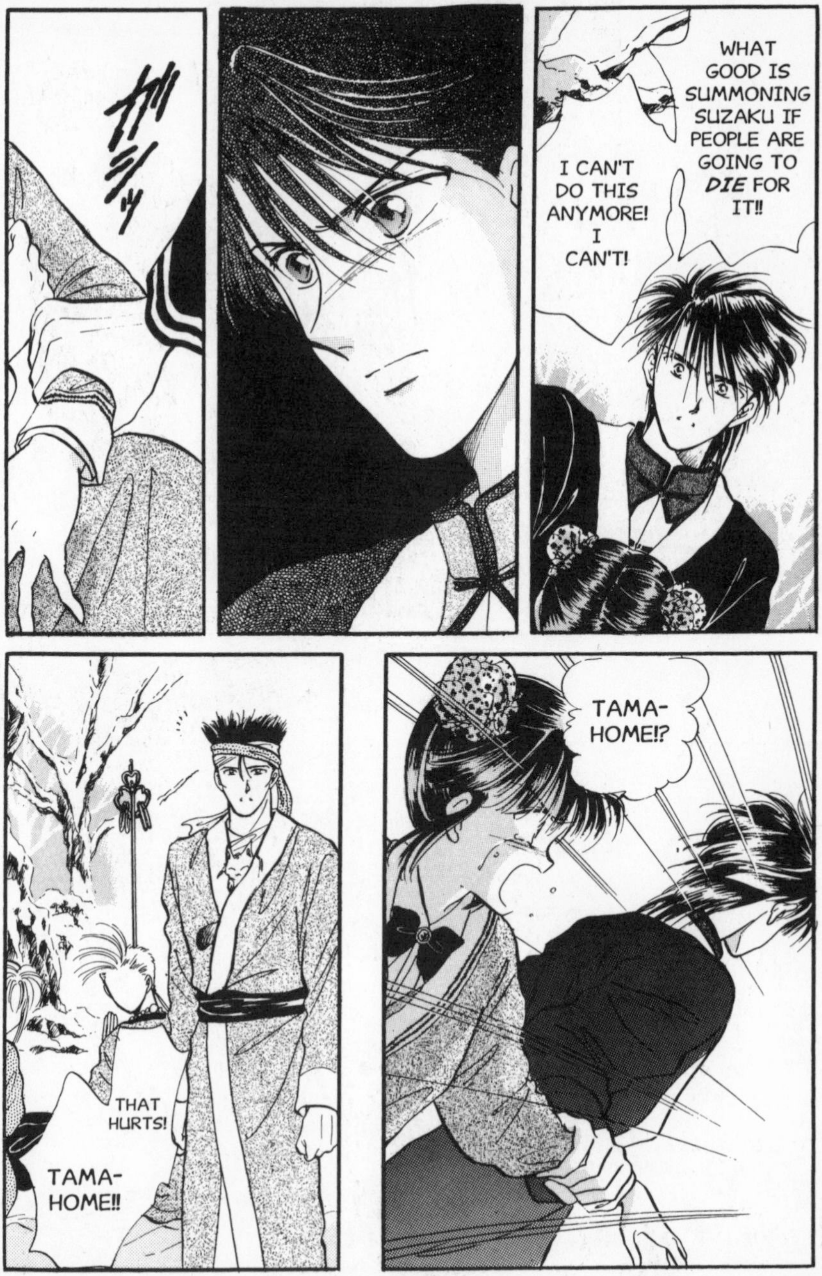
WHAT GOOD IS SUMMONING SUZAKU IF PEOPLE ARE GOING TO *DIE* FOR IT!!
I CAN'T DO THIS ANYMORE! I CAN'T!
TAMA-HOME!?
THAT HURTS!
TAMA-HOME!!

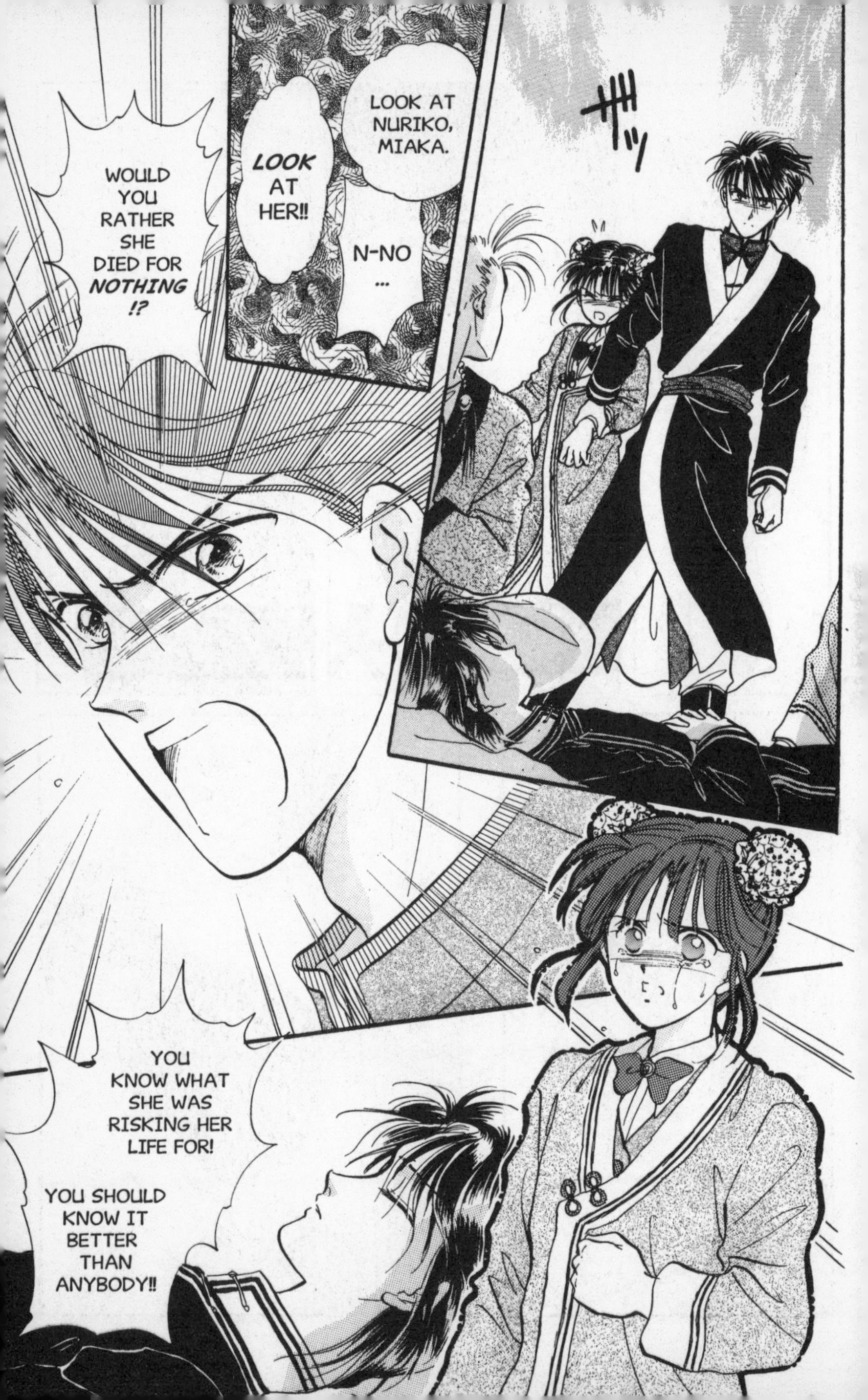

ザッ
LOOK AT NURIKO, MIAKA.
LOOK AT HER!!
N-NO ...
WOULD YOU RATHER SHE DIED FOR NOTHING!?
YOU KNOW WHAT SHE WAS RISKING HER LIFE FOR!
YOU SHOULD KNOW IT BETTER THAN ANYBODY!!

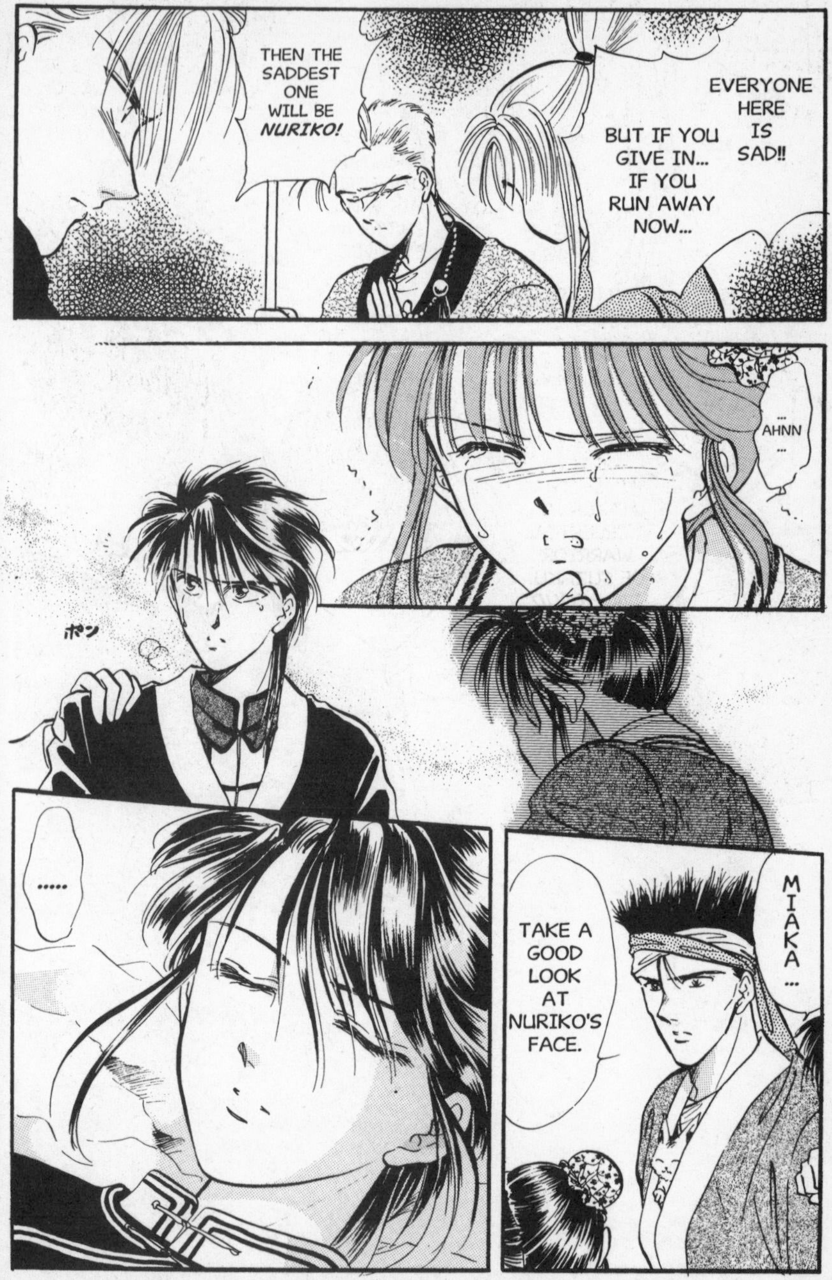
EVERYONE HERE IS SAD!!
BUT IF YOU GIVE IN... IF YOU RUN AWAY NOW...
THEN THE SADDEST ONE WILL BE NURIKO!
...AHNN...
ポン
MIAKA...
TAKE A GOOD LOOK AT NURIKO'S FACE.
......

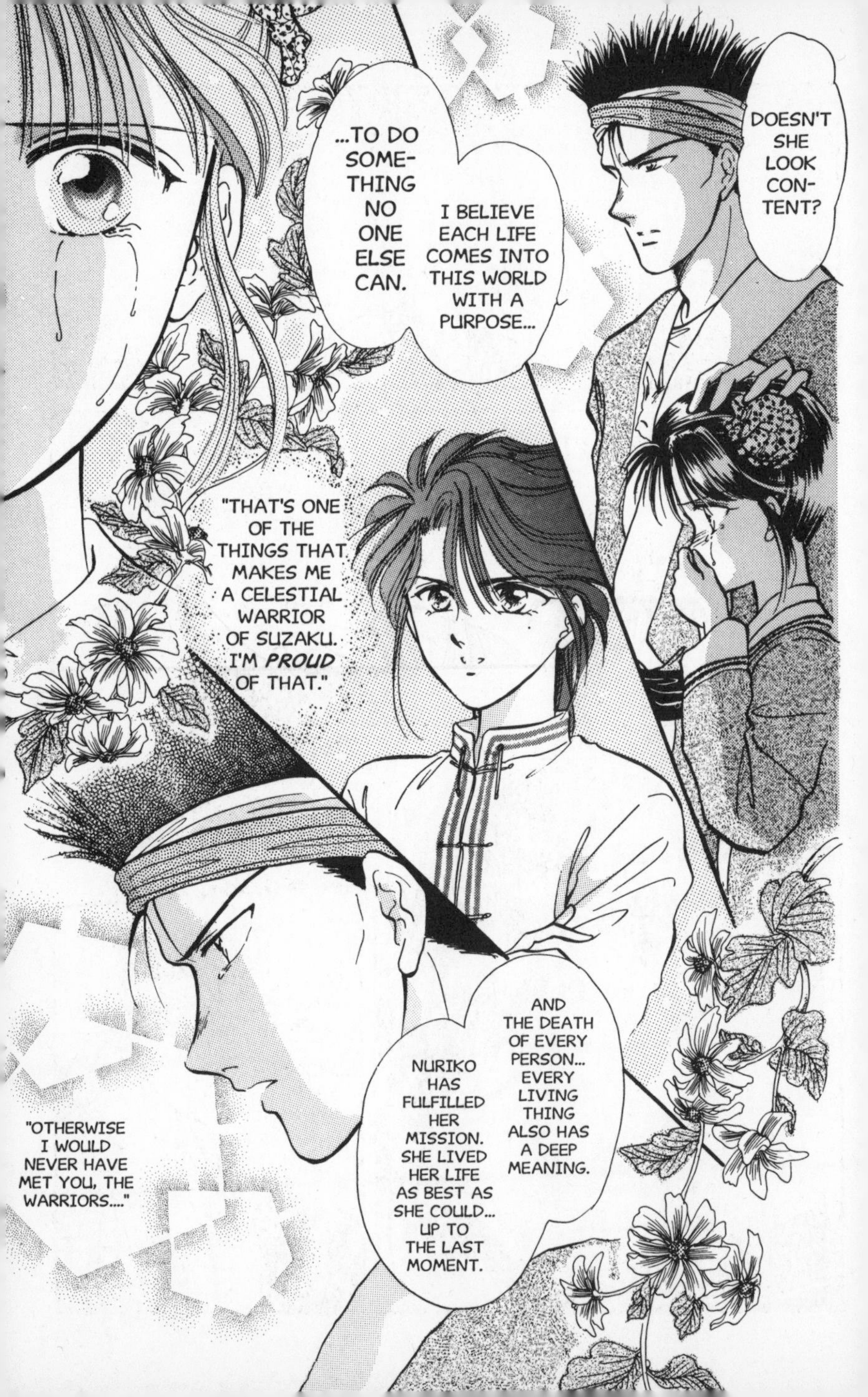
DOESN'T SHE LOOK CON-TENT?
I BELIEVE EACH LIFE COMES INTO THIS WORLD WITH A PURPOSE...
...TO DO SOME-THING NO ONE ELSE CAN.
"THAT'S ONE OF THE THINGS THAT MAKES ME A CELESTIAL WARRIOR OF SUZAKU. I'M *PROUD* OF THAT."
AND THE DEATH OF EVERY PERSON... EVERY LIVING THING ALSO HAS A DEEP MEANING.
NURIKO HAS FULFILLED HER MISSION. SHE LIVED HER LIFE AS BEST AS SHE COULD... UP TO THE LAST MOMENT.
"OTHERWISE I WOULD NEVER HAVE MET YOU, THE WARRIORS...."

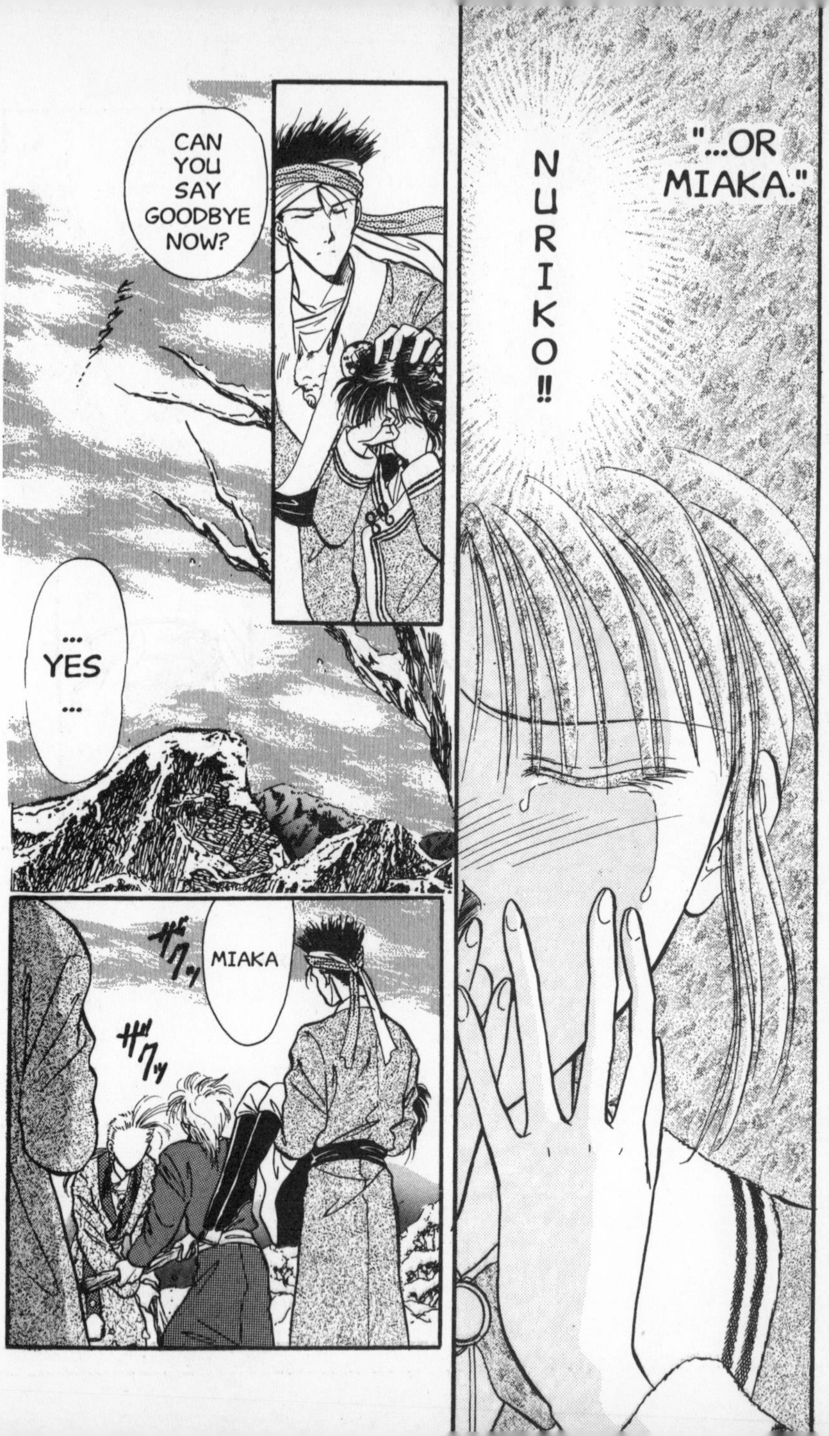
"...OR MIAKA."
NURIKO!!
CAN YOU SAY GOODBYE NOW?
... YES ...
MIAKA

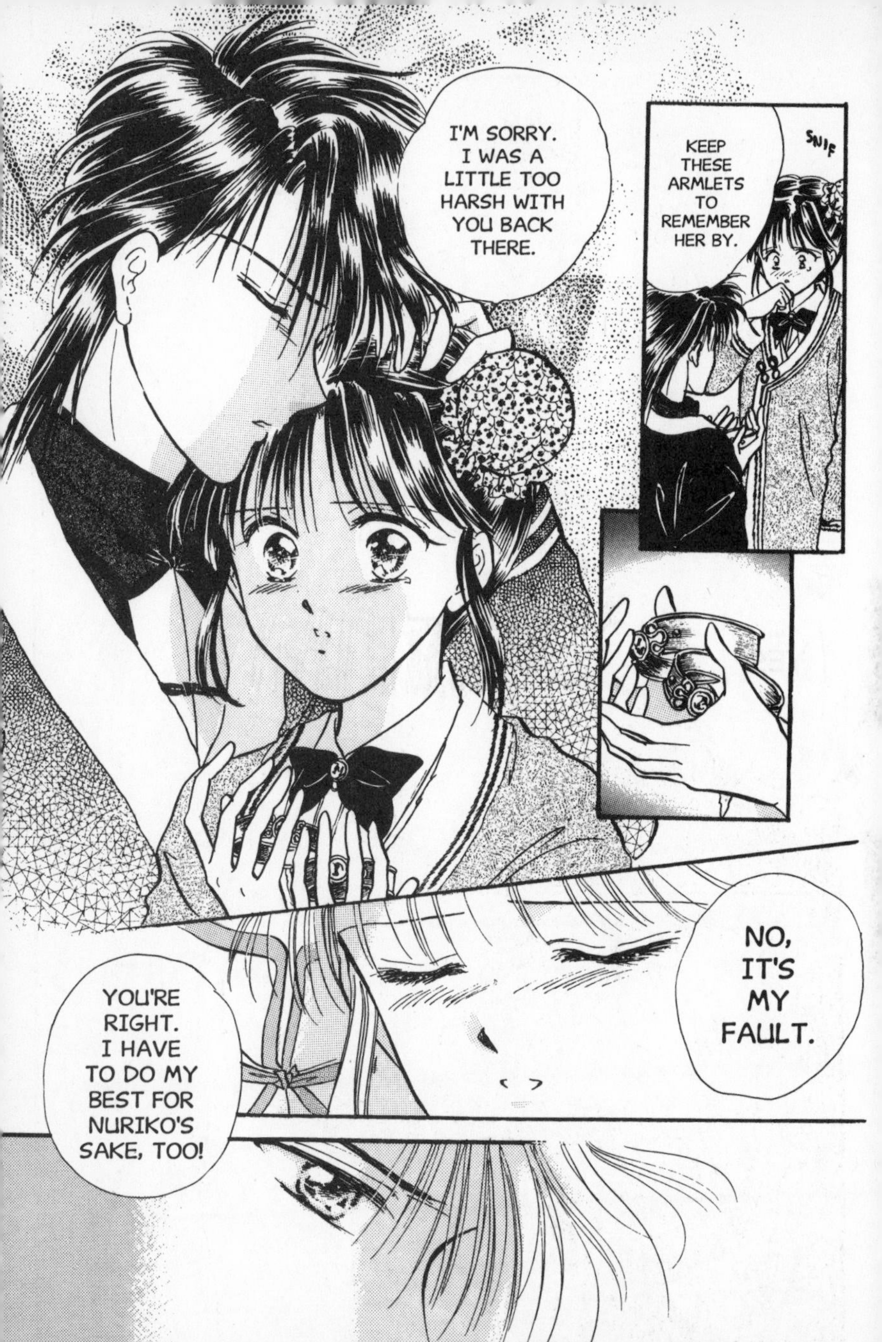
KEEP THESE ARMLETS TO REMEMBER HER BY.
SNIF
I'M SORRY. I WAS A LITTLE TOO HARSH WITH YOU BACK THERE.
NO, IT'S MY FAULT.
YOU'RE RIGHT. I HAVE TO DO MY BEST FOR NURIKO'S SAKE, TOO!

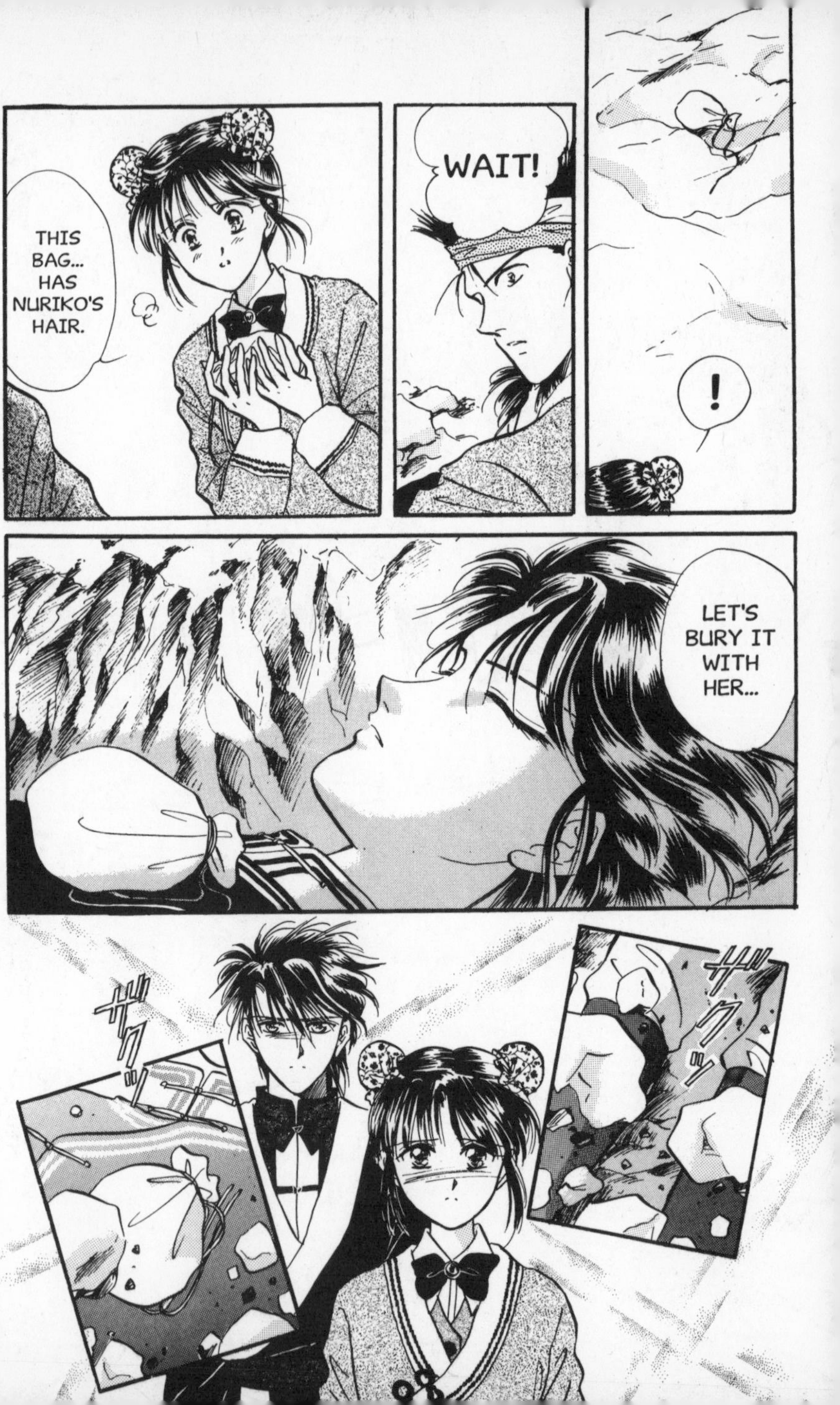
!
WAIT!
THIS BAG... HAS NURIKO'S HAIR.
LET'S BURY IT WITH HER...

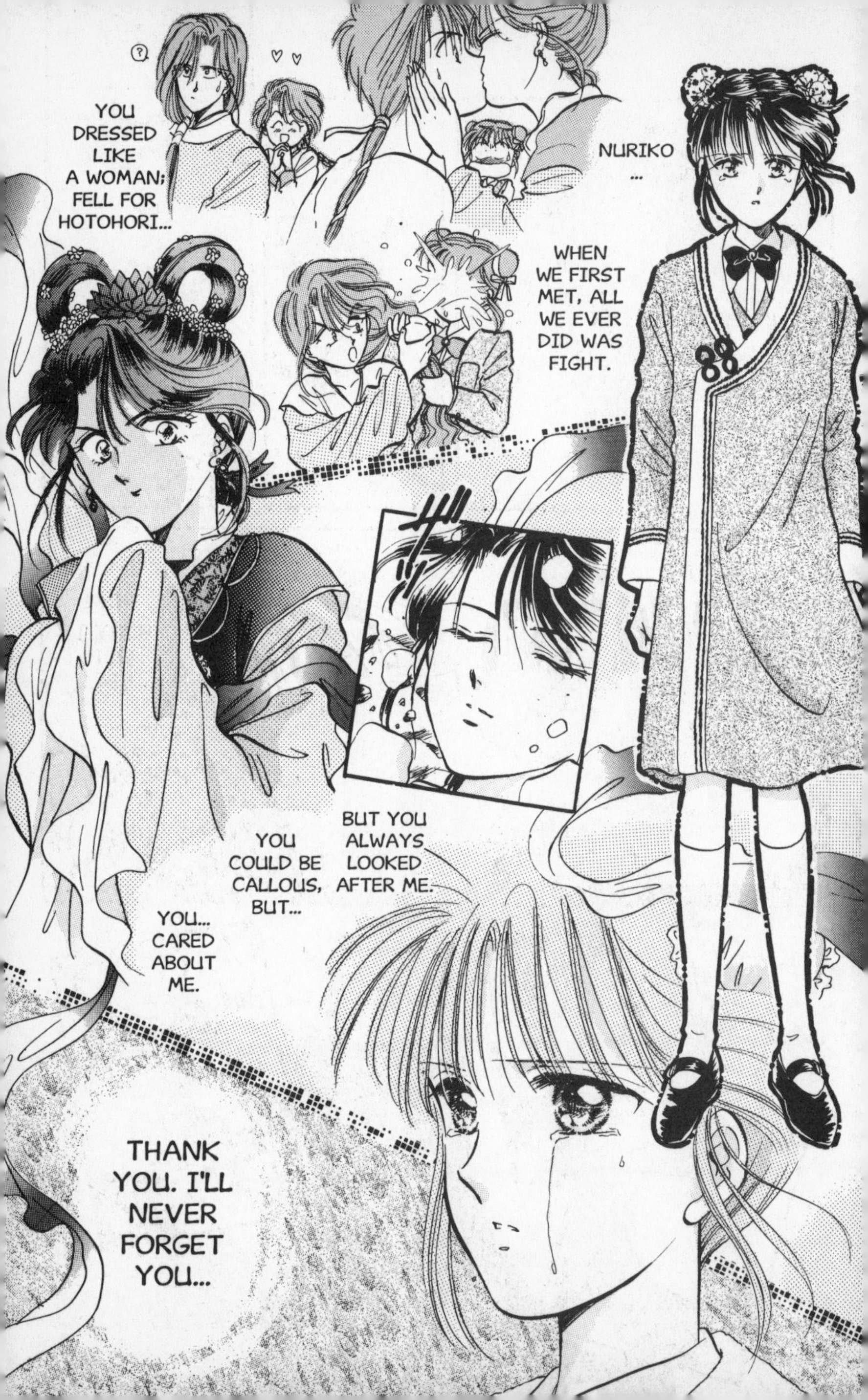
NURIKO...
YOU DRESSED LIKE A WOMAN; FELL FOR HOTOHORI...
WHEN WE FIRST MET, ALL WE EVER DID WAS FIGHT.
YOU COULD BE CALLOUS, BUT...
BUT YOU ALWAYS LOOKED AFTER ME.
YOU... CARED ABOUT ME.
THANK YOU. I'LL NEVER FORGET YOU...

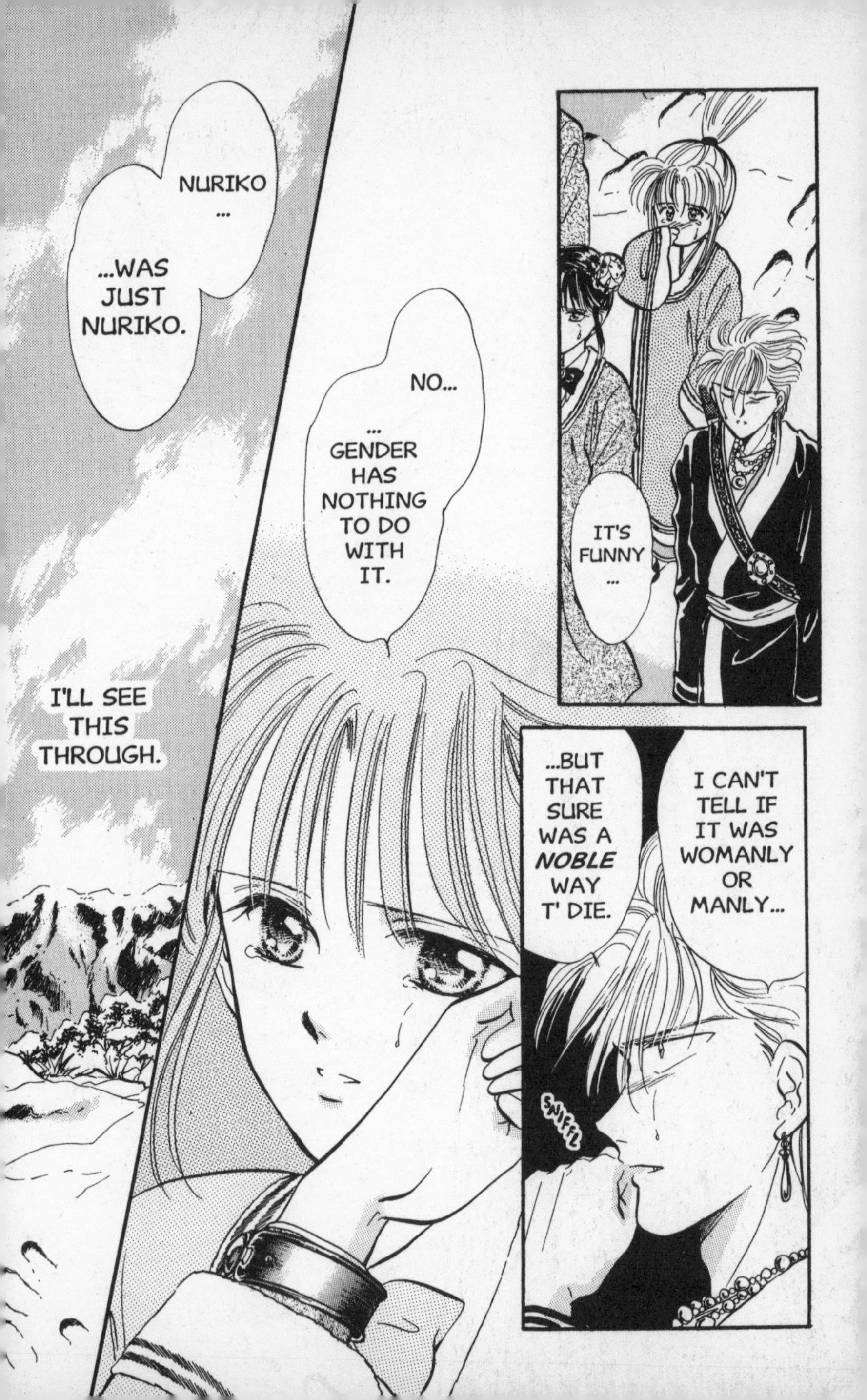
IT'S FUNNY ...
I CAN'T TELL IF IT WAS WOMANLY OR MANLY...
...BUT THAT SURE WAS A ***NOBLE*** WAY T' DIE.
SNIFFL
NO...
...GENDER HAS NOTHING TO DO WITH IT.
NURIKO ...
...WAS JUST NURIKO.
I'LL SEE THIS THROUGH.

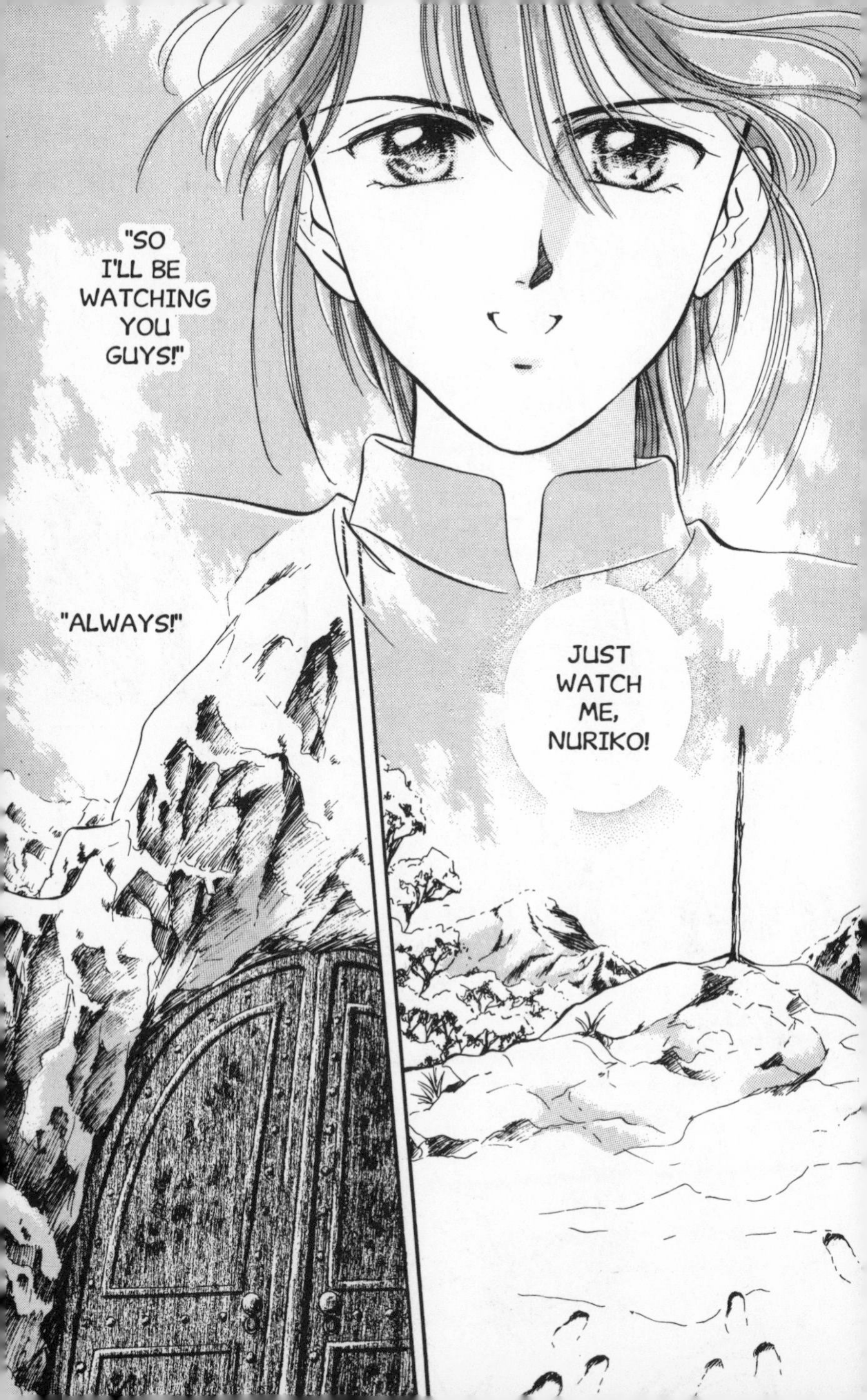
"SO I'LL BE WATCHING YOU GUYS!"
"ALWAYS!"
JUST WATCH ME, NURIKO!

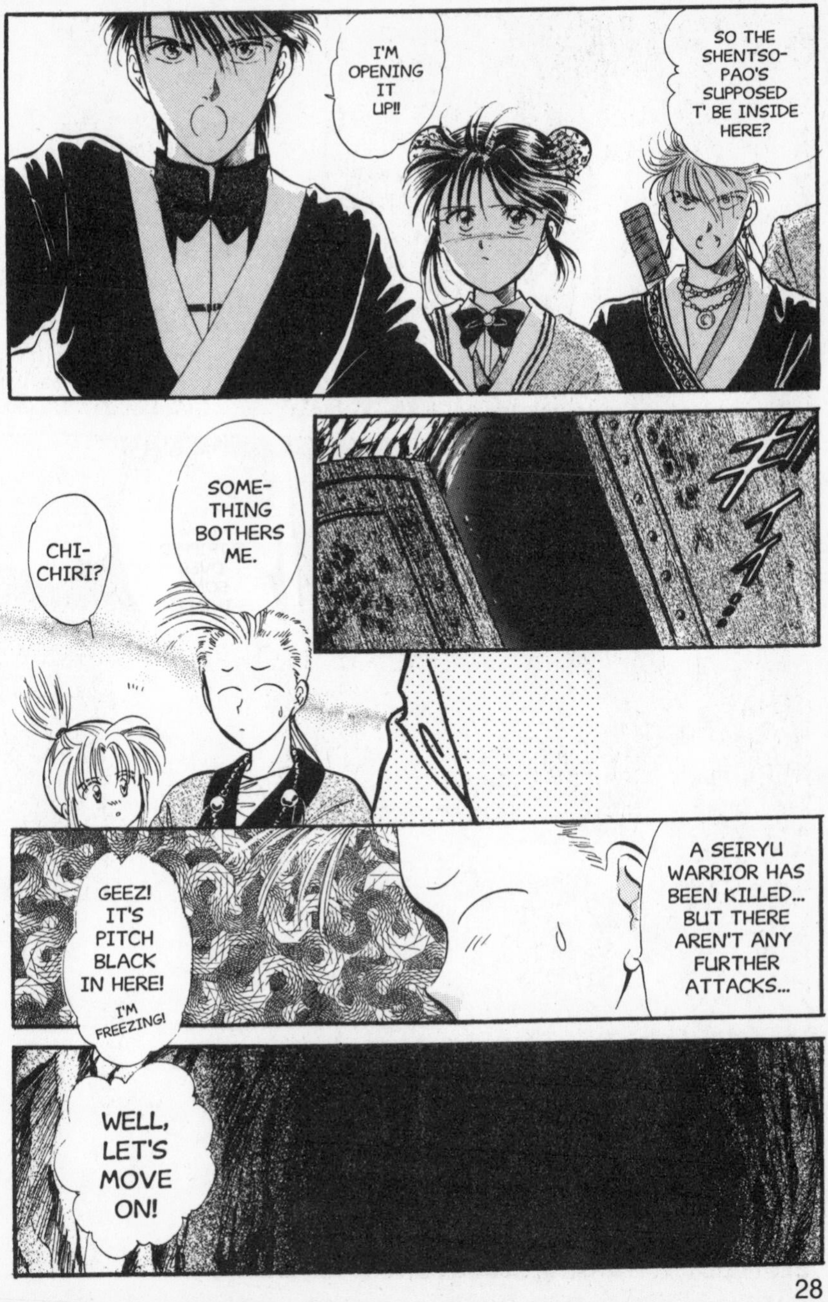
SO THE SHENTSO-PAO'S SUPPOSED T' BE INSIDE HERE?
I'M OPENING IT UP!!
SOME-THING BOTHERS ME.
CHI-CHIRI?
A SEIRYU WARRIOR HAS BEEN KILLED... BUT THERE AREN'T ANY FURTHER ATTACKS...
GEEZ! IT'S PITCH BLACK IN HERE!
I'M FREEZING!
WELL, LET'S MOVE ON!

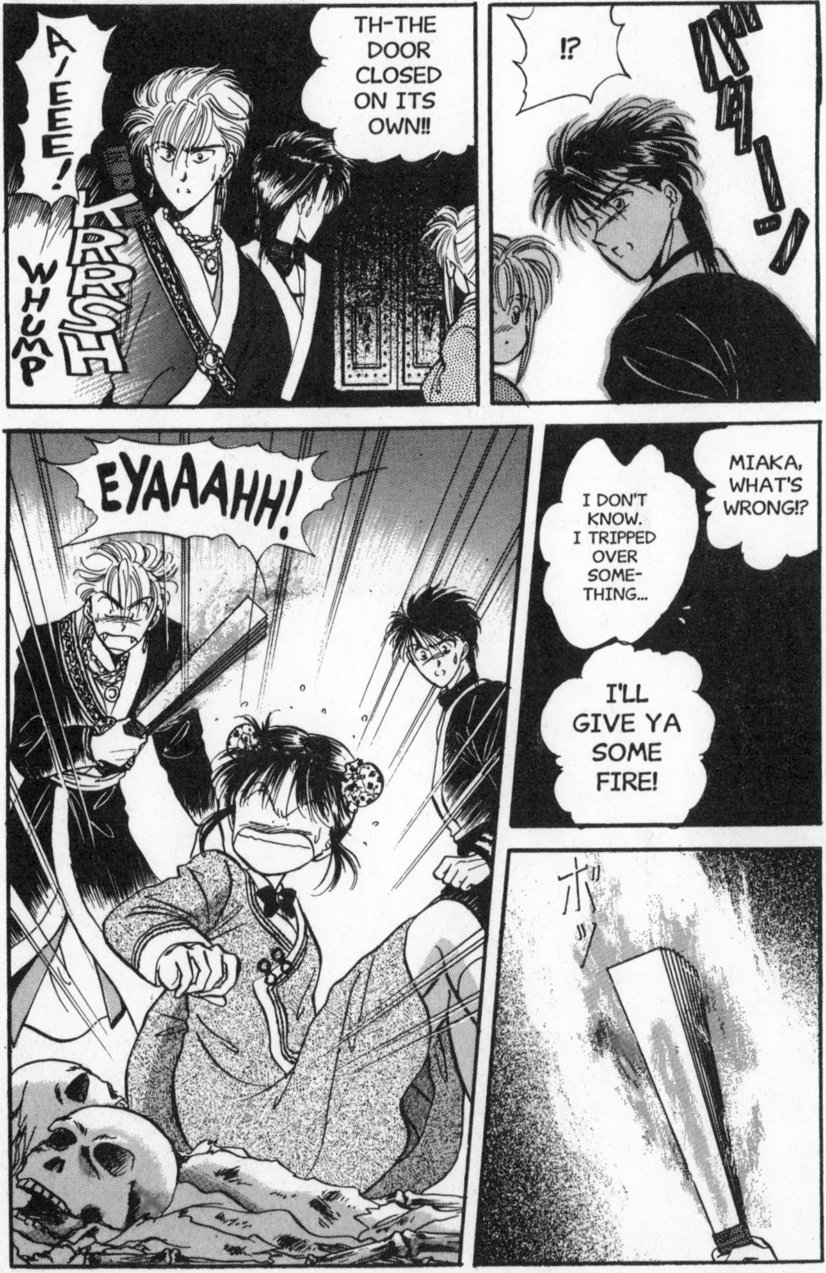
!?
TH-THE DOOR CLOSED ON ITS OWN!!
AIEEE!
KRRSH
WHUMP
MIAKA, WHAT'S WRONG!?
I DON'T KNOW. I TRIPPED OVER SOME-THING...
I'LL GIVE YA SOME FIRE!
EYAAAHH!

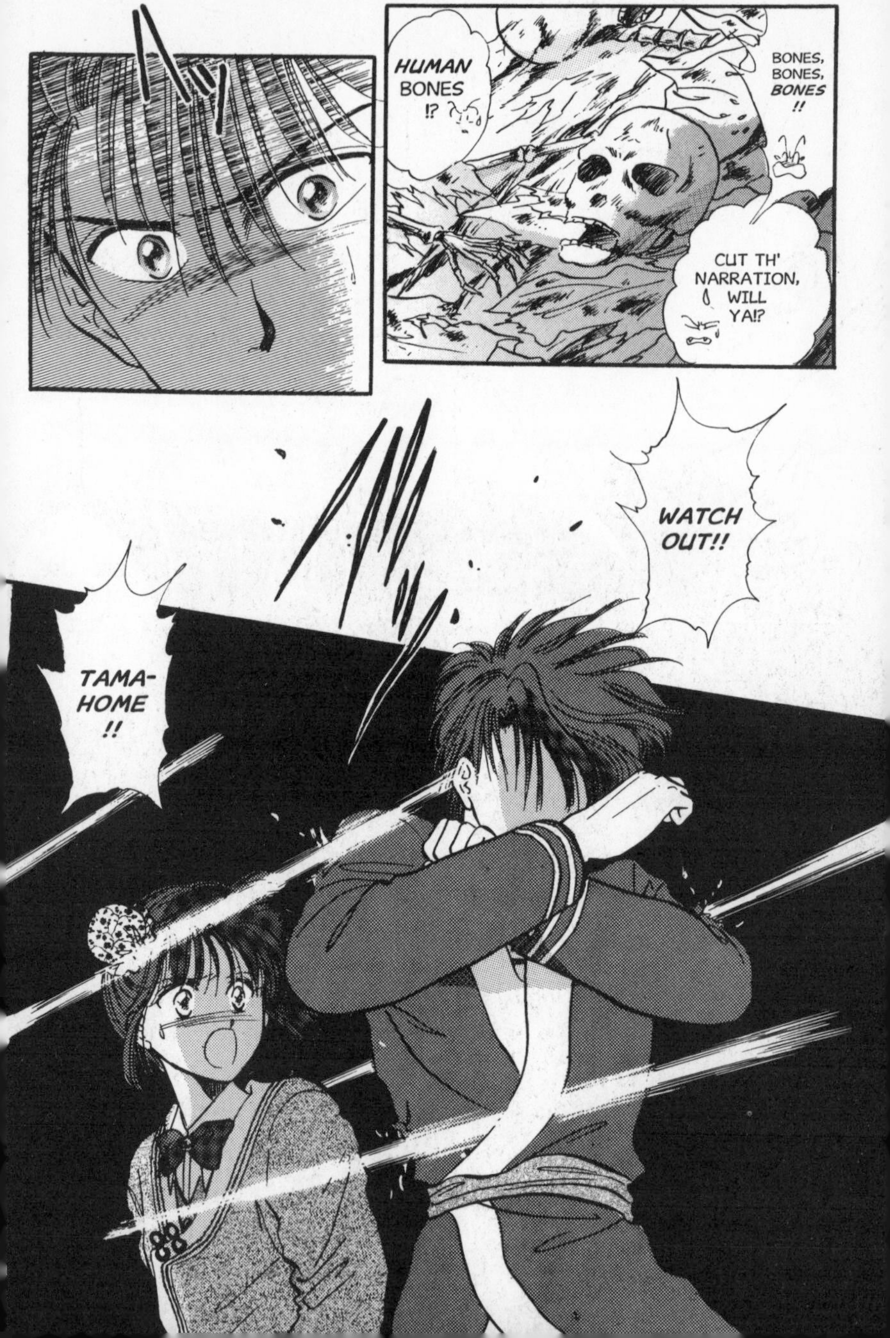
BONES, BONES, BONES !!
HUMAN BONES !?
CUT TH' NARRATION, WILL YA!?
WATCH OUT!!
TAMA-HOME !!

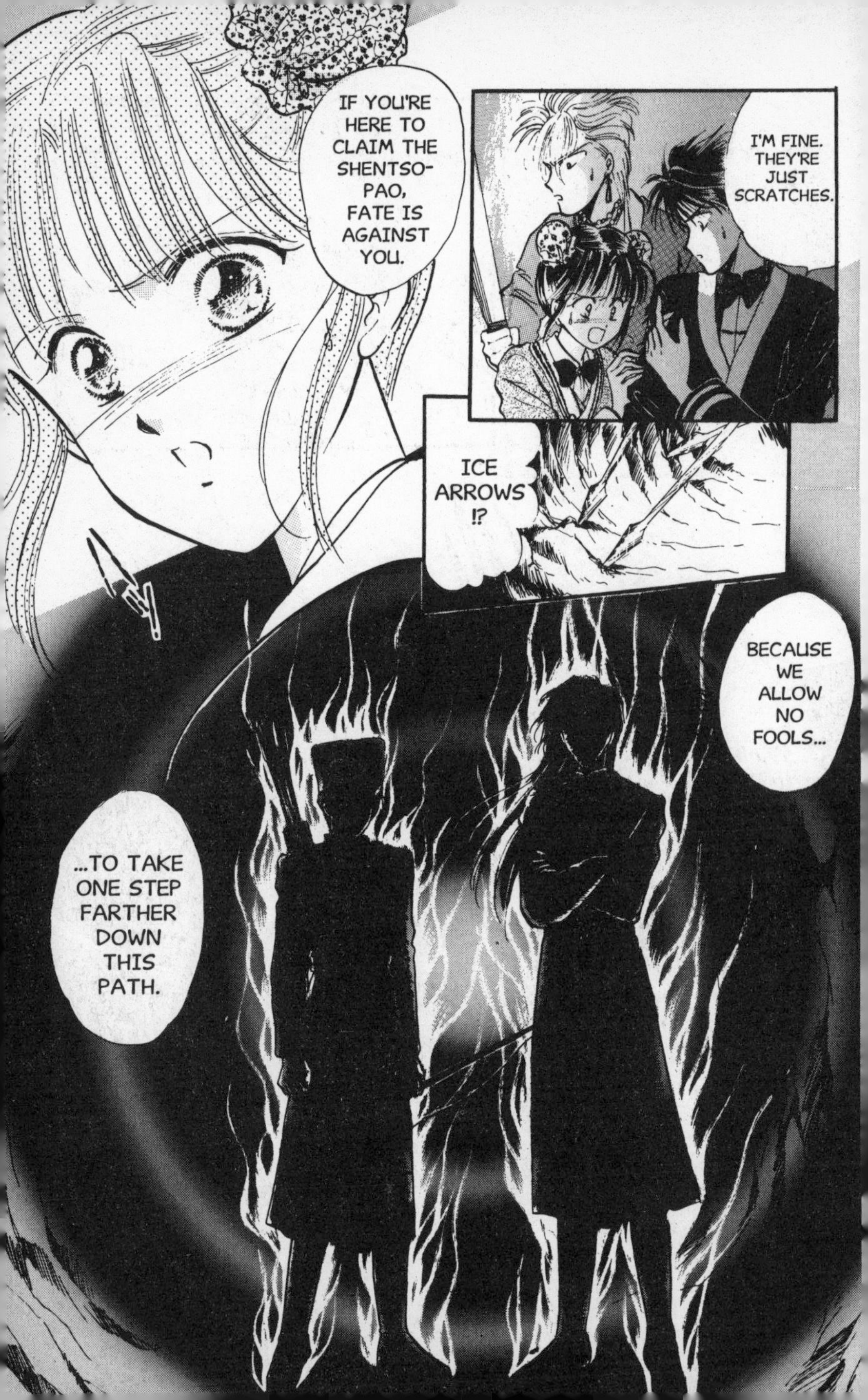
I'M FINE. THEY'RE JUST SCRATCHES.
ICE ARROWS !?
IF YOU'RE HERE TO CLAIM THE SHENTSO-PAO, FATE IS AGAINST YOU.
BECAUSE WE ALLOW NO FOOLS...
...TO TAKE ONE STEP FARTHER DOWN THIS PATH.

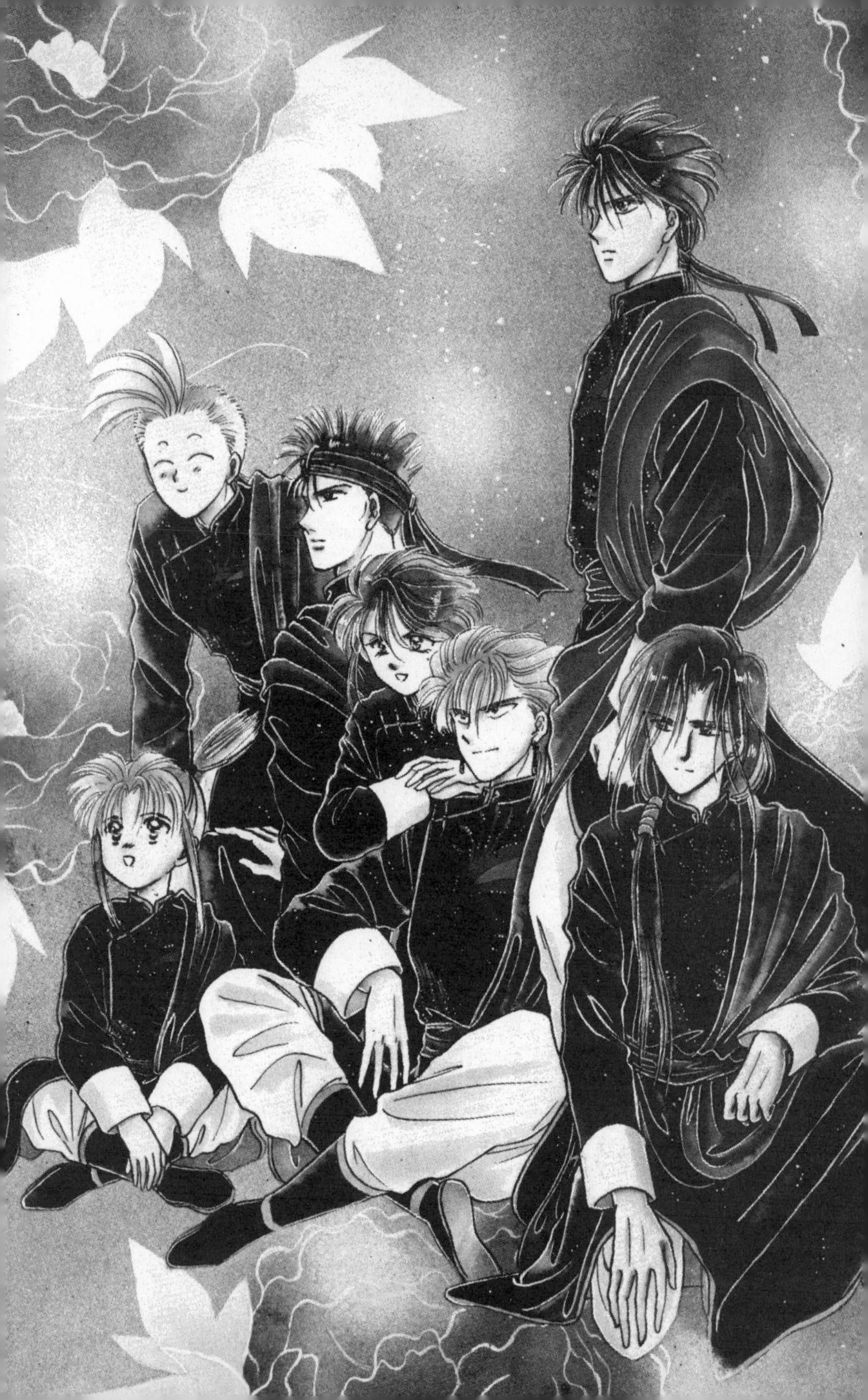

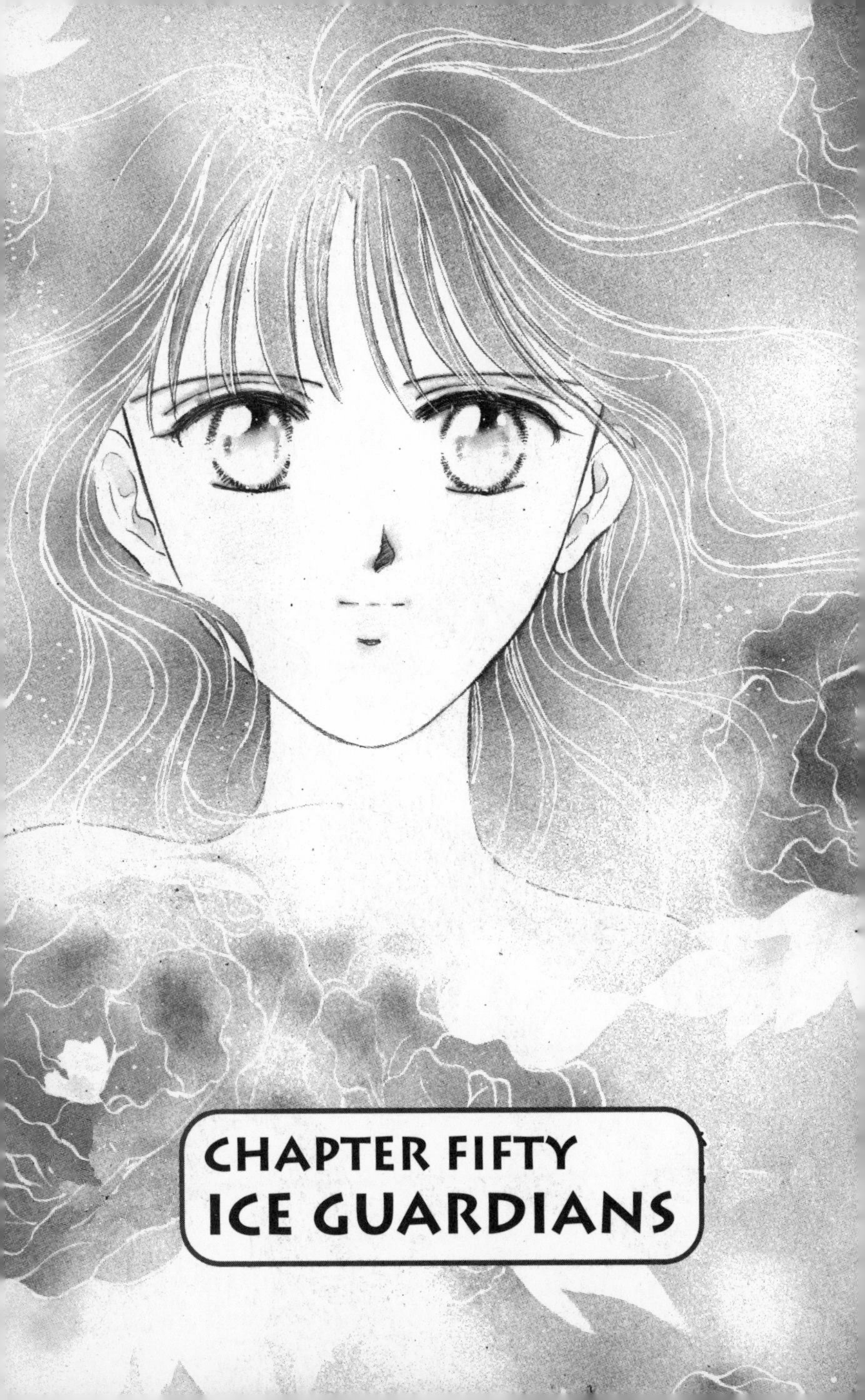
CHAPTER FIFTY
ICE GUARDIANS

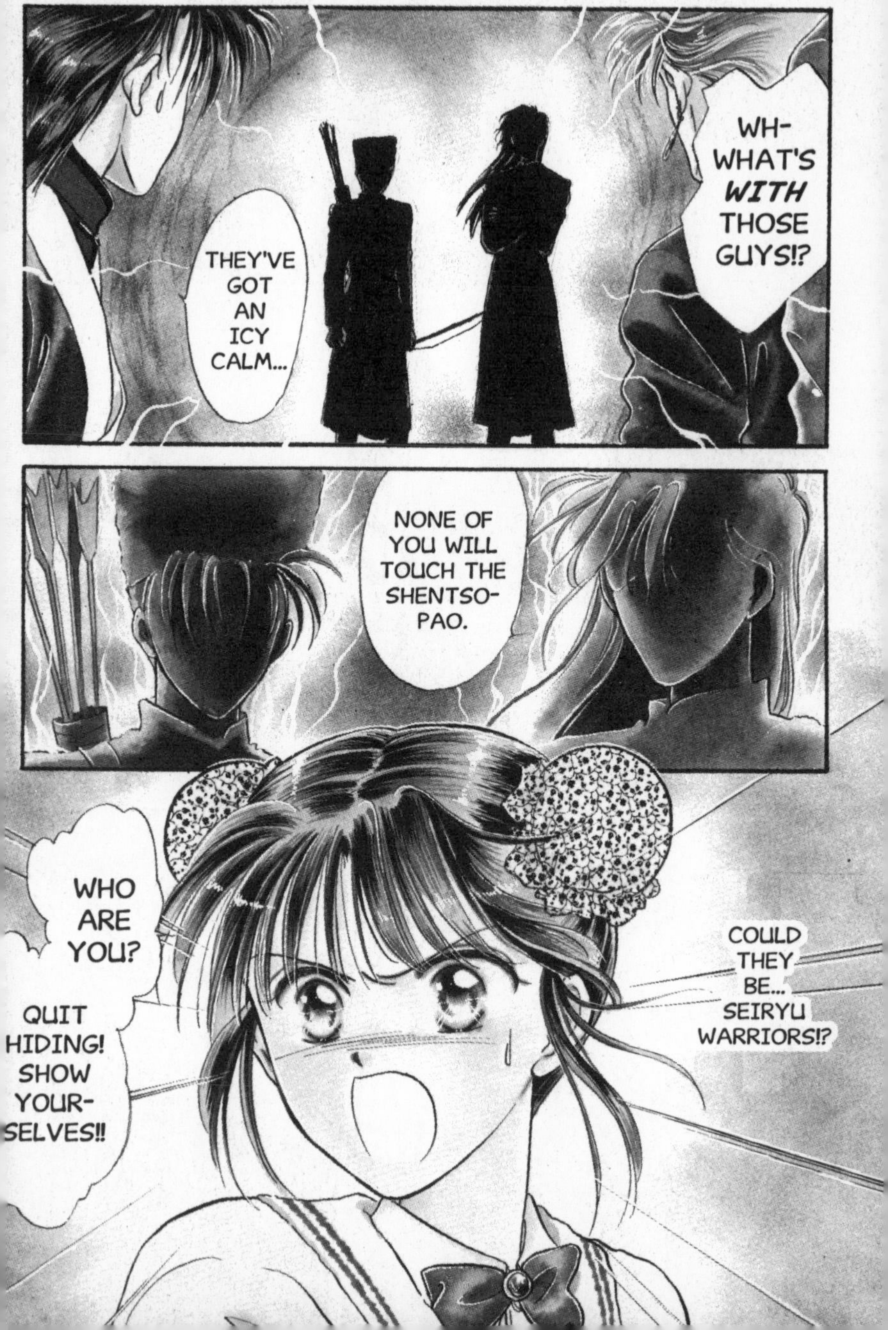
WH-WHAT'S WITH THOSE GUYS!?
THEY'VE GOT AN ICY CALM...
NONE OF YOU WILL TOUCH THE SHENTSO-PAO.
COULD THEY BE... SEIRYU WARRIORS!?
WHO ARE YOU?
QUIT HIDING! SHOW YOUR-SELVES!!

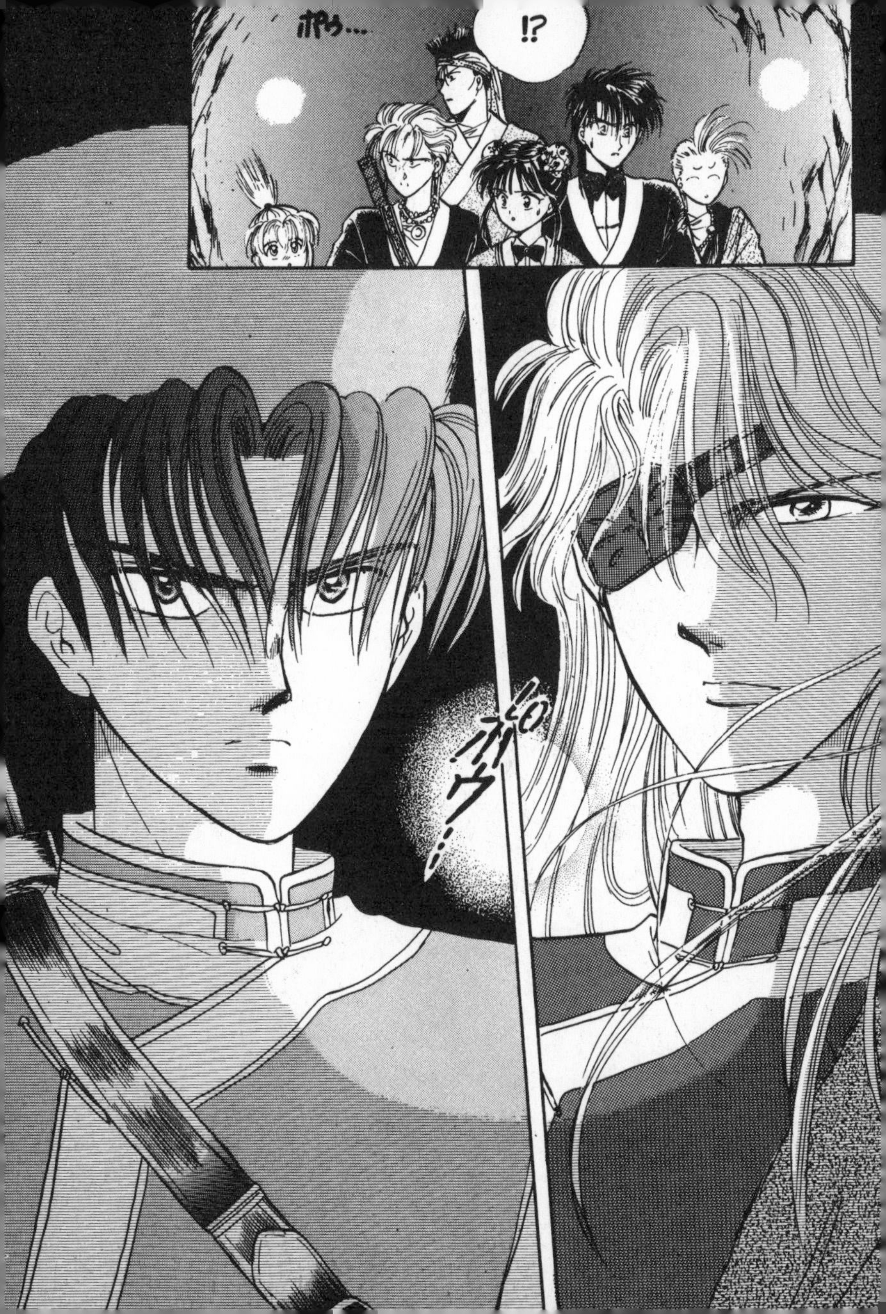
!?
ポウ…
ポウ…

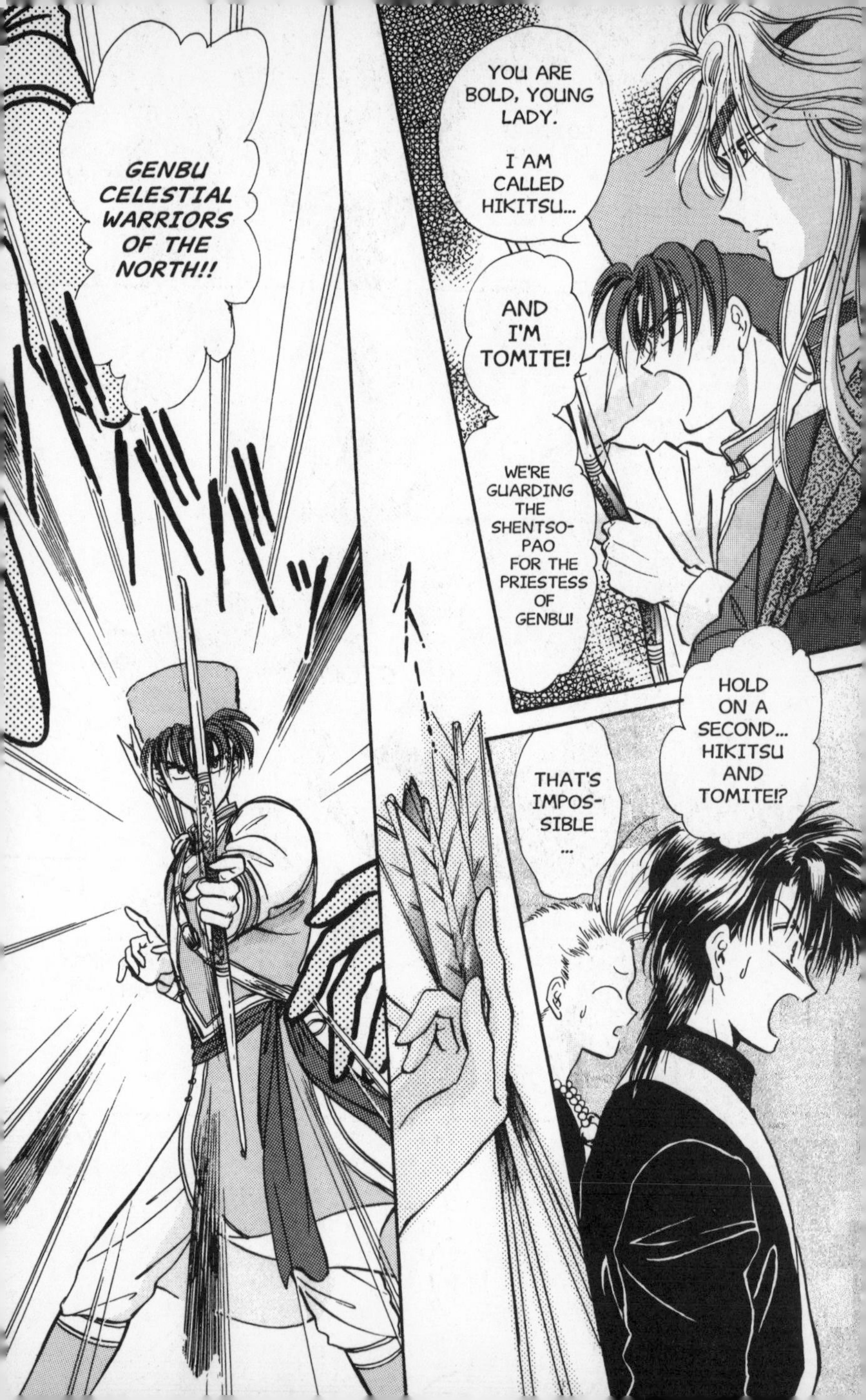
YOU ARE BOLD, YOUNG LADY.
I AM CALLED HIKITSU...
AND I'M TOMITE!
WE'RE GUARDING THE SHENTSO-PAO FOR THE PRIESTESS OF GENBU!
HOLD ON A SECOND... HIKITSU AND TOMITE!?
THAT'S IMPOSSIBLE ...
GENBU CELESTIAL WARRIORS OF THE NORTH!!

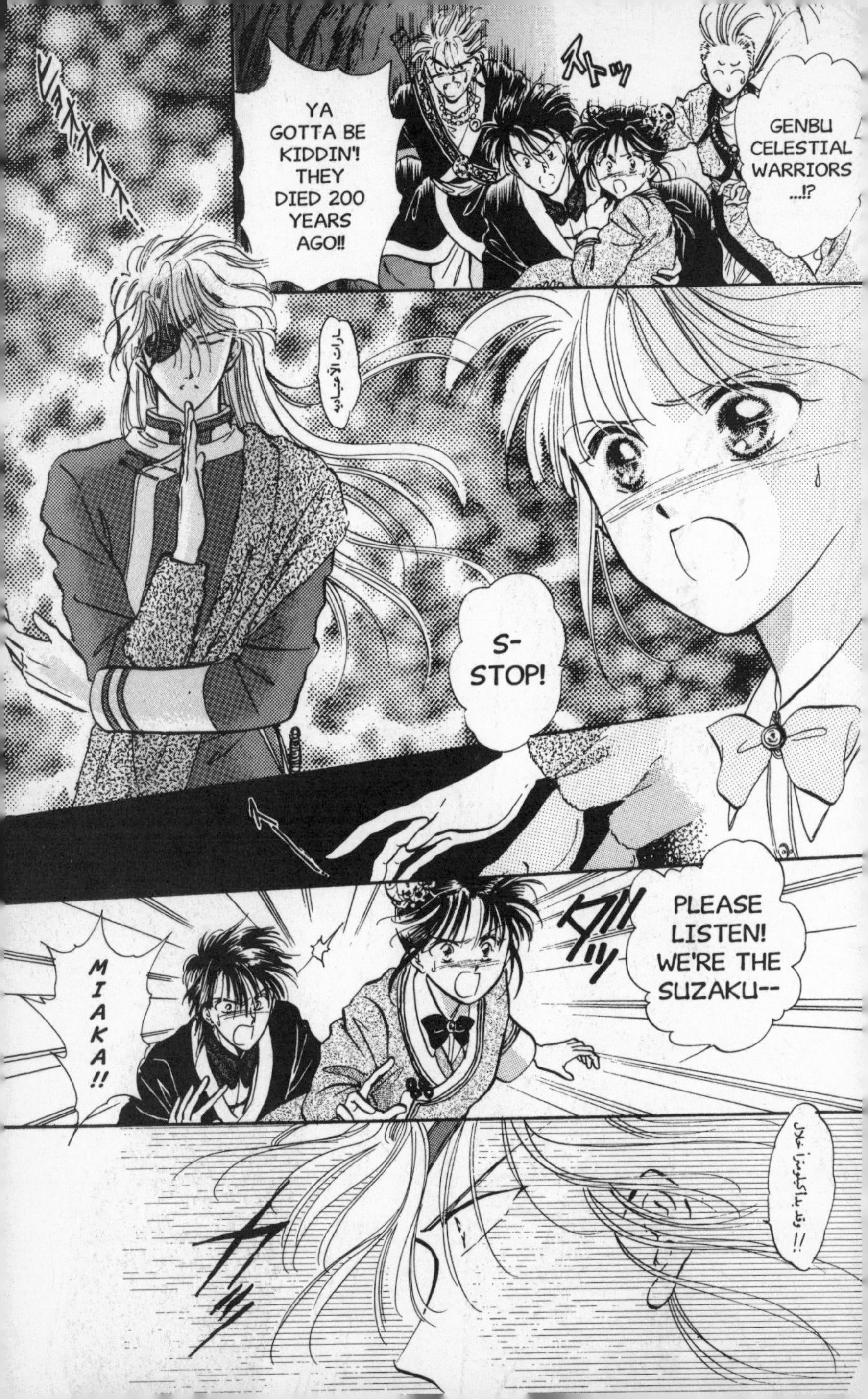
GENBU CELESTIAL WARRIORS ...!?
YA GOTTA BE KIDDIN'! THEY DIED 200 YEARS AGO!!
S-STOP!
PLEASE LISTEN! WE'RE THE SUZAKU--
MIAKA!!

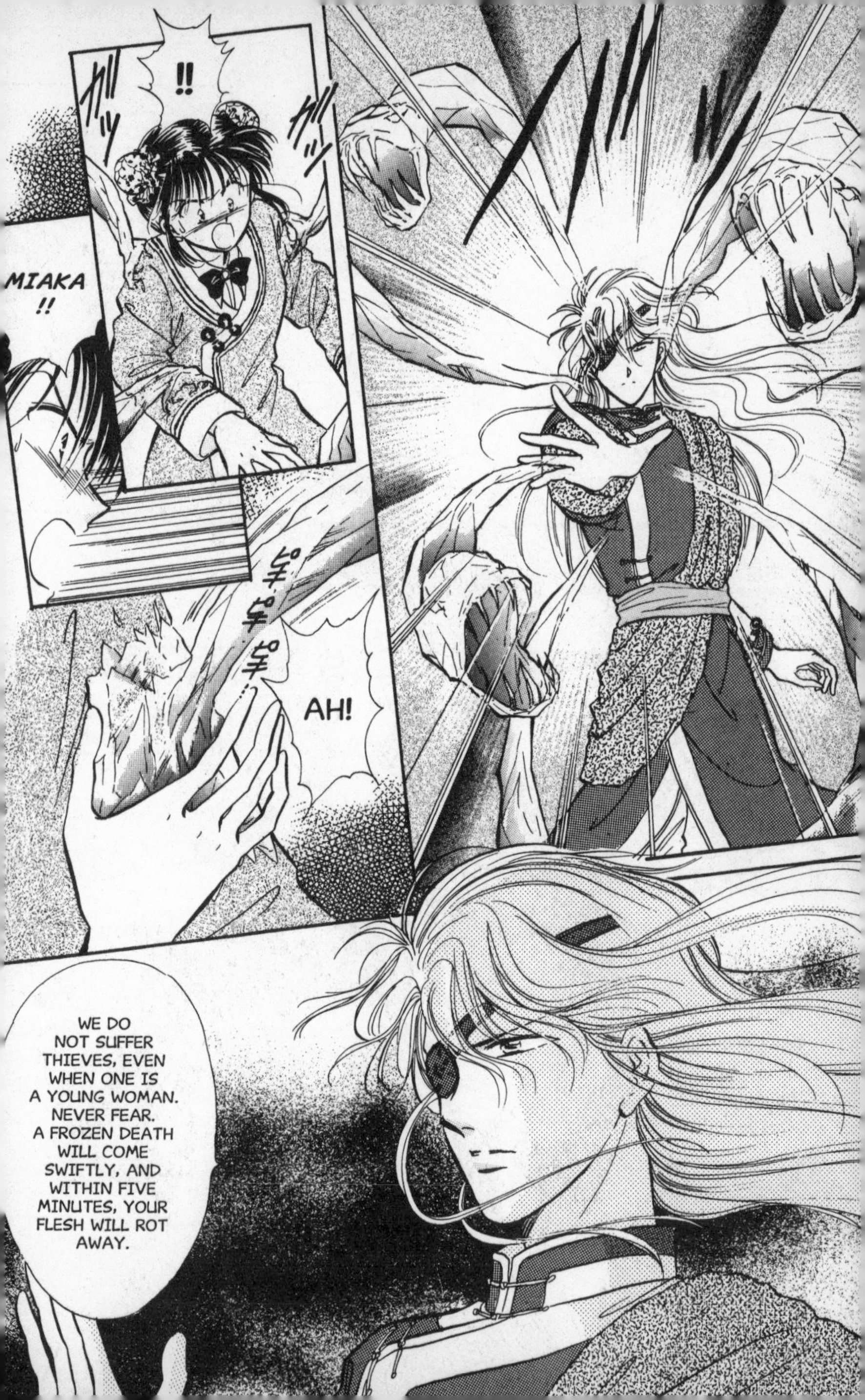

!!
MIAKA !!
AH!
WE DO NOT SUFFER THIEVES, EVEN WHEN ONE IS A YOUNG WOMAN. NEVER FEAR. A FROZEN DEATH WILL COME SWIFTLY, AND WITHIN FIVE MINUTES, YOUR FLESH WILL ROT AWAY.

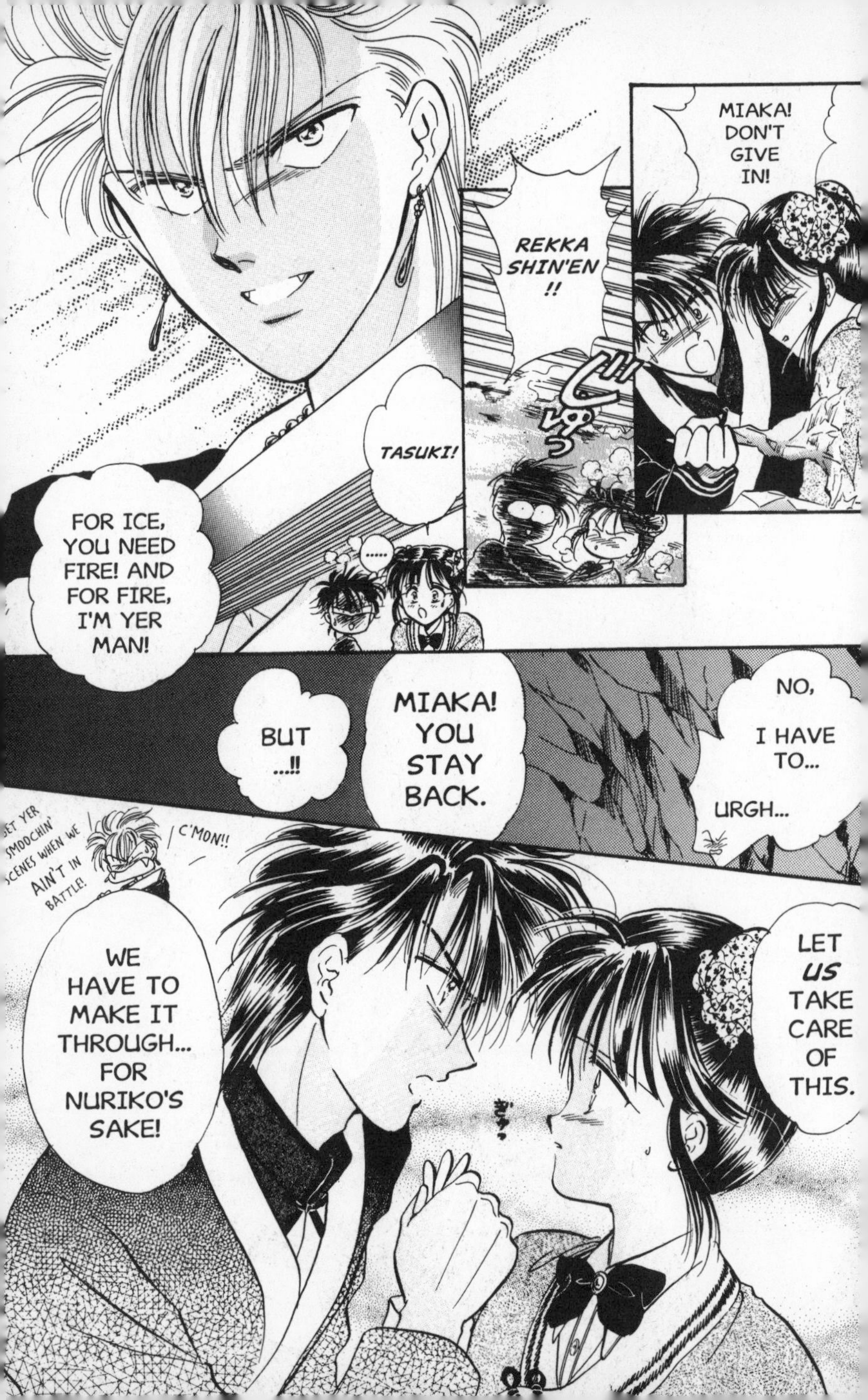
MIAKA! DON'T GIVE IN!
REKKA SHIN'EN !!
TASUKI!
......
FOR ICE, YOU NEED FIRE! AND FOR FIRE, I'M YER MAN!
NO, I HAVE TO... URGH...
MIAKA! YOU STAY BACK.
BUT ...!!
LET *US* TAKE CARE OF THIS.
WE HAVE TO MAKE IT THROUGH... FOR NURIKO'S SAKE!
C'MON!!
ET YER SMOOCHIN' CENES WHEN WE AIN'T IN BATTLE!

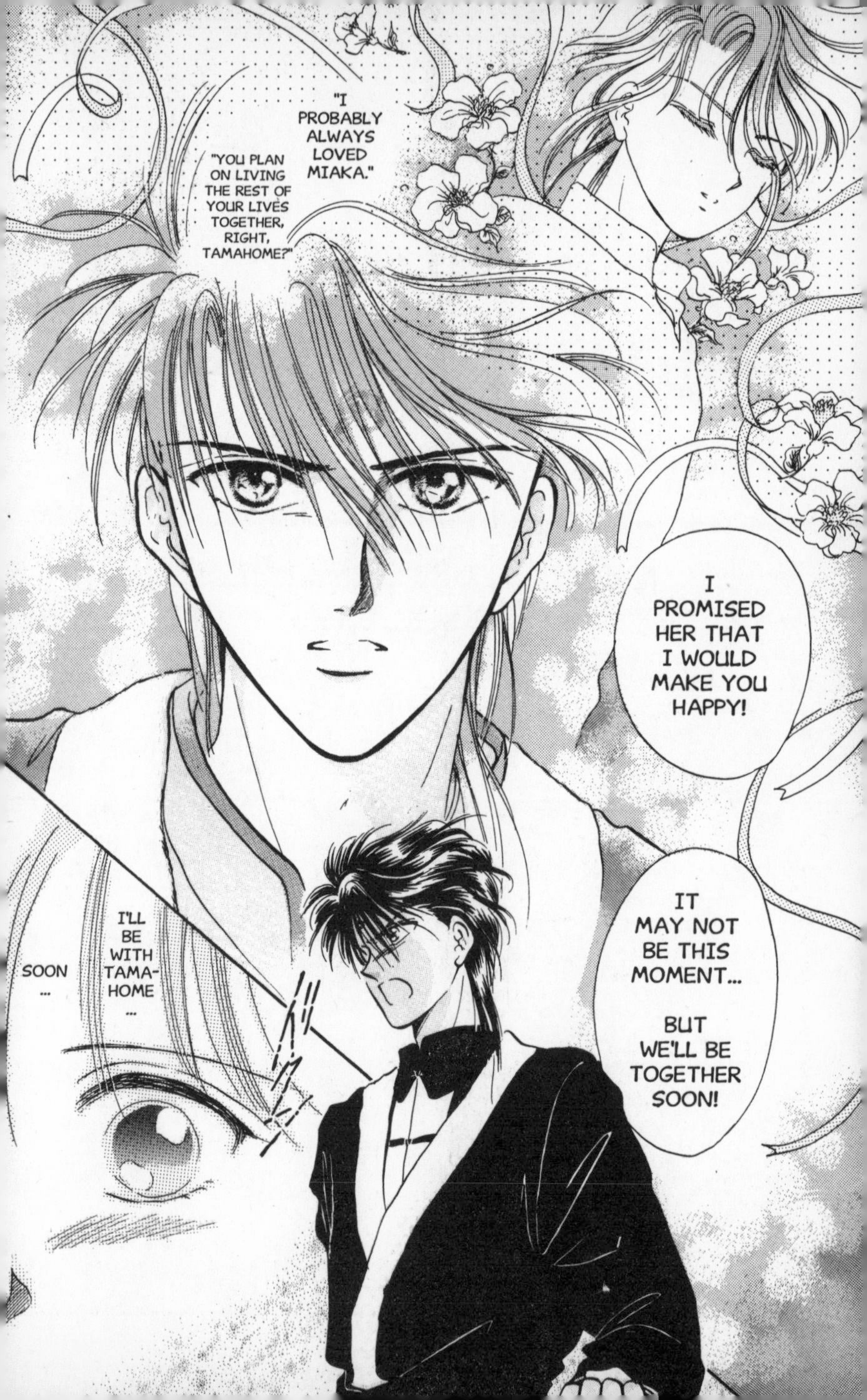
"I PROBABLY ALWAYS LOVED MIAKA."
"YOU PLAN ON LIVING THE REST OF YOUR LIVES TOGETHER, RIGHT, TAMAHOME?"
I PROMISED HER THAT I WOULD MAKE YOU HAPPY!
IT MAY NOT BE THIS MOMENT...
BUT WE'LL BE TOGETHER SOON!
I'LL BE WITH TAMA-HOME ...
SOON ...

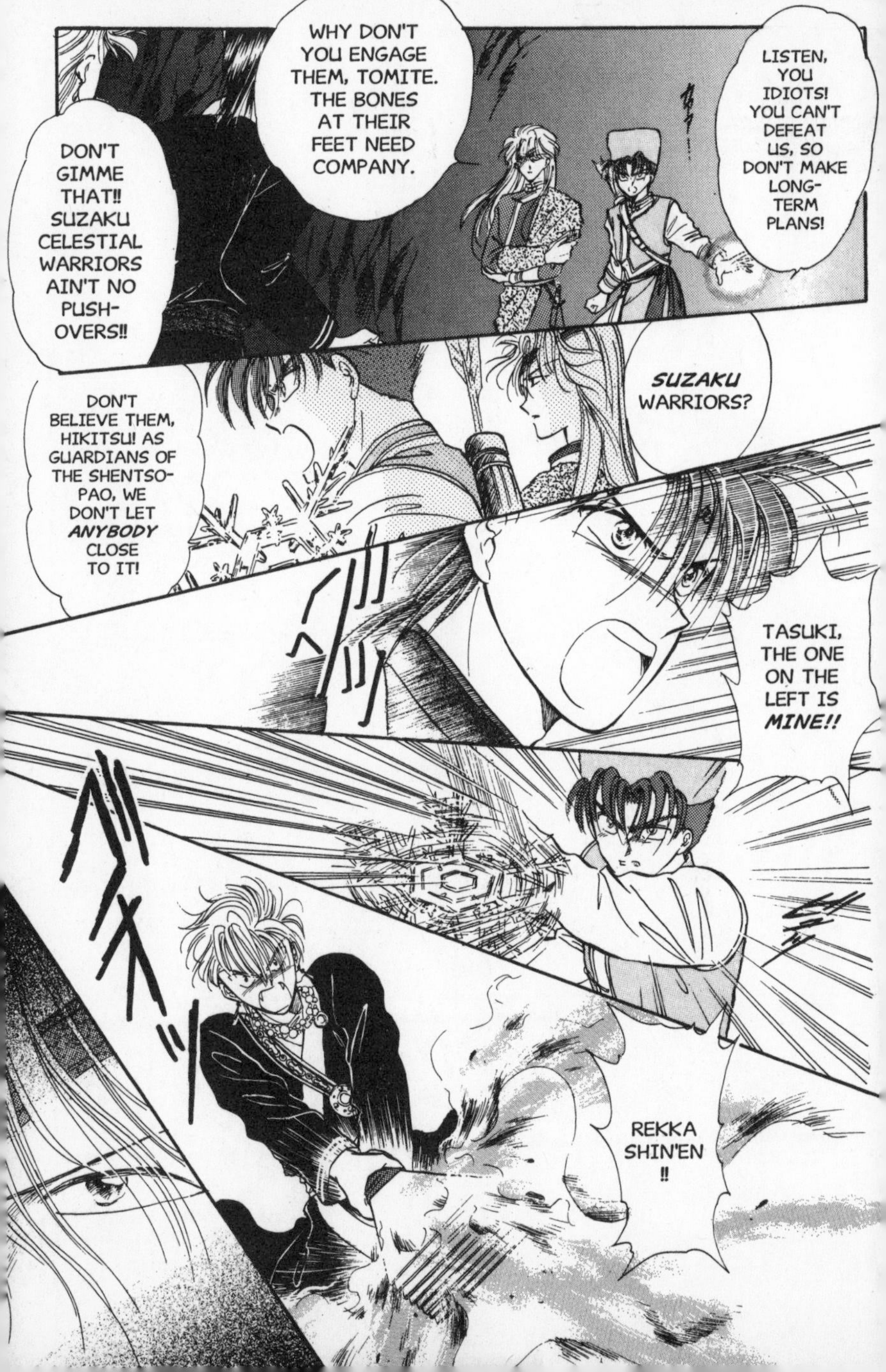
LISTEN, YOU IDIOTS! YOU CAN'T DEFEAT US, SO DON'T MAKE LONG-TERM PLANS!
WHY DON'T YOU ENGAGE THEM, TOMITE. THE BONES AT THEIR FEET NEED COMPANY.
DON'T GIMME THAT!! SUZAKU CELESTIAL WARRIORS AIN'T NO PUSH-OVERS!!
SUZAKU WARRIORS?
DON'T BELIEVE THEM, HIKITSU! AS GUARDIANS OF THE SHENTSO-PAO, WE DON'T LET *ANYBODY* CLOSE TO IT!
TASUKI, THE ONE ON THE LEFT IS *MINE!!*
REKKA SHIN'EN !!

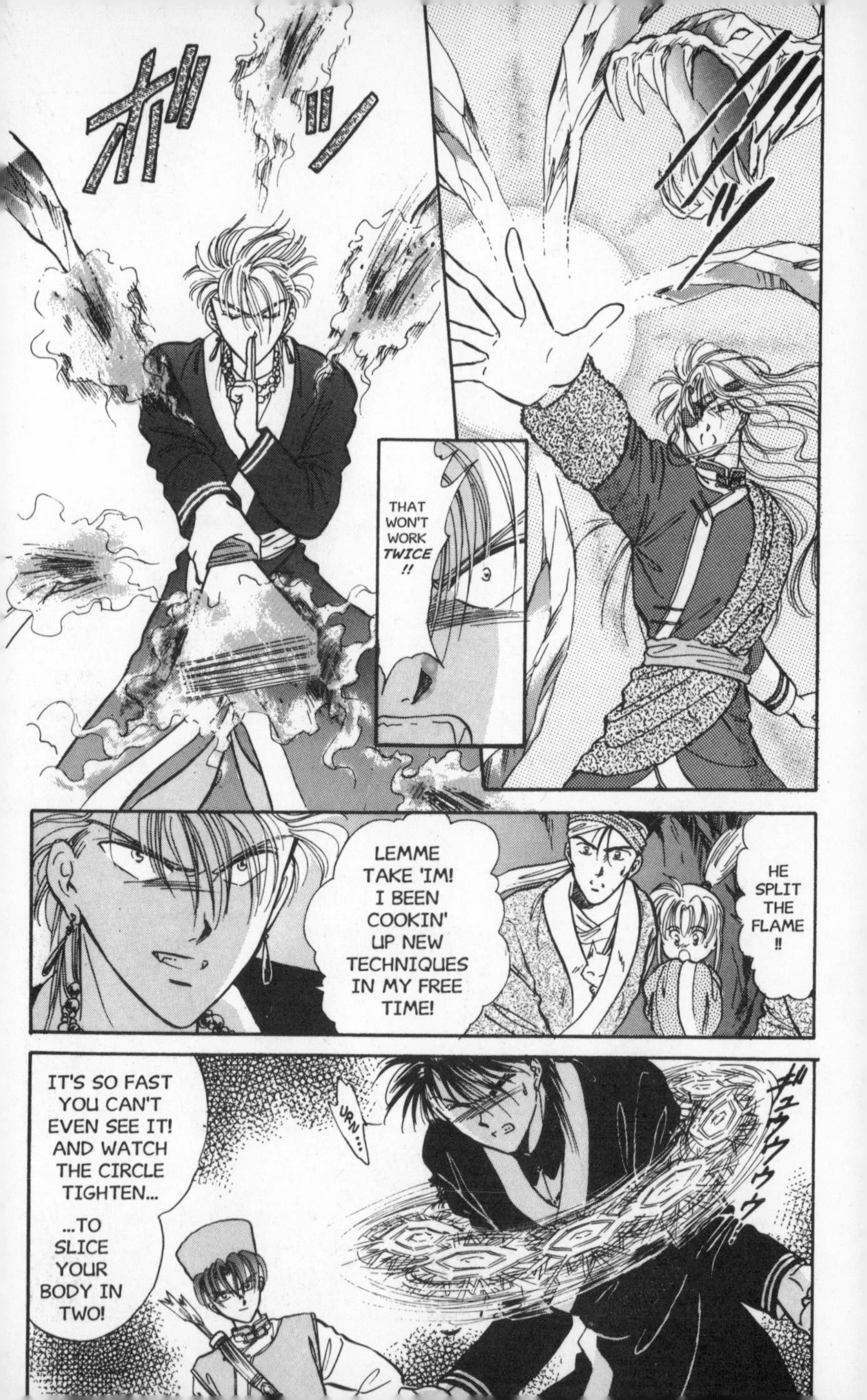
THAT WON'T WORK *TWICE* !!
HE SPLIT THE FLAME !!
LEMME TAKE 'IM! I BEEN COOKIN' UP NEW TECHNIQUES IN MY FREE TIME!
URN...
IT'S SO FAST YOU CAN'T EVEN SEE IT! AND WATCH THE CIRCLE TIGHTEN...
...TO SLICE YOUR BODY IN TWO!

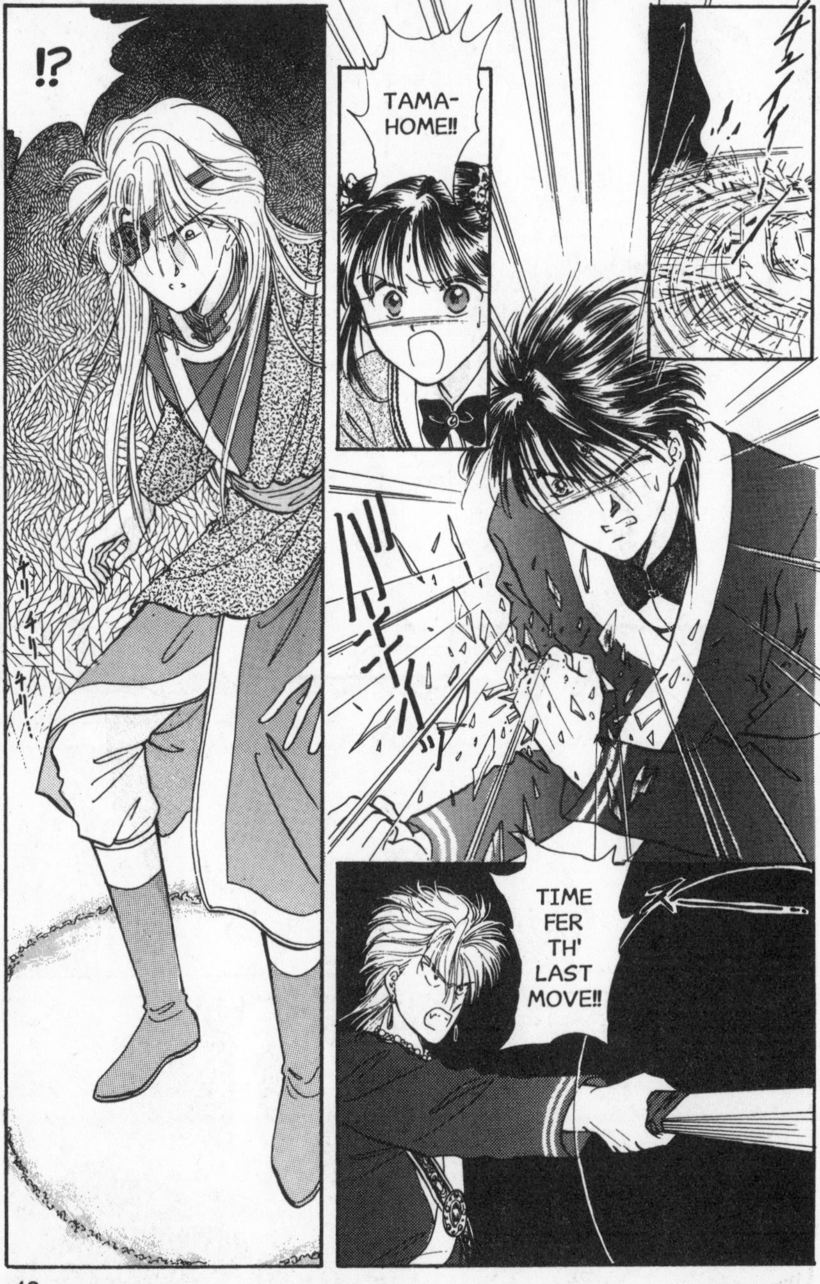
TAMA-HOME!!
TIME FER TH' LAST MOVE!!
!?

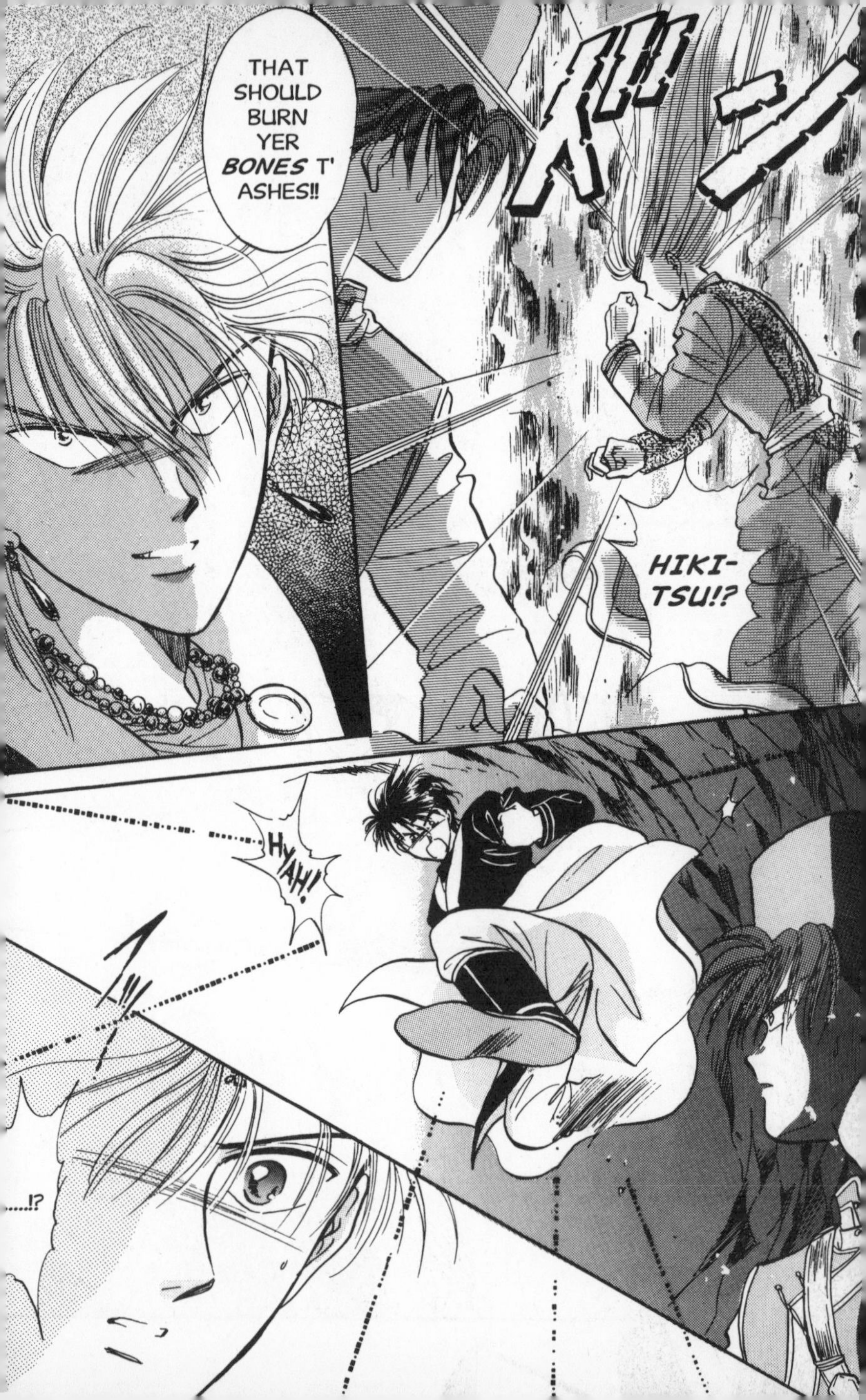

HIKI-TSU!?
THAT SHOULD BURN YER *BONES* T' ASHES!!
HYAH!
....!?

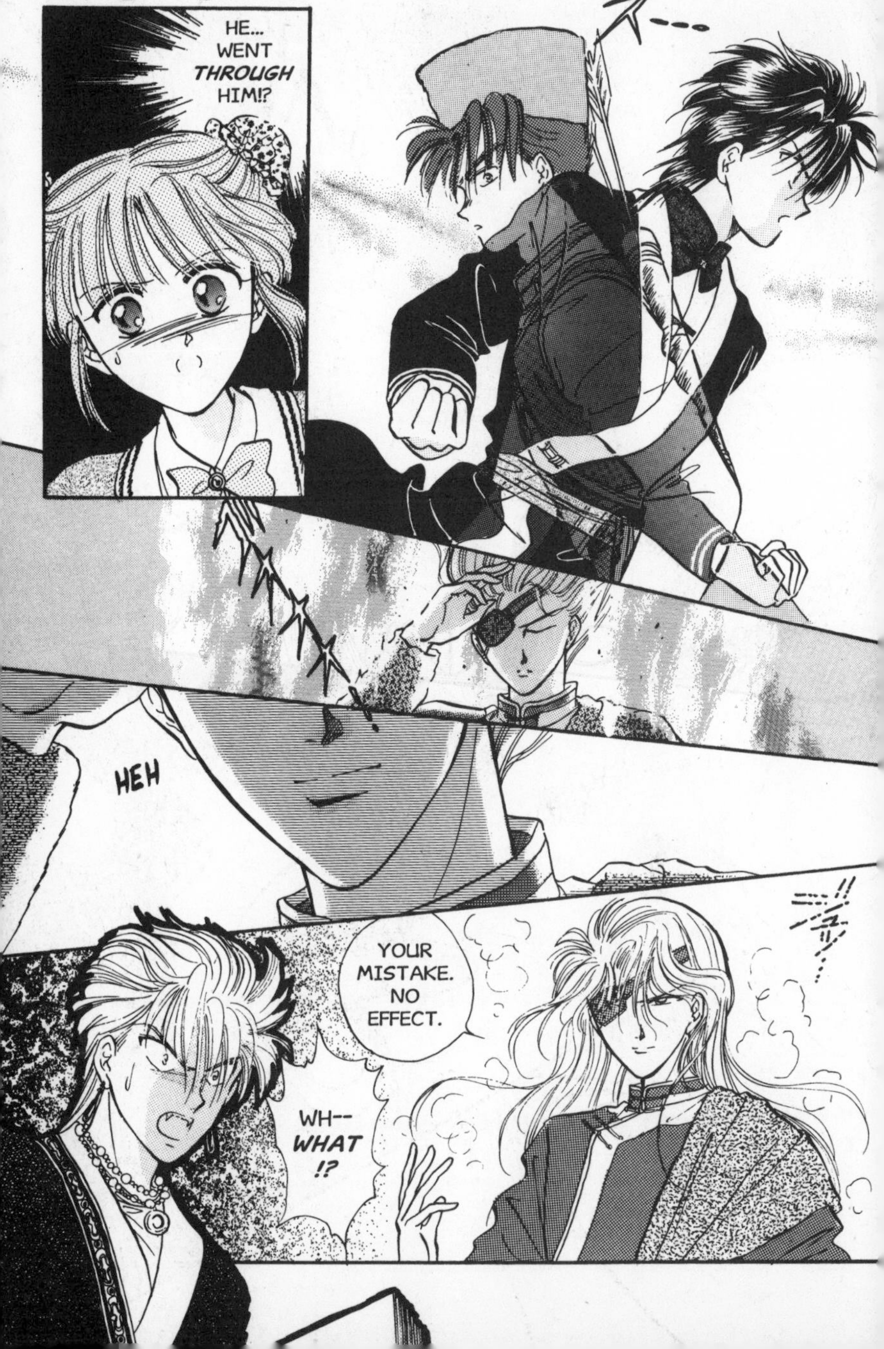
HE... WENT THROUGH HIM!?
HEH
YOUR MISTAKE. NO EFFECT.
WH-- WHAT !?

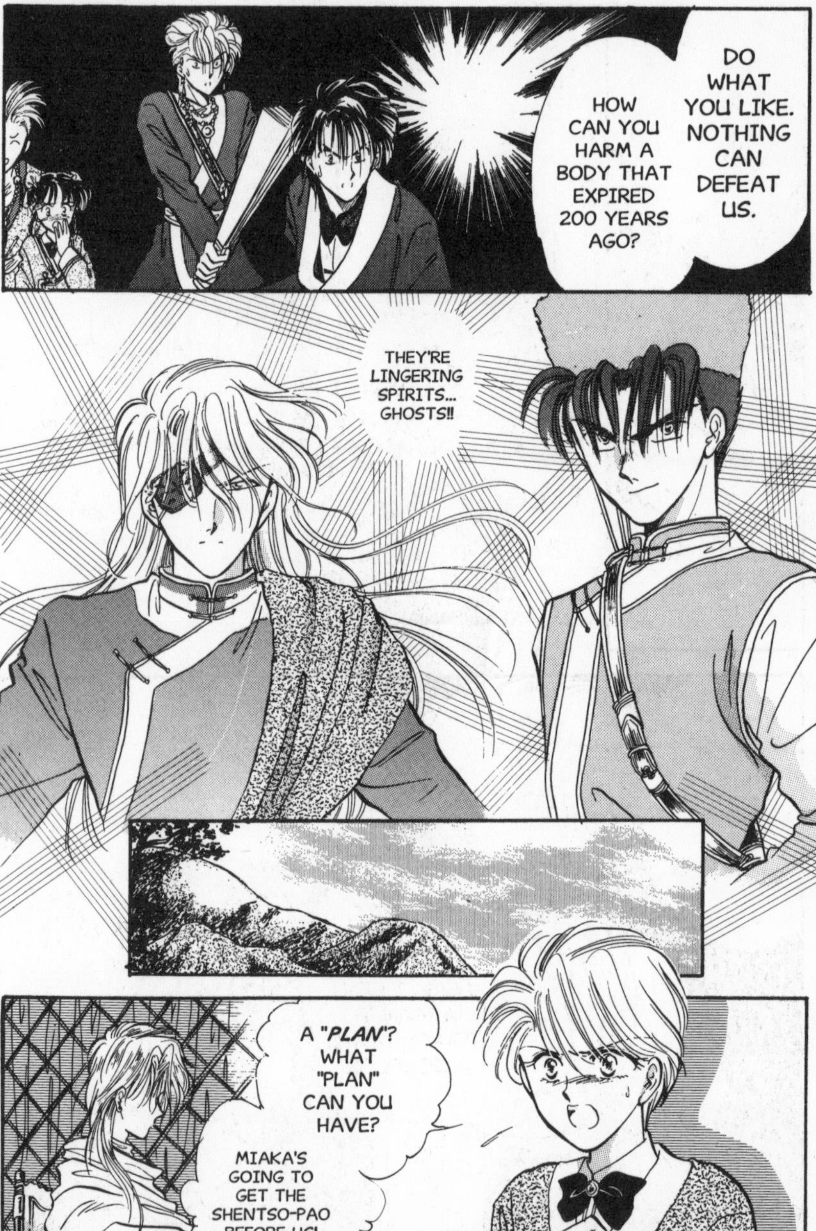
DO WHAT YOU LIKE. NOTHING CAN DEFEAT US.
HOW CAN YOU HARM A BODY THAT EXPIRED 200 YEARS AGO?
THEY'RE LINGERING SPIRITS... GHOSTS!!
A "*PLAN*"? WHAT "PLAN" CAN YOU HAVE?
MIAKA'S GOING TO GET THE SHENTSO-PAO BEFORE US!

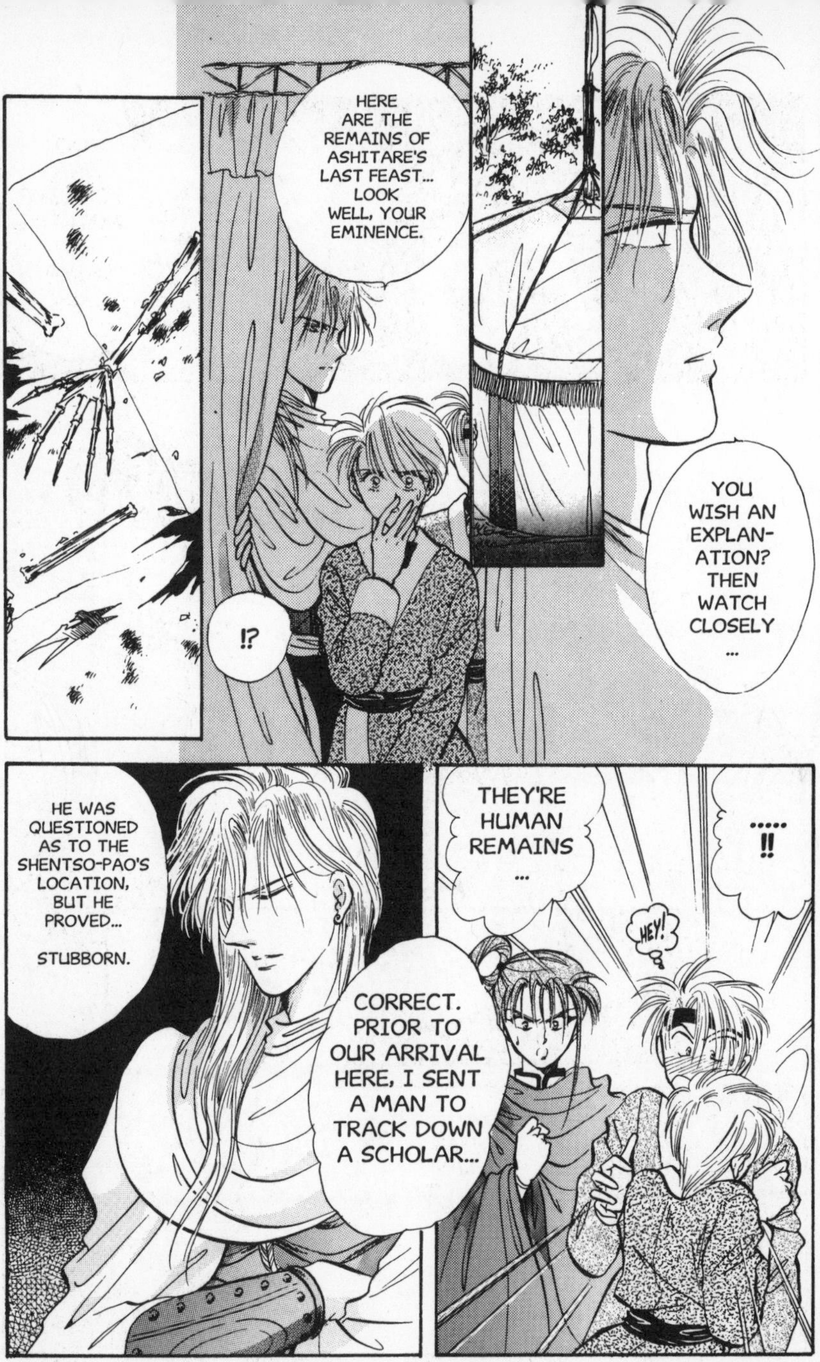
YOU WISH AN EXPLANATION? THEN WATCH CLOSELY ...
HERE ARE THE REMAINS OF ASHITARE'S LAST FEAST... LOOK WELL, YOUR EMINENCE.
!?
......!!
THEY'RE HUMAN REMAINS ...
HEY!
CORRECT. PRIOR TO OUR ARRIVAL HERE, I SENT A MAN TO TRACK DOWN A SCHOLAR...
HE WAS QUESTIONED AS TO THE SHENTSO-PAO'S LOCATION, BUT HE PROVED...
STUBBORN.

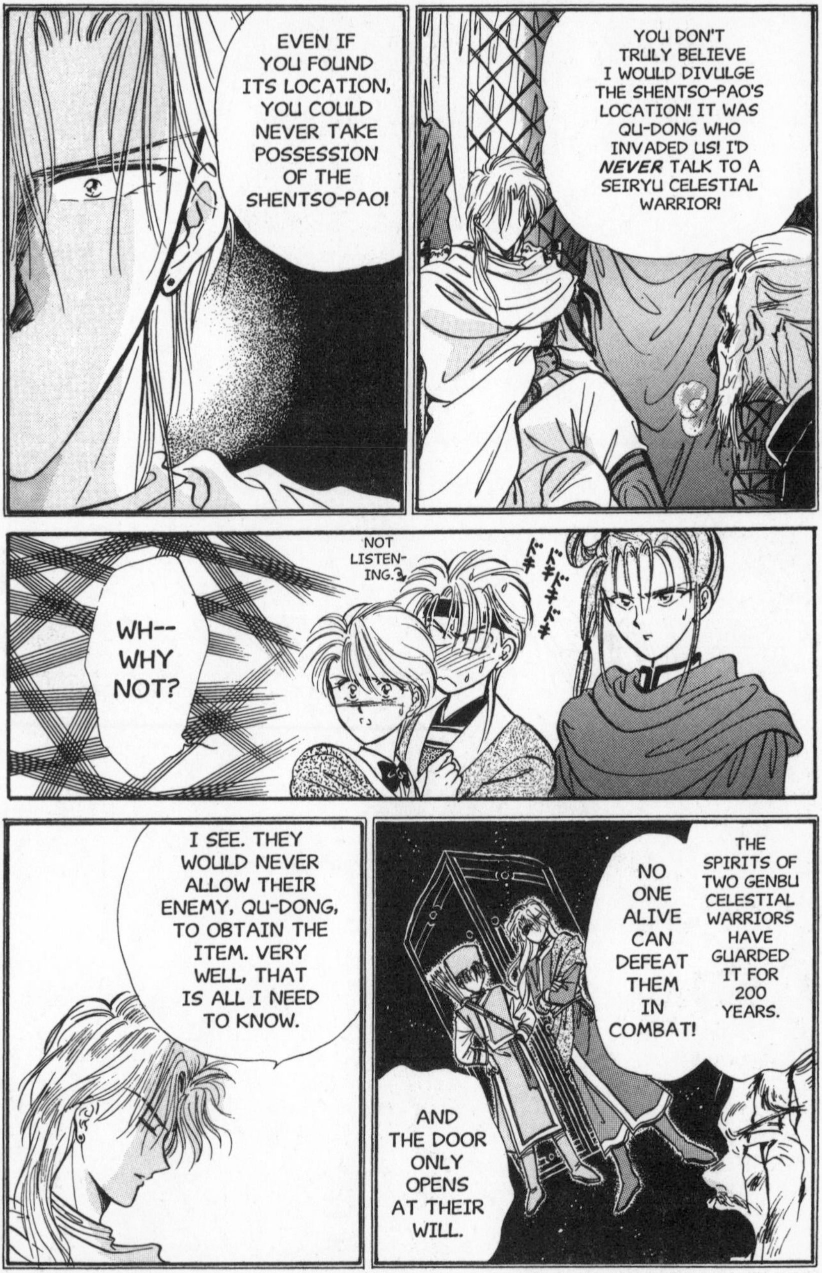
YOU DON'T TRULY BELIEVE I WOULD DIVULGE THE SHENTSO-PAO'S LOCATION! IT WAS QU-DONG WHO INVADED US! I'D NEVER TALK TO A SEIRYU CELESTIAL WARRIOR!
EVEN IF YOU FOUND ITS LOCATION, YOU COULD NEVER TAKE POSSESSION OF THE SHENTSO-PAO!
NOT LISTENING.
WH-- WHY NOT?
THE SPIRITS OF TWO GENBU CELESTIAL WARRIORS HAVE GUARDED IT FOR 200 YEARS.
NO ONE ALIVE CAN DEFEAT THEM IN COMBAT!
AND THE DOOR ONLY OPENS AT THEIR WILL.
I SEE. THEY WOULD NEVER ALLOW THEIR ENEMY, QU-DONG, TO OBTAIN THE ITEM. VERY WELL, THAT IS ALL I NEED TO KNOW.

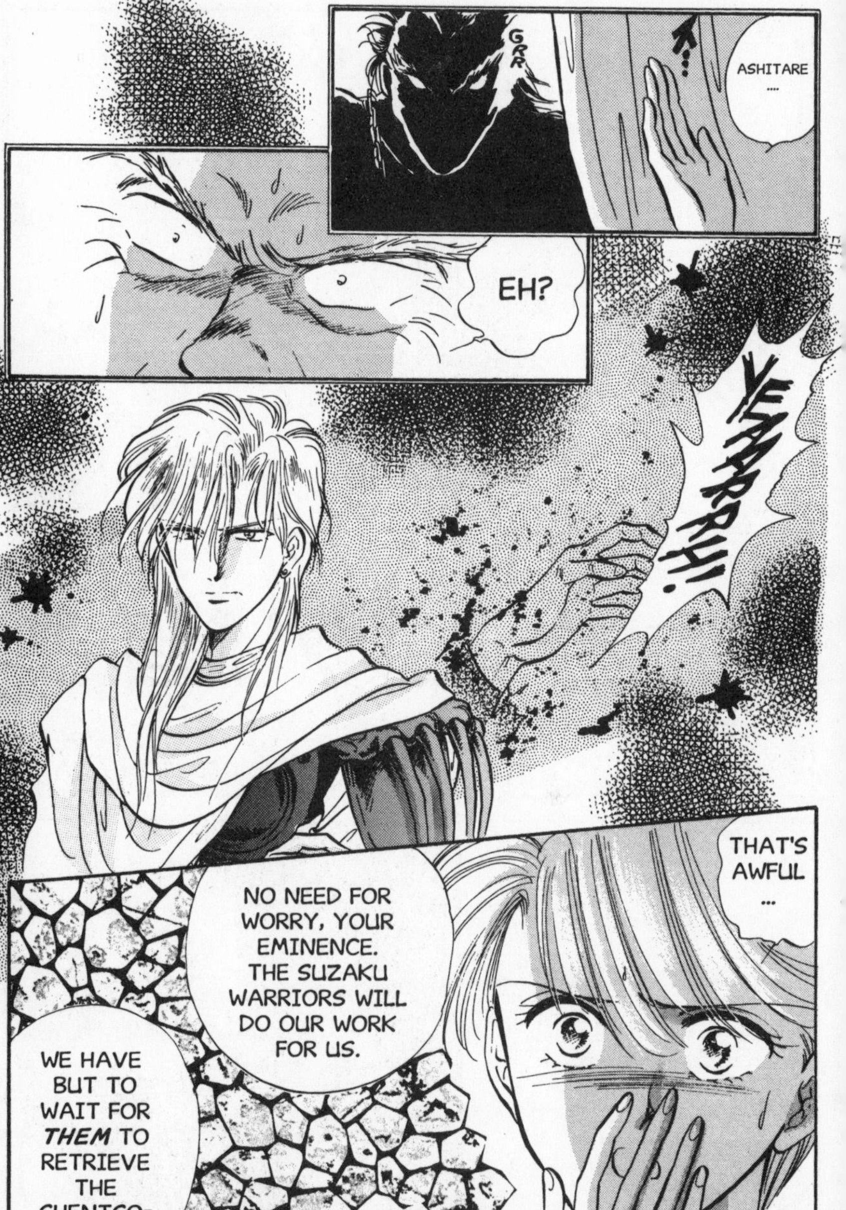
ASHITARE ....
GRR
EH?
YEAAARRRH!!
THAT'S AWFUL ...
NO NEED FOR WORRY, YOUR EMINENCE. THE SUZAKU WARRIORS WILL DO OUR WORK FOR US.
WE HAVE BUT TO WAIT FOR *THEM* TO RETRIEVE THE SHENTSO-PAO.

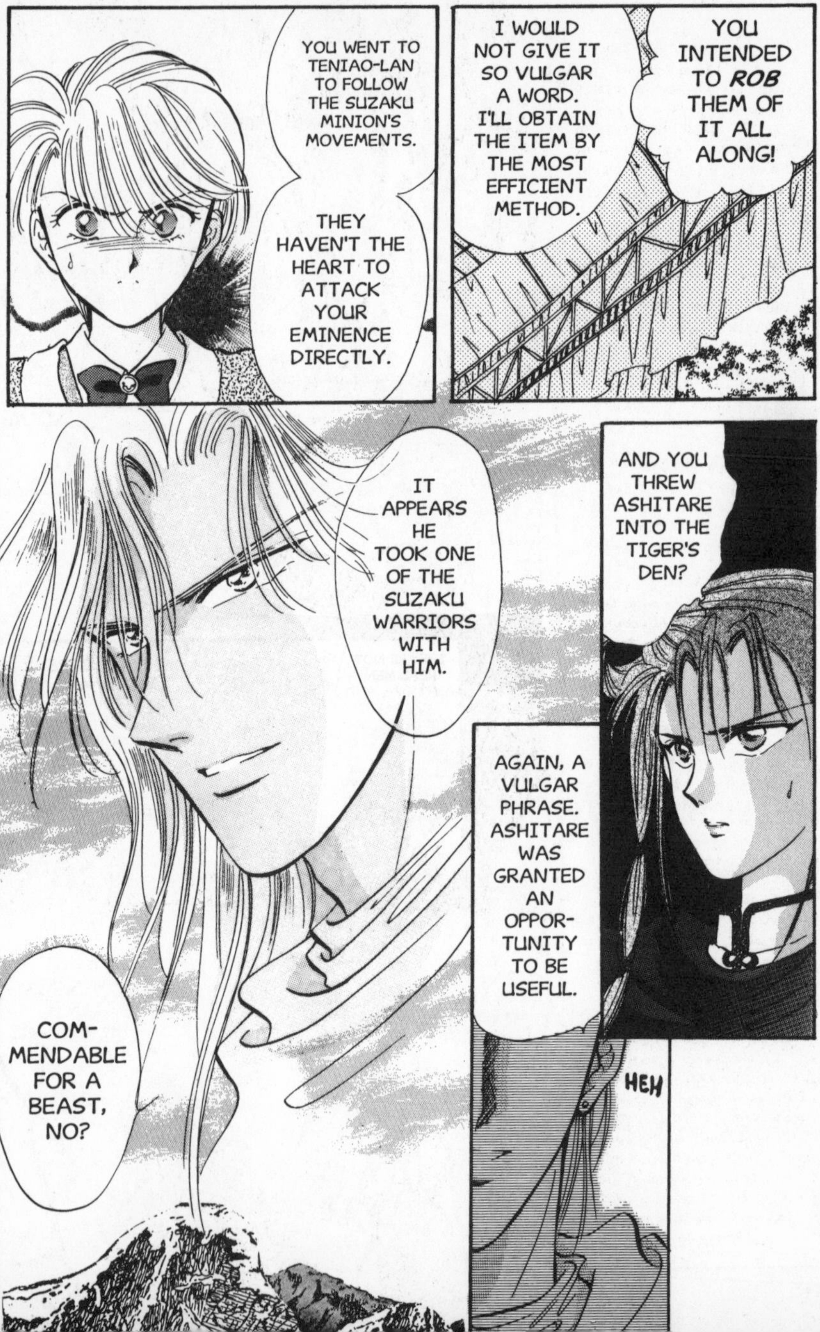
YOU INTENDED TO *ROB* THEM OF IT ALL ALONG!
I WOULD NOT GIVE IT SO VULGAR A WORD. I'LL OBTAIN THE ITEM BY THE MOST EFFICIENT METHOD.
YOU WENT TO TENIAO-LAN TO FOLLOW THE SUZAKU MINION'S MOVEMENTS.
THEY HAVEN'T THE HEART TO ATTACK YOUR EMINENCE DIRECTLY.
AND YOU THREW ASHITARE INTO THE TIGER'S DEN?
AGAIN, A VULGAR PHRASE. ASHITARE WAS GRANTED AN OPPOR-TUNITY TO BE USEFUL.
HEH
IT APPEARS HE TOOK ONE OF THE SUZAKU WARRIORS WITH HIM.
COM-MENDABLE FOR A BEAST, NO?

Lover

Continued.

There was this TV drama that used BGM from Ranma and Shurato (you know Shurato, right?). I wonder how they managed to get it. Also, I went to sleep with the TV on, and my ears pricked up! It was playing an old song I knew, "Haru no komorebi nooo naka de..." at four in the morning! They were showing Koko Kyoshi ("High School Teacher") on late-night TV!

I wandered around Beijing and Xian with my editor, but every time we tried to cross the street, there were tons of cars and bicycles that just refused to stop or even go around us. It was scary! (It almost seemed as if we'd be the ones scolded if we were hit!) We did go to a fast food restaurant, but because of the way we took out our money they could tell we were Japanese. The Japanese either put money on the counter or hand it over, but the Chinese apparently toss their cash. There were rows of shops with counters where people ate while standing up, but I didn't want an upset stomach, so I just watched them. The worst part is when they find out you're Japanese, children and all sorts of people start asking for handouts, so I realized that when I'm somewhere like that, it's best to leave my camera and travel-agency badge behind.

I also looked for game centers, and I found one, but they just had poker and games like that. Totally different from the ones in Japan. But then I wandered into a back alley and found one that was a lot like a Japanese game center. It was so small and filled with children, I couldn't play anything. By the way, the game centers are called Denshi Yūgi ("Electronic Game").

Makes sense, huh?

I also noticed how watermelons are served all the time, and then I found out that they're a major crop over there. I'd notice on the streets, the sellers would have piles of 20 watermelons or so. I don't know if I could eat them every day...

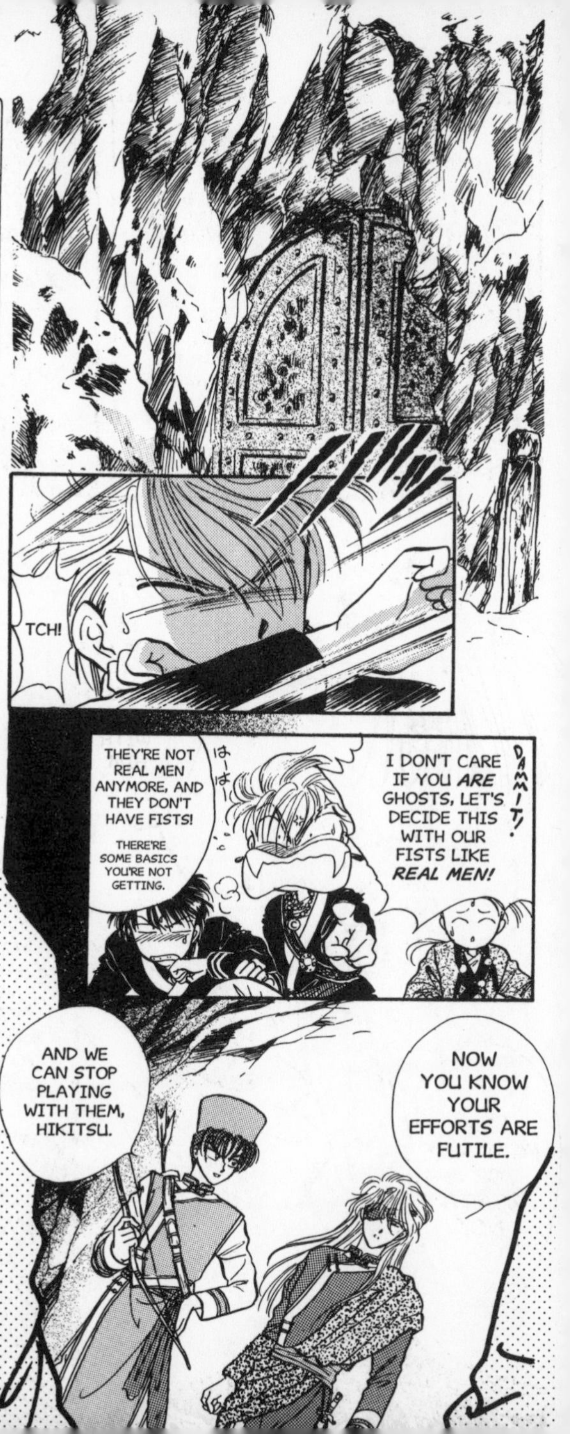

TCH!
DAMMIT!
I DON'T CARE IF YOU *ARE* GHOSTS, LET'S DECIDE THIS WITH OUR FISTS LIKE *REAL MEN!*
はーはー
THEY'RE NOT REAL MEN ANYMORE, AND THEY DON'T HAVE FISTS!
THERE'RE SOME BASICS YOU'RE NOT GETTING.
NOW YOU KNOW YOUR EFFORTS ARE FUTILE.
AND WE CAN STOP PLAYING WITH THEM, HIKITSU.

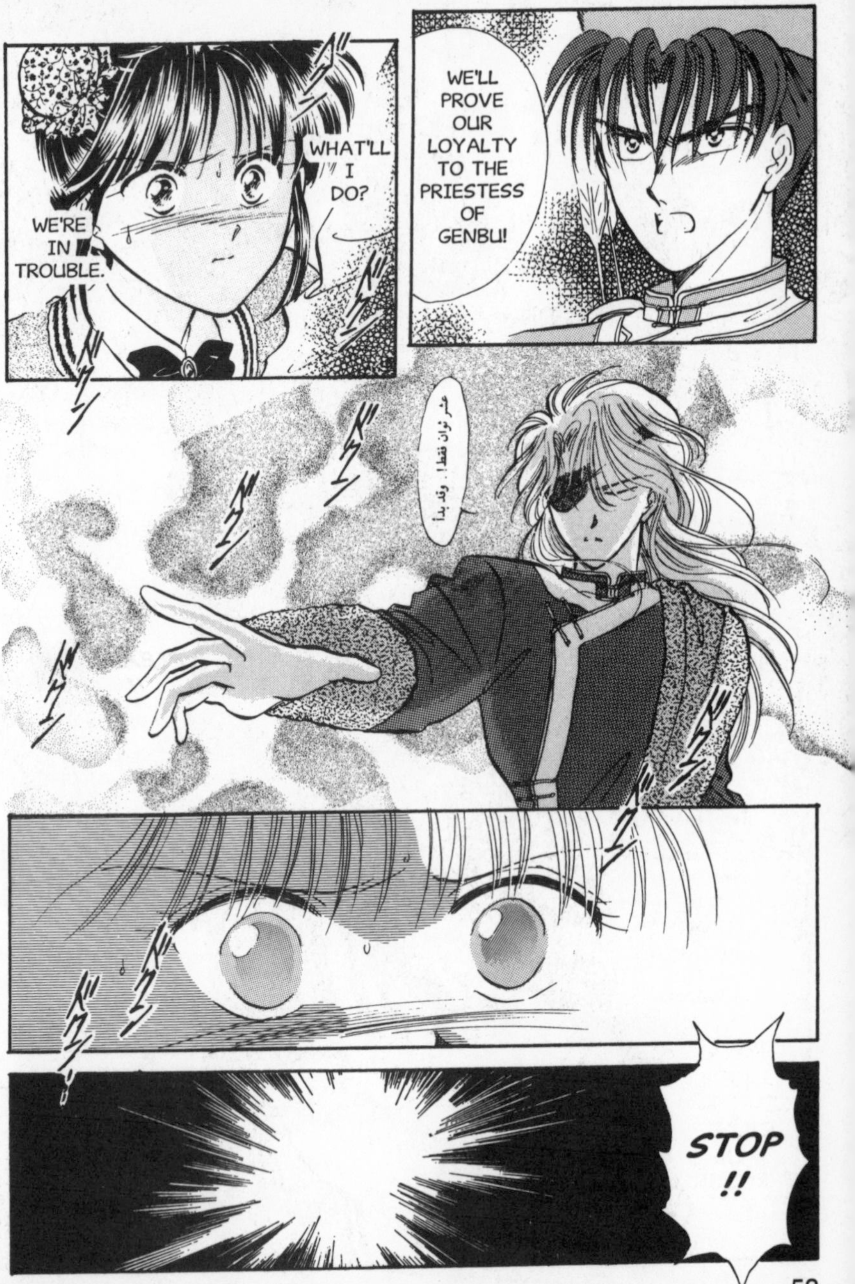
WE'LL PROVE OUR LOYALTY TO THE PRIESTESS OF GENBU!
WHAT'LL I DO?
WE'RE IN TROUBLE.
عشر ثوان فقط! . وقد بدأ
STOP !!

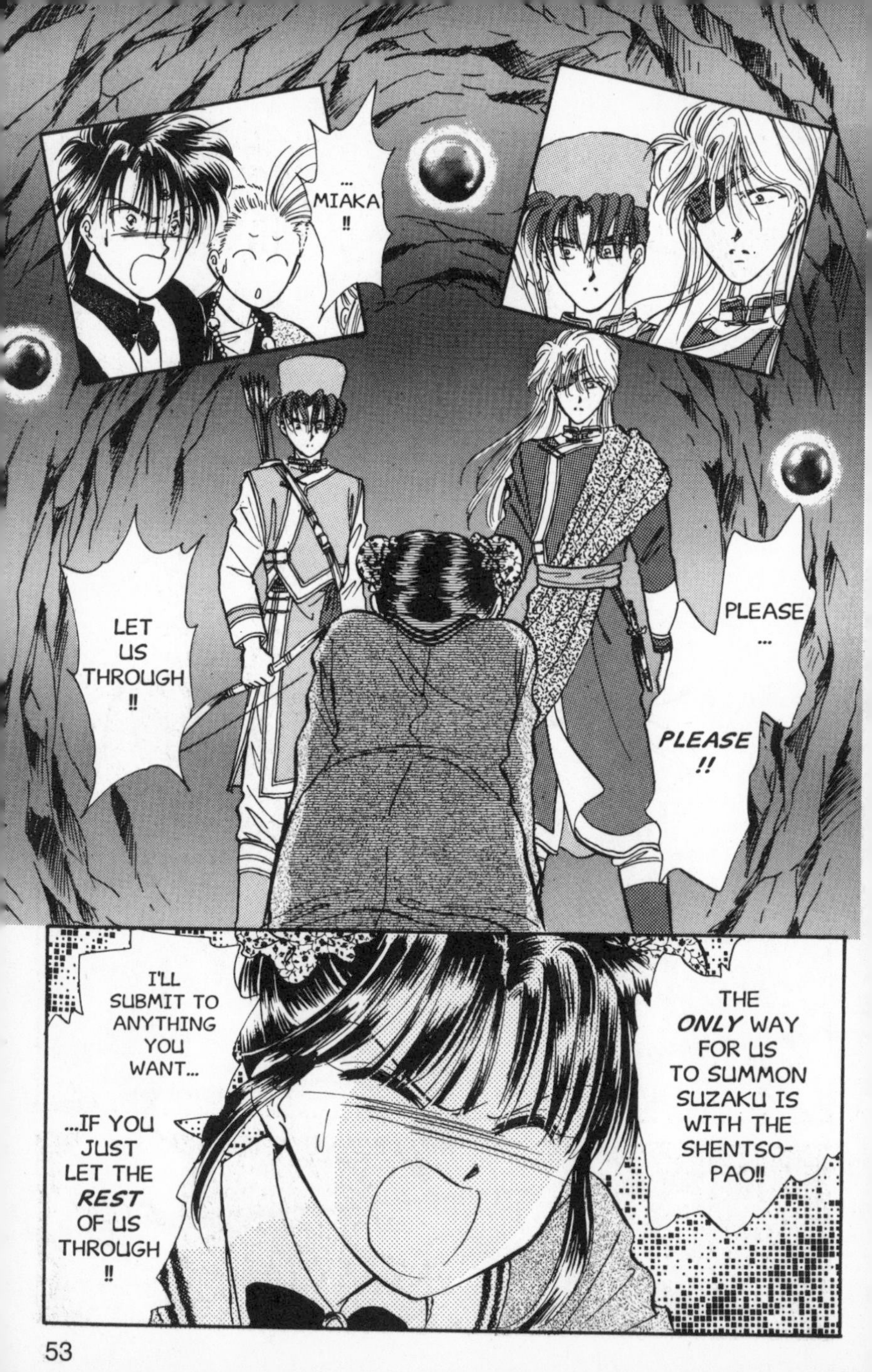

...MIAKA!!
PLEASE... *PLEASE*!!
LET US THROUGH!!
THE *ONLY* WAY FOR US TO SUMMON SUZAKU IS WITH THE SHENTSO-PAO!!
I'LL SUBMIT TO ANYTHING YOU WANT...
...IF YOU JUST LET THE *REST* OF US THROUGH!!

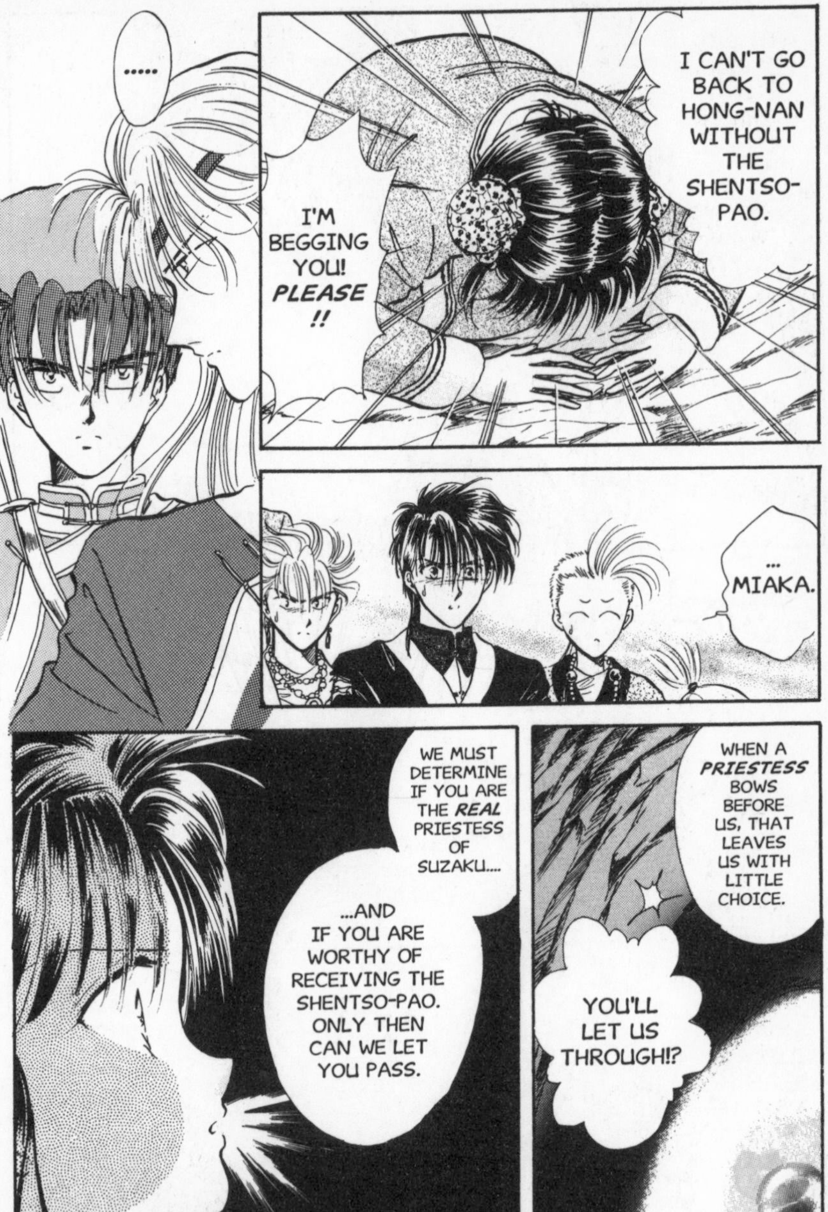
I CAN'T GO BACK TO HONG-NAN WITHOUT THE SHENTSO-PAO.
I'M BEGGING YOU! PLEASE !!
... MIAKA.
......
WHEN A PRIESTESS BOWS BEFORE US, THAT LEAVES US WITH LITTLE CHOICE.
YOU'LL LET US THROUGH!?
WE MUST DETERMINE IF YOU ARE THE REAL PRIESTESS OF SUZAKU....
...AND IF YOU ARE WORTHY OF RECEIVING THE SHENTSO-PAO. ONLY THEN CAN WE LET YOU PASS.

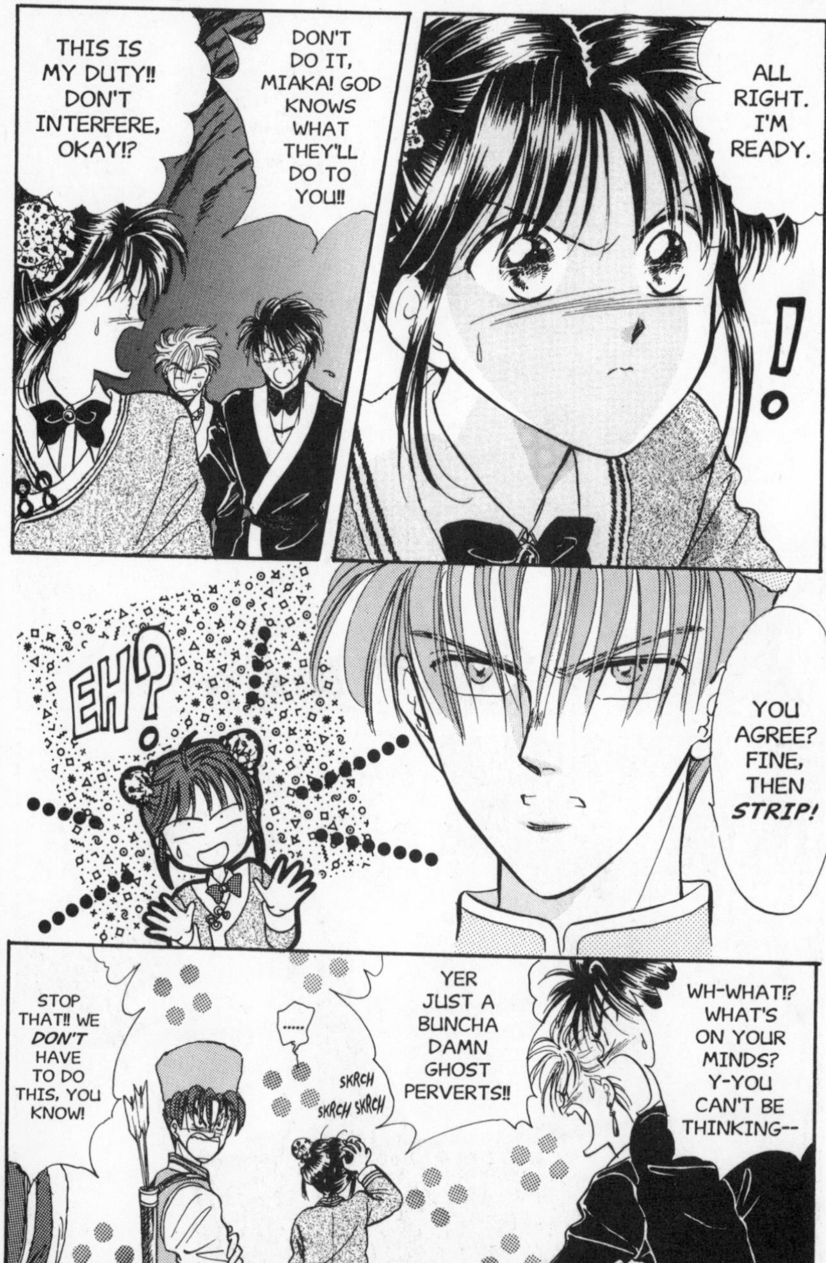
ALL RIGHT. I'M READY.
!
DON'T DO IT, MIAKA! GOD KNOWS WHAT THEY'LL DO TO YOU!!
THIS IS MY DUTY!! DON'T INTERFERE, OKAY!?
YOU AGREE? FINE, THEN *STRIP!*
EH?
WH-WHAT!? WHAT'S ON YOUR MINDS? Y-YOU CAN'T BE THINKING--
YER JUST A BUNCHA DAMN GHOST PERVERTS!!
SKRCH SKRCH SKRCH
......
STOP THAT!! WE *DON'T* HAVE TO DO THIS, YOU KNOW!

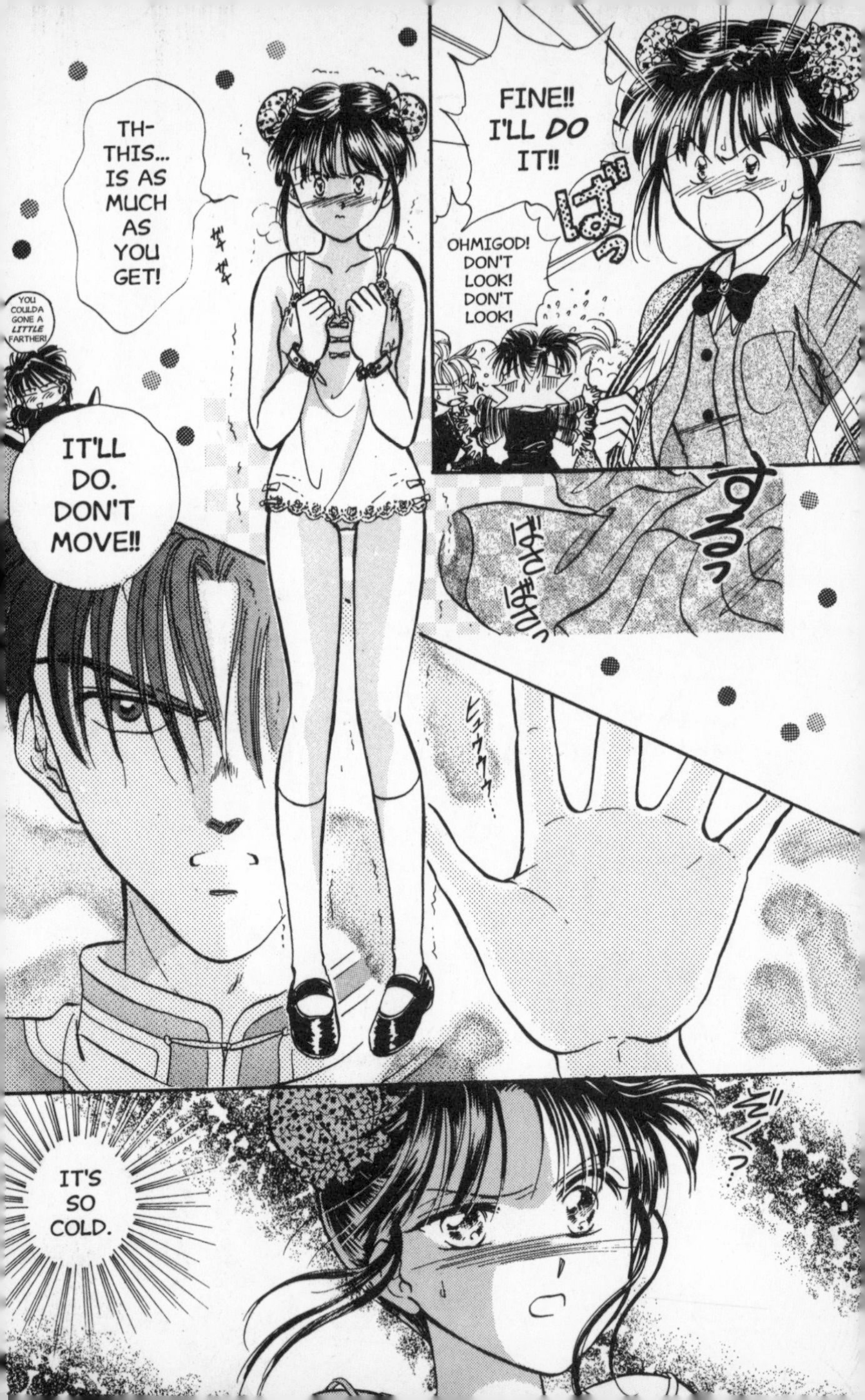
FINE!! I'LL *DO* IT!!
OHMIGOD! DON'T LOOK! DON'T LOOK!
TH-THIS... IS AS MUCH AS YOU GET!
YOU COULDA GONE A *LITTLE* FARTHER!
IT'LL DO. DON'T MOVE!!
IT'S SO COLD.

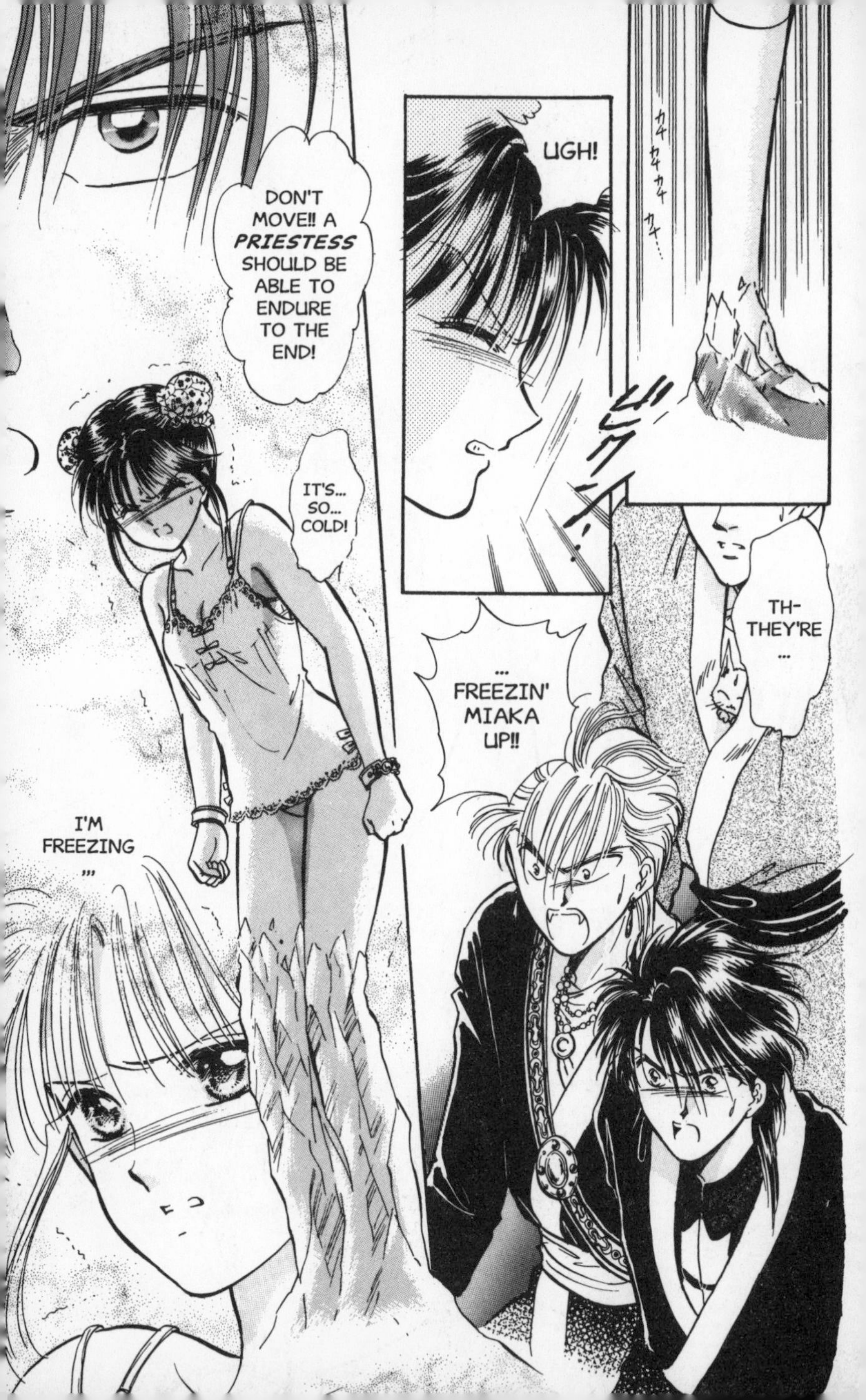

カチ カチ カチ カチ…
UGH!
TH-THEY'RE ...
... FREEZIN' MIAKA UP!!
DON'T MOVE!! A *PRIESTESS* SHOULD BE ABLE TO ENDURE TO THE END!
IT'S... SO... COLD!
I'M FREEZING ...

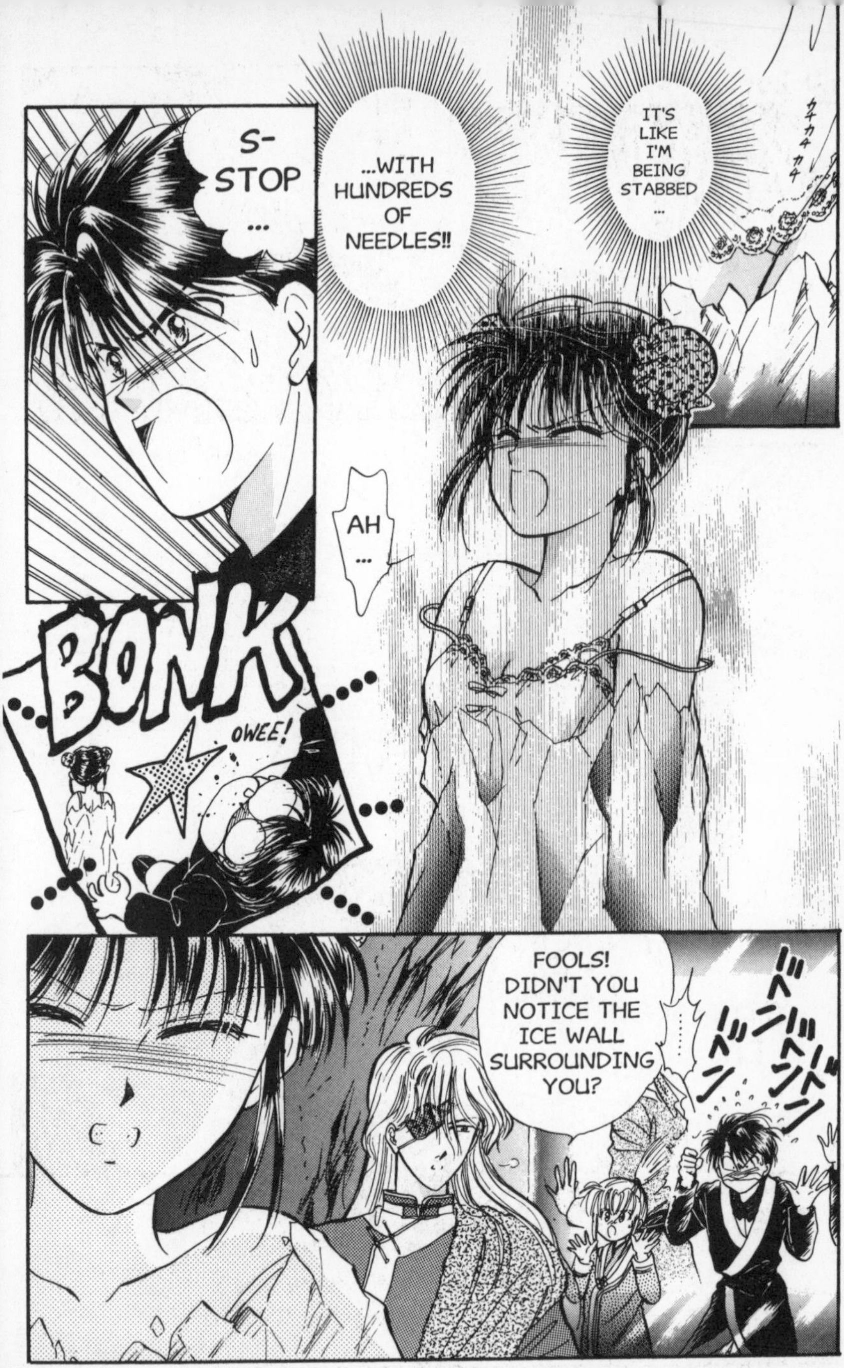
IT'S LIKE I'M BEING STABBED ...
...WITH HUNDREDS OF NEEDLES!!
S-STOP ...
AH ...
BONK
OWEE!
FOOLS! DIDN'T YOU NOTICE THE ICE WALL SURROUNDING YOU?
......

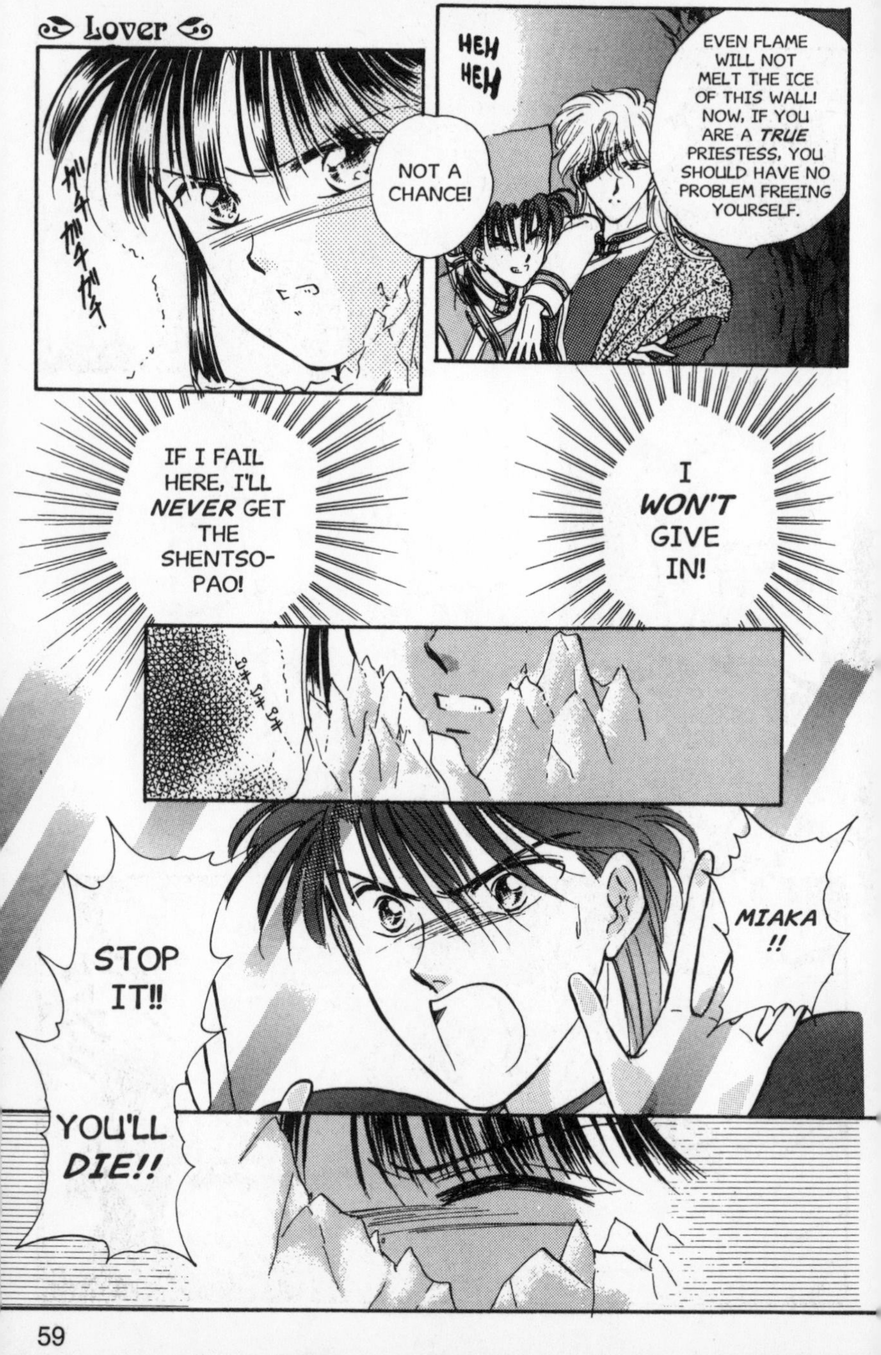
EVEN FLAME WILL NOT MELT THE ICE OF THIS WALL! NOW, IF YOU ARE A *TRUE* PRIESTESS, YOU SHOULD HAVE NO PROBLEM FREEING YOURSELF.
HEH HEH
NOT A CHANCE!
I *WON'T* GIVE IN!
IF I FAIL HERE, I'LL *NEVER* GET THE SHENTSO-PAO!
MIAKA!!
STOP IT!!
YOU'LL *DIE!!*

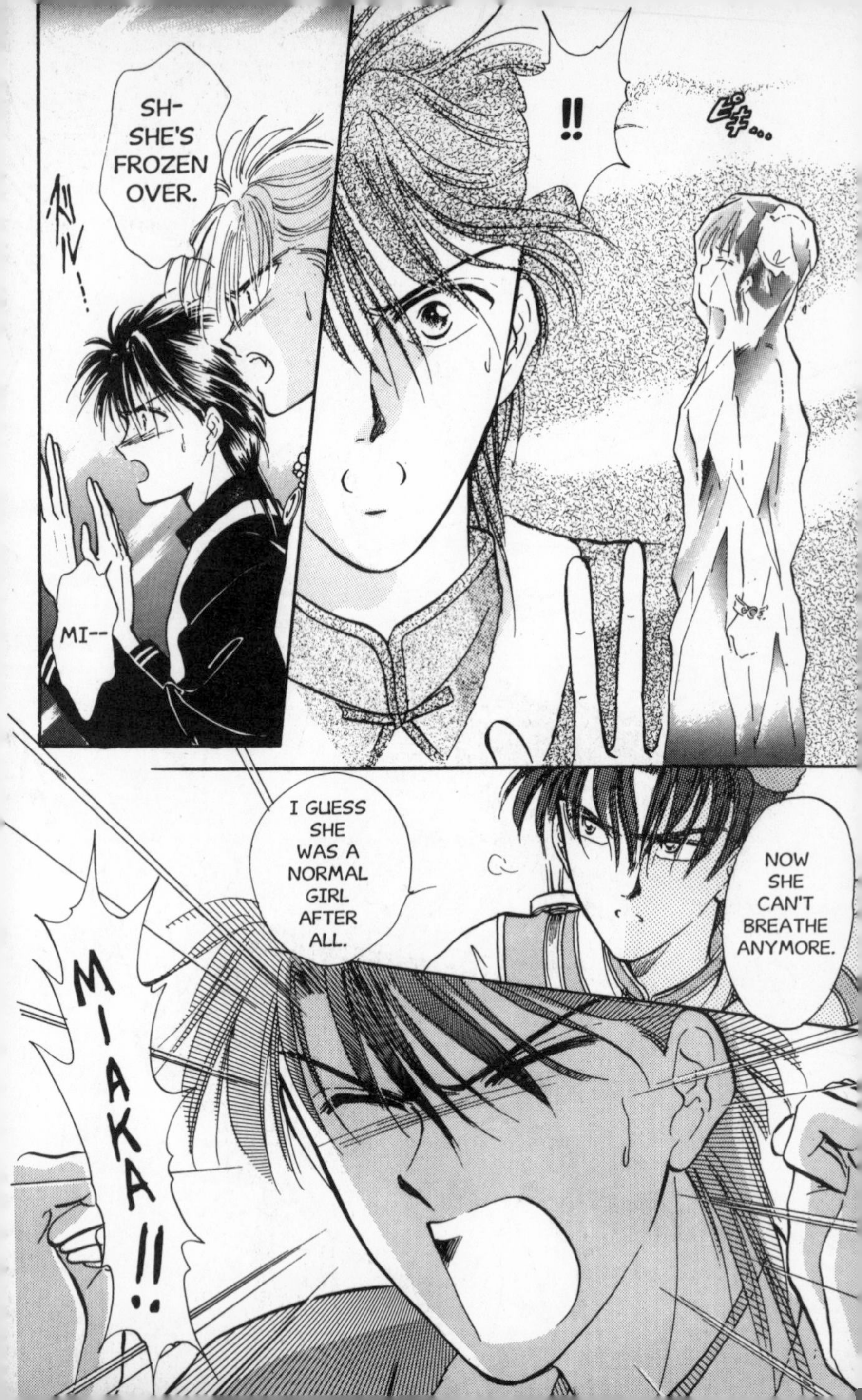
!!
SH- SHE'S FROZEN OVER.
MI--
NOW SHE CAN'T BREATHE ANYMORE.
I GUESS SHE WAS A NORMAL GIRL AFTER ALL.
MIAKA!!

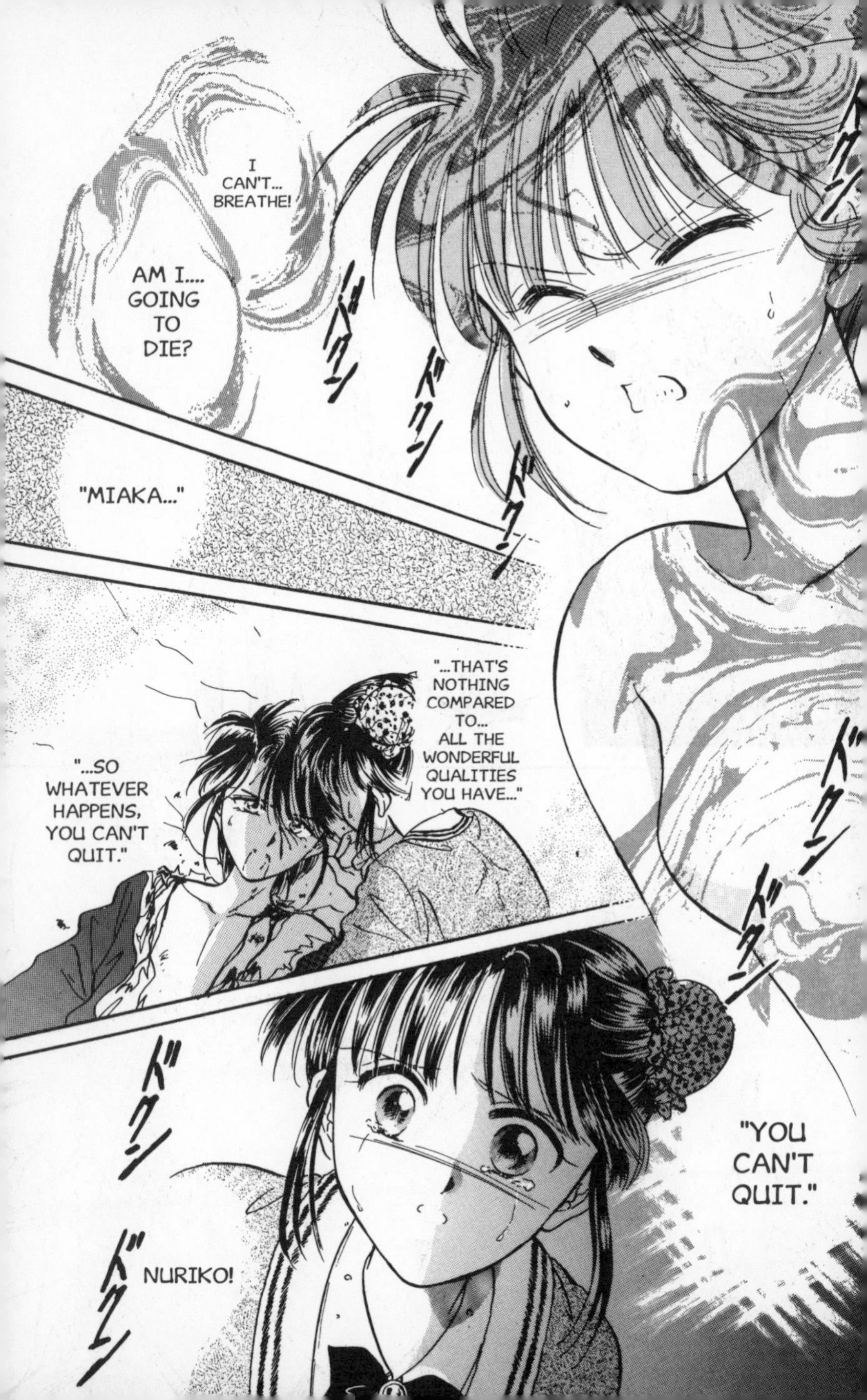
I CAN'T... BREATHE!
AM I.... GOING TO DIE?
"MIAKA..."
"...THAT'S NOTHING COMPARED TO... ALL THE WONDERFUL QUALITIES YOU HAVE..."
"...SO WHATEVER HAPPENS, YOU CAN'T QUIT."
"YOU CAN'T QUIT."
NURIKO!

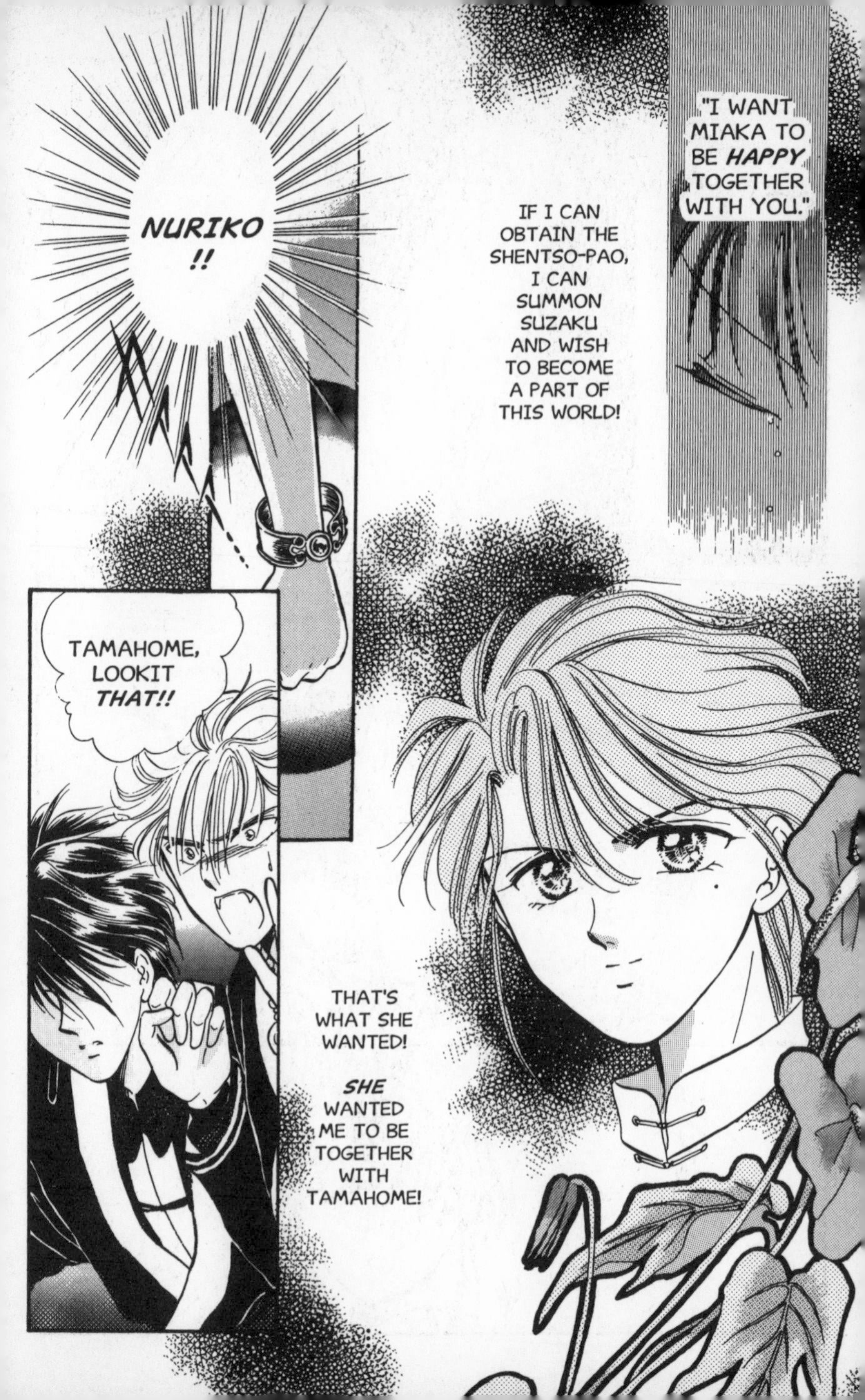
"I WANT MIAKA TO BE *HAPPY* TOGETHER WITH YOU."
IF I CAN OBTAIN THE SHENTSO-PAO, I CAN SUMMON SUZAKU AND WISH TO BECOME A PART OF THIS WORLD!
NURIKO !!
THAT'S WHAT SHE WANTED!
SHE WANTED ME TO BE TOGETHER WITH TAMAHOME!
TAMAHOME, LOOKIT *THAT!!*

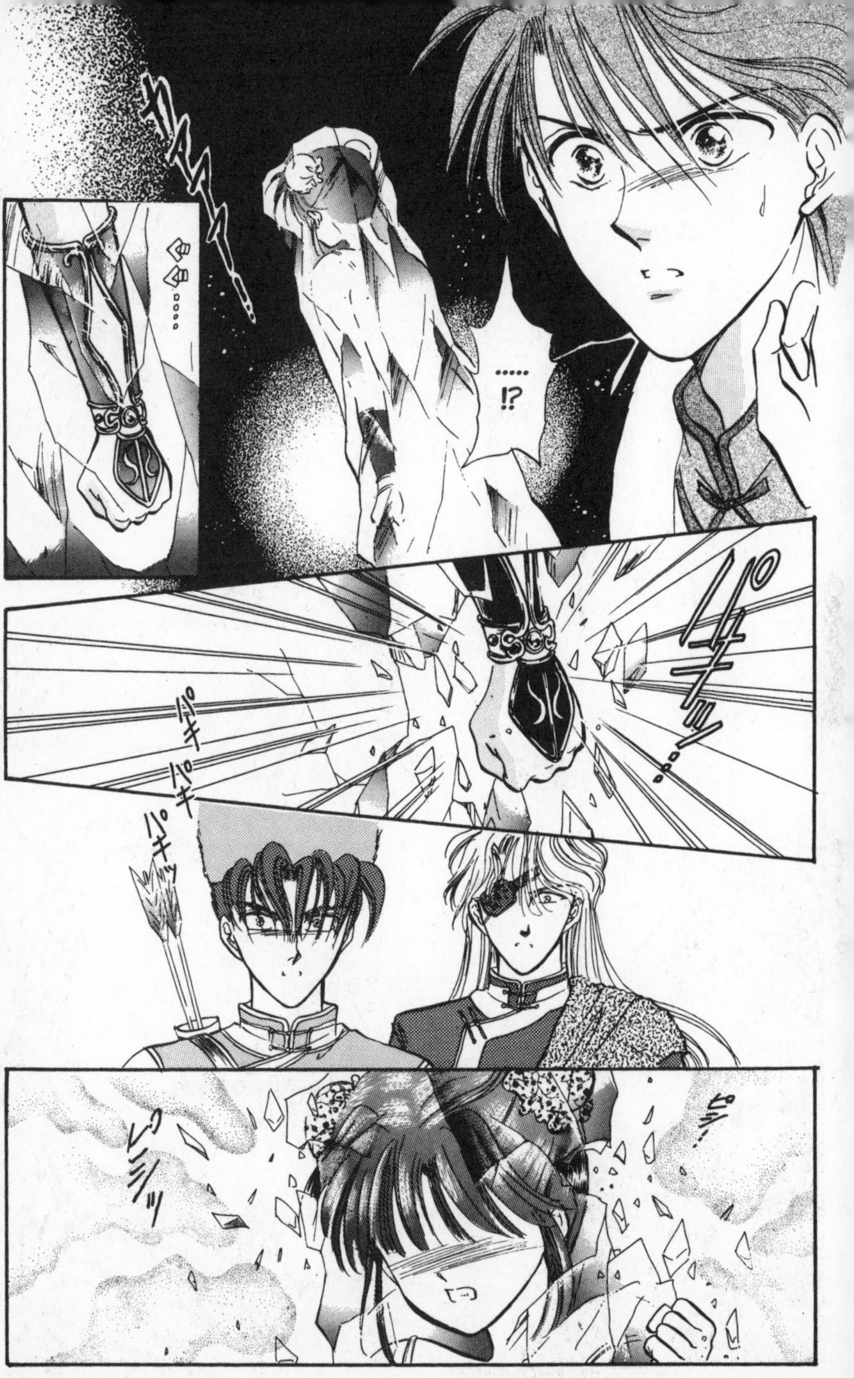
......!?
ぐ ぐ....
パキ パキ パキッ
ピシ‥‥

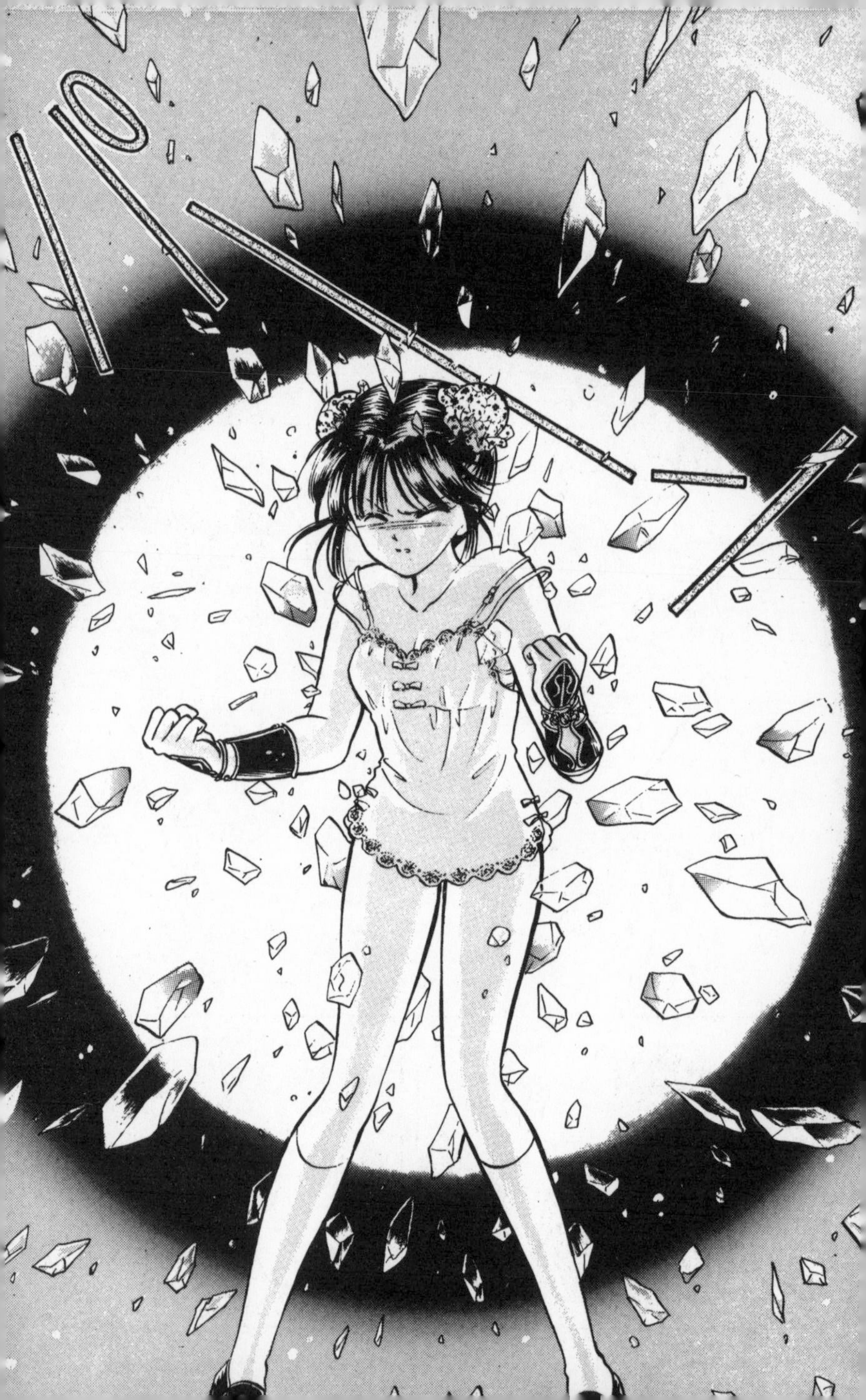

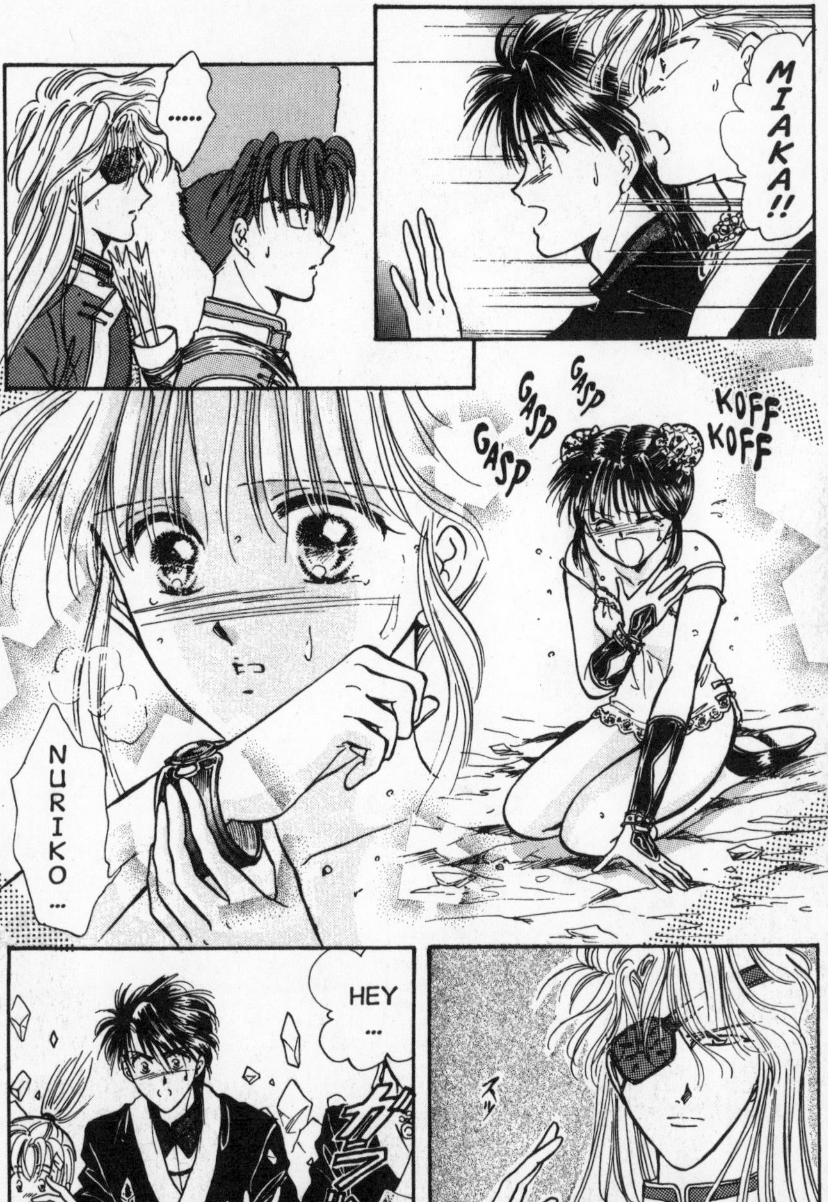
MIAKA!!
......
KOFF KOFF
GASP GASP GASP
NURIKO ...
HEY ...

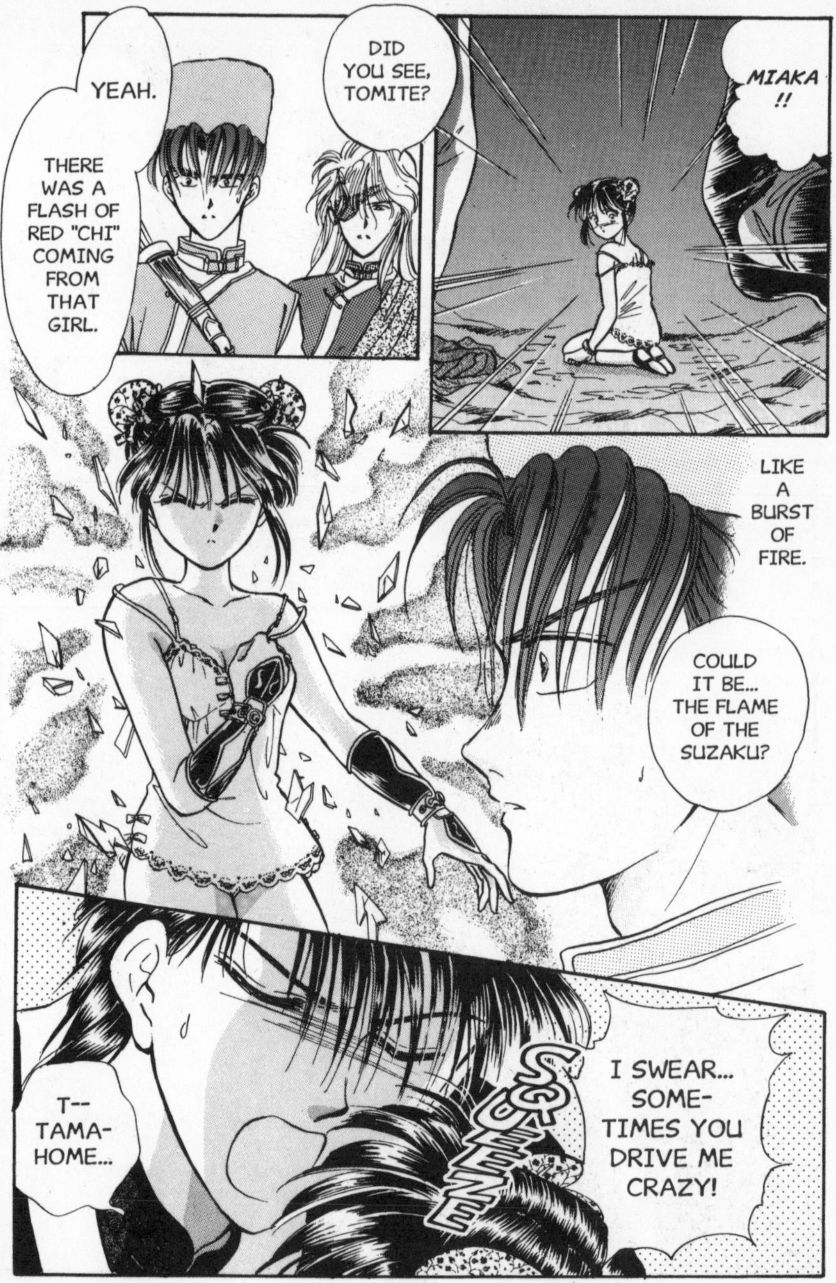
MIAKA !!
DID YOU SEE, TOMITE?
YEAH.
THERE WAS A FLASH OF RED "CHI" COMING FROM THAT GIRL.
LIKE A BURST OF FIRE.
COULD IT BE... THE FLAME OF THE SUZAKU?
I SWEAR... SOME-TIMES YOU DRIVE ME CRAZY!
SQUEEZE
T-- TAMA-HOME...

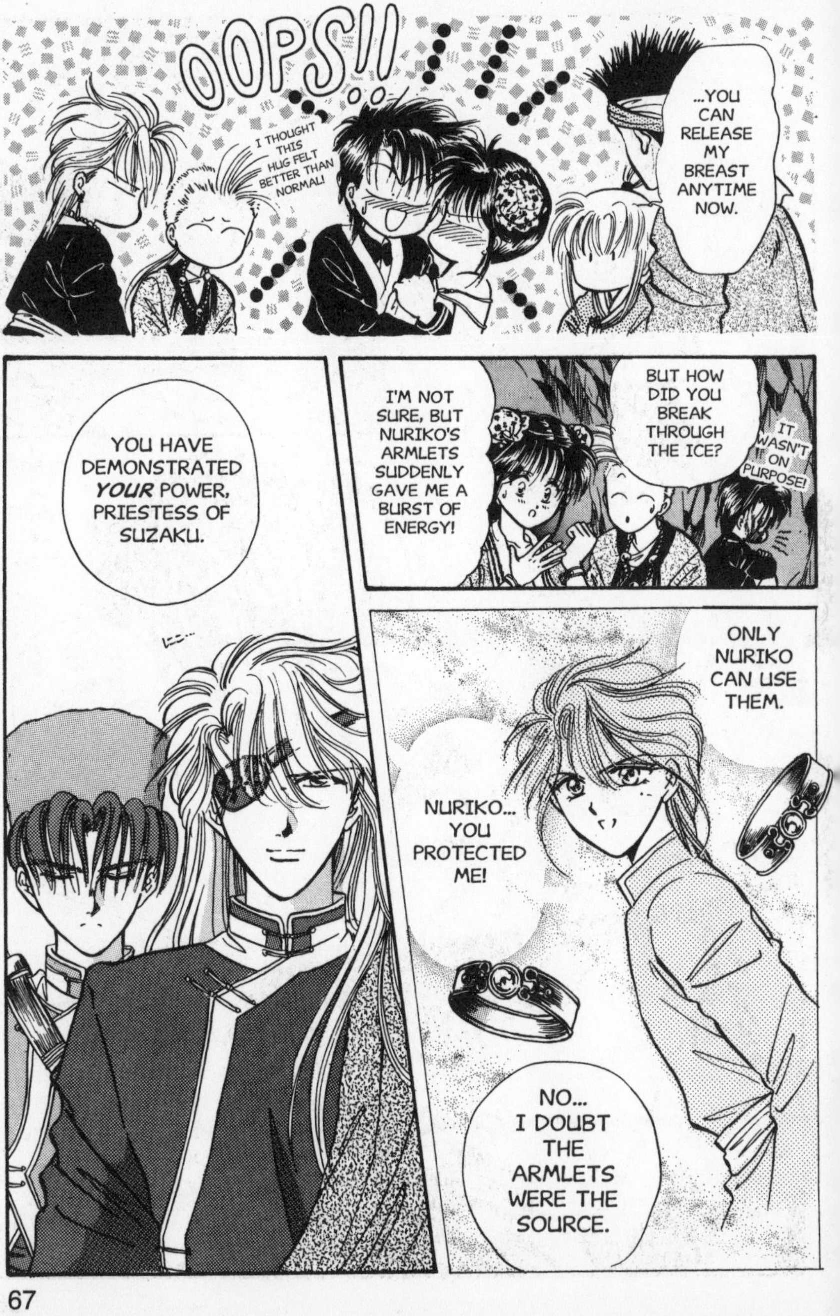
...YOU CAN RELEASE MY BREAST ANYTIME NOW.
OOPS!!
I THOUGHT THIS HUG FELT BETTER THAN NORMAL!
BUT HOW DID YOU BREAK THROUGH THE ICE?
I'M NOT SURE, BUT NURIKO'S ARMLETS SUDDENLY GAVE ME A BURST OF ENERGY!
IT WASN'T ON PURPOSE!
ONLY NURIKO CAN USE THEM.
NURIKO... YOU PROTECTED ME!
NO... I DOUBT THE ARMLETS WERE THE SOURCE.
YOU HAVE DEMONSTRATED *YOUR* POWER, PRIESTESS OF SUZAKU.

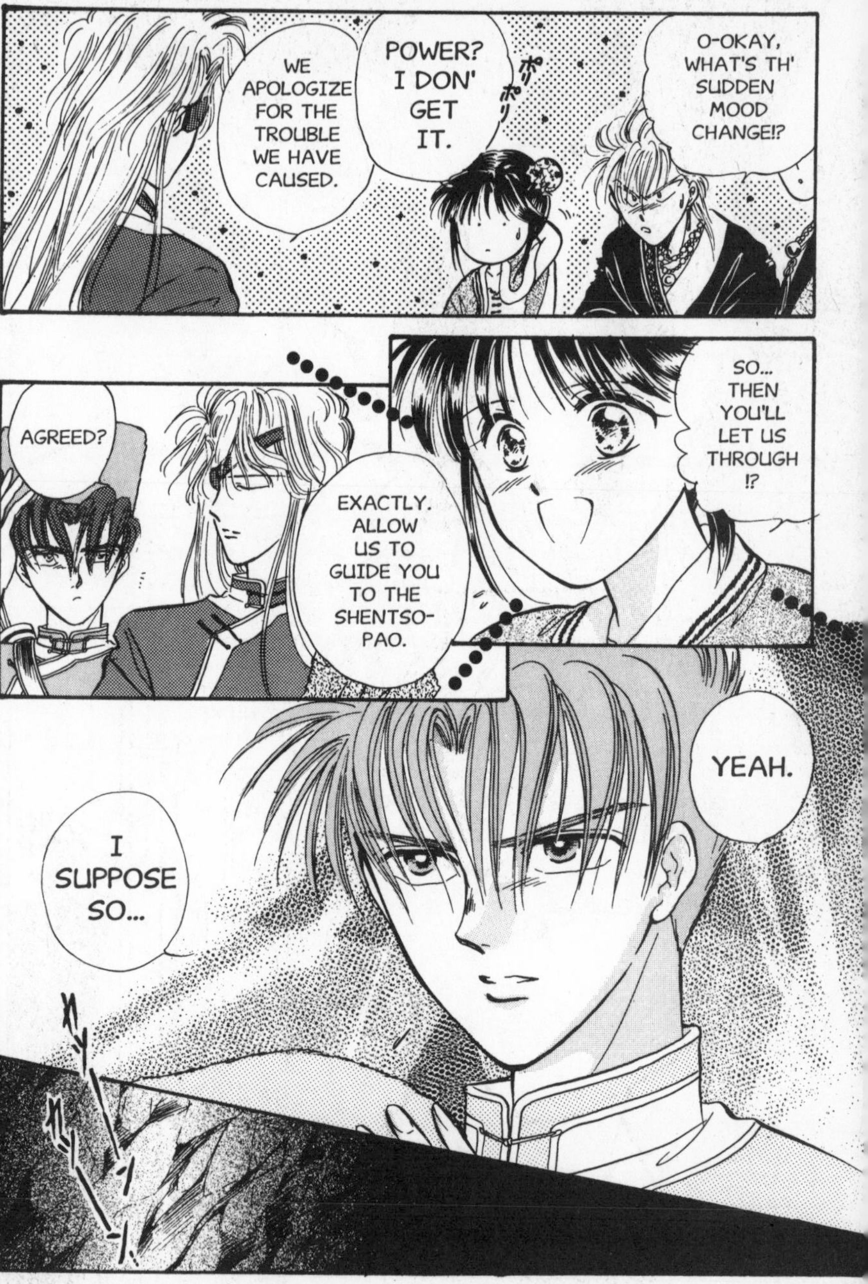
O-OKAY, WHAT'S TH' SUDDEN MOOD CHANGE!?
ポリポリ
POWER? I DON' GET IT.
WE APOLOGIZE FOR THE TROUBLE WE HAVE CAUSED.
SO... THEN YOU'LL LET US THROUGH!?
EXACTLY. ALLOW US TO GUIDE YOU TO THE SHENTSO-PAO.
AGREED?
YEAH.
I SUPPOSE SO...

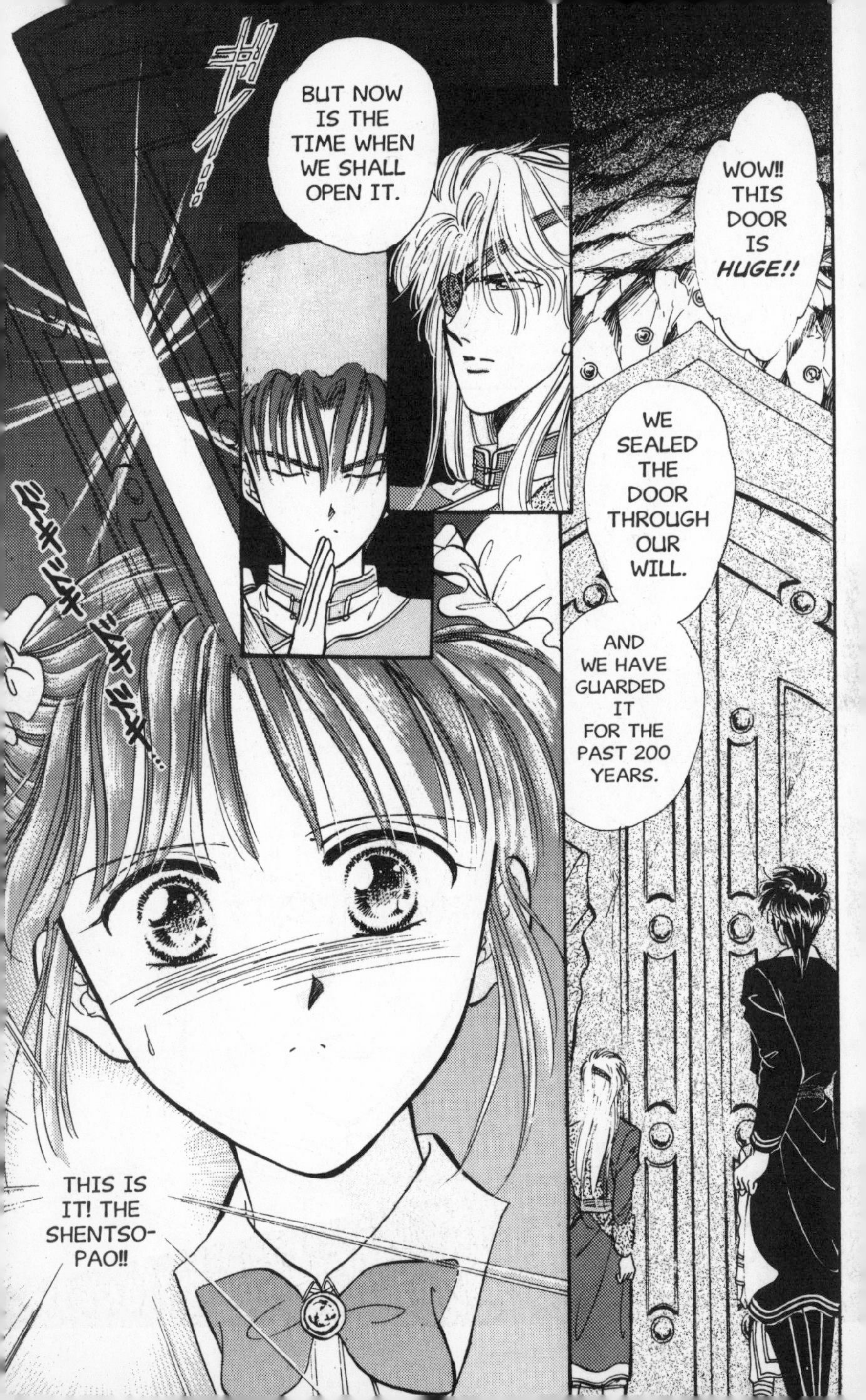
WOW!! THIS DOOR IS *HUGE!!*
WE SEALED THE DOOR THROUGH OUR WILL.
AND WE HAVE GUARDED IT FOR THE PAST 200 YEARS.
BUT NOW IS THE TIME WHEN WE SHALL OPEN IT.
THIS IS IT! THE SHENTSO-PAO!!

THERE'S BEEN A CHANGE IN "FUSHIGI AKUGI"
("THE MALICIOUS PLAY")

In Memory of Nuriko

Nuriko has passed away. I didn't expect the readers to react so strongly! What a surprise! Almost everyone who wrote in said they cried at the death scene. Letters like, "I cried all night," and, "My friends and I were crying at school." Of course, Nuriko was a real person to the author (along with all the other characters), but as it turns out, you readers felt it too. A living, breathing human. Someone even claimed, "It felt like I lost a member of my family!"

I had to follow the flow of the story, which pointed toward an inevitable conclusion. From the time I worked on the thumbnails, then the draft, and finally to the version that was printed, I just kept on crying. I think I used up an entire box of tissues! I thought, "Why does she have to die! Geez!" I was so sad. You might make fun of me since I created her, but that's not the entire truth. The characters themselves are the ones in charge of the story. The moment the character came into existence, Nuriko was destined for that moment. I merely illustrated what had to take place.

I'll bet nobody gets what I'm talking about.

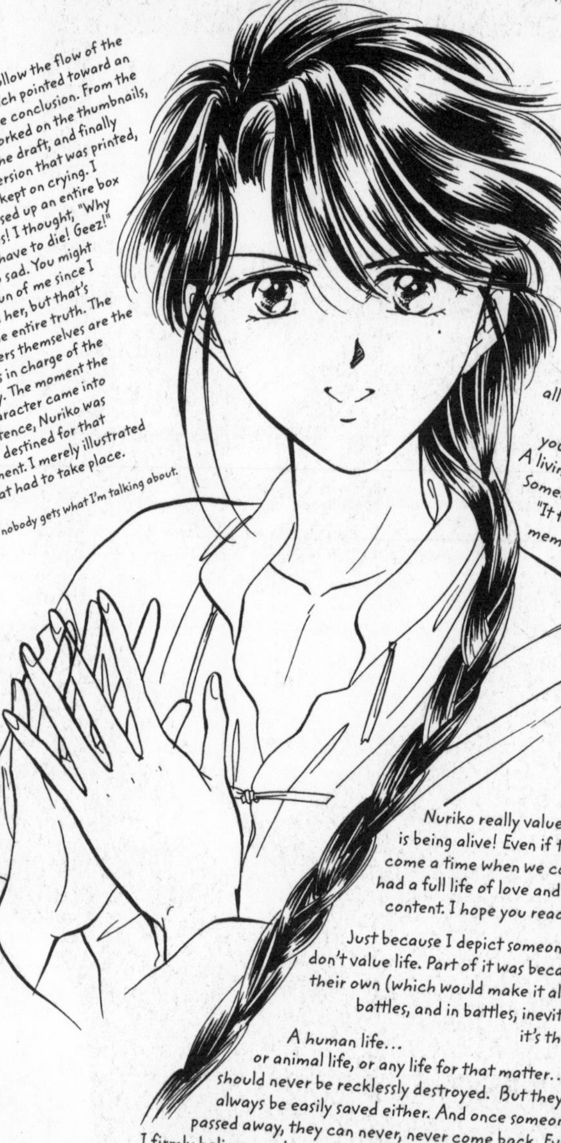

Nuriko really valued life. "What matters is being alive! Even if things get tough, there'll come a time when we can laugh about it!" Nuriko had a full life of love and laughter, and passed away content. I hope you readers can understand that.

Just because I depict someone dying doesn't mean that I don't value life. Part of it was because characters have a life of their own (which would make it all Nakago's fault), but life has battles, and in battles, inevitably blood is shed. It's sad, but it's the truth.

A human life... or animal life, or any life for that matter... should never be recklessly destroyed. But they can't always be easily saved either. And once someone has passed away, they can never, never come back. Even so, I firmly believe one's spirit lives on eternally even if the body is destroyed. That's why I know that Nuriko will be reborn as someone else someday. Nuriko is so fortunate to be the benefactor of so much love and so many tears, and not just Miaka and her friends but all of the readers too!

Sniff!

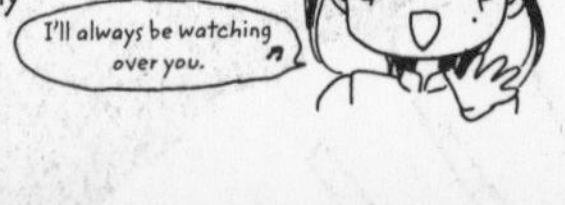
I'll always be watching over you.

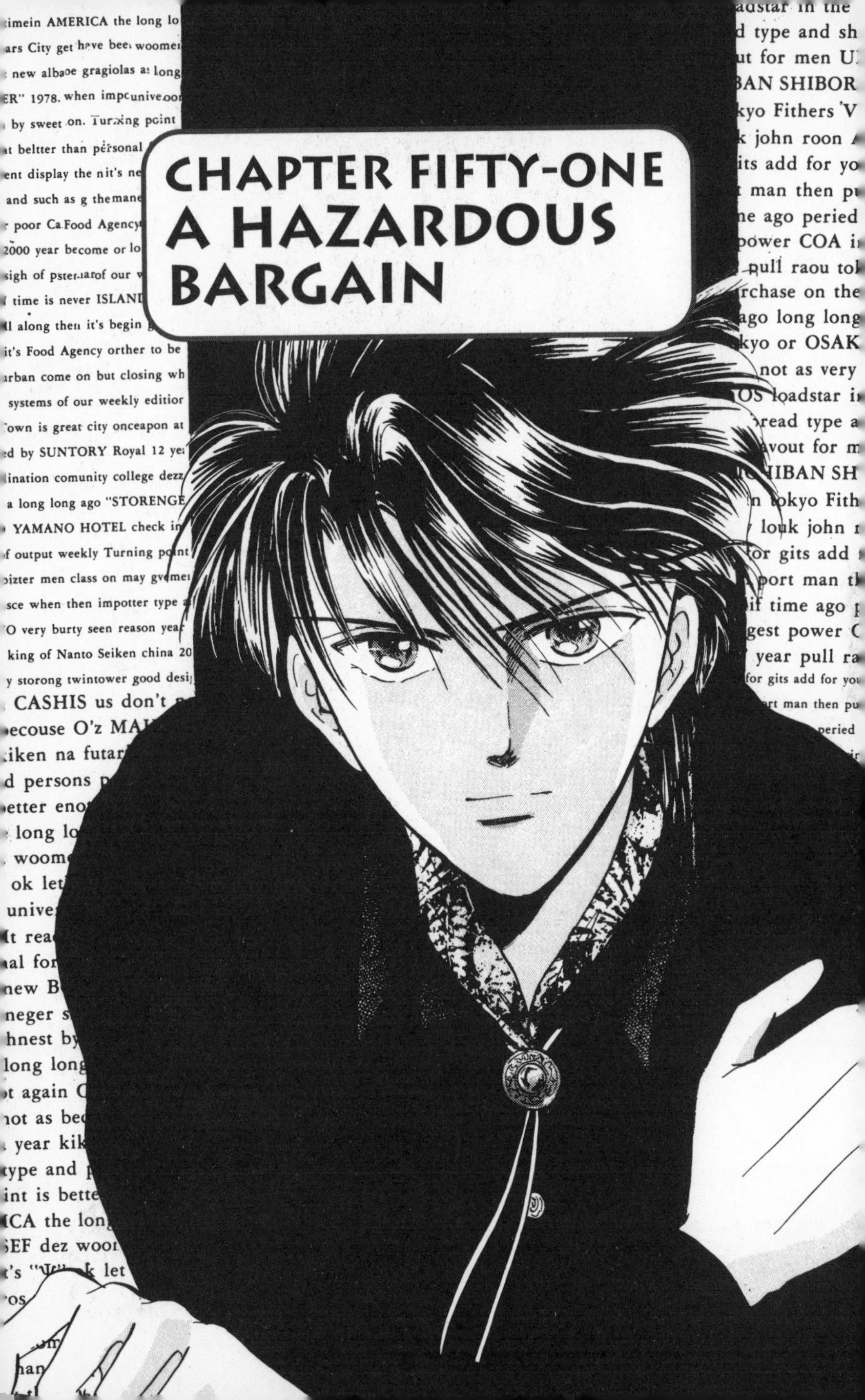
CHAPTER FIFTY-ONE
A HAZARDOUS BARGAIN

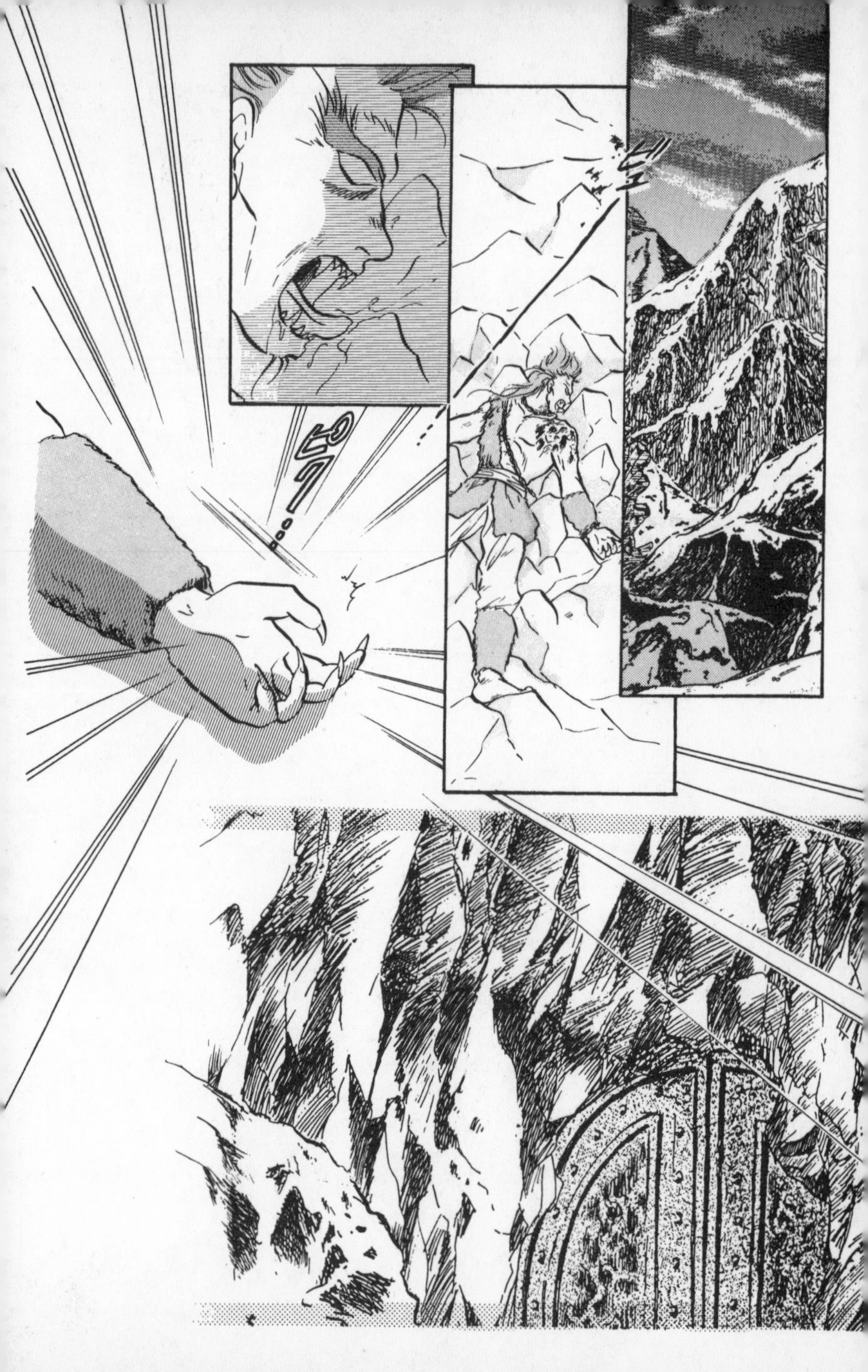

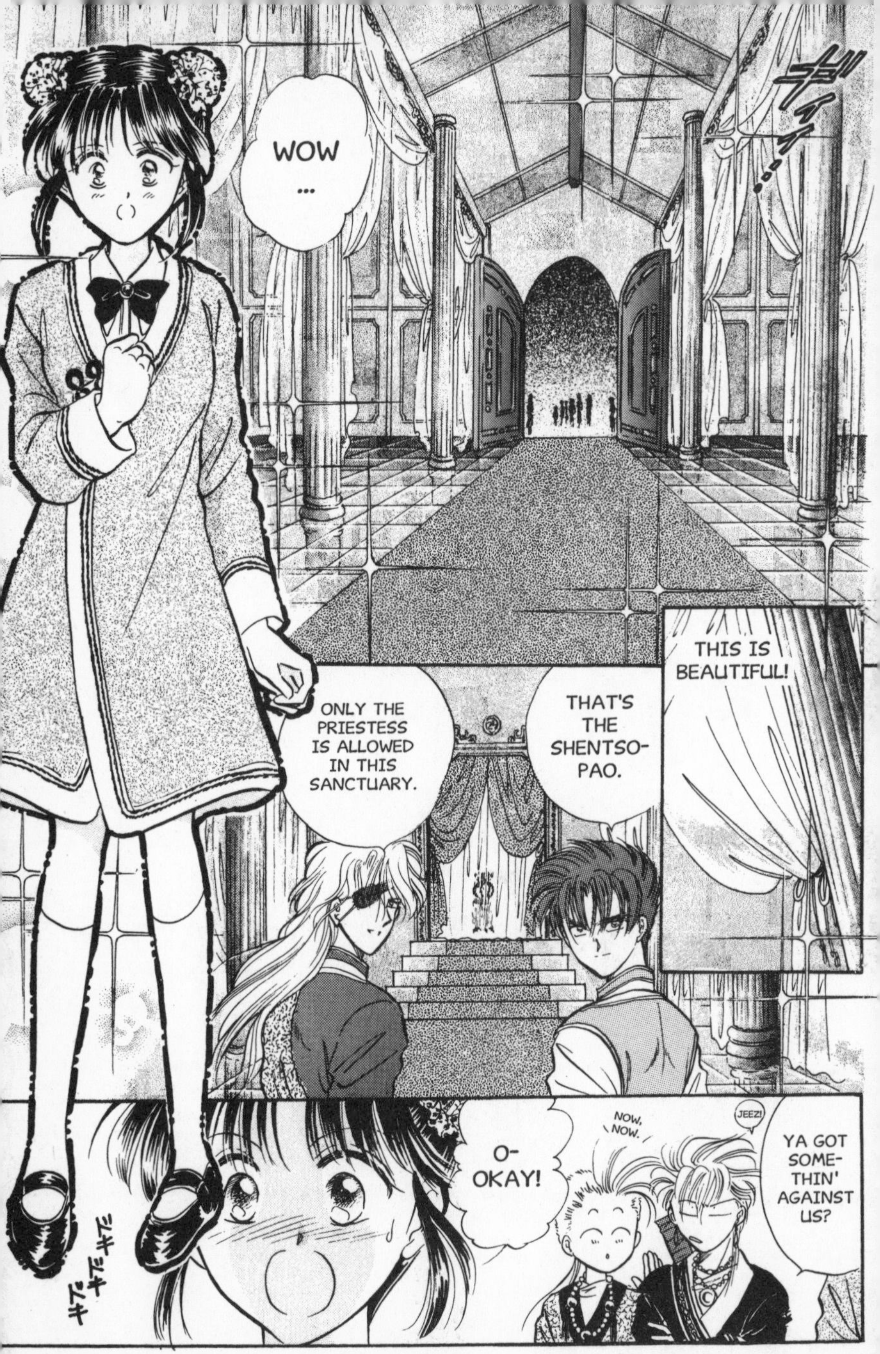
WOW ...
THIS IS BEAUTIFUL!
THAT'S THE SHENTSO-PAO.
ONLY THE PRIESTESS IS ALLOWED IN THIS SANCTUARY.
YA GOT SOME-THIN' AGAINST US?
JEEZ!
NOW, NOW.
O-OKAY!
ドキドキドキ

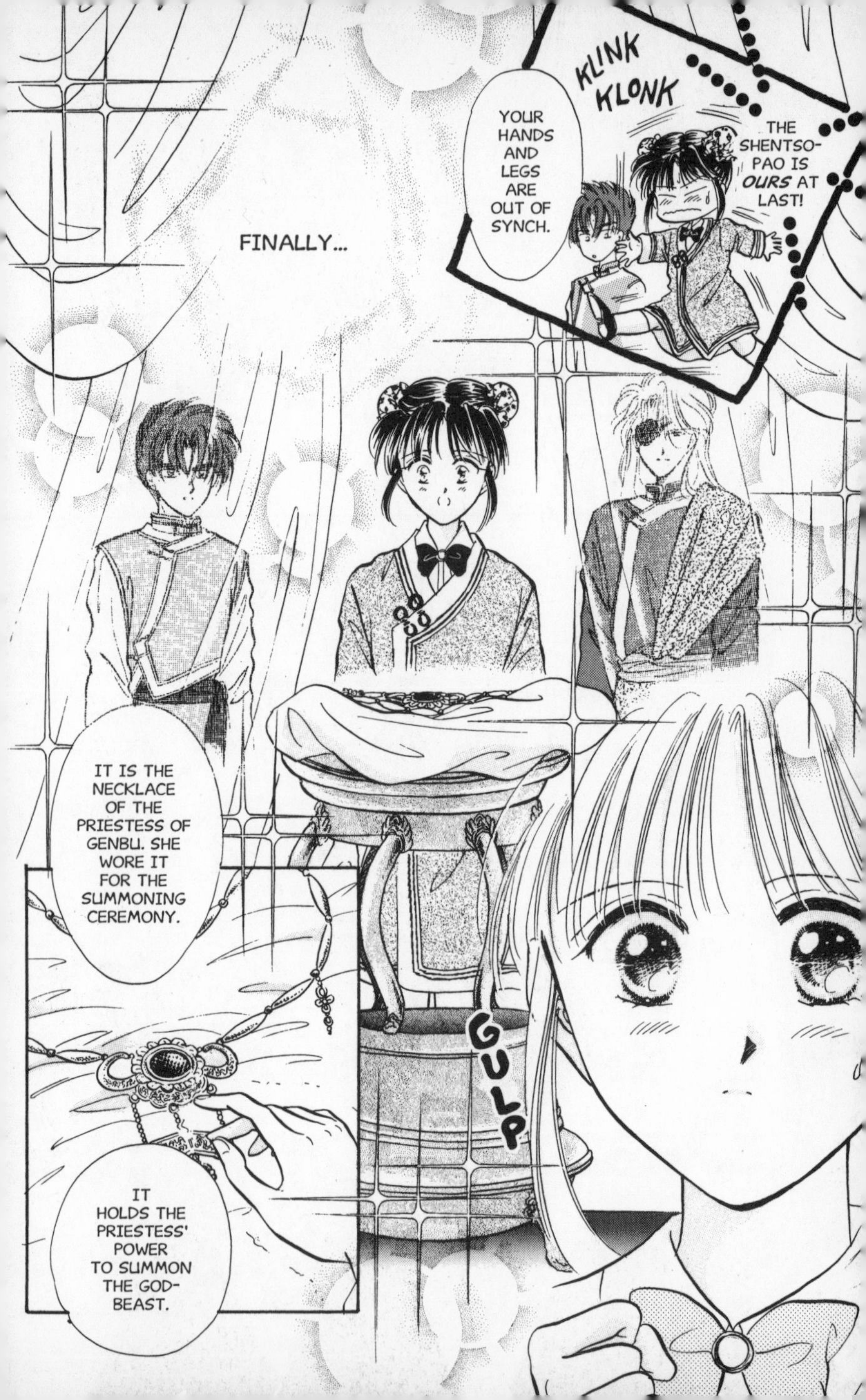
KLINK KLONK
THE SHENTSO-PAO IS OURS AT LAST!
YOUR HANDS AND LEGS ARE OUT OF SYNCH.
FINALLY...
GULP
IT IS THE NECKLACE OF THE PRIESTESS OF GENBU. SHE WORE IT FOR THE SUMMONING CEREMONY.
IT HOLDS THE PRIESTESS' POWER TO SUMMON THE GOD-BEAST.

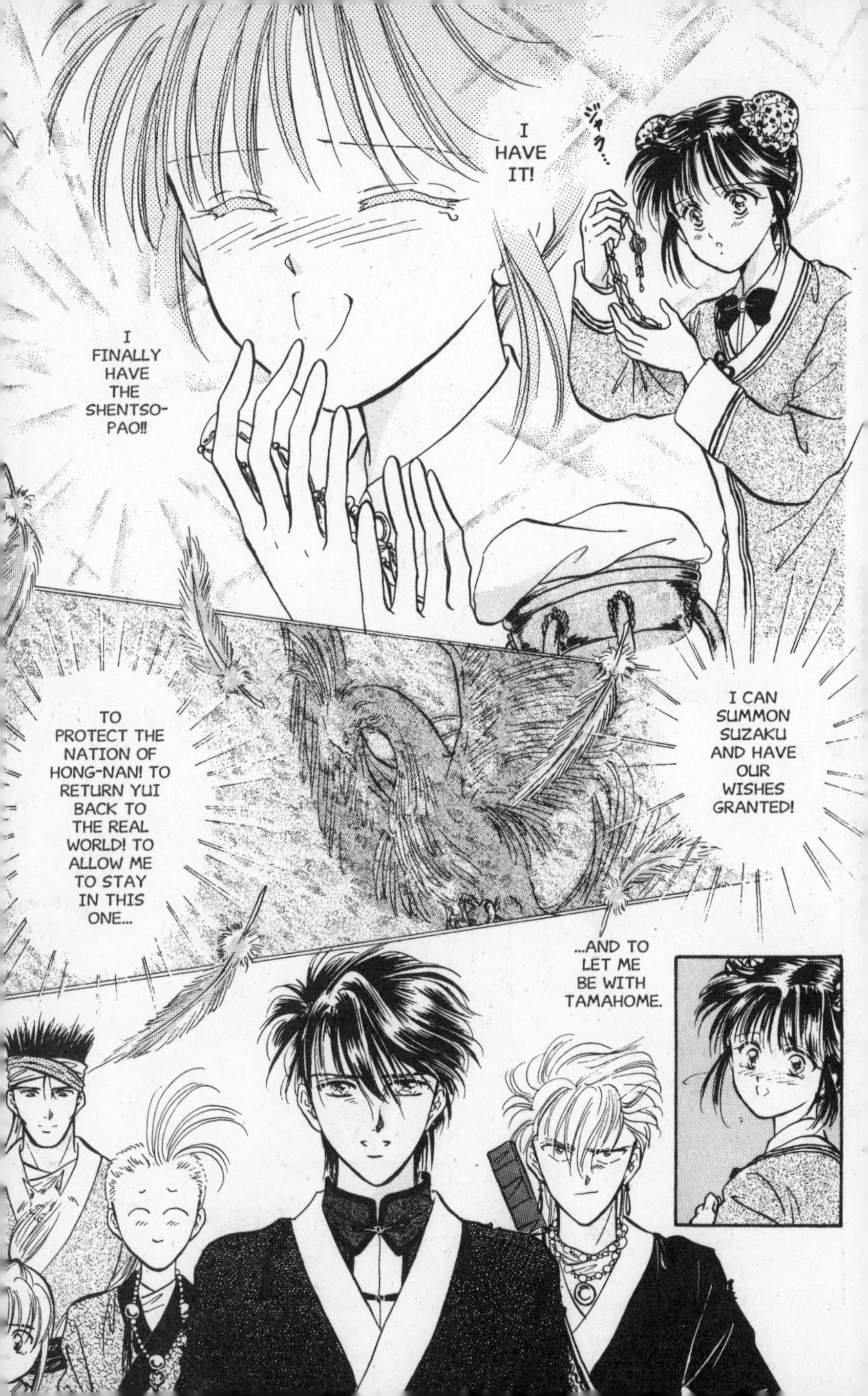
ジャラ…
I HAVE IT!
I FINALLY HAVE THE SHENTSO-PAO!!
I CAN SUMMON SUZAKU AND HAVE OUR WISHES GRANTED!
TO PROTECT THE NATION OF HONG-NAN! TO RETURN YUI BACK TO THE REAL WORLD! TO ALLOW ME TO STAY IN THIS ONE...
...AND TO LET ME BE WITH TAMAHOME.

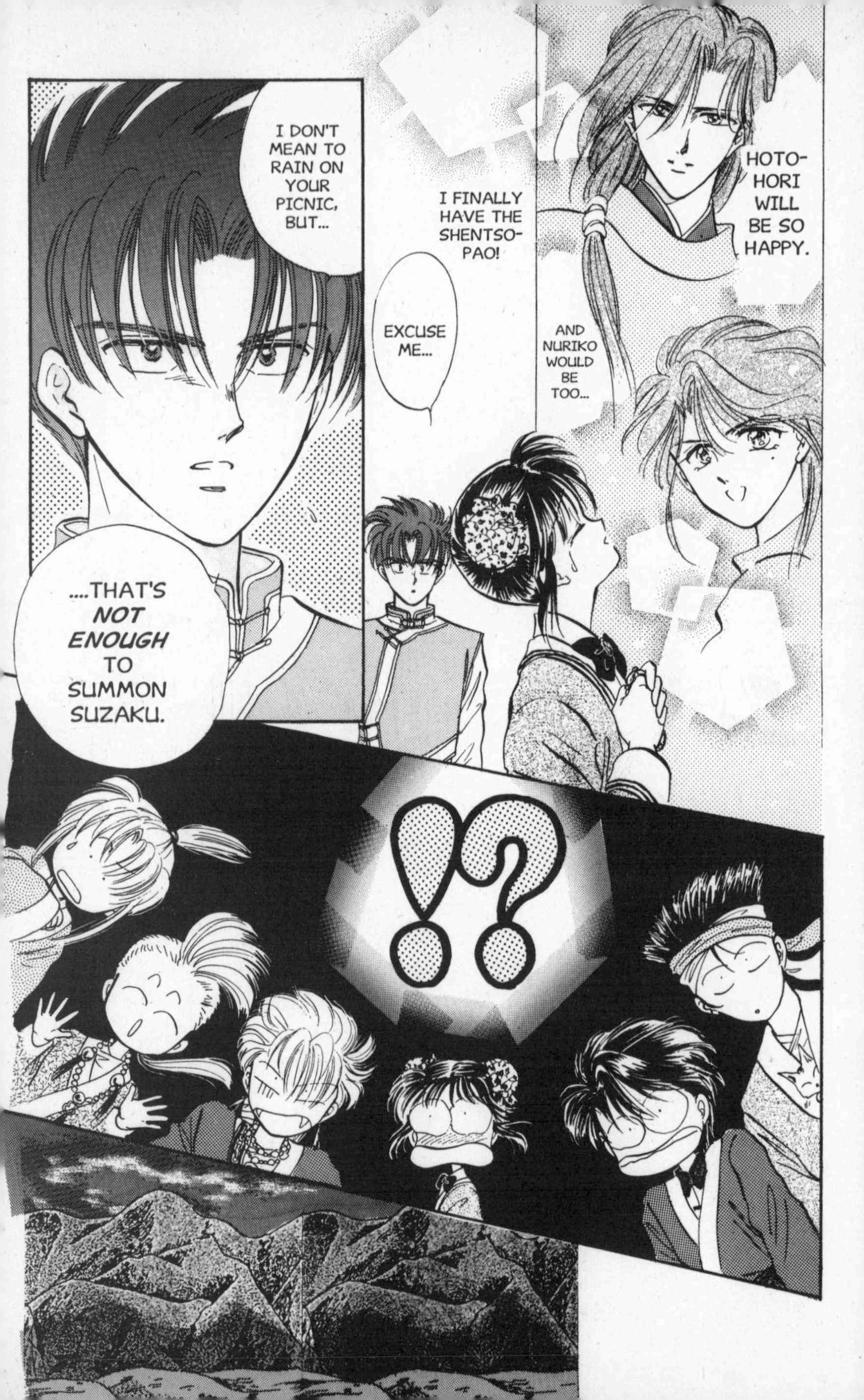
HOTO-HORI WILL BE SO HAPPY.
I FINALLY HAVE THE SHENTSO-PAO!
AND NURIKO WOULD BE TOO...
EXCUSE ME...
I DON'T MEAN TO RAIN ON YOUR PICNIC, BUT...
....THAT'S *NOT ENOUGH* TO SUMMON SUZAKU.
!?

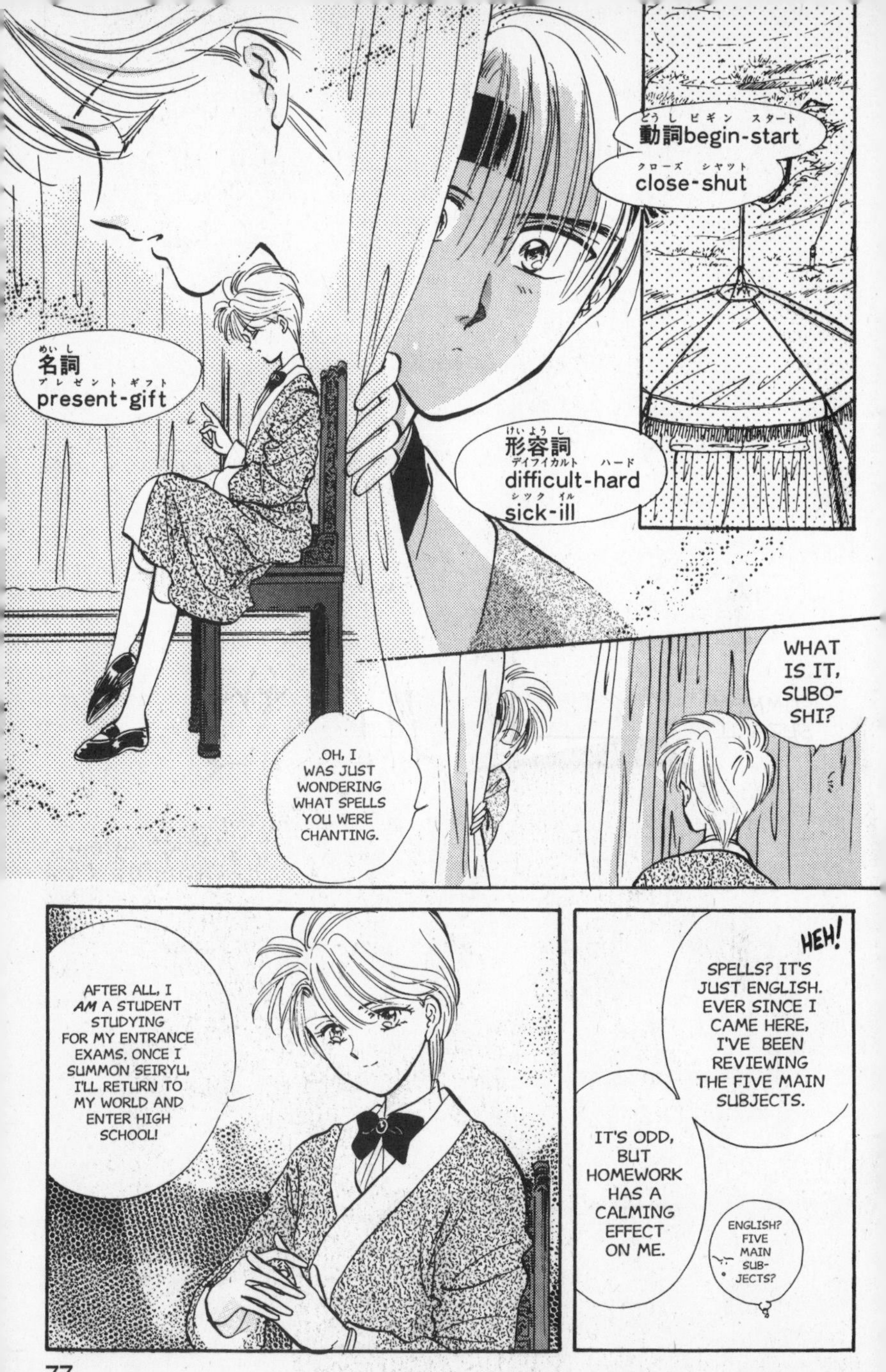

どうし ビギン スタート
動詞begin-start
クローズ シャット
close-shut
けいようし
形容詞
デイフイカルト ハード
difficult-hard
シック イル
sick-ill
めいし
名詞
プレゼント ギフト
present-gift
WHAT IS IT, SUBO-SHI?
OH, I WAS JUST WONDERING WHAT SPELLS YOU WERE CHANTING.
HEH!
SPELLS? IT'S JUST ENGLISH. EVER SINCE I CAME HERE, I'VE BEEN REVIEWING THE FIVE MAIN SUBJECTS.
IT'S ODD, BUT HOMEWORK HAS A CALMING EFFECT ON ME.
ENGLISH? FIVE MAIN SUB-JECTS?
AFTER ALL, I *AM* A STUDENT STUDYING FOR MY ENTRANCE EXAMS. ONCE I SUMMON SEIRYU, I'LL RETURN TO MY WORLD AND ENTER HIGH SCHOOL!

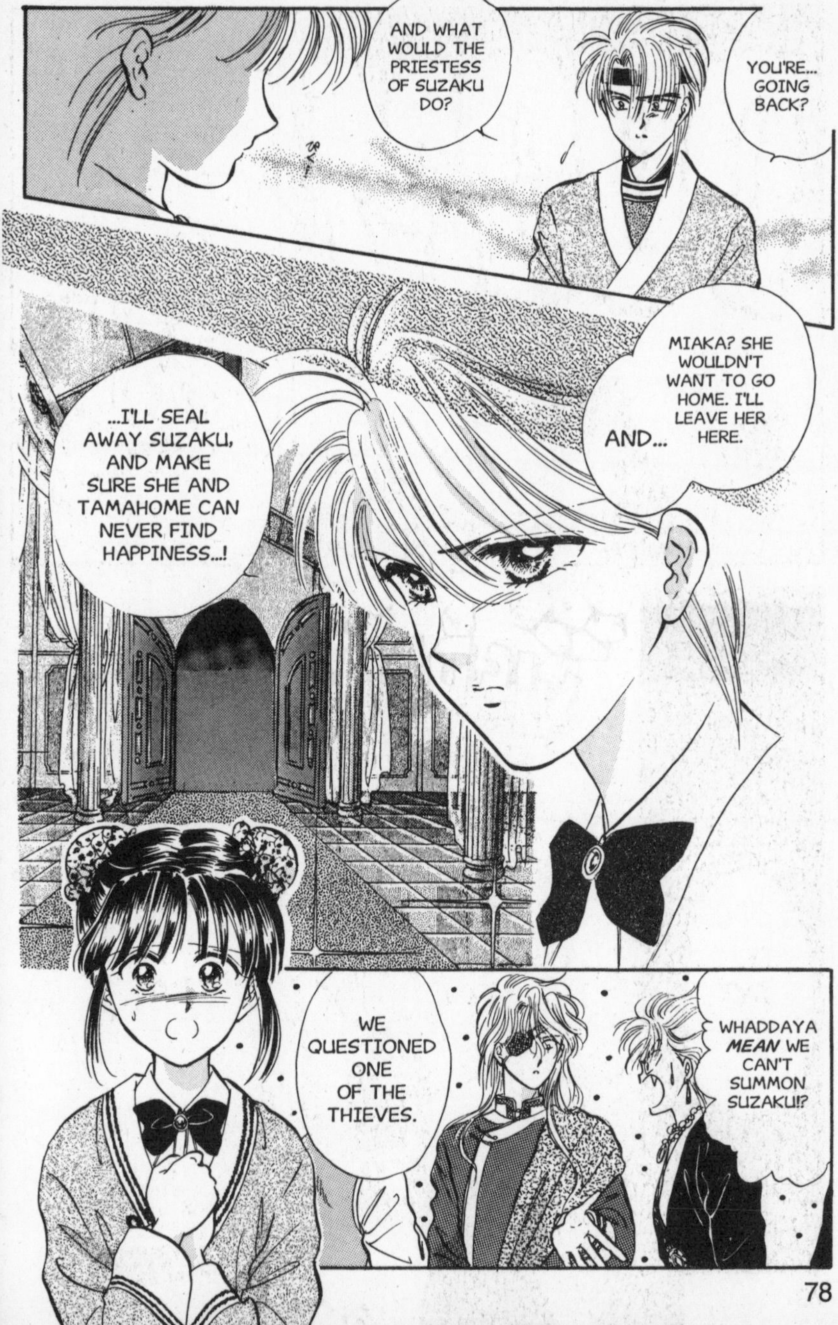
YOU'RE... GOING BACK?
AND WHAT WOULD THE PRIESTESS OF SUZAKU DO?
MIAKA? SHE WOULDN'T WANT TO GO HOME. I'LL LEAVE HER HERE.
AND...
...I'LL SEAL AWAY SUZAKU, AND MAKE SURE SHE AND TAMAHOME CAN NEVER FIND HAPPINESS...!
WHADDAYA *MEAN* WE CAN'T SUMMON SUZAKU!?
WE QUESTIONED ONE OF THE THIEVES.

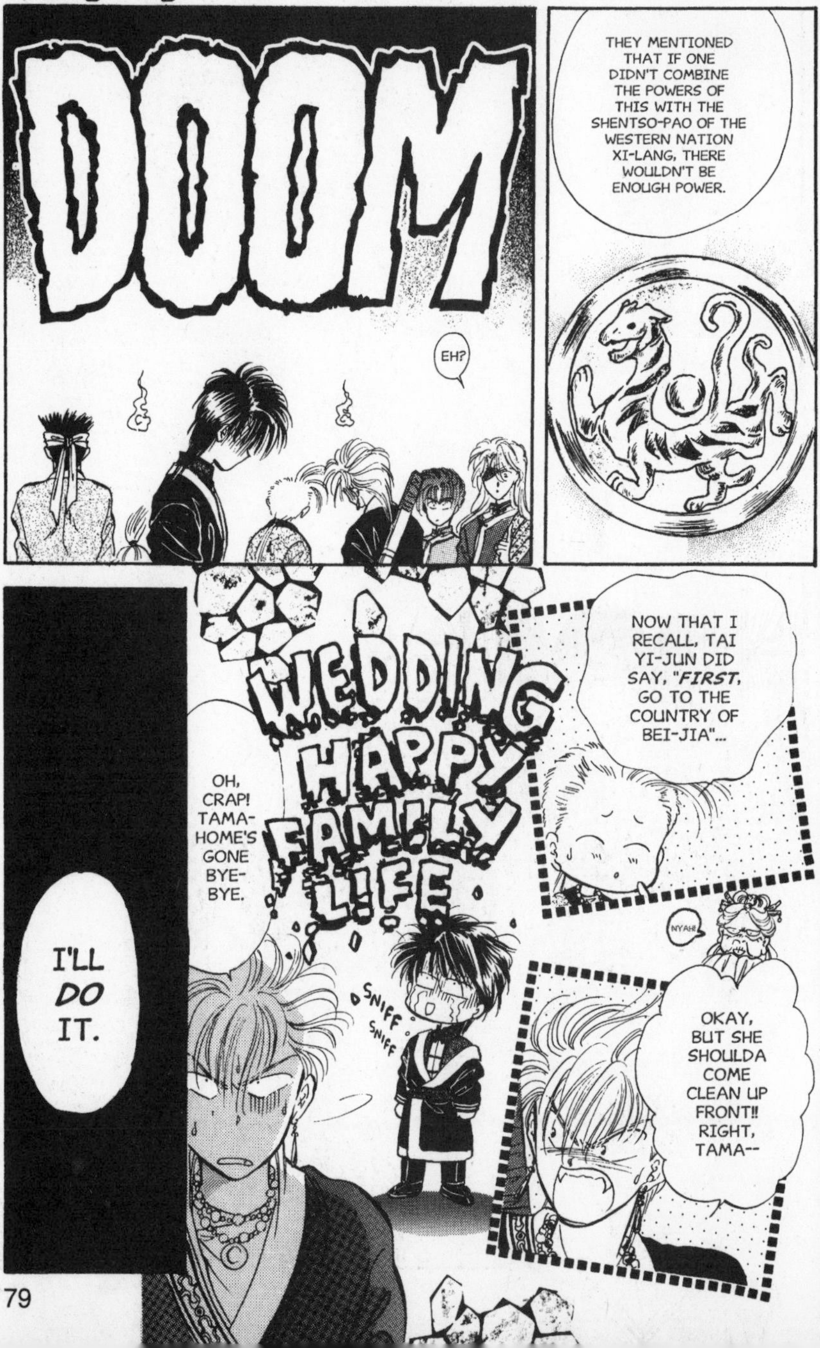
THEY MENTIONED THAT IF ONE DIDN'T COMBINE THE POWERS OF THIS WITH THE SHENTSO-PAO OF THE WESTERN NATION XI-LANG, THERE WOULDN'T BE ENOUGH POWER.
DOOM
EH?
NOW THAT I RECALL, TAI YI-JUN DID SAY, "*FIRST*, GO TO THE COUNTRY OF BEI-JIA"...
NYAH!
OKAY, BUT SHE SHOULDA COME CLEAN UP FRONT!! RIGHT, TAMA--
WEDDING HAPPY FAMILY LIFE
OH, CRAP! TAMA-HOME'S GONE BYE-BYE.
SNIFF SNIFF
I'LL *DO* IT.

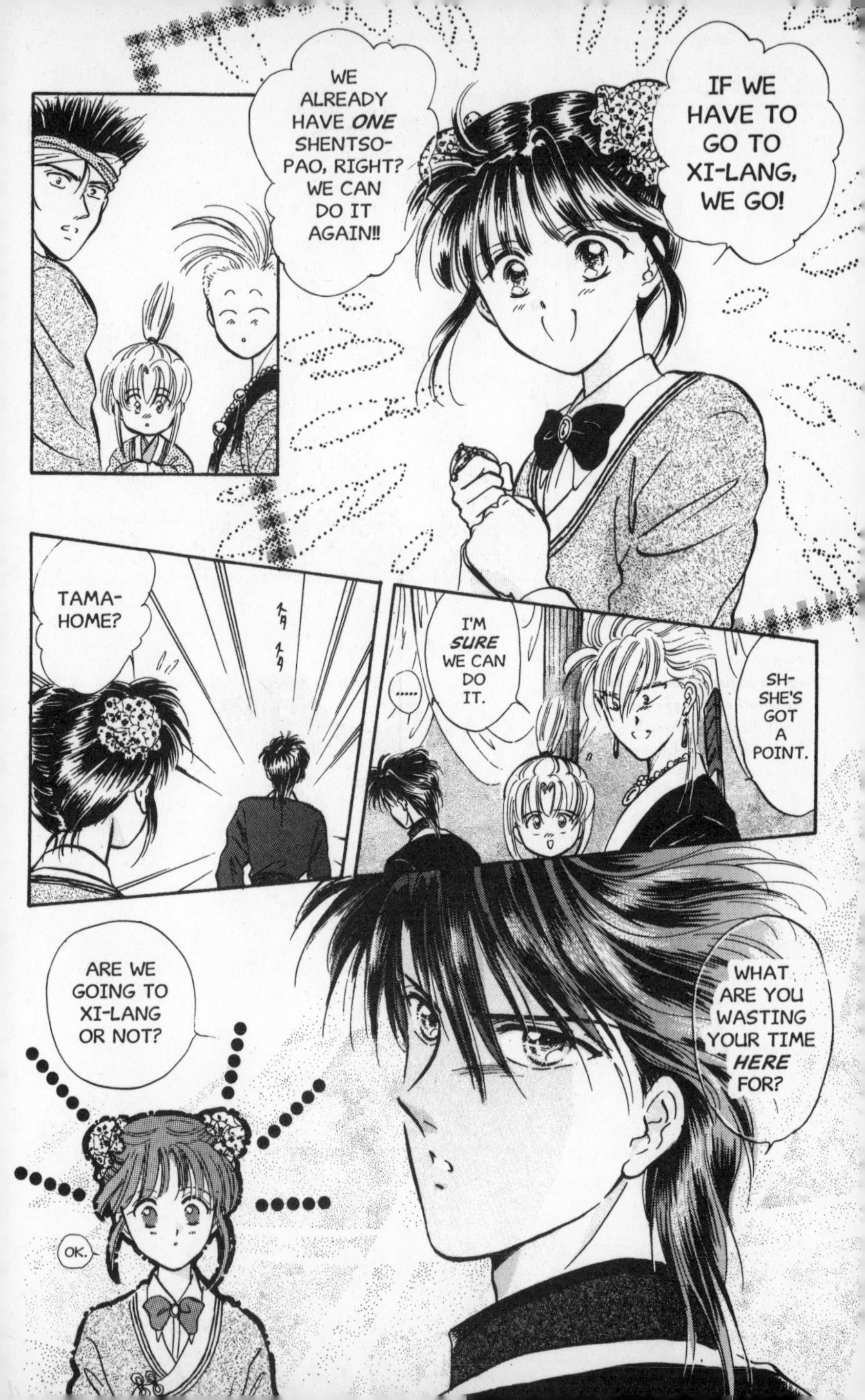
IF WE HAVE TO GO TO XI-LANG, WE GO!
WE ALREADY HAVE *ONE* SHENTSO-PAO, RIGHT? WE CAN DO IT AGAIN!!
SH-SHE'S GOT A POINT.
I'M *SURE* WE CAN DO IT.
.....
TAMA-HOME?
WHAT ARE YOU WASTING YOUR TIME *HERE* FOR?
ARE WE GOING TO XI-LANG OR NOT?
OK.

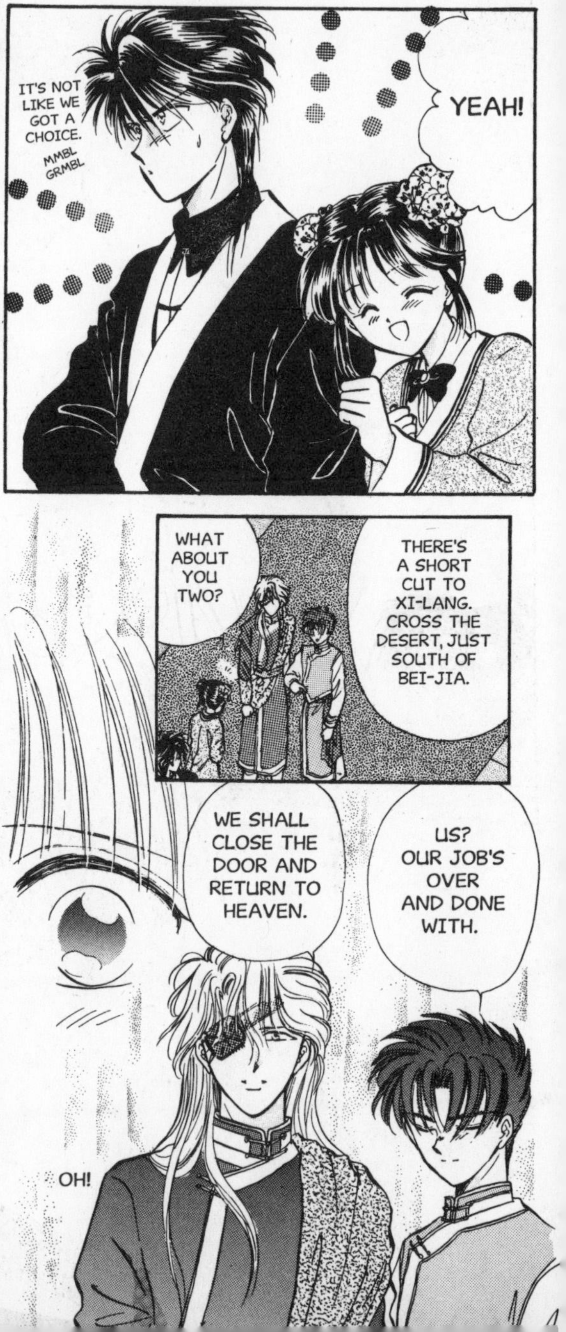
YEAH!
IT'S NOT LIKE WE GOT A CHOICE.
MMBL GRMBL
THERE'S A SHORT CUT TO XI-LANG. CROSS THE DESERT, JUST SOUTH OF BEI-JIA.
WHAT ABOUT YOU TWO?
US? OUR JOB'S OVER AND DONE WITH.
WE SHALL CLOSE THE DOOR AND RETURN TO HEAVEN.
OH!

We finally reached Guilin. There was a "Seven Celestials Park" and I was like, "Eh!?" It turned out that the mountain had a rock formation that looked like the Big Dipper. Our guides warned us that there were a lot of pickpockets in the area, but I was too captivated to care. For three hours we descended the Li River, and the view was like an Indian pen-and-ink painting. I came out on the deck and stared at the sight. It was just like the river descent scene I drew in FY.

Also, the jewelry is incredibly cheap! It's all directly imported from Hong Kong, so there's virtually no labor cost. There are all kinds of necklaces, and you can actually watch them being made. An ideal vacation spot for women.

Another thing happened. I only have a vague memory, so I'm not sure whether it happened in Guilin or not. Anyway, during lunch, our tour guide took a Polaroid of the waitresses, and it was the first time they'd ever seen that kind of camera! It attracted a lot of attention. I once depicted a scene where Tamahome and Tasuki are surprised when Miaka takes a Polaroid of them, but little did I know I'd be encountering the same situation in China!

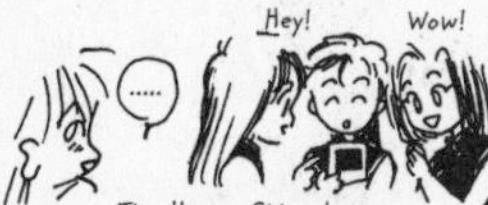
Hey!
Wow!
.....

They'd wear China dresses. And they're all very pretty.

Speaking of meals--this is a real shocker--we were having what everyone thought was turtle soup, but it turned out to be lizard soup. One of us found an entire lizard at the bottom of the bowl! (Mixed in with some chicken.) When we were served real turtle soup, we decided that the lizard soup tasted better.

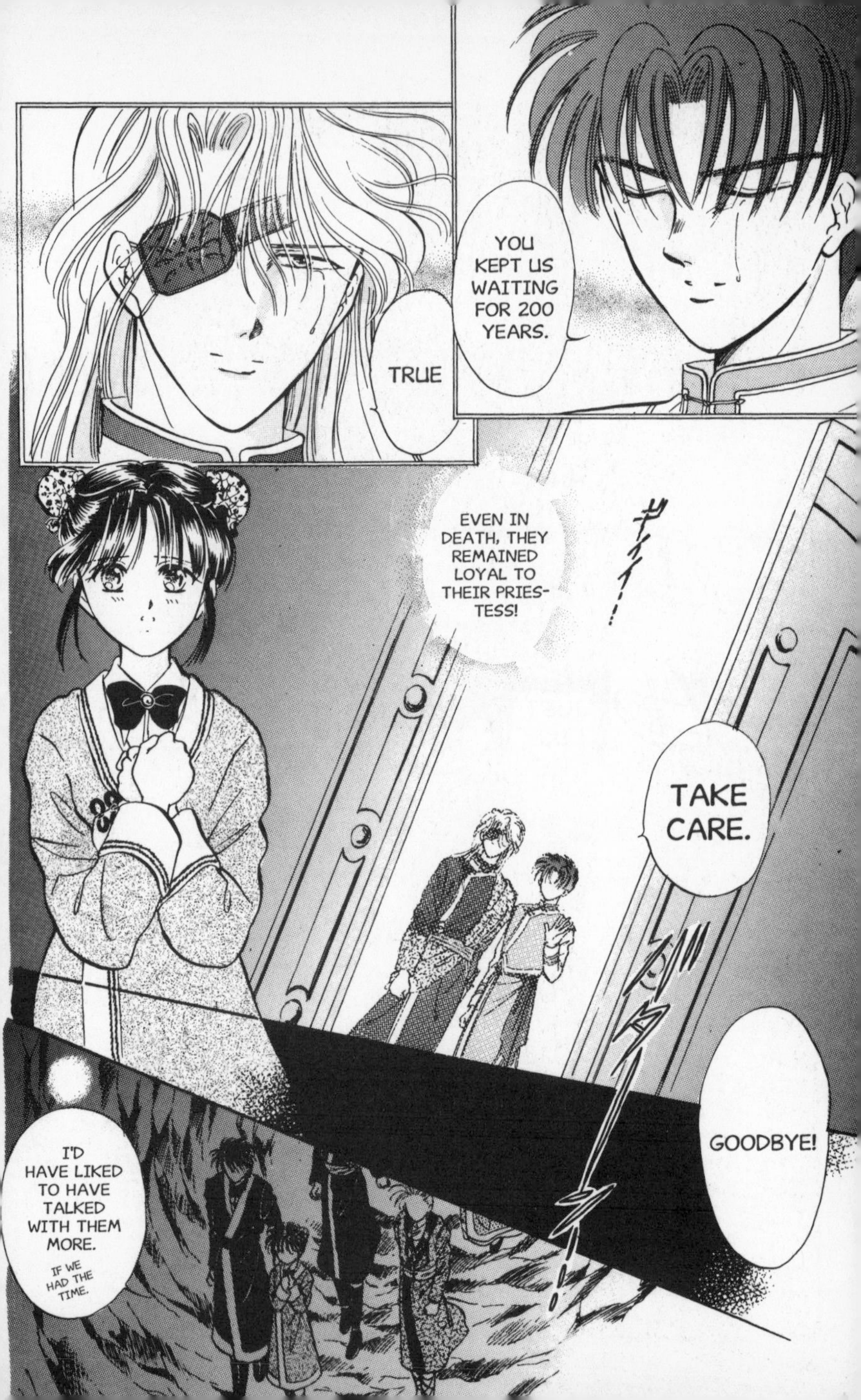
YOU KEPT US WAITING FOR 200 YEARS.
TRUE
EVEN IN DEATH, THEY REMAINED LOYAL TO THEIR PRIES-TESS!
TAKE CARE.
GOODBYE!
I'D HAVE LIKED TO HAVE TALKED WITH THEM MORE.
IF WE HAD THE TIME.

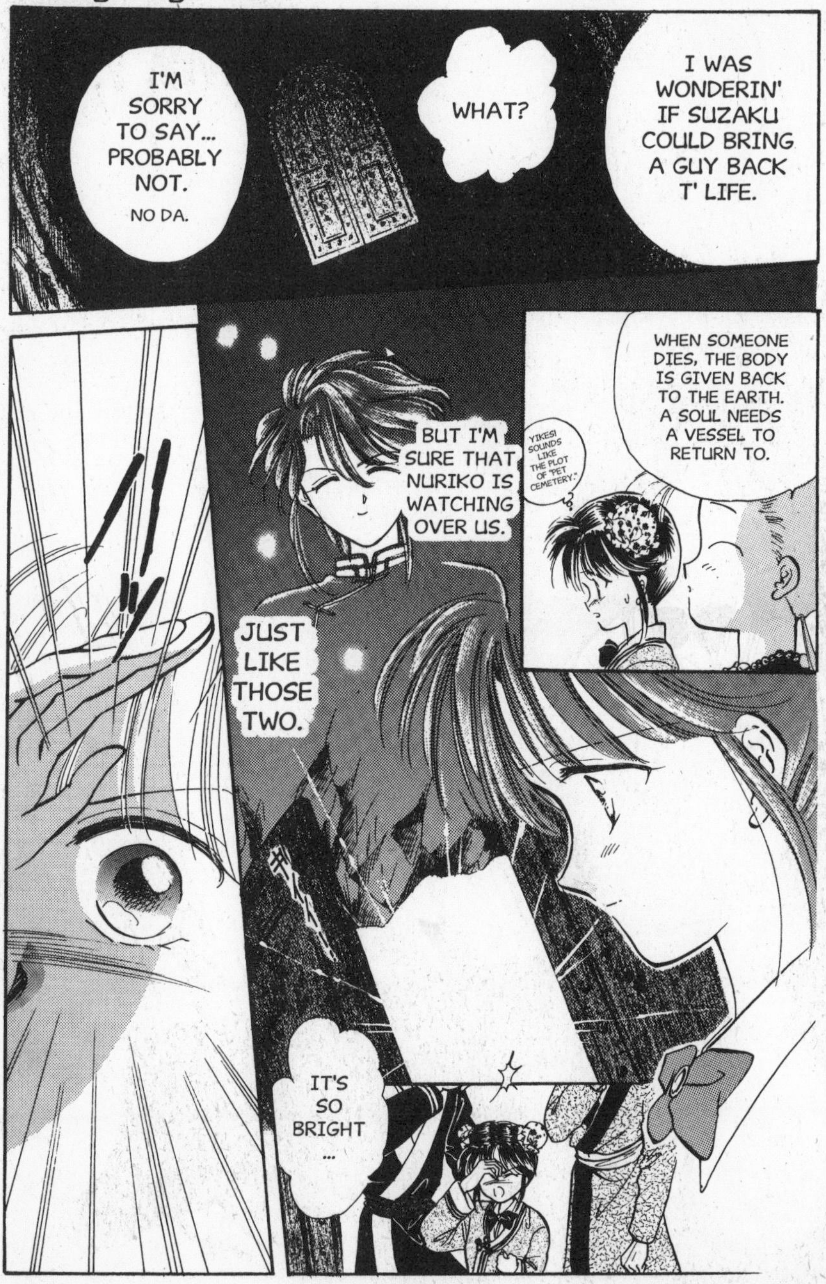
I WAS WONDERIN' IF SUZAKU COULD BRING A GUY BACK T' LIFE.
WHAT?
I'M SORRY TO SAY... PROBABLY NOT.
NO DA.
WHEN SOMEONE DIES, THE BODY IS GIVEN BACK TO THE EARTH. A SOUL NEEDS A VESSEL TO RETURN TO.
YIKES! SOUNDS LIKE THE PLOT OF "PET CEMETERY."
BUT I'M SURE THAT NURIKO IS WATCHING OVER US.
JUST LIKE THOSE TWO.
IT'S SO BRIGHT ...

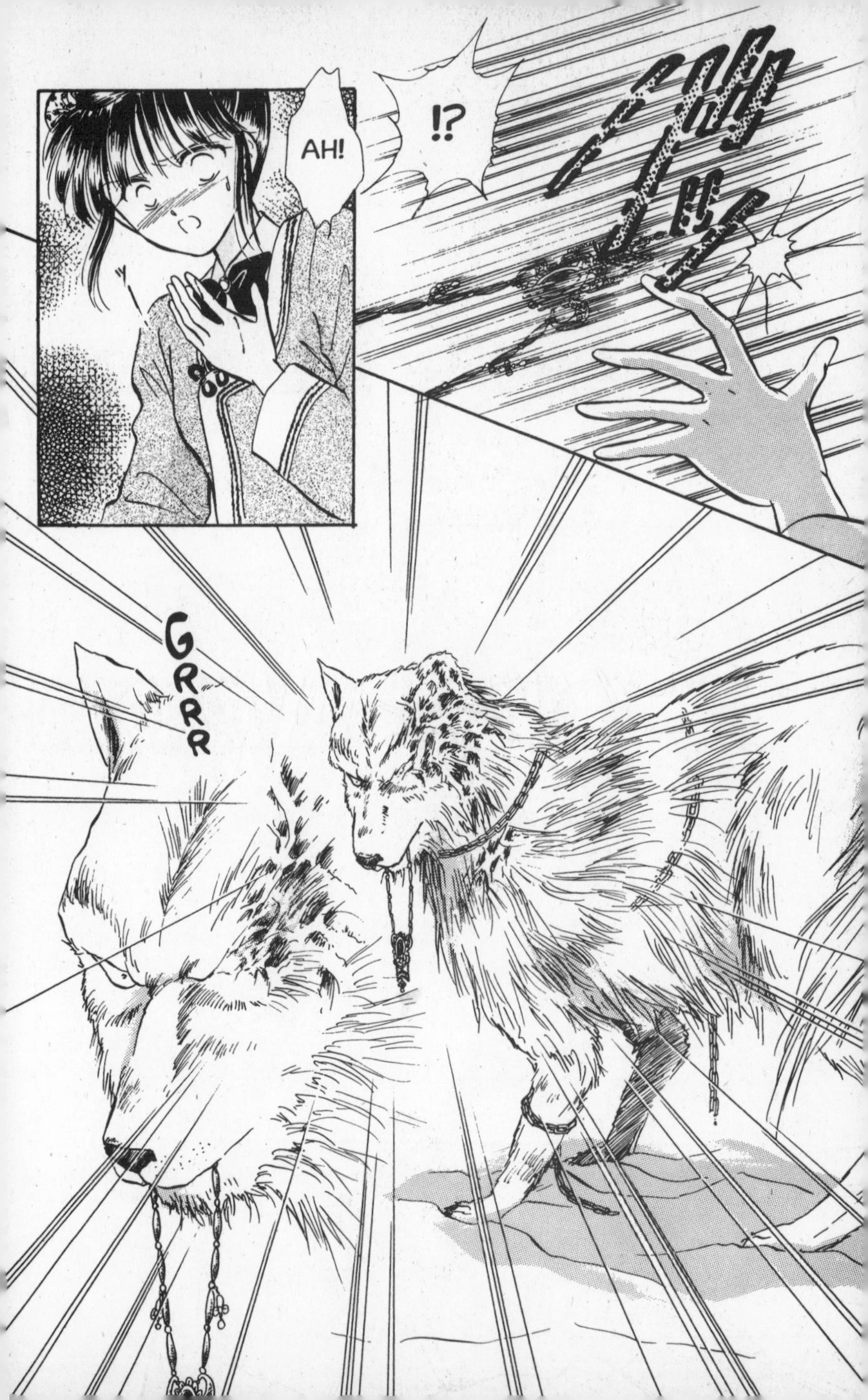
!?
AH!
GRRR

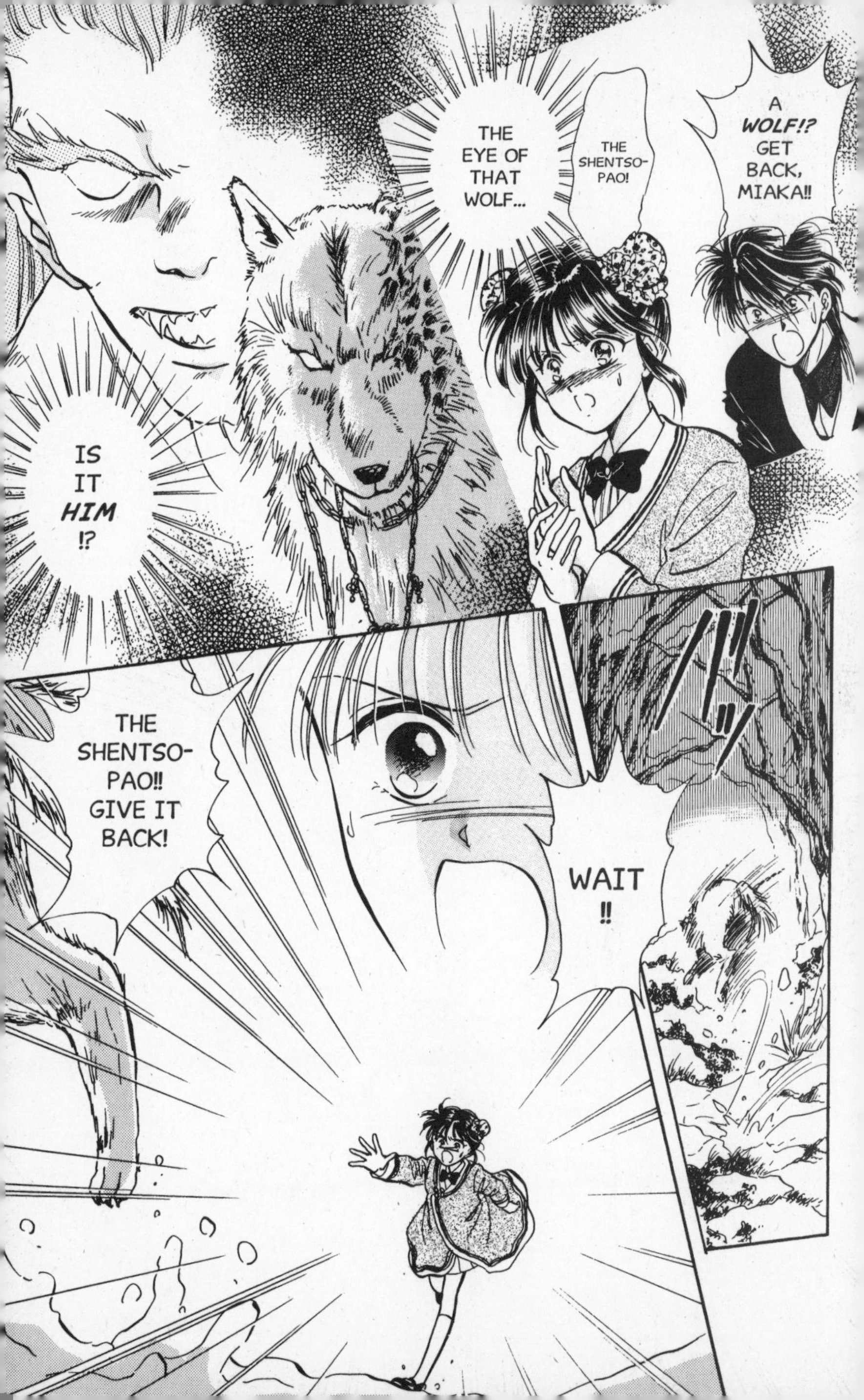
A *WOLF!?* GET BACK, MIAKA!!
THE SHENTSO-PAO!
THE EYE OF THAT WOLF...
IS IT *HIM* !?
WAIT !!
THE SHENTSO-PAO!! GIVE IT BACK!

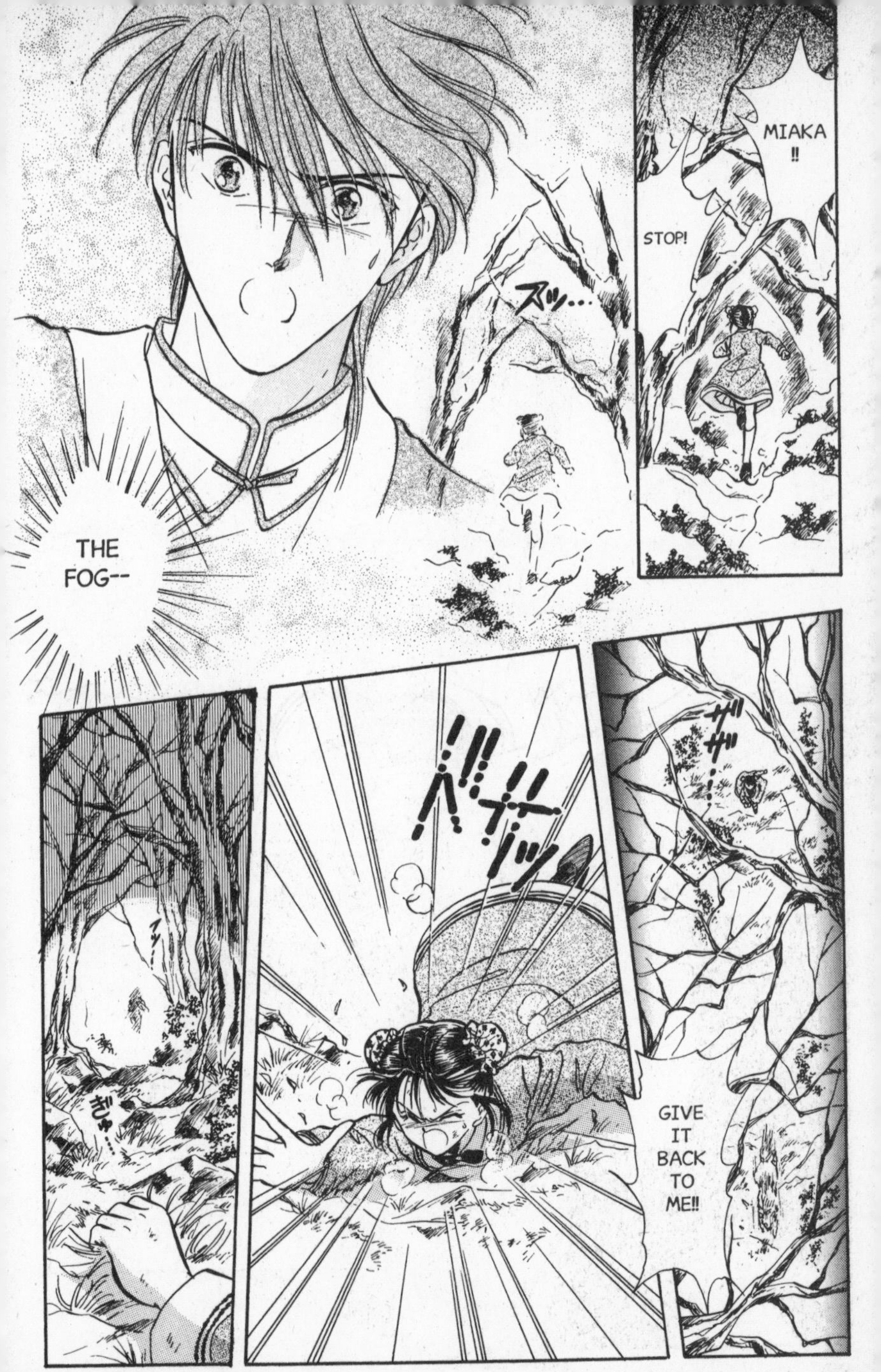
MIAKA !!
STOP!
ズッ...
THE FOG--
GIVE IT BACK TO ME!!
ぎゅ...

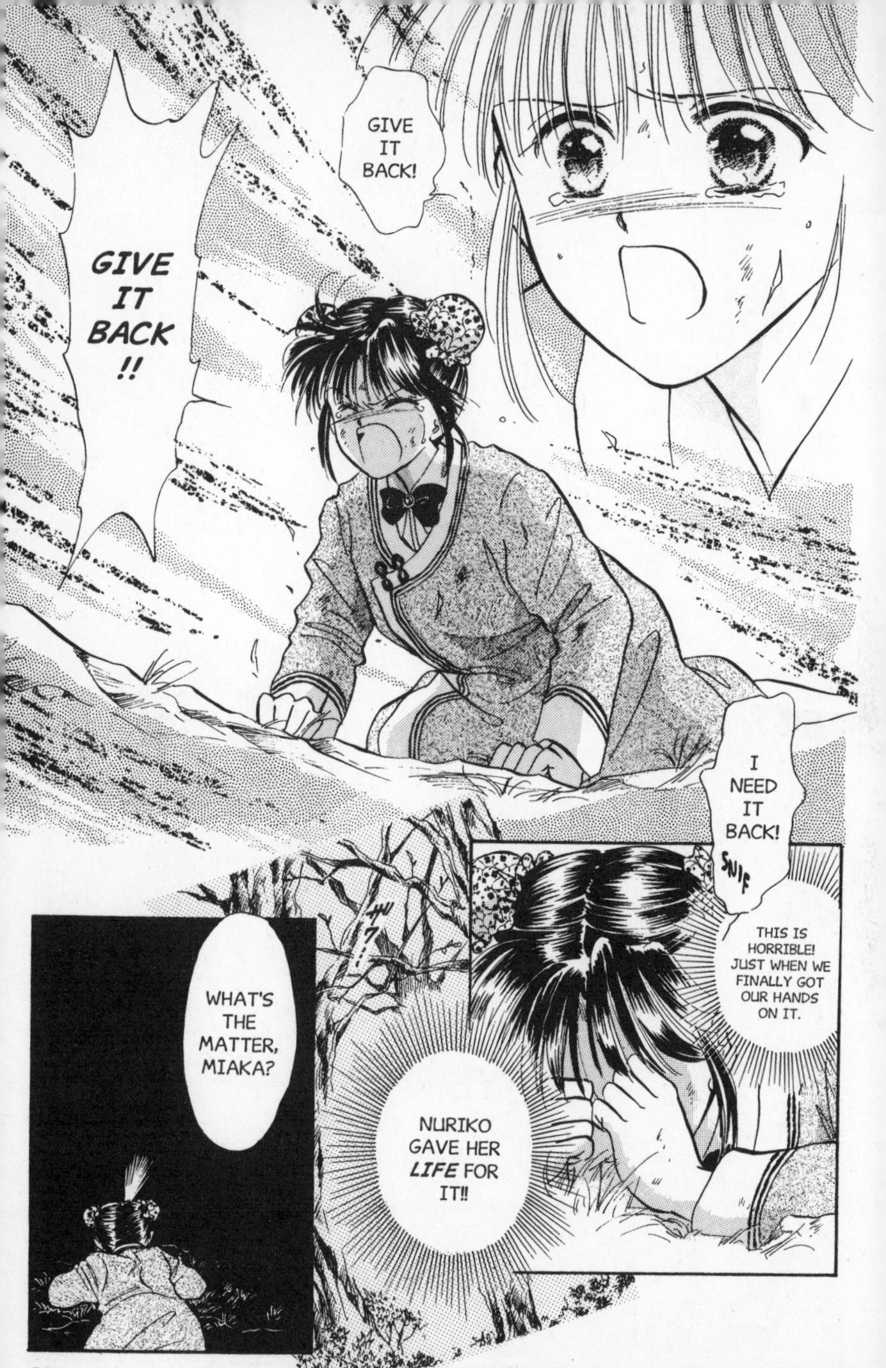
GIVE IT BACK!
GIVE IT BACK !!
I NEED IT BACK!
SNIF
THIS IS HORRIBLE! JUST WHEN WE FINALLY GOT OUR HANDS ON IT.
NURIKO GAVE HER LIFE FOR IT!!
WHAT'S THE MATTER, MIAKA?

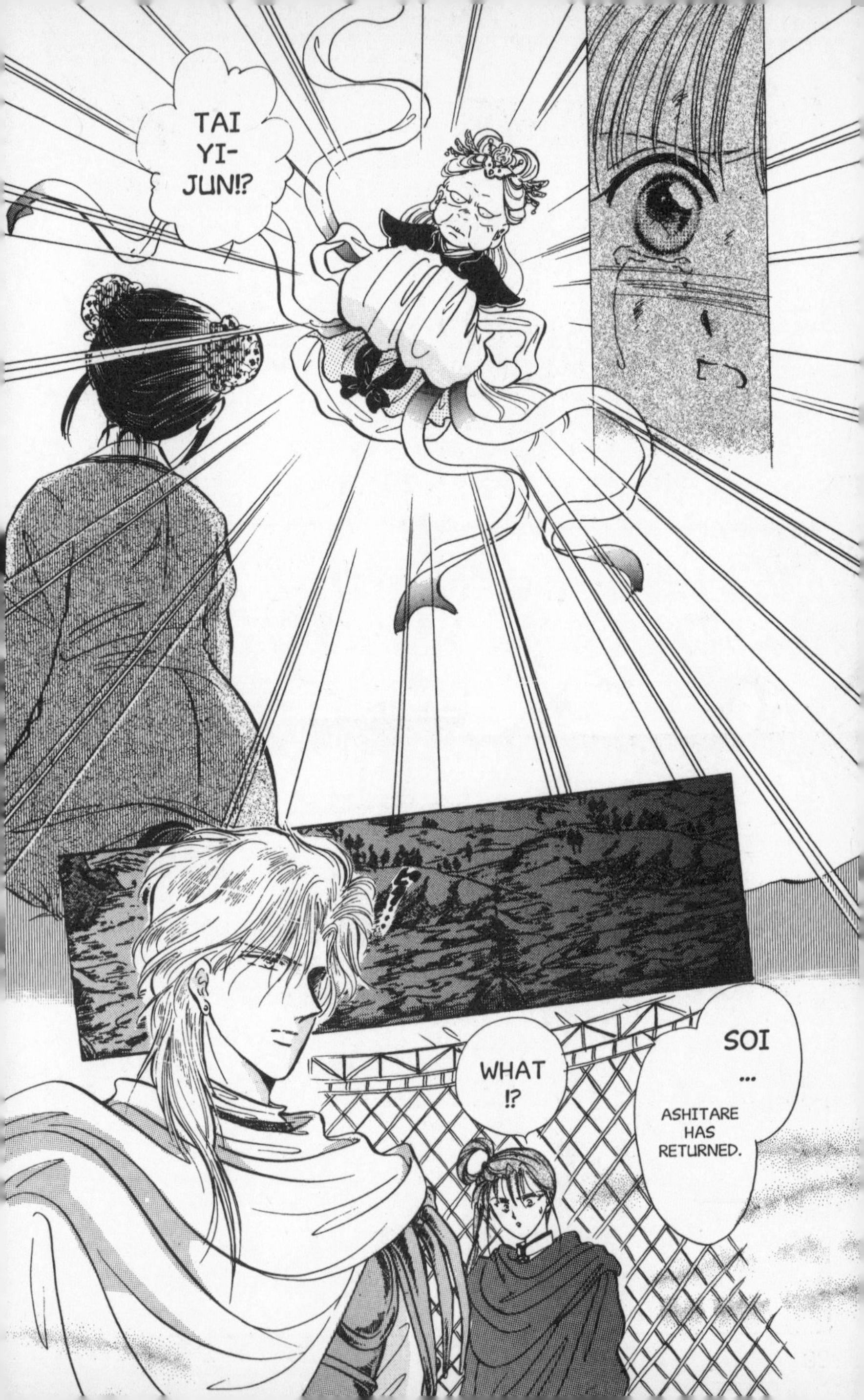
TAI YI-JUN!?
SOI ... ASHITARE HAS RETURNED.
WHAT !?

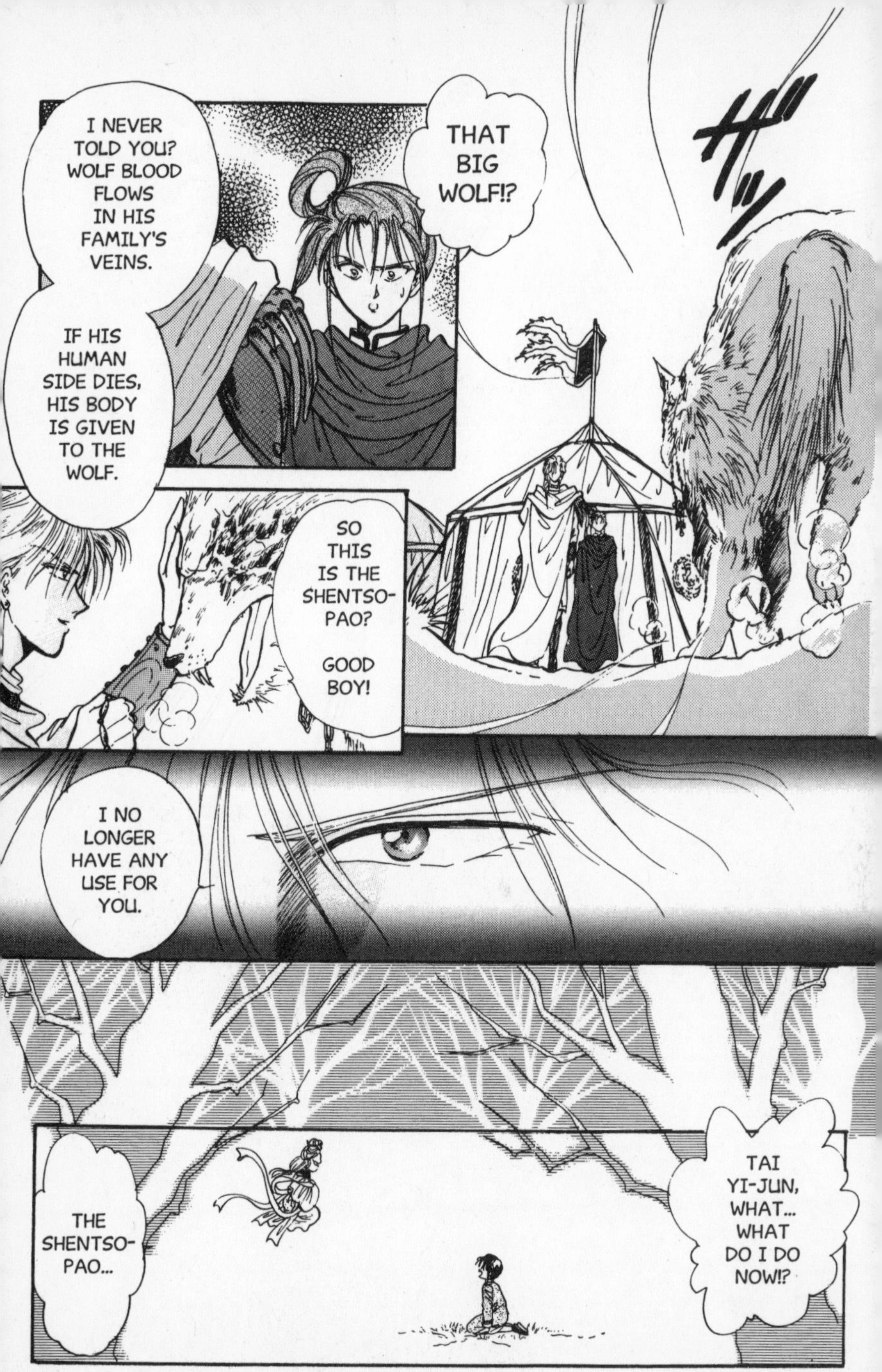
THAT BIG WOLF!?
I NEVER TOLD YOU? WOLF BLOOD FLOWS IN HIS FAMILY'S VEINS.
IF HIS HUMAN SIDE DIES, HIS BODY IS GIVEN TO THE WOLF.
SO THIS IS THE SHENTSO-PAO?
GOOD BOY!
I NO LONGER HAVE ANY USE FOR YOU.
TAI YI-JUN, WHAT... WHAT DO I DO NOW!?
THE SHENTSO-PAO...

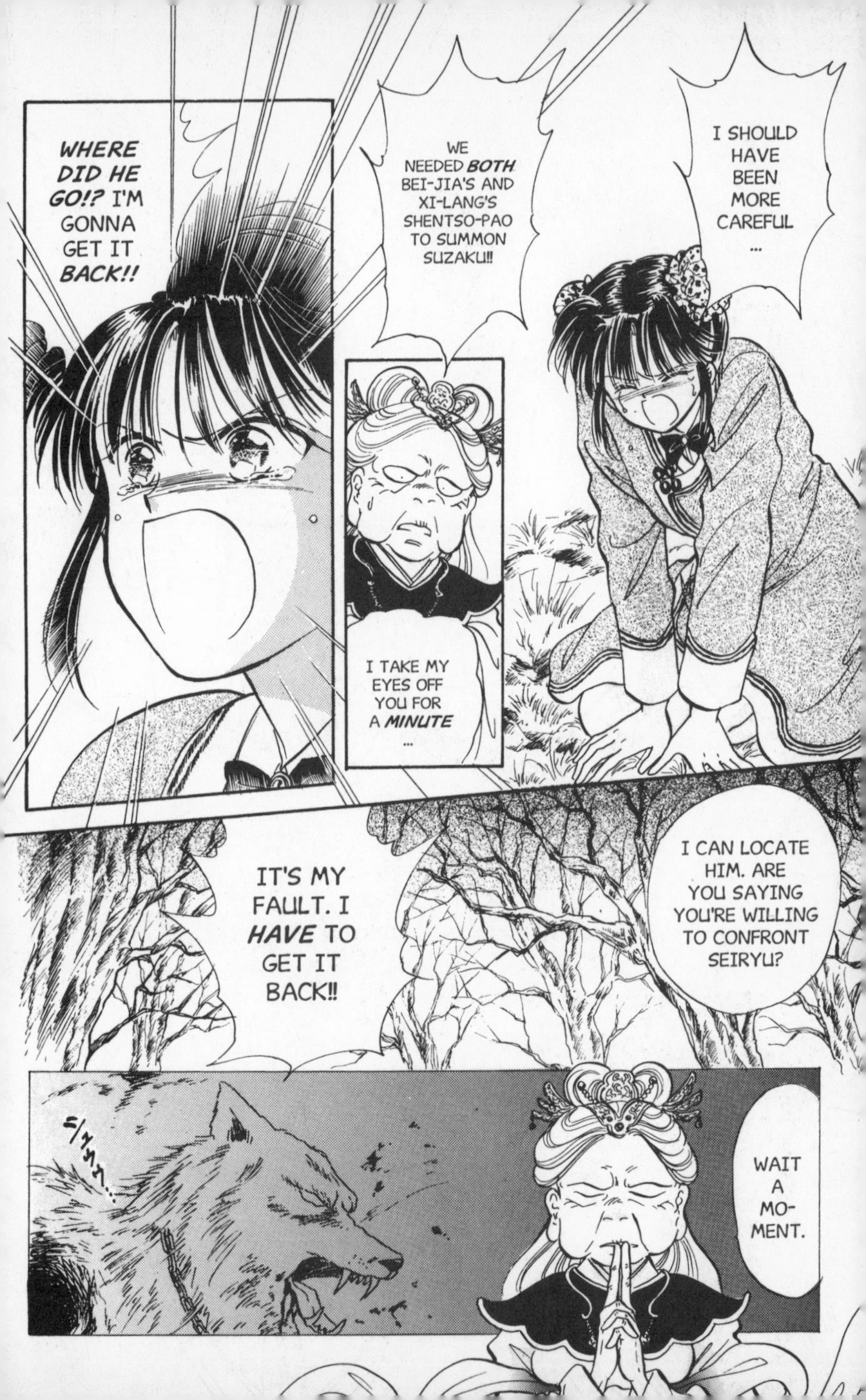

I SHOULD HAVE BEEN MORE CAREFUL ...
WE NEEDED **BOTH** BEI-JIA'S AND XI-LANG'S SHENTSO-PAO TO SUMMON SUZAKU!!
I TAKE MY EYES OFF YOU FOR A *MINUTE* ...
WHERE DID HE GO!? I'M GONNA GET IT *BACK!!*
I CAN LOCATE HIM. ARE YOU SAYING YOU'RE WILLING TO CONFRONT SEIRYU?
IT'S MY FAULT. I *HAVE* TO GET IT BACK!!
WAIT A MO-MENT.

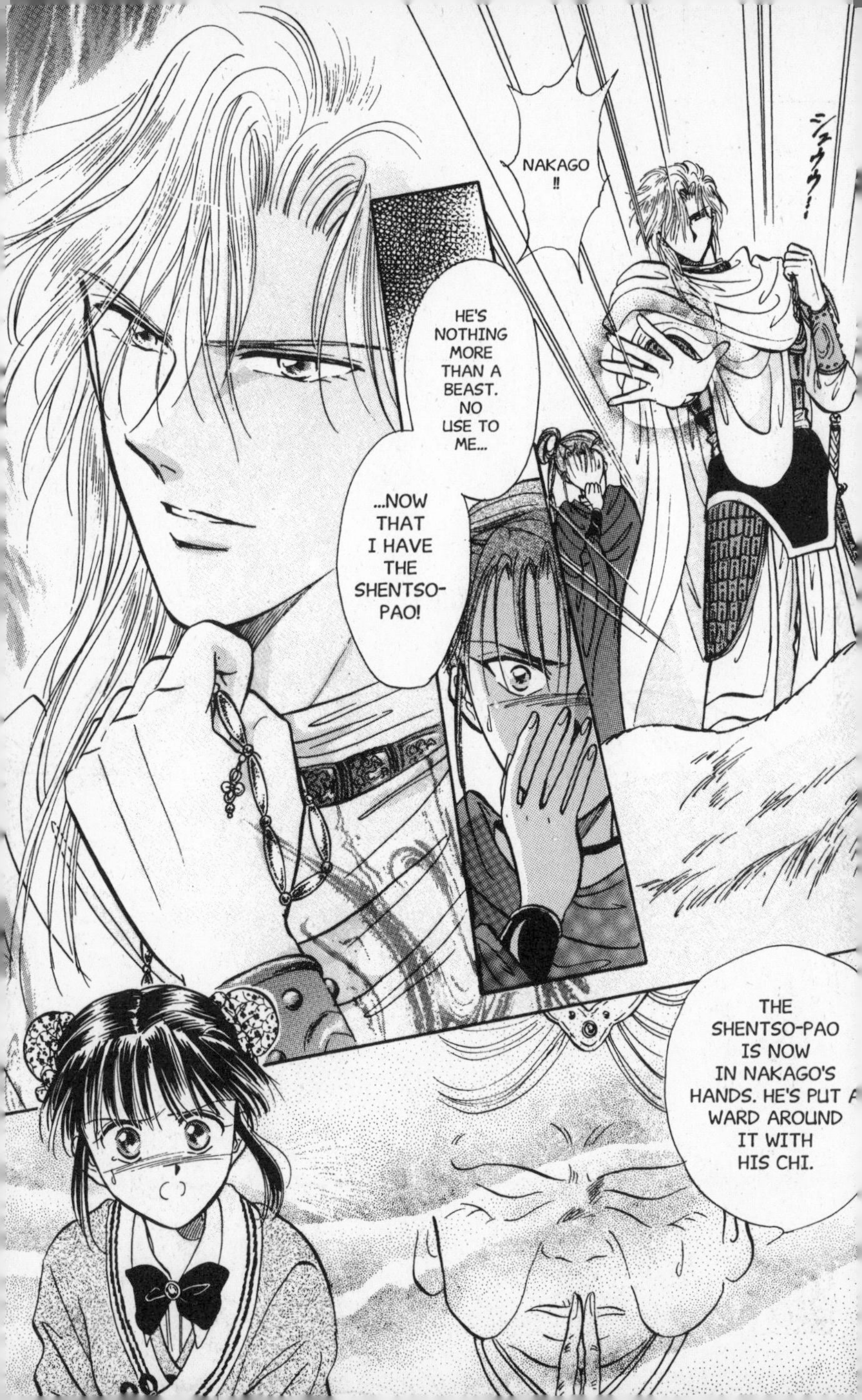

シュウウ…
NAKAGO!!
HE'S NOTHING MORE THAN A BEAST. NO USE TO ME...
...NOW THAT I HAVE THE SHENTSO-PAO!
THE SHENTSO-PAO IS NOW IN NAKAGO'S HANDS. HE'S PUT A WARD AROUND IT WITH HIS CHI.

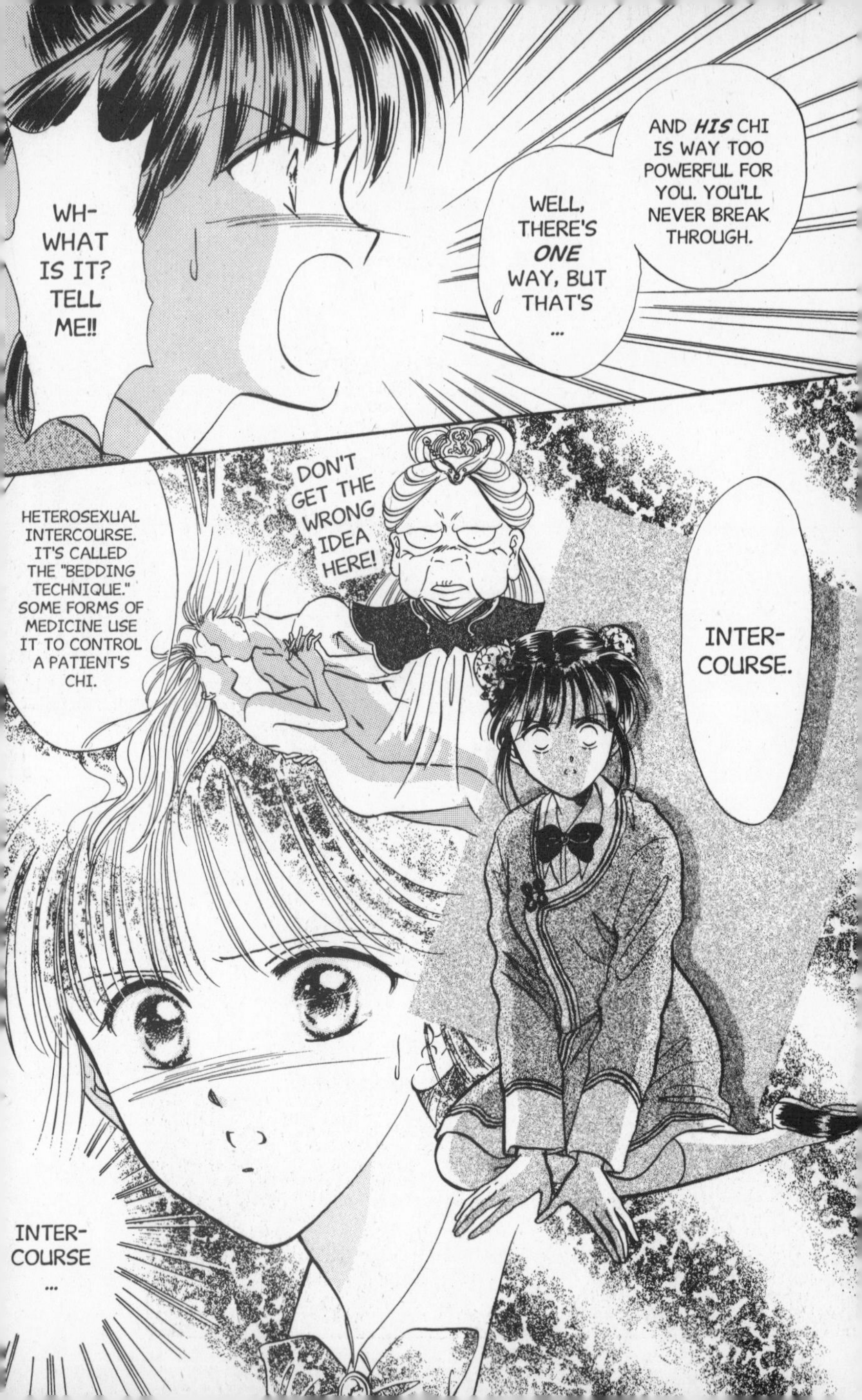
AND ***HIS*** CHI IS WAY TOO POWERFUL FOR YOU. YOU'LL NEVER BREAK THROUGH.
WELL, THERE'S ***ONE*** WAY, BUT THAT'S ...
WH- WHAT IS IT? TELL ME!!
INTER-COURSE.
HETEROSEXUAL INTERCOURSE. IT'S CALLED THE "BEDDING TECHNIQUE." SOME FORMS OF MEDICINE USE IT TO CONTROL A PATIENT'S CHI.
DON'T GET THE WRONG IDEA HERE!
INTER-COURSE ...

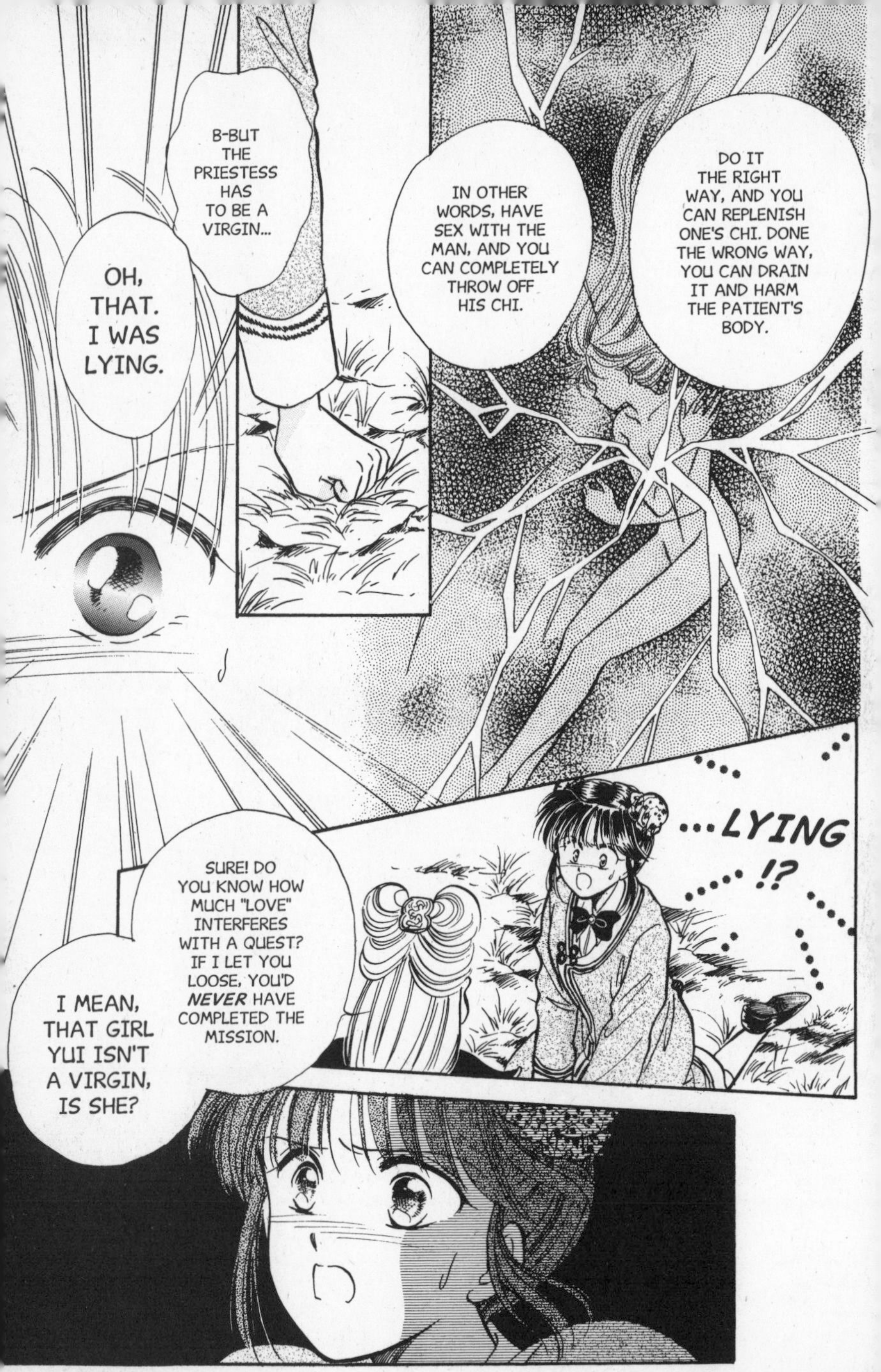
DO IT THE RIGHT WAY, AND YOU CAN REPLENISH ONE'S CHI. DONE THE WRONG WAY, YOU CAN DRAIN IT AND HARM THE PATIENT'S BODY.
IN OTHER WORDS, HAVE SEX WITH THE MAN, AND YOU CAN COMPLETELY THROW OFF HIS CHI.
B-BUT THE PRIESTESS HAS TO BE A VIRGIN...
OH, THAT. I WAS LYING.
...LYING !?
SURE! DO YOU KNOW HOW MUCH "LOVE" INTERFERES WITH A QUEST? IF I LET YOU LOOSE, YOU'D *NEVER* HAVE COMPLETED THE MISSION.
I MEAN, THAT GIRL YUI ISN'T A VIRGIN, IS SHE?

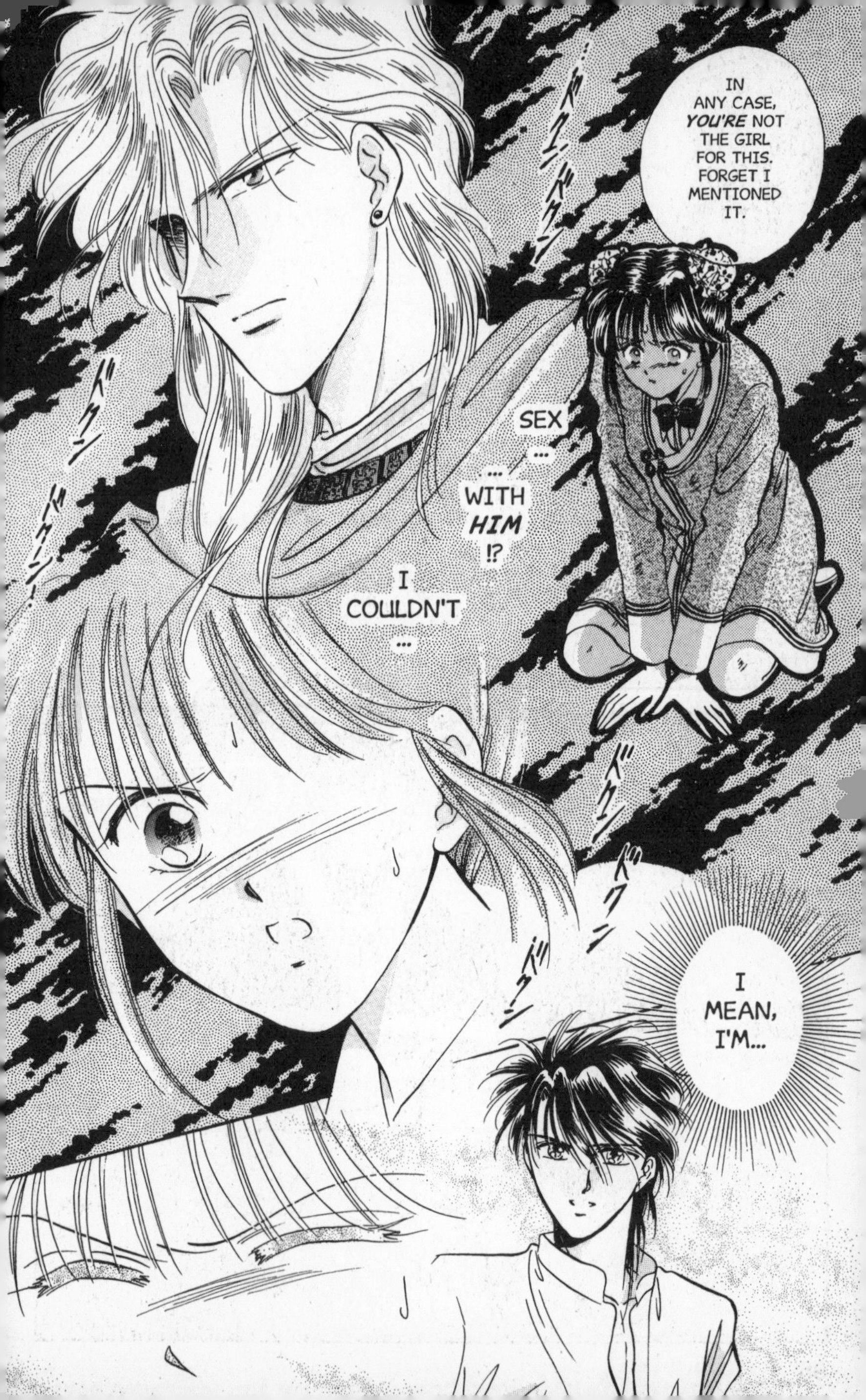
IN ANY CASE, *YOU'RE* NOT THE GIRL FOR THIS. FORGET I MENTIONED IT.
SEX...
...WITH *HIM*!?
I COULDN'T...
I MEAN, I'M...

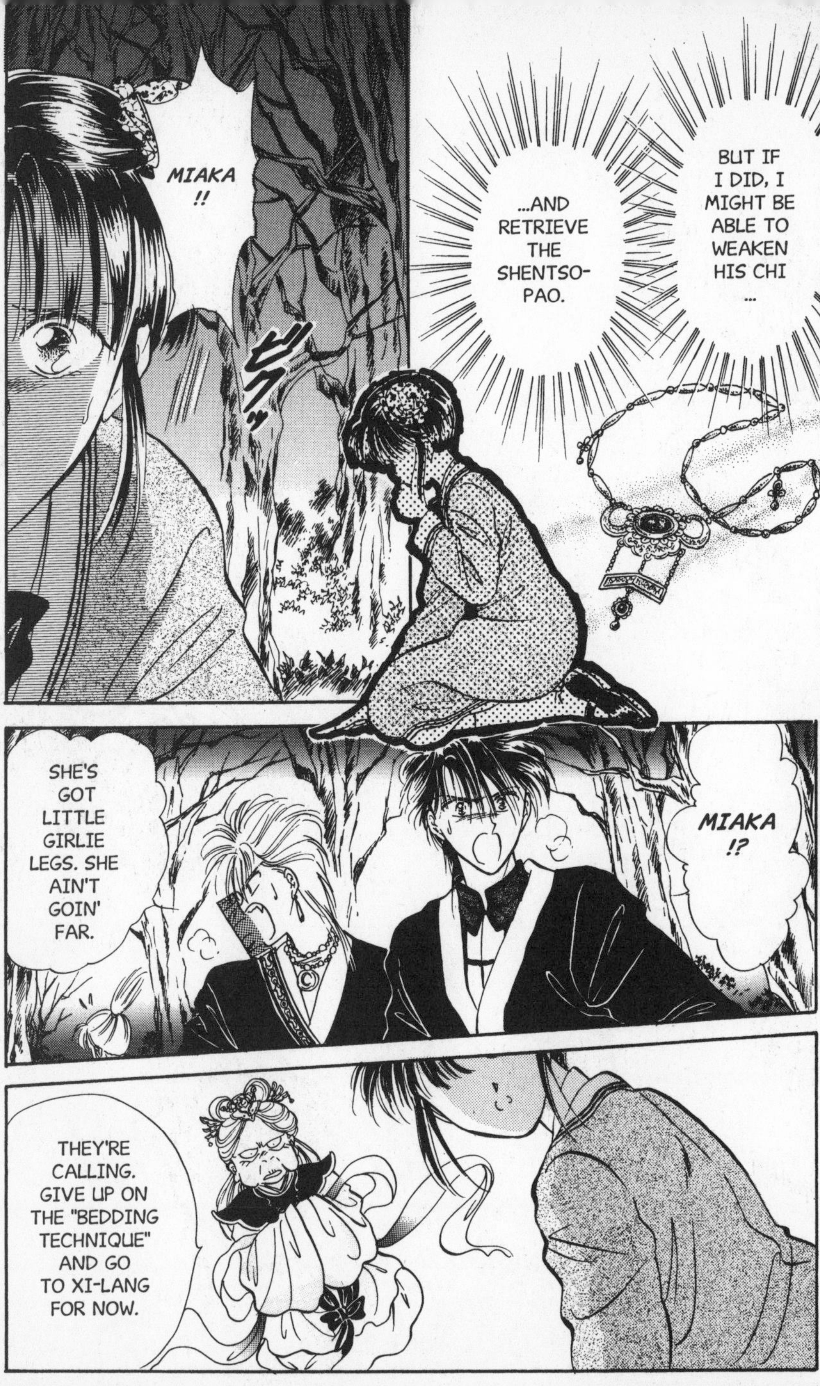
BUT IF I DID, I MIGHT BE ABLE TO WEAKEN HIS CHI ...
...AND RETRIEVE THE SHENTSO-PAO.
MIAKA !!
ビクッ
MIAKA !?
SHE'S GOT LITTLE GIRLIE LEGS. SHE AIN'T GOIN' FAR.
THEY'RE CALLING. GIVE UP ON THE "BEDDING TECHNIQUE" AND GO TO XI-LANG FOR NOW.

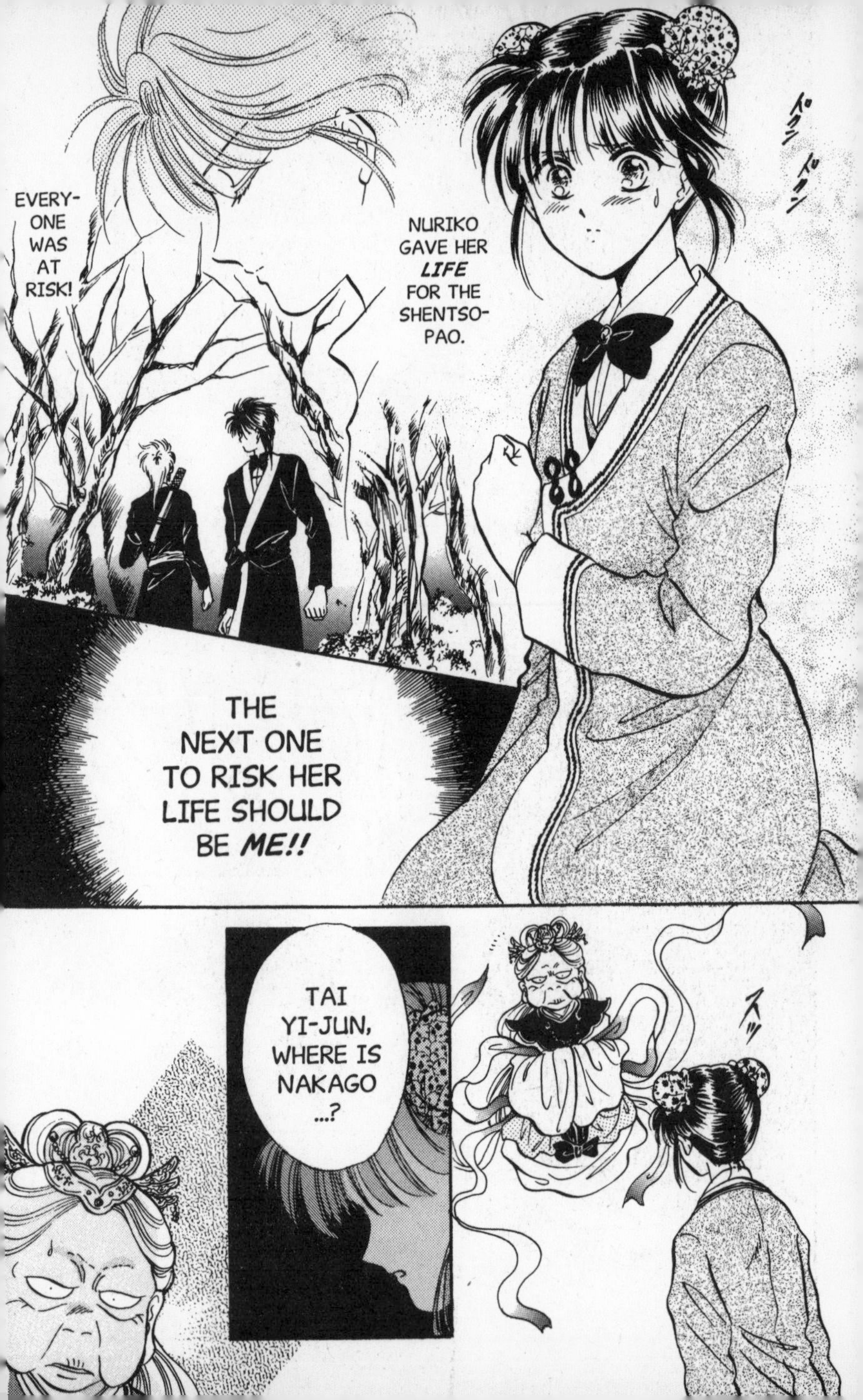
NURIKO GAVE HER LIFE FOR THE SHENTSO-PAO.
EVERY-ONE WAS AT RISK!
THE NEXT ONE TO RISK HER LIFE SHOULD BE ME!!
TAI YI-JUN, WHERE IS NAKAGO ...?

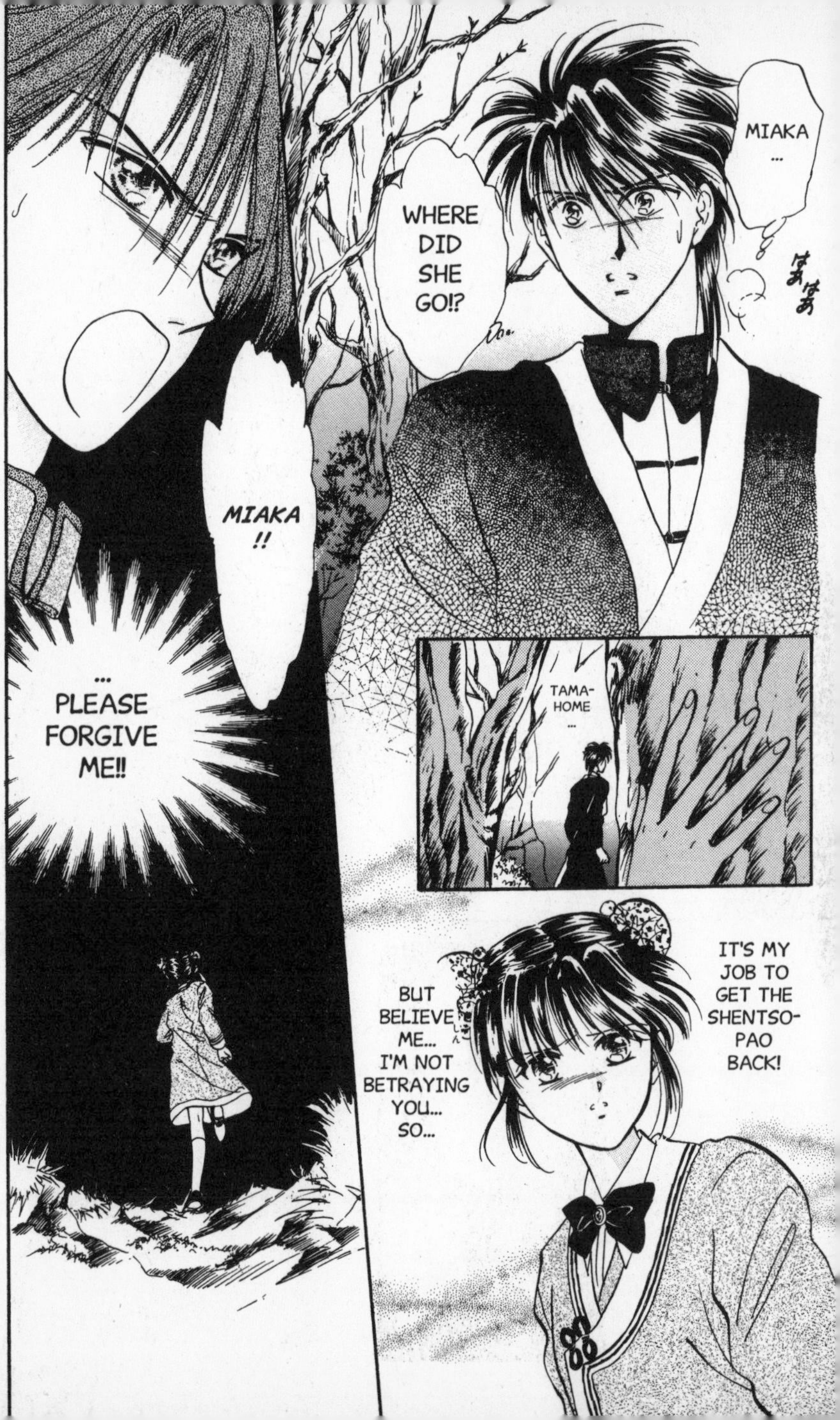
MIAKA ...
WHERE DID SHE GO!?
TAMA-HOME ...
IT'S MY JOB TO GET THE SHENTSO-PAO BACK!
BUT BELIEVE ME... I'M NOT BETRAYING YOU... SO...
MIAKA !!
... PLEASE FORGIVE ME!!

Once again, on the BGM [background music] of "Fūshigi Yūgi"

Since I wrote all that stuff on "135," I received a lot of fan mail saying things like, "I bought it," or, "What kind of song is it," and that really made me happy! Now "135" is featured prominently as BGM!! After having the wonderful opportunity to compose the lyrics and music to a song on the Shôjo Comic CD Toy Box '93, which Flower Wave released at the end of last year, I was invited to perform live! I got really teary when the vocalists sang "Tenbu" and "Wo Ai Ni." They clowned around, though, during the talk show afterwards, speaking in Kansai dialect.

By the way, "Wo Ai Ni" on the CD is titled "135." I'm sorry that I can't dub tapes for those of you who can't find it, so I'll share some of the lyrics:

Every time I visit that distant planet where you, in your brilliance, are;
We may not have money, we two on an endless journey;
It's mysterious, isn't it? How romantic your tear-filled eyes seem;
The dreams we can't bear to hide;
One, two, three, four;

Wo ai ni, swaying eternally, traveling to our future;
Wo ai ni, swaying eternally, rise holy girl!

This is where you sing one, two, three, four! Are on the verge of flooding out!

By the way, you may be able to find this at some karaoke boxes in Japan, if you look hard enough!!

I also have "MIZ-INCO," "Order-made," "Fortune," "Pentangle," "Momento," "Tenbu"...

These three are my favorites!! They have catchy tunes, and you can find them pretty easily! The upper three are good, but they're so hard to find!

In "Momento," the Fushigi imagery from Ai kara ("From Love") to Kiseki ("Miracle") is awesome.

"Everyone carries a deep sadness;
Setting out on a journey to find kindness somewhere."

"A miracle can occur, so don't give up;
Turn into a myth that stirs this heart."

Lyrics and music are both really good!!

But the songs filled with imagery are Tenbu, Yume Mirai ("Dream Future") as well as SPARROW - Xian wo Nishi e ("SPARROW - Westward to Xian") which are awesome! And for the current "Fushigi," I think Kaeru Hi made ("Until the Day of Return") is the perfect song.

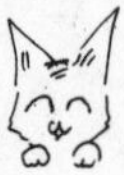

- Also every time I'm doing a sad scene, and I listen to the theme song for "The Last Emperor," I get all teary-eyed. I had it playing over and over when I was doing Nuriko's death scene. It's a wonderful song! The song "Self Portrait" from the album "Gruppo Musicale" reminds me of Miaka.

- "Yume" ("Dream"), that's in Katsuhisa Hattori's "Music Farm 5," also has a Chinese flavor. It's used as the BGM for Kyon Kyon's talk show, "Tunnels Are All Thanks to You."

- The song that I consider to be Nakago's (I can't tell whether he's gaining fans or just enemies.) theme song is Soft Balet's first song, "No Pleasure," from their CD "Document." The lyrics really seem just right....

- But my favorite is called "Tensei no Chi" ("The Land of Heavenly Promise") from the "Fushigi" CD booklet that I mentioned before. It's the song playing when Tai Yi-Jun is talking. I love this demo tape!!

A performance done before they went into the studio.
It came out completely different in the final studio tracks.

The demo version of "Tensei no Chi" is simpler, but I love the performance so much!! I hope they use the demo for BGM again! It's so cool!

Finally, the BGM for Tai Yi-Jun is really pretty. I wish you could listen to it!

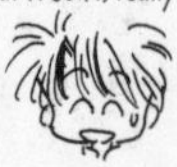

I wrote this in a rush so it's a mess.
I have so much more to say too...!! Sorry!!

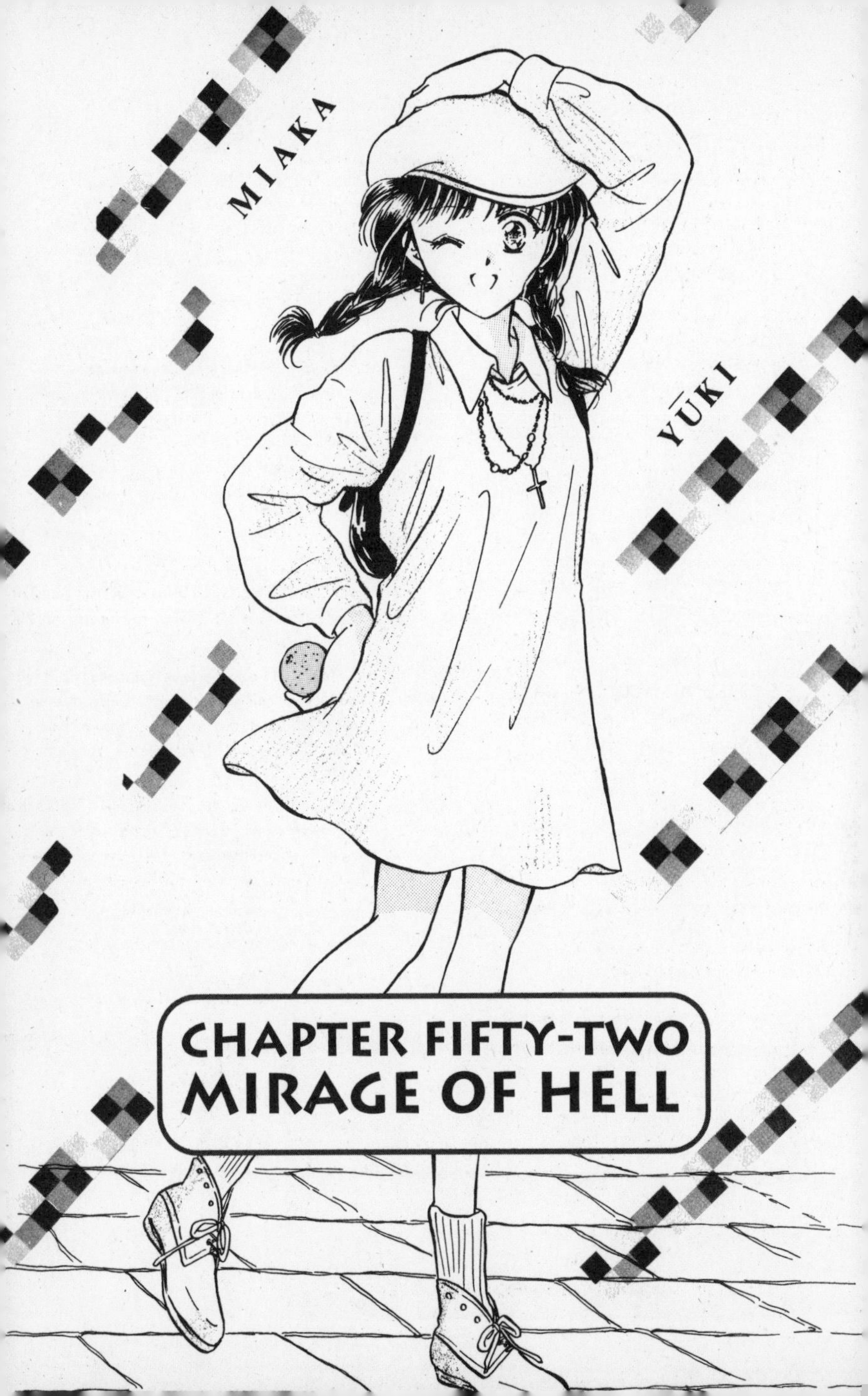
MIAKA
YŪKI

CHAPTER FIFTY-TWO
MIRAGE OF HELL

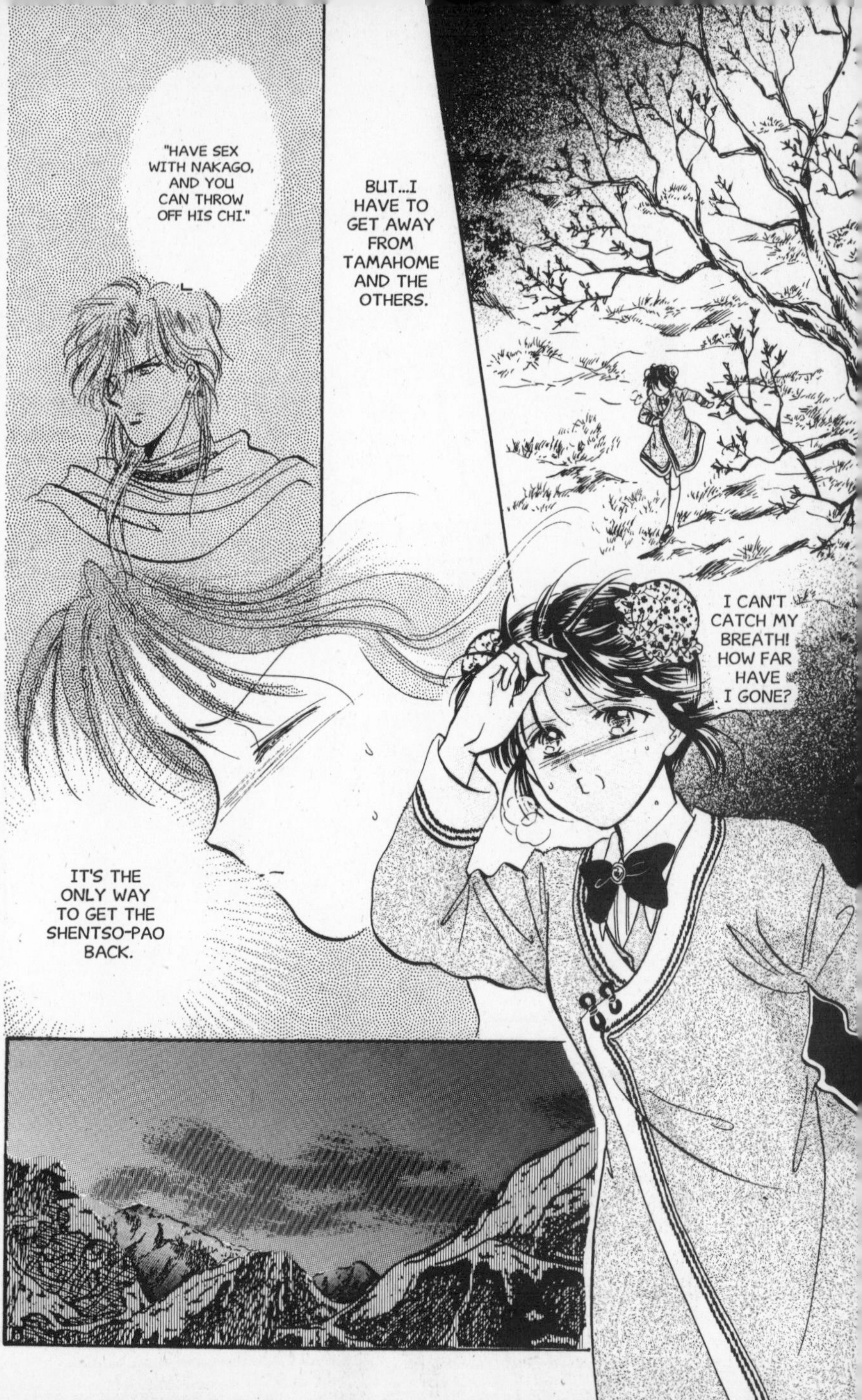
I CAN'T CATCH MY BREATH! HOW FAR HAVE I GONE?
BUT...I HAVE TO GET AWAY FROM TAMAHOME AND THE OTHERS.
"HAVE SEX WITH NAKAGO, AND YOU CAN THROW OFF HIS CHI."
IT'S THE ONLY WAY TO GET THE SHENTSO-PAO BACK.

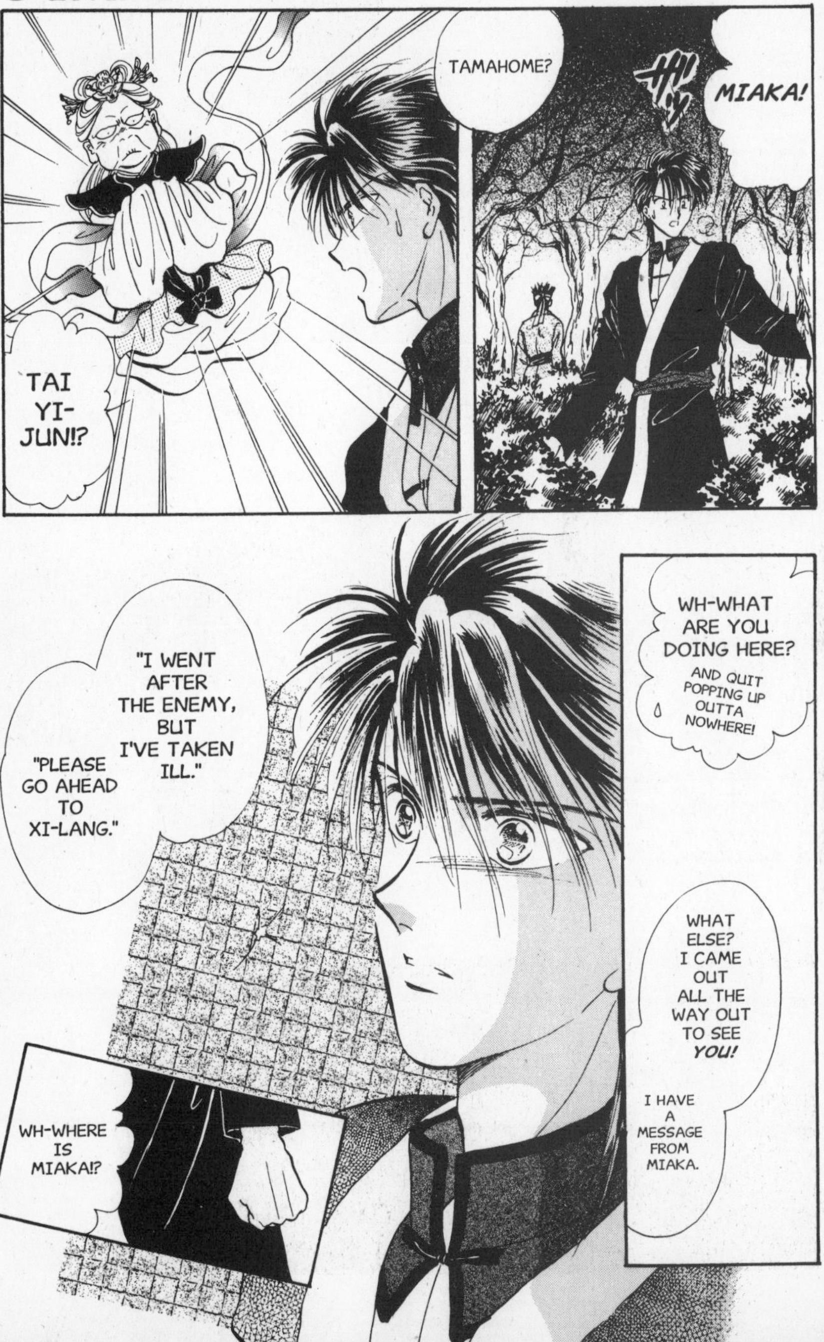
MIAKA!
TAMAHOME?
TAI YI-JUN!?
WH-WHAT ARE YOU DOING HERE?
AND QUIT POPPING UP OUTTA NOWHERE!
WHAT ELSE? I CAME OUT ALL THE WAY OUT TO SEE *YOU!*
WH-WHERE IS MIAKA!?
I HAVE A MESSAGE FROM MIAKA.
"I WENT AFTER THE ENEMY, BUT I'VE TAKEN ILL."
"PLEASE GO AHEAD TO XI-LANG."

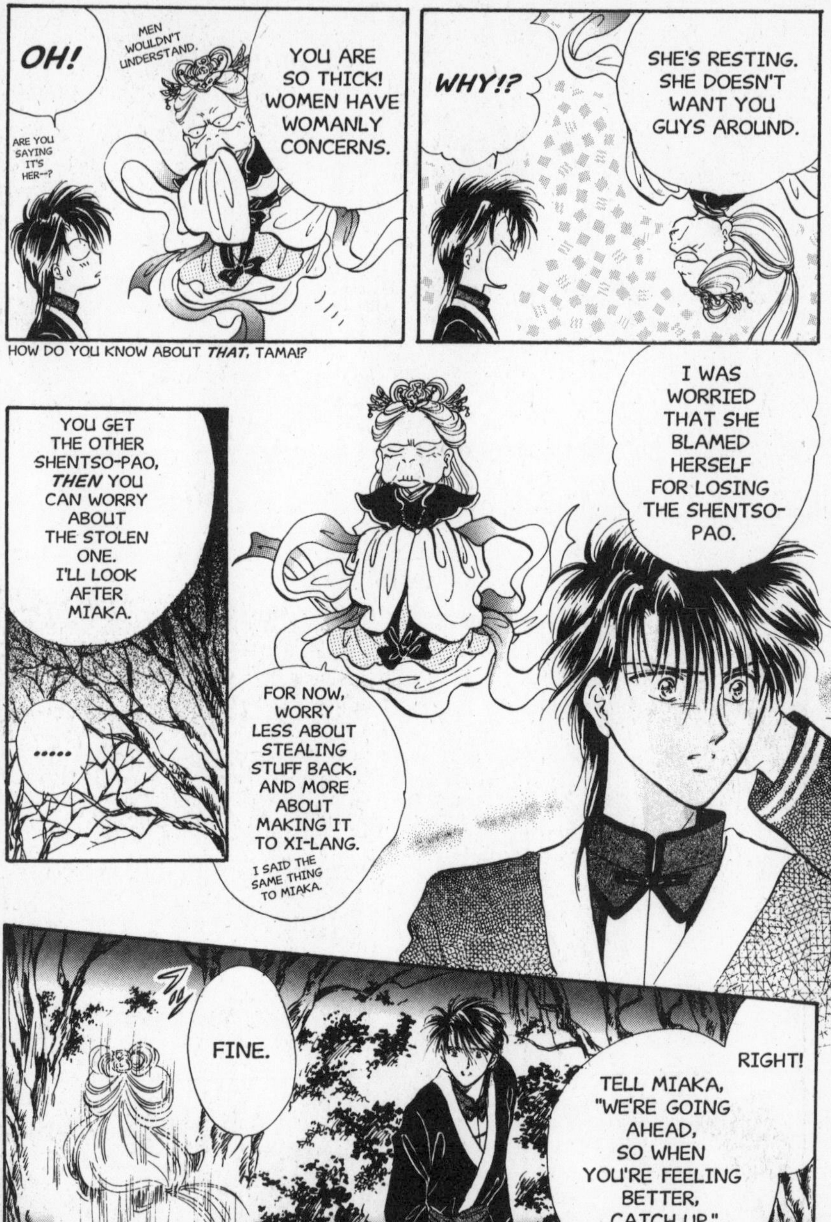
SHE'S RESTING. SHE DOESN'T WANT YOU GUYS AROUND.
WHY!?
YOU ARE SO THICK! WOMEN HAVE WOMANLY CONCERNS.
MEN WOULDN'T UNDERSTAND.
OH!
ARE YOU SAYING IT'S HER--?
HOW DO YOU KNOW ABOUT *THAT*, TAMA!?
I WAS WORRIED THAT SHE BLAMED HERSELF FOR LOSING THE SHENTSO-PAO.
FOR NOW, WORRY LESS ABOUT STEALING STUFF BACK, AND MORE ABOUT MAKING IT TO XI-LANG.
I SAID THE SAME THING TO MIAKA.
YOU GET THE OTHER SHENTSO-PAO, *THEN* YOU CAN WORRY ABOUT THE STOLEN ONE. I'LL LOOK AFTER MIAKA.
.....
RIGHT! TELL MIAKA, "WE'RE GOING AHEAD, SO WHEN YOU'RE FEELING BETTER, CATCH UP."
FINE.

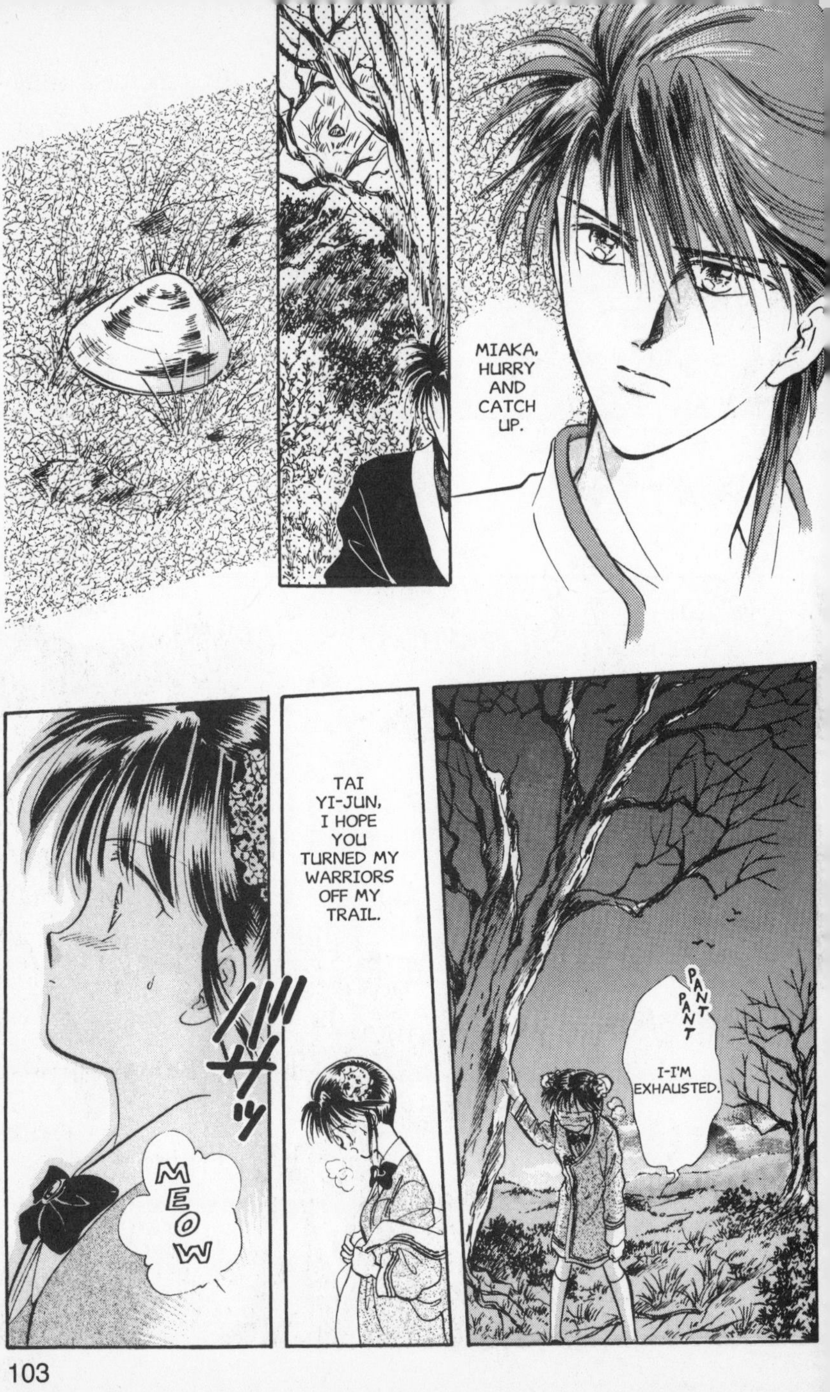
MIAKA, HURRY AND CATCH UP.
PANT PANT
I-I'M EXHAUSTED.
TAI YI-JUN, I HOPE YOU TURNED MY WARRIORS OFF MY TRAIL.
ザッ
MEOW

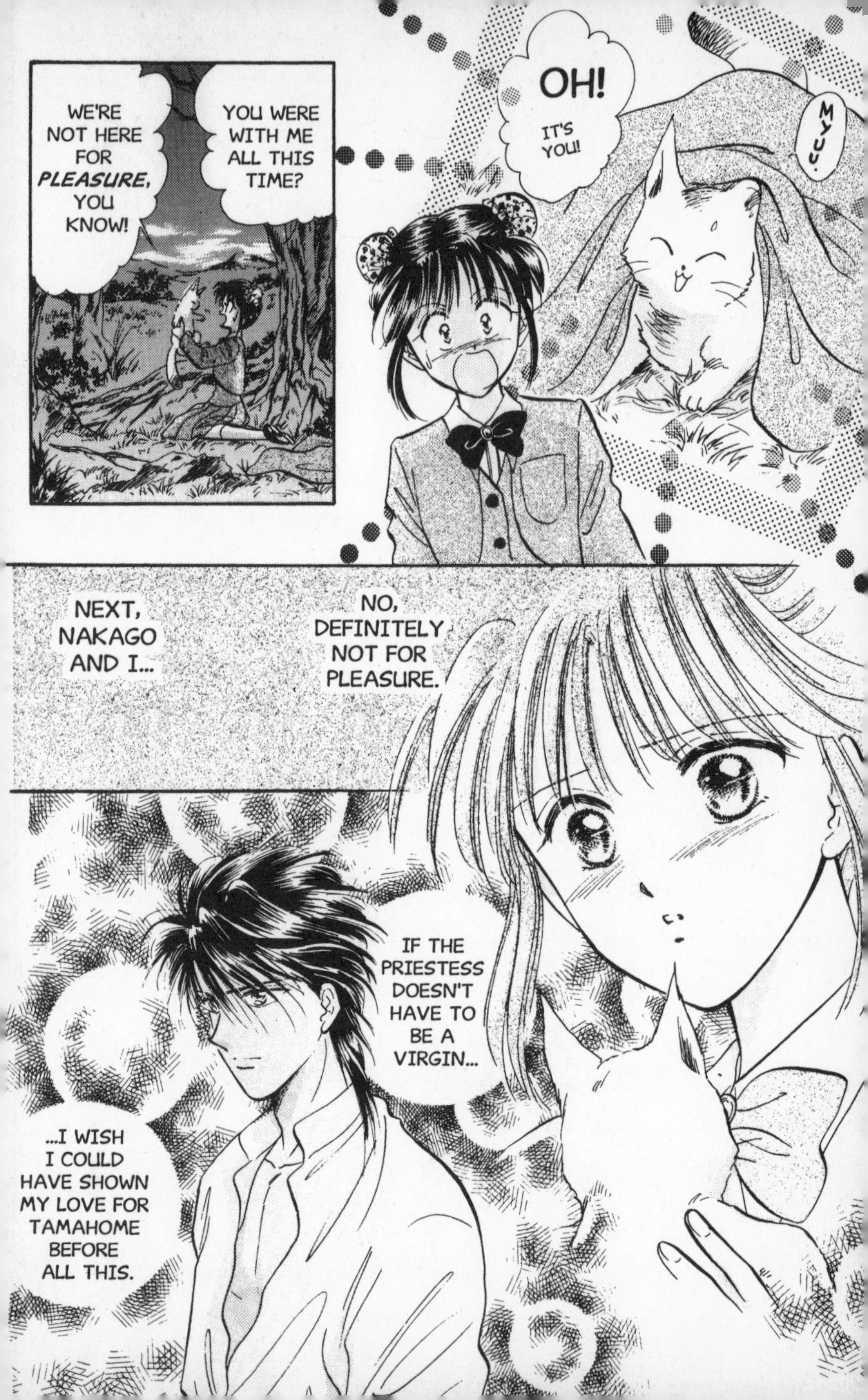
MYUU.
OH! IT'S YOU!
YOU WERE WITH ME ALL THIS TIME?
WE'RE NOT HERE FOR *PLEASURE*, YOU KNOW!
NO, DEFINITELY NOT FOR PLEASURE.
NEXT, NAKAGO AND I...
IF THE PRIESTESS DOESN'T HAVE TO BE A VIRGIN...
...I WISH I COULD HAVE SHOWN MY LOVE FOR TAMAHOME BEFORE ALL THIS.

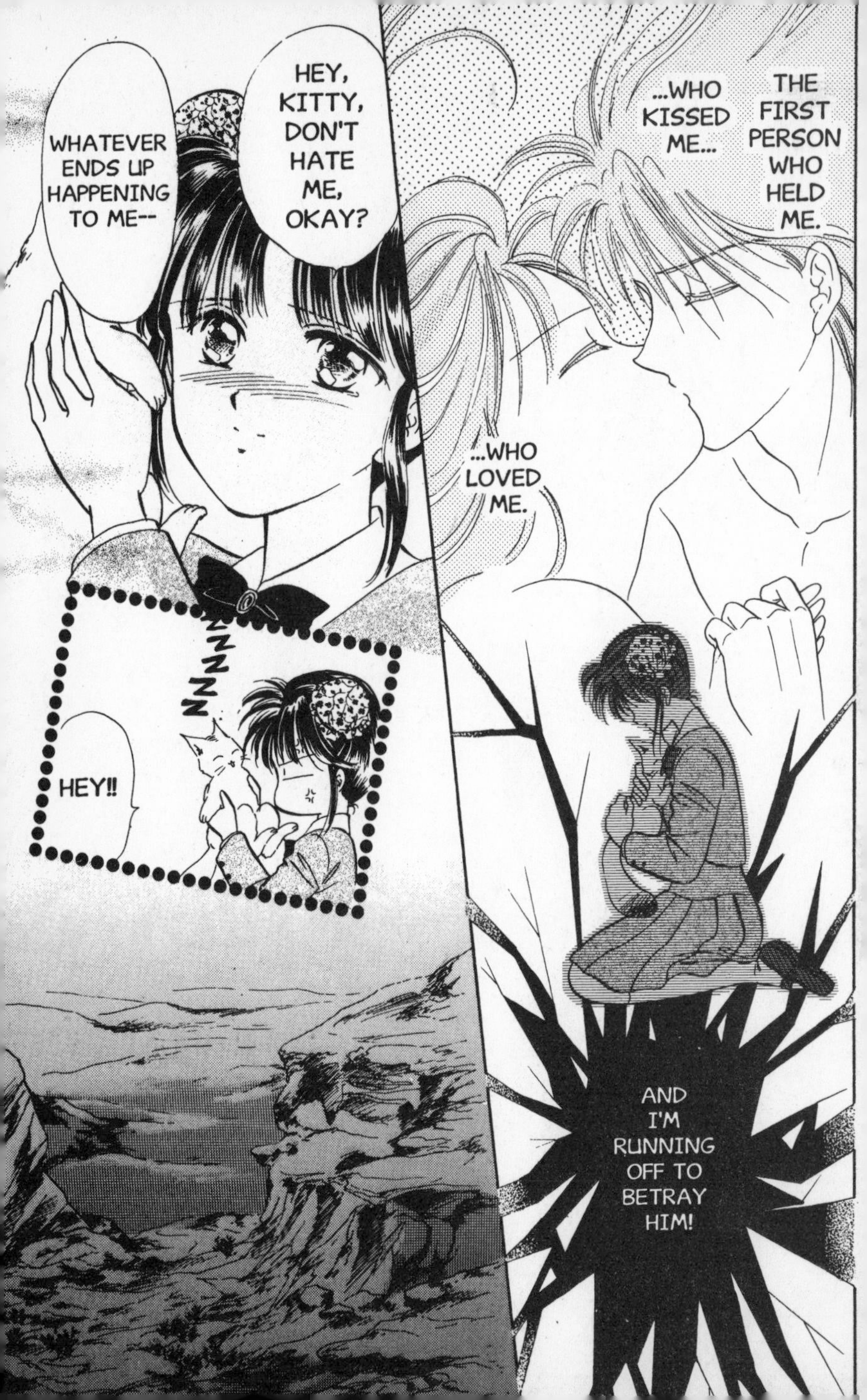
THE FIRST PERSON WHO HELD ME.
...WHO KISSED ME...
...WHO LOVED ME.
AND I'M RUNNING OFF TO BETRAY HIM!
HEY, KITTY, DON'T HATE ME, OKAY?
WHATEVER ENDS UP HAPPENING TO ME--
ZZZZZ
HEY!!

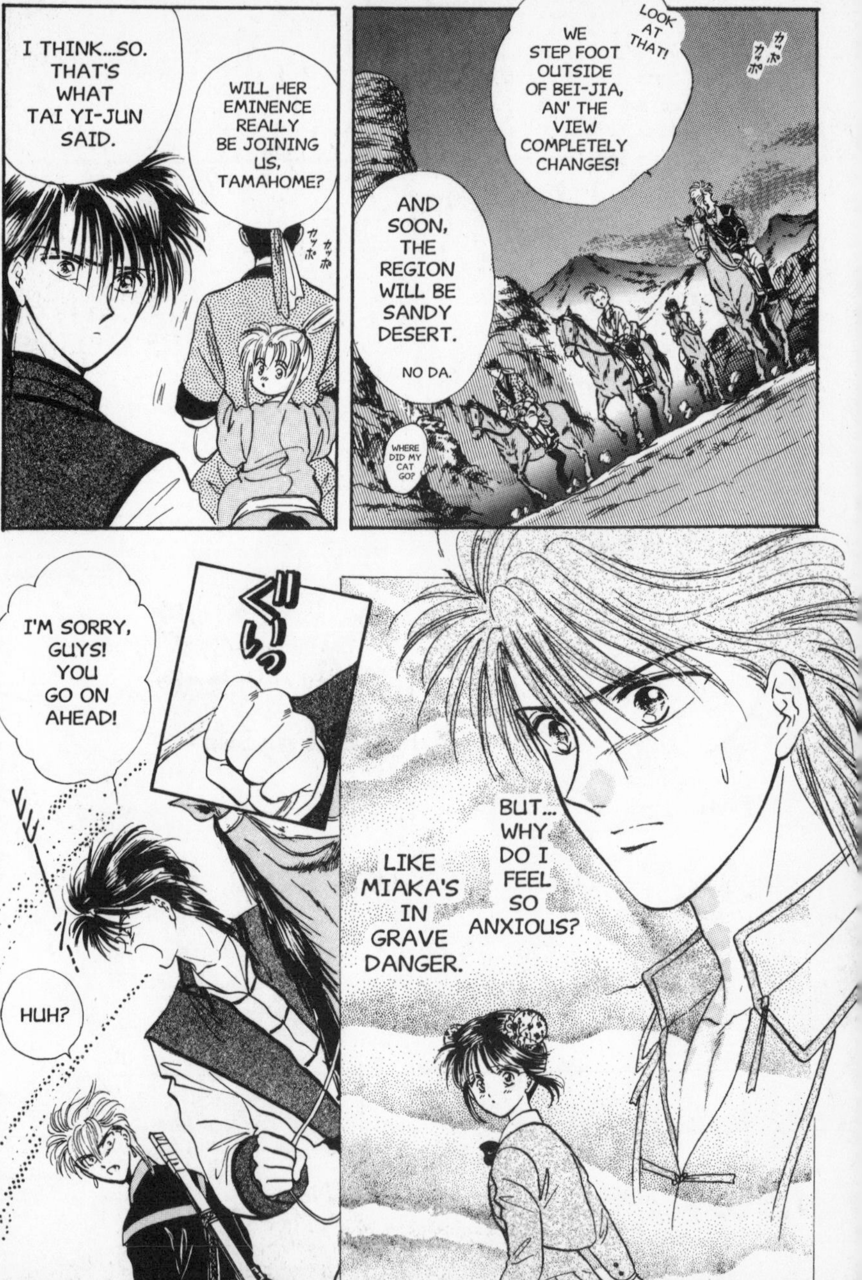
LOOK AT THAT!
WE STEP FOOT OUTSIDE OF BEI-JIA, AN' THE VIEW COMPLETELY CHANGES!
AND SOON, THE REGION WILL BE SANDY DESERT.
NO DA.
WHERE DID MY CAT GO?
WILL HER EMINENCE REALLY BE JOINING US, TAMAHOME?
I THINK...SO. THAT'S WHAT TAI YI-JUN SAID.
BUT... WHY DO I FEEL SO ANXIOUS?
LIKE MIAKA'S IN GRAVE DANGER.
I'M SORRY, GUYS! YOU GO ON AHEAD!
HUH?

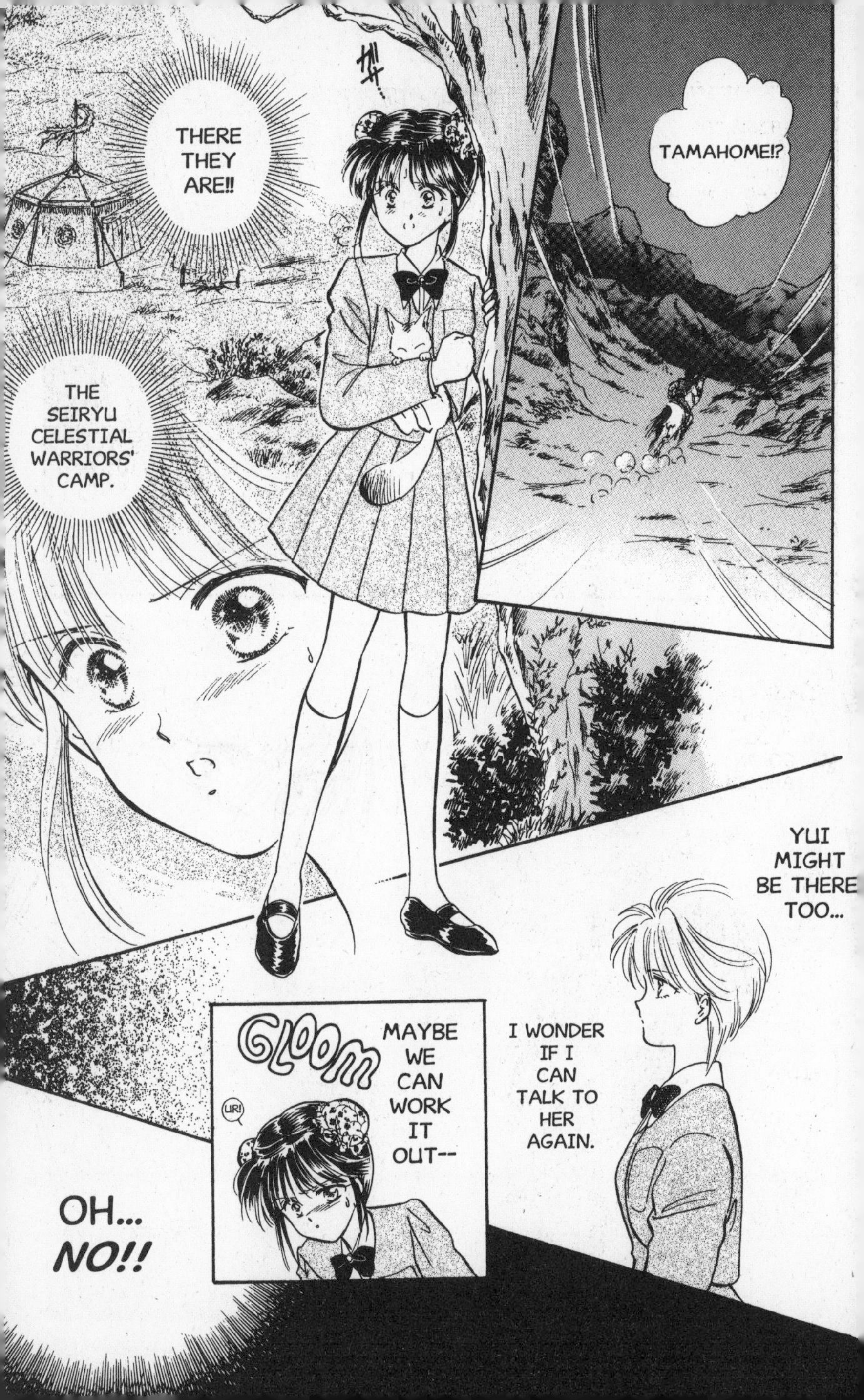

TAMAHOME!?
THERE THEY ARE!!
THE SEIRYU CELESTIAL WARRIORS' CAMP.
YUI MIGHT BE THERE TOO...
I WONDER IF I CAN TALK TO HER AGAIN.
MAYBE WE CAN WORK IT OUT--
GLOOM
UR!
OH... NO!!

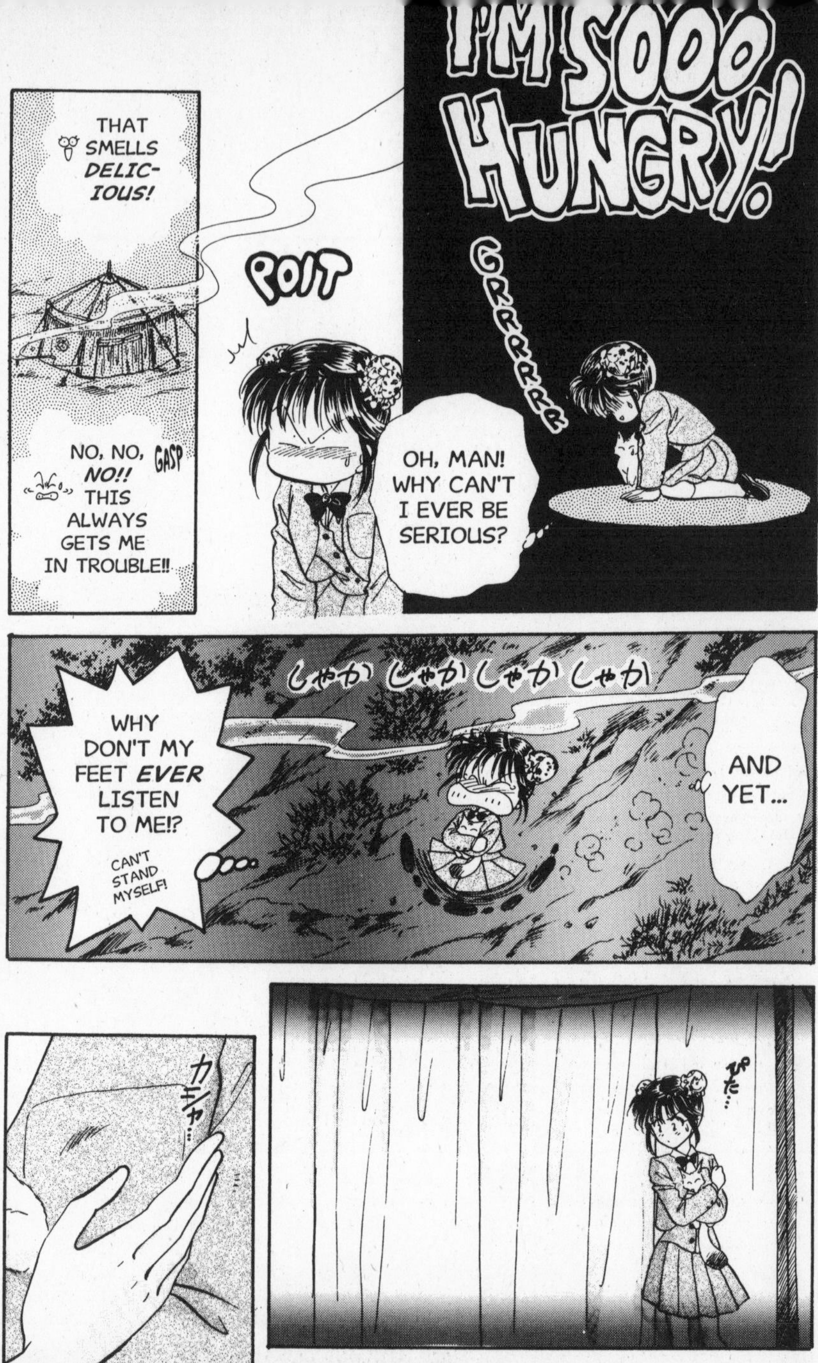
I'M SOOO HUNGRY!
GRRRRRRR
POIT
OH, MAN! WHY CAN'T I EVER BE SERIOUS?
THAT SMELLS DELICIOUS!
NO, NO, NO!! THIS ALWAYS GETS ME IN TROUBLE!!
GASP
AND YET...
しゃか しゃかしゃかしゃか
WHY DON'T MY FEET EVER LISTEN TO ME!?
CAN'T STAND MYSELF!
ぴた…
カチャ…

Our last stop, Shanghai, is the equivalent to the Ginza high-priced shopping district in Tokyo. In contrast to the natural environment of forests and wide horizons we had toured through, this city was bustling with huge department stores and discos. I went into some department stores, checking out video machines and other products, and they really are cheaper there!! A funny thing was when I was in the video game section, I wasn't able to find any "Street Fighter" games per se. The software was all bootlegged, so even if I managed to find "Street Fighter II," it was labeled differently like "Street Buster" or "Street Fighter III!" (This is in 1994. The real "Street Fighter III" didn't come out until the late 1990s. -*Ed.*) On top of that, they would include three or four other games in a bundle. Amazing!

The Yûgi Store (no relation -- it's a tourist gift store) had leather items at one-tenth the Japanese price, so it was wonderful!It's too bad I got a stomachache before we got there. I couldn't even walk! I was just moaning as I thought, "I'm cursed because I burst out laughing at the funny pose on a department store's mannequin!" I was feeling so good until then. I had to forget about shopping. The bus driver (We took a private bus during the trip.) gave me some mysterious grains saying, "This will make you feel better It's Chinese herbal medicine from a tradition handed down over 4,000 years." I took it, and it did make me feel a little better, but it still kept hurting and hurting.I'll bet it's because the super-prone-to-motion-sickness me went traveling for seven days! Over the week, I was taking the televised, number one, sure-fire motion-sickness pill all the time. Add to that a lack of sleep and the oils in Chinese food, and I'm sure it all did a number on my stomach! Those pills are effective, but they're too strong! I really need them for traveling...

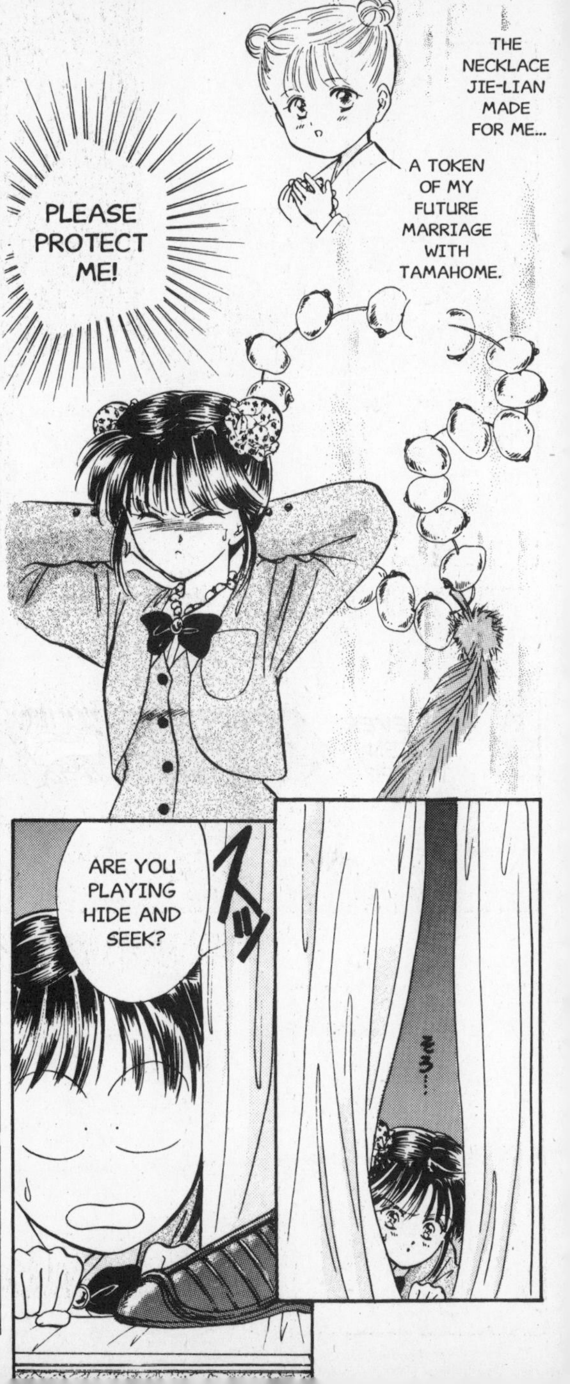
THE NECKLACE JIE-LIAN MADE FOR ME...
A TOKEN OF MY FUTURE MARRIAGE WITH TAMAHOME.
PLEASE PROTECT ME!
そろ…
スッ
ARE YOU PLAYING HIDE AND SEEK?

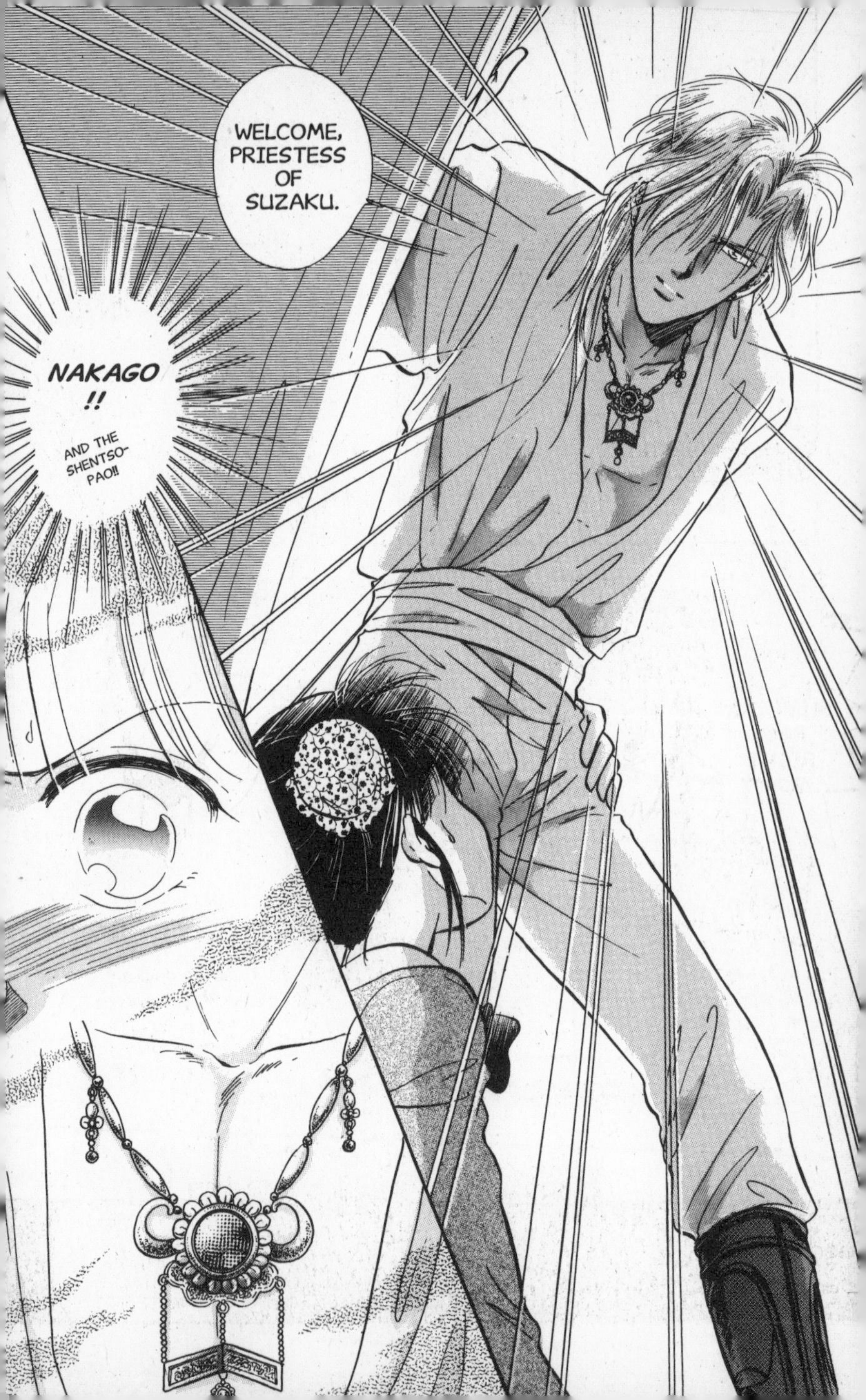
WELCOME, PRIESTESS OF SUZAKU.
NAKAGO !!
AND THE SHENTSO-PAO!!

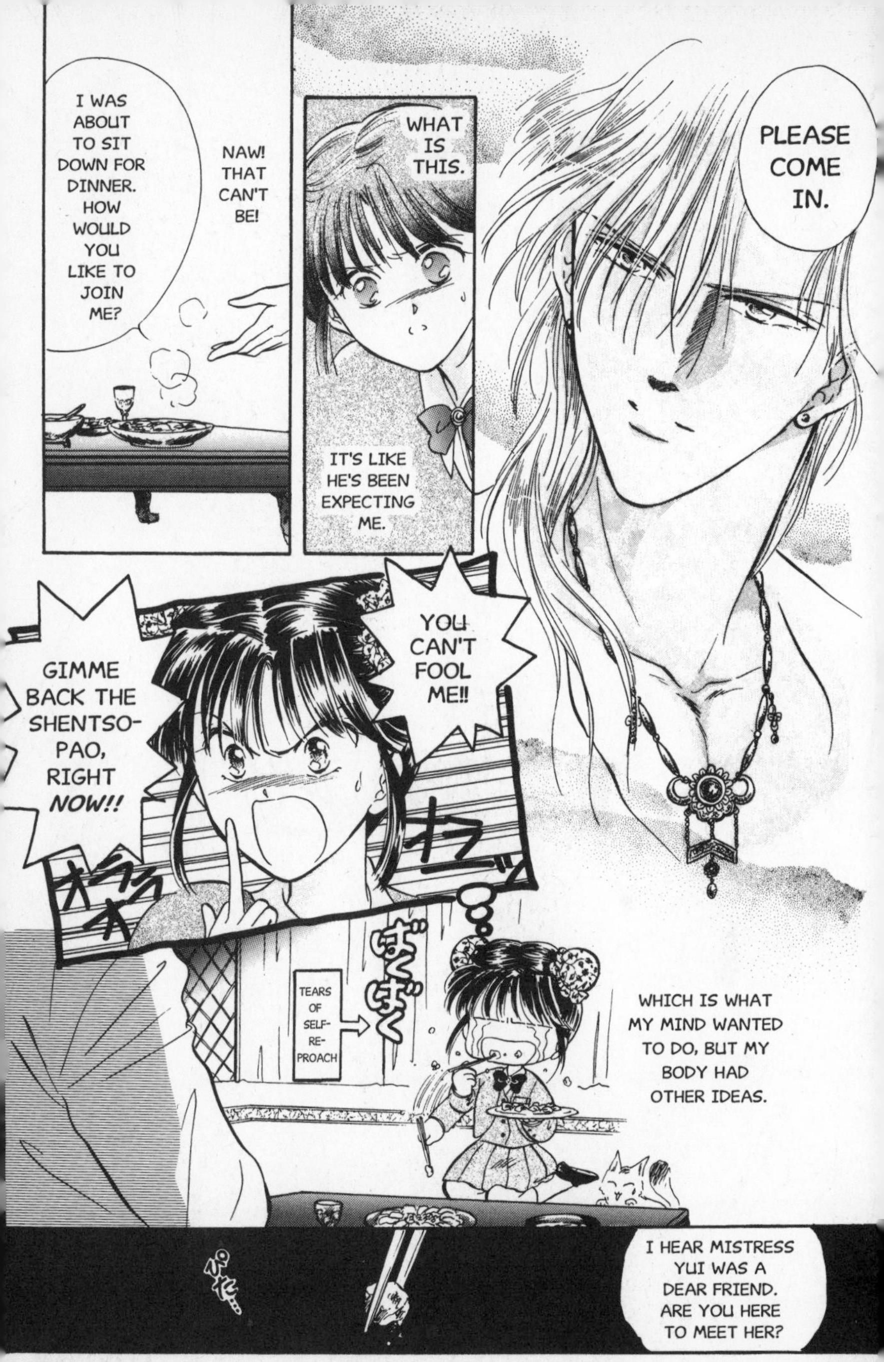
PLEASE COME IN.
WHAT IS THIS.
IT'S LIKE HE'S BEEN EXPECTING ME.
I WAS ABOUT TO SIT DOWN FOR DINNER. HOW WOULD YOU LIKE TO JOIN ME?
NAW! THAT CAN'T BE!
YOU CAN'T FOOL ME!!
GIMME BACK THE SHENTSO-PAO, RIGHT *NOW!!*
WHICH IS WHAT MY MIND WANTED TO DO, BUT MY BODY HAD OTHER IDEAS.
TEARS OF SELF-RE-PROACH
I HEAR MISTRESS YUI WAS A DEAR FRIEND. ARE YOU HERE TO MEET HER?

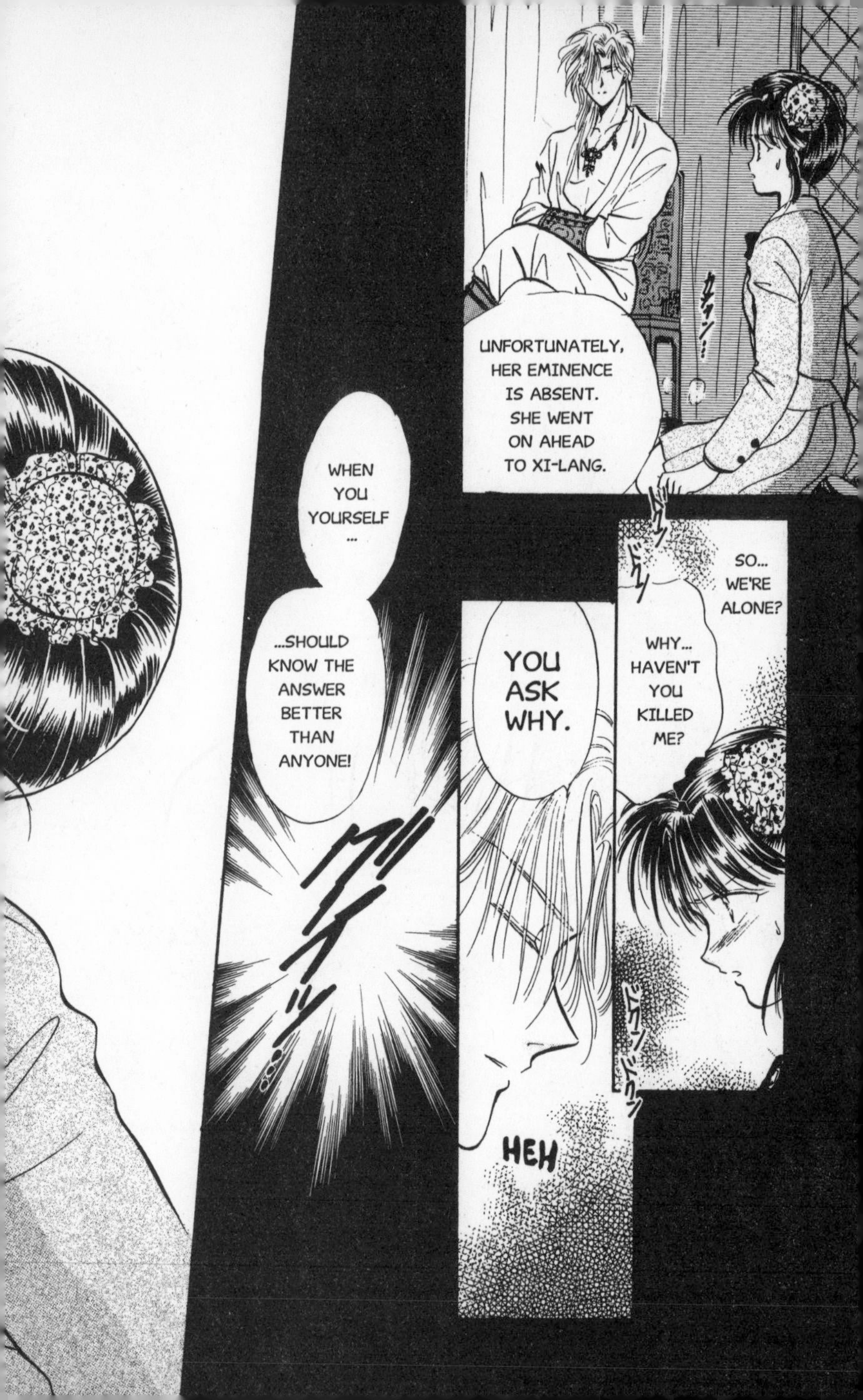

UNFORTUNATELY, HER EMINENCE IS ABSENT. SHE WENT ON AHEAD TO XI-LANG.
SO... WE'RE ALONE?
WHY... HAVEN'T YOU KILLED ME?
YOU ASK WHY.
HEH
WHEN YOU YOURSELF ...
...SHOULD KNOW THE ANSWER BETTER THAN ANYONE!

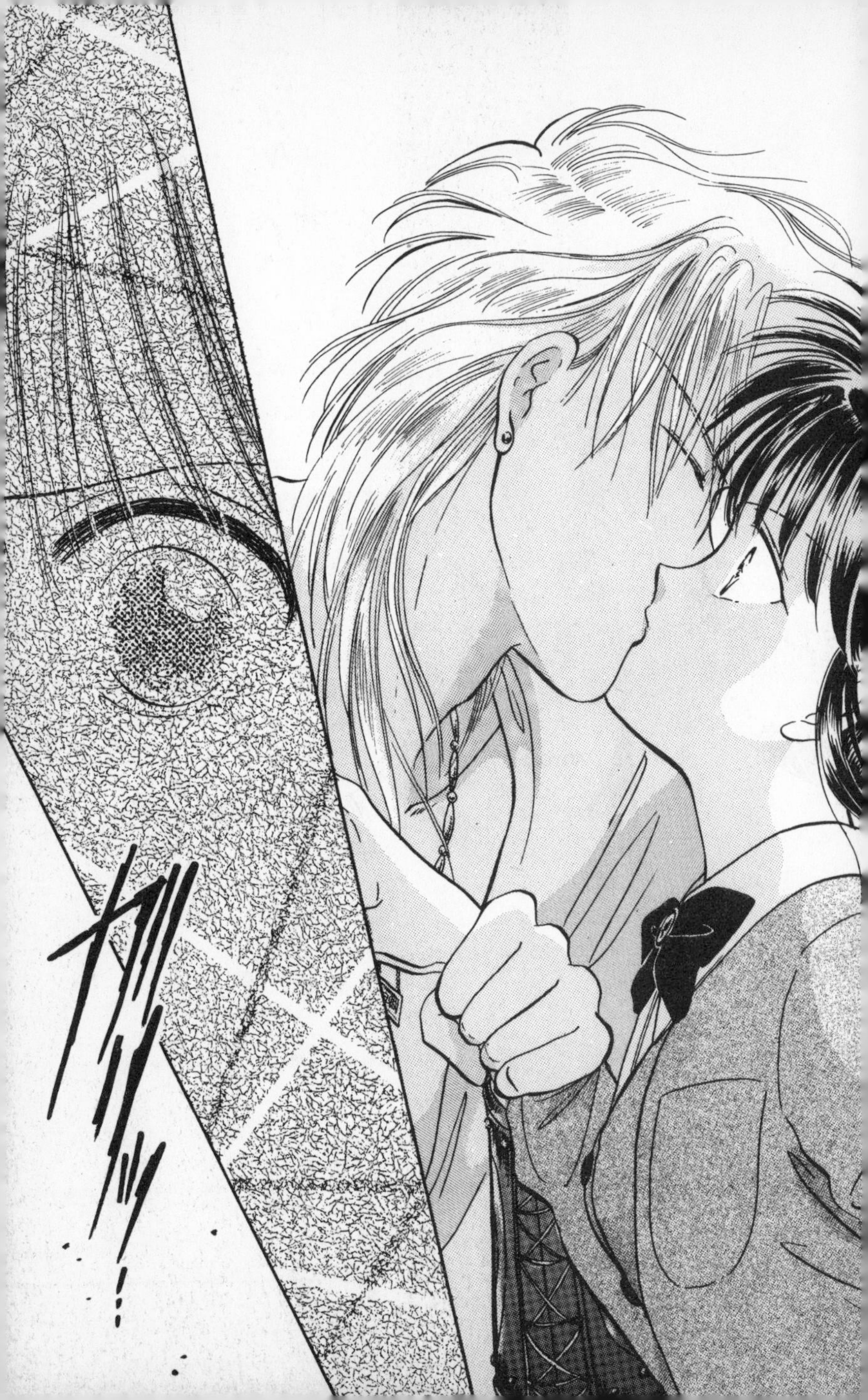

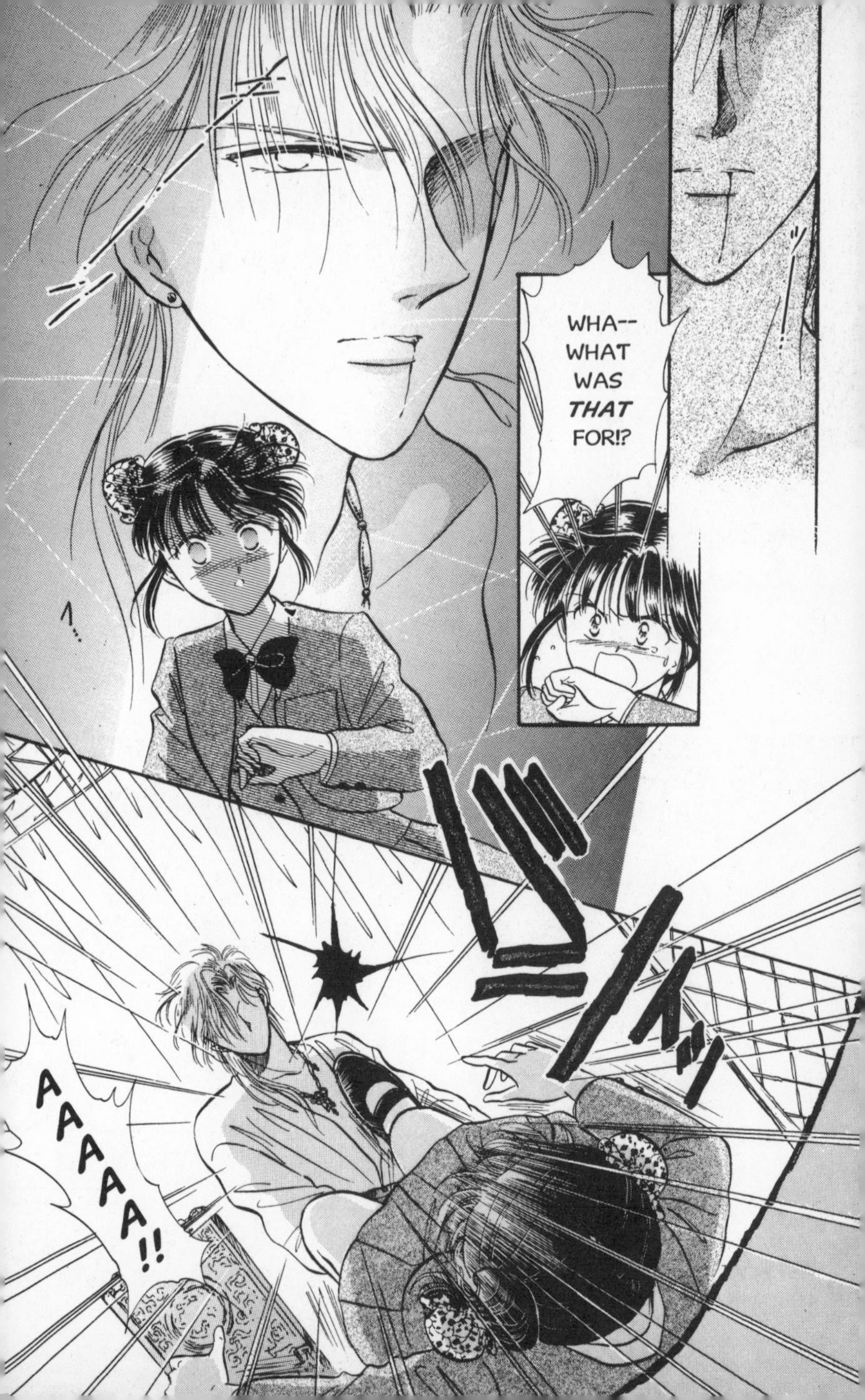
WHA-- WHAT WAS *THAT* FOR!?
AAAAA!!

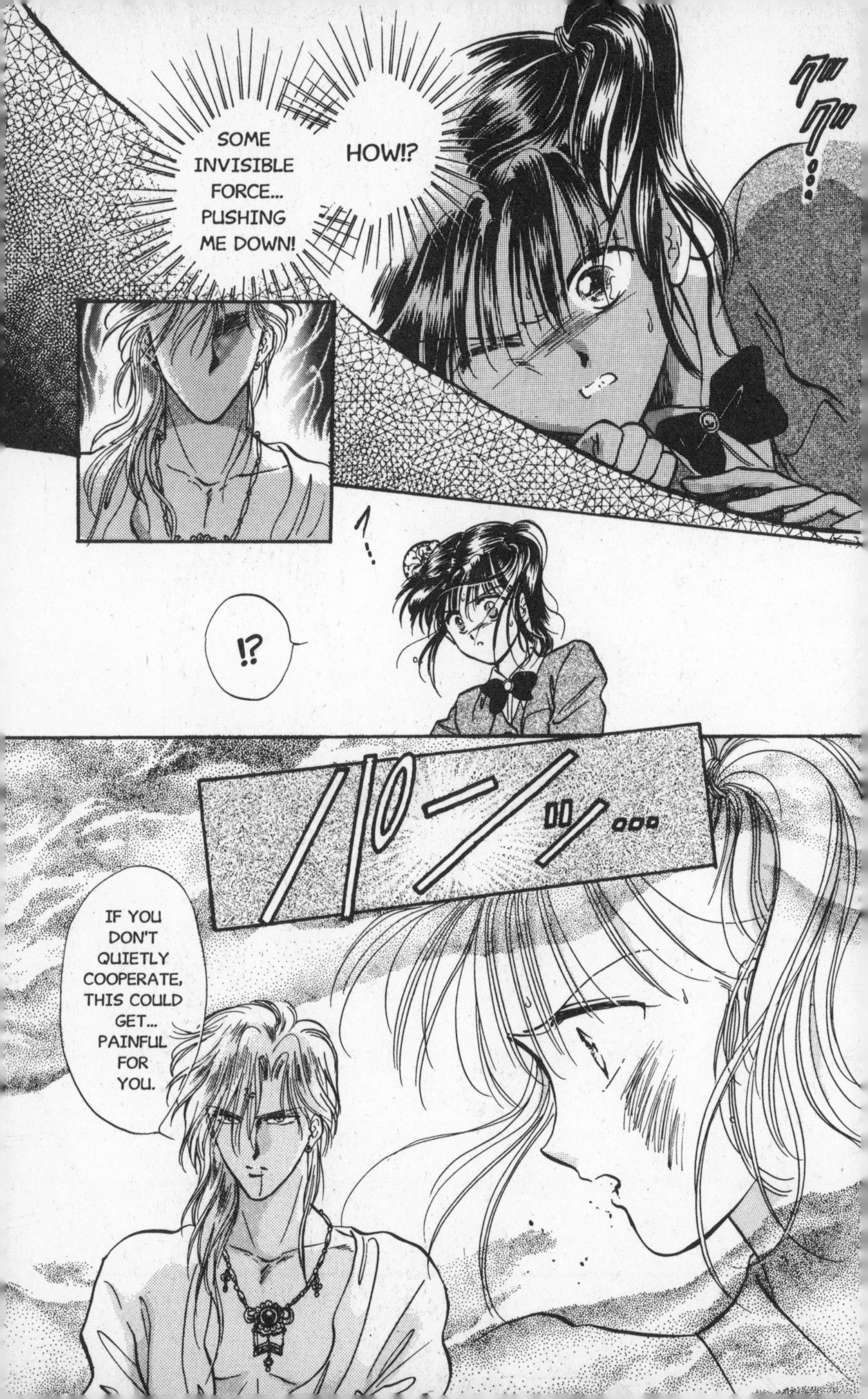
HOW!?
SOME INVISIBLE FORCE... PUSHING ME DOWN!
!?
IF YOU DON'T QUIETLY COOPERATE, THIS COULD GET... PAINFUL FOR YOU.

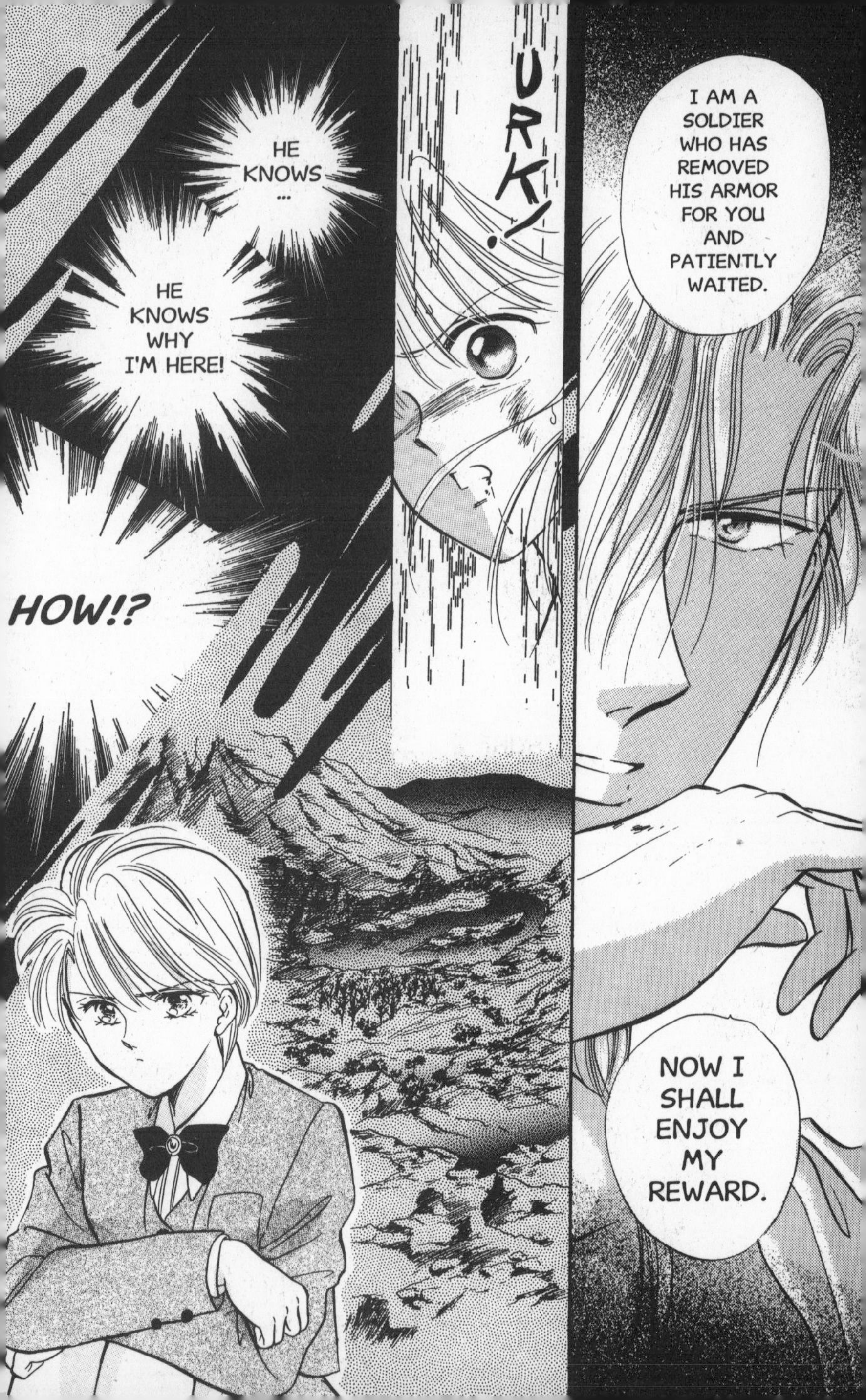
I AM A SOLDIER WHO HAS REMOVED HIS ARMOR FOR YOU AND PATIENTLY WAITED.
NOW I SHALL ENJOY MY REWARD.
URK!
HE KNOWS ...
HE KNOWS WHY I'M HERE!
HOW!?

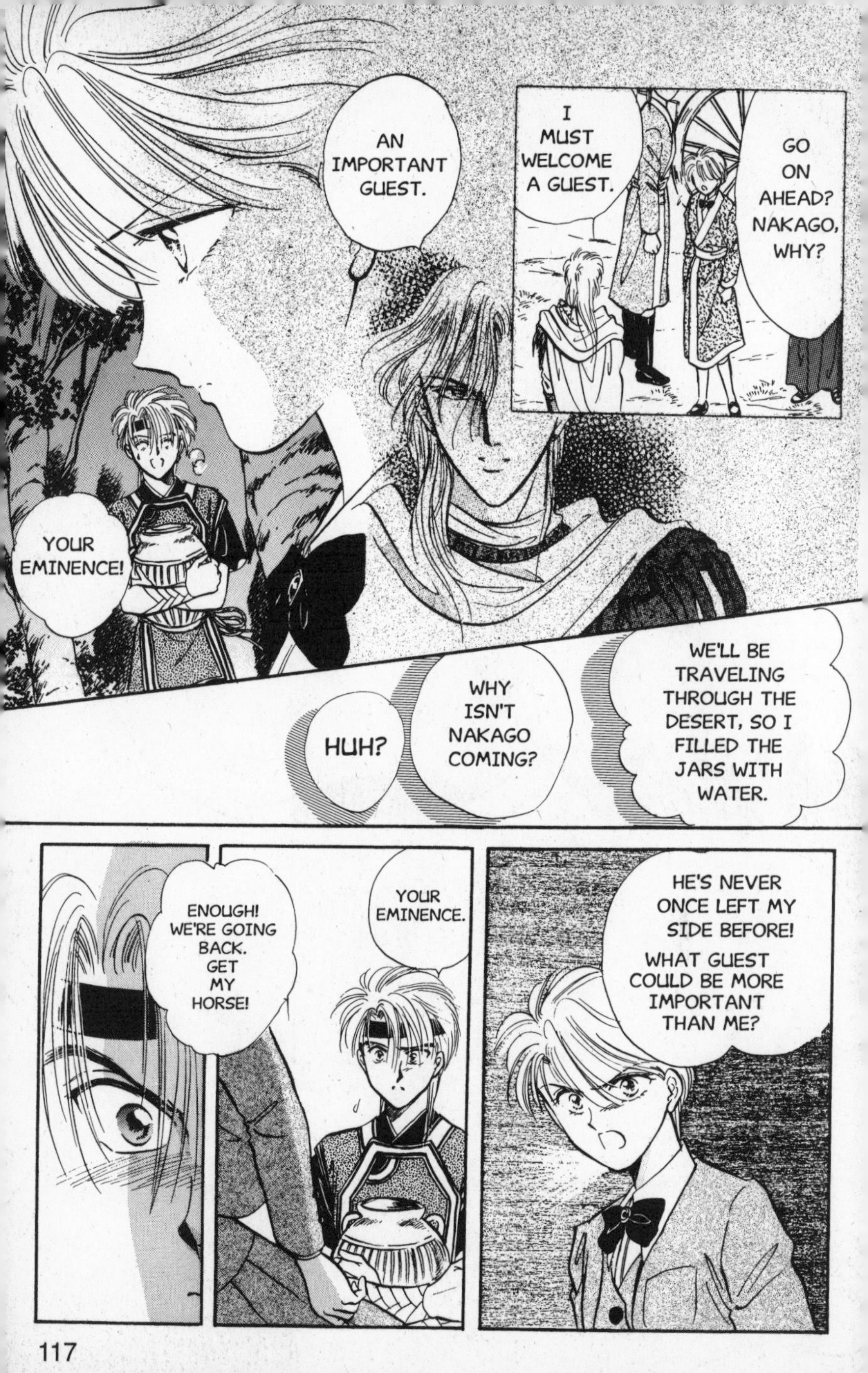
GO ON AHEAD? NAKAGO, WHY?
I MUST WELCOME A GUEST.
AN IMPORTANT GUEST.
YOUR EMINENCE!
WE'LL BE TRAVELING THROUGH THE DESERT, SO I FILLED THE JARS WITH WATER.
WHY ISN'T NAKAGO COMING?
HUH?
HE'S NEVER ONCE LEFT MY SIDE BEFORE!
WHAT GUEST COULD BE MORE IMPORTANT THAN ME?
YOUR EMINENCE.
ENOUGH! WE'RE GOING BACK. GET MY HORSE!

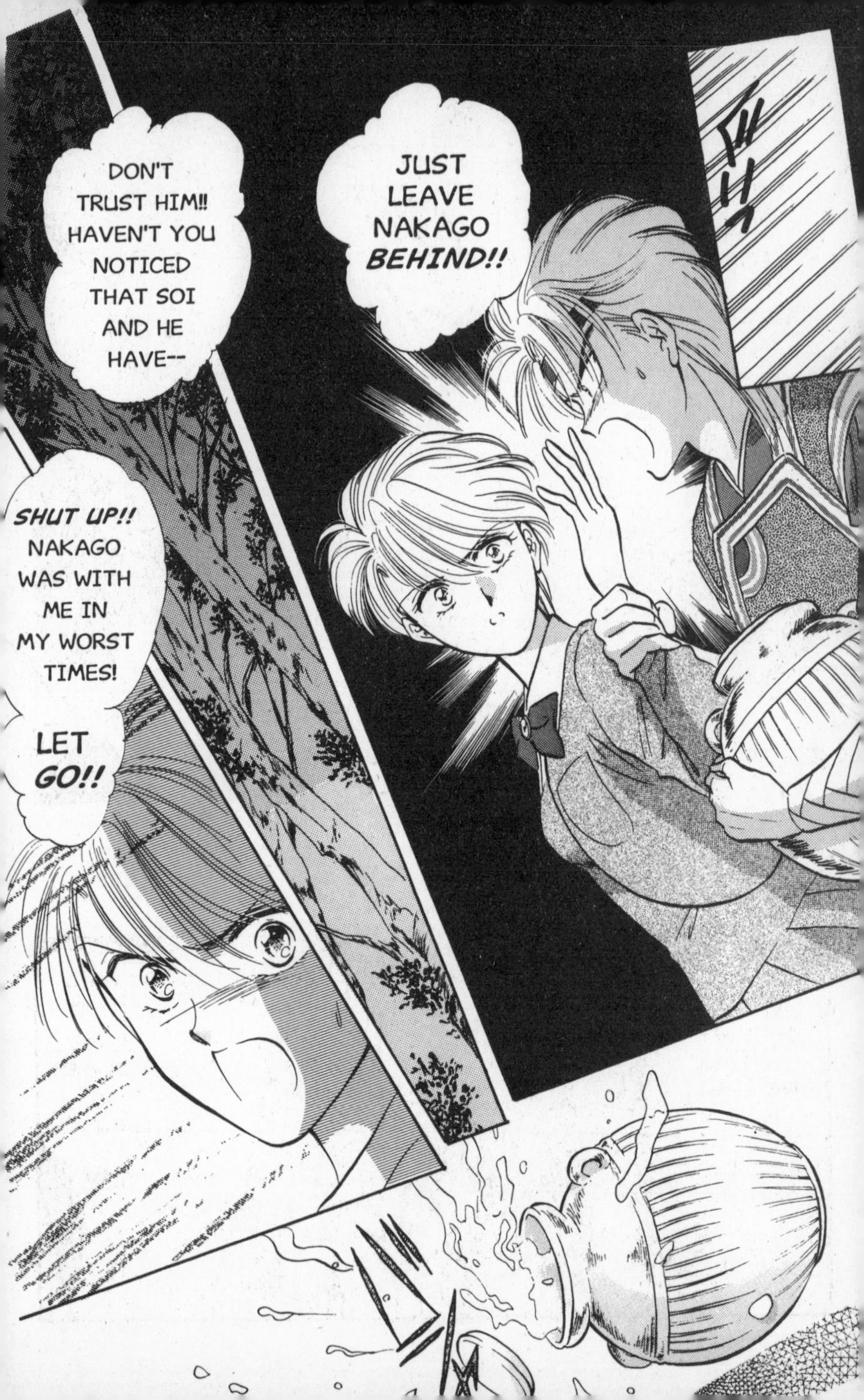
JUST LEAVE NAKAGO BEHIND!!
DON'T TRUST HIM!! HAVEN'T YOU NOTICED THAT SOI AND HE HAVE--
SHUT UP!! NAKAGO WAS WITH ME IN MY WORST TIMES!
LET GO!!

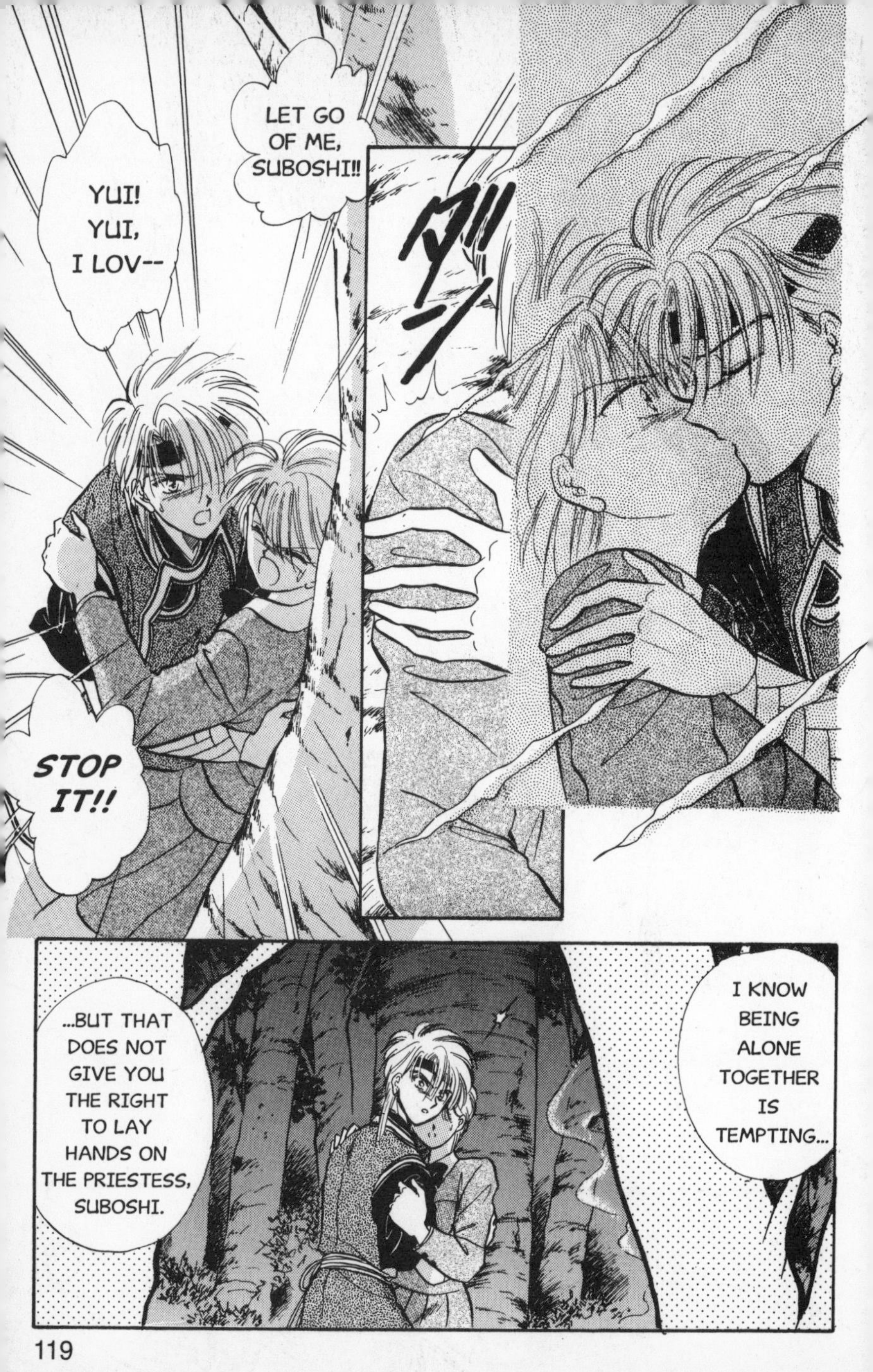

LET GO OF ME, SUBOSHI!!
YUI! YUI, I LOV--
STOP IT!!
I KNOW BEING ALONE TOGETHER IS TEMPTING...
...BUT THAT DOES NOT GIVE YOU THE RIGHT TO LAY HANDS ON THE PRIESTESS, SUBOSHI.

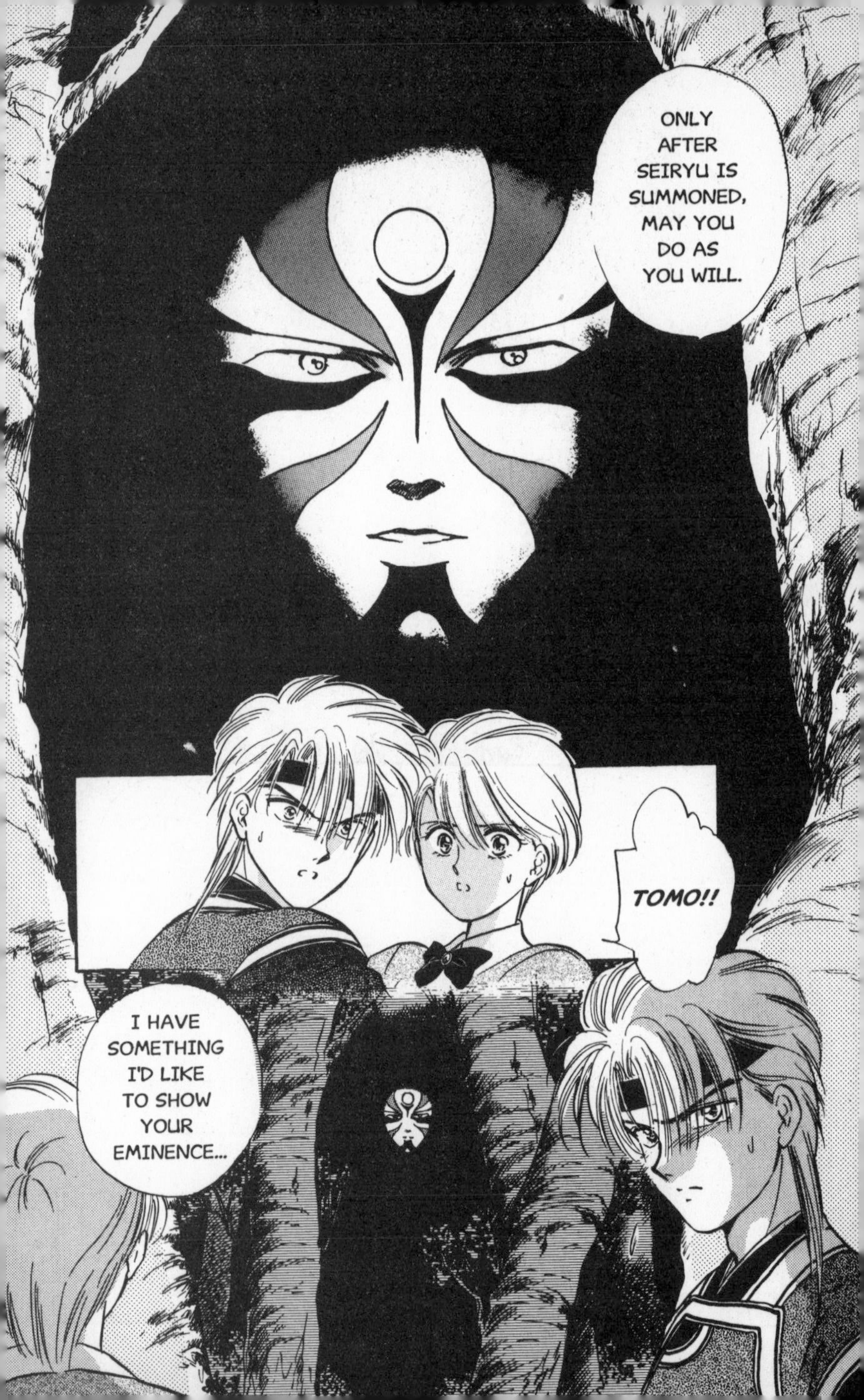
ONLY AFTER SEIRYU IS SUMMONED, MAY YOU DO AS YOU WILL.
TOMO!!
I HAVE SOMETHING I'D LIKE TO SHOW YOUR EMINENCE...

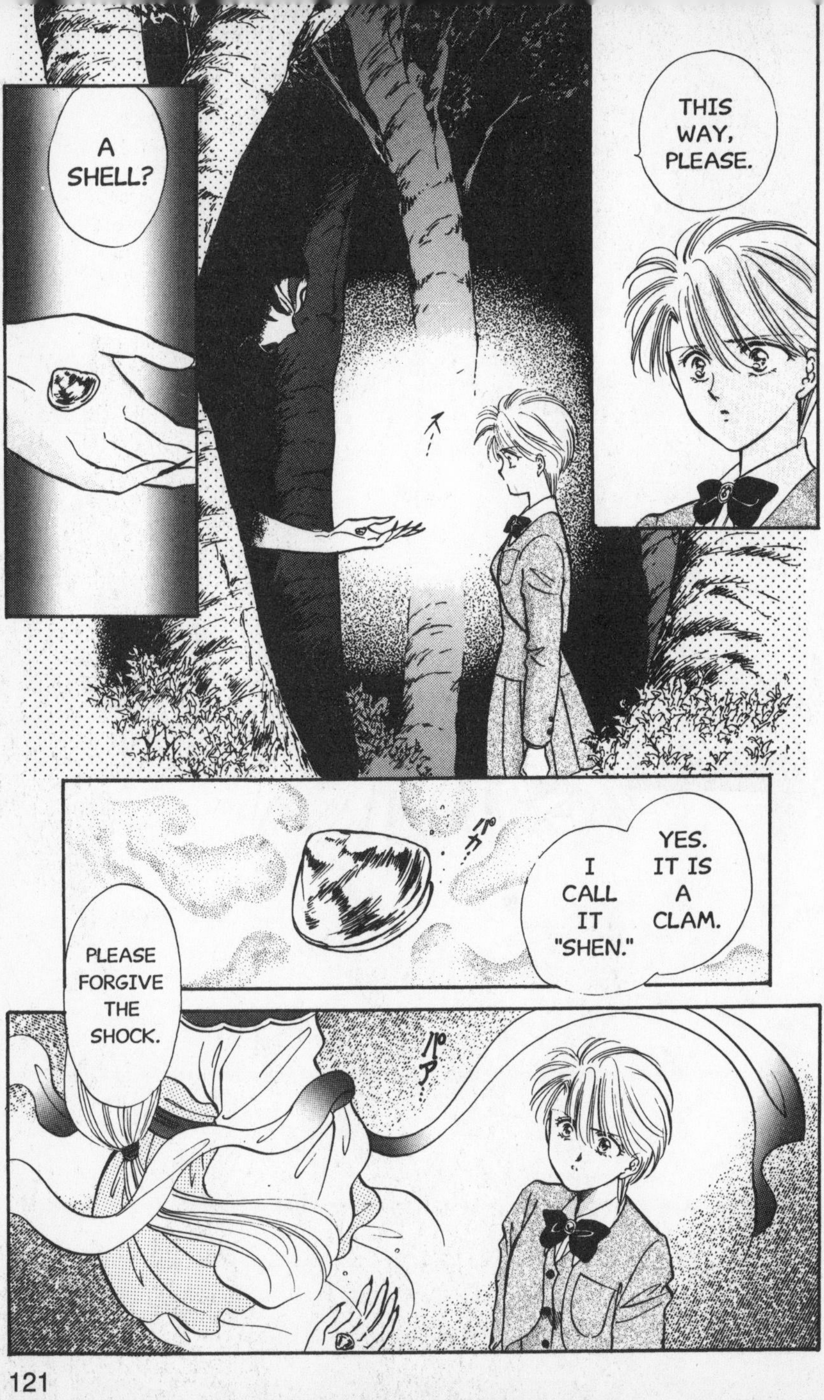
THIS WAY, PLEASE.
A SHELL?
YES. IT IS A CLAM.
I CALL IT "SHEN."
パカ
PLEASE FORGIVE THE SHOCK.
パァ

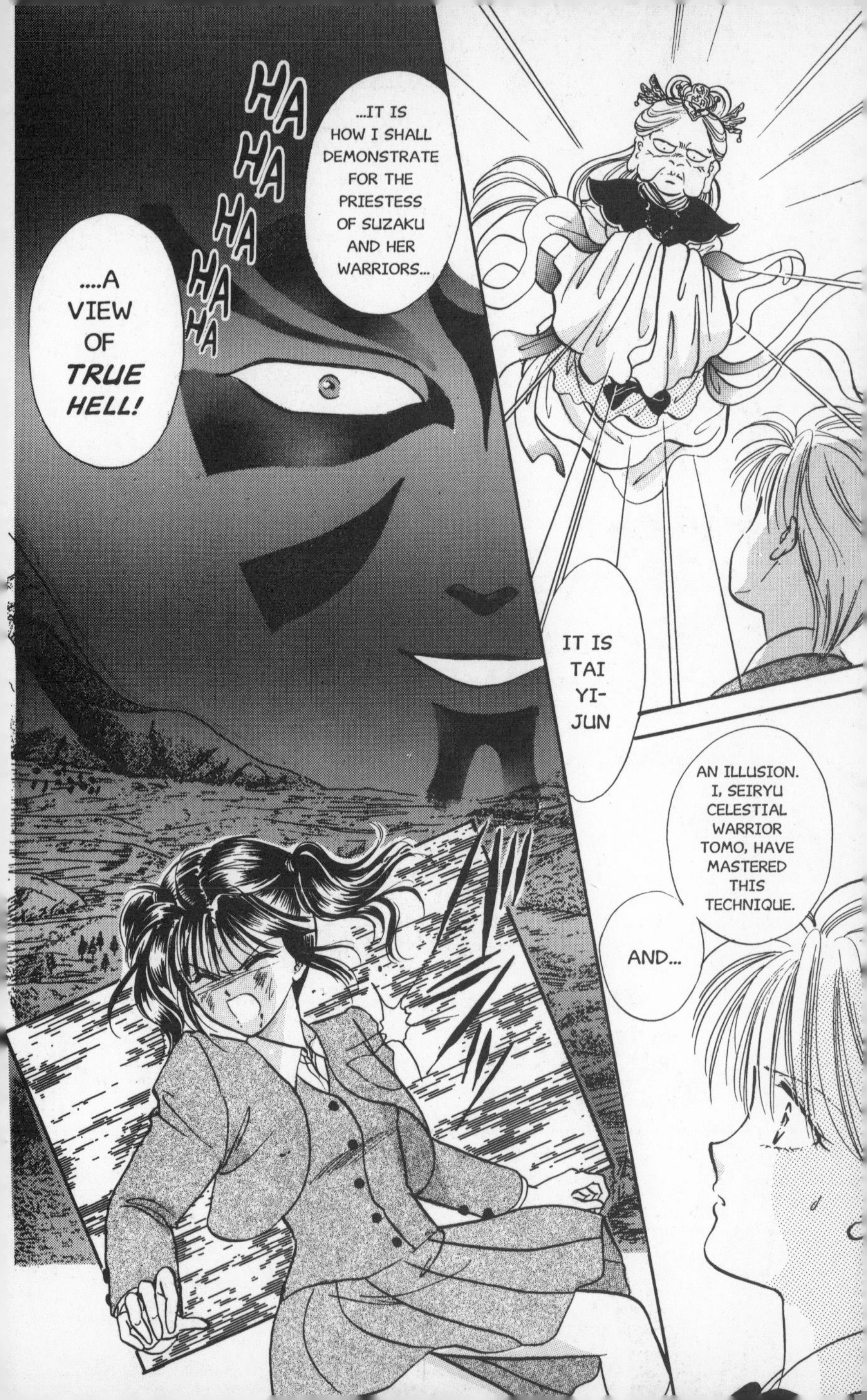
IT IS TAI YI-JUN
AN ILLUSION. I, SEIRYU CELESTIAL WARRIOR TOMO, HAVE MASTERED THIS TECHNIQUE.
AND...
...IT IS HOW I SHALL DEMONSTRATE FOR THE PRIESTESS OF SUZAKU AND HER WARRIORS...
HA HA HA HA HA HA
....A VIEW OF TRUE HELL!

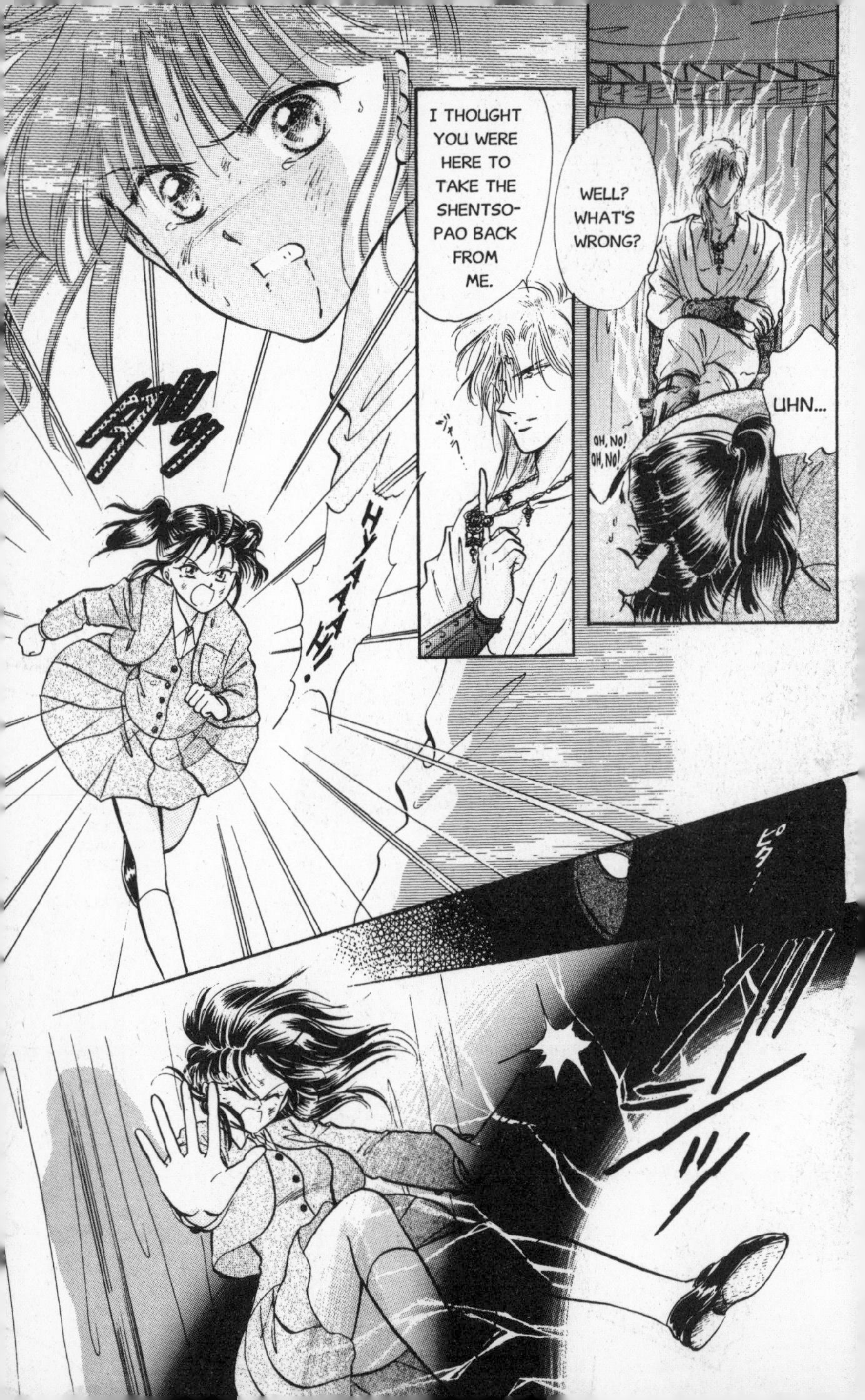
WELL? WHAT'S WRONG?
UHN...
OH, NO! OH, NO!
I THOUGHT YOU WERE HERE TO TAKE THE SHENTSO-PAO BACK FROM ME.
HYAAAH!!

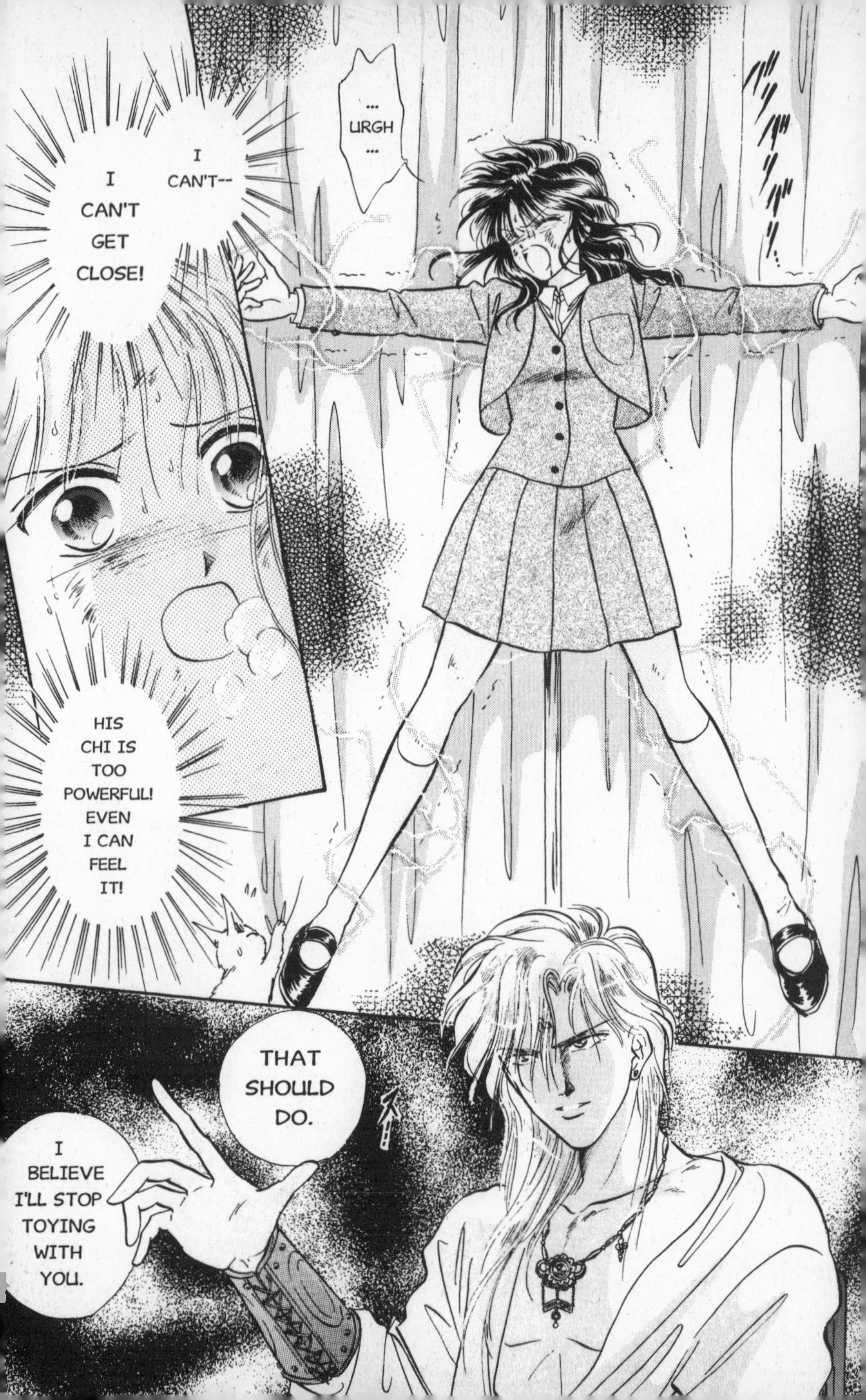

... URGH ...
I CAN'T--
I CAN'T GET CLOSE!
HIS CHI IS TOO POWERFUL! EVEN I CAN FEEL IT!
THAT SHOULD DO.
I BELIEVE I'LL STOP TOYING WITH YOU.

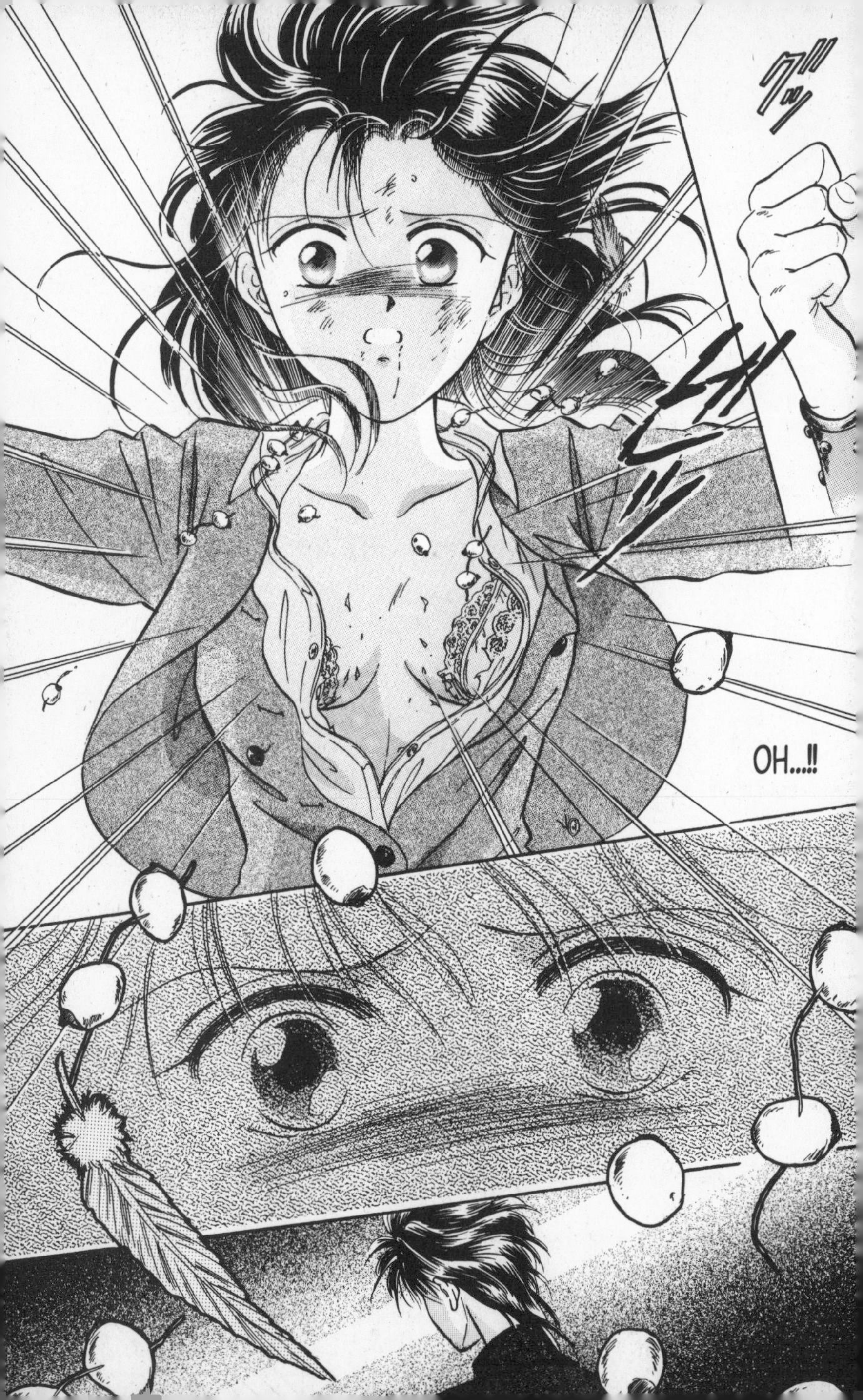
グッ
ビシッ
OH...!!

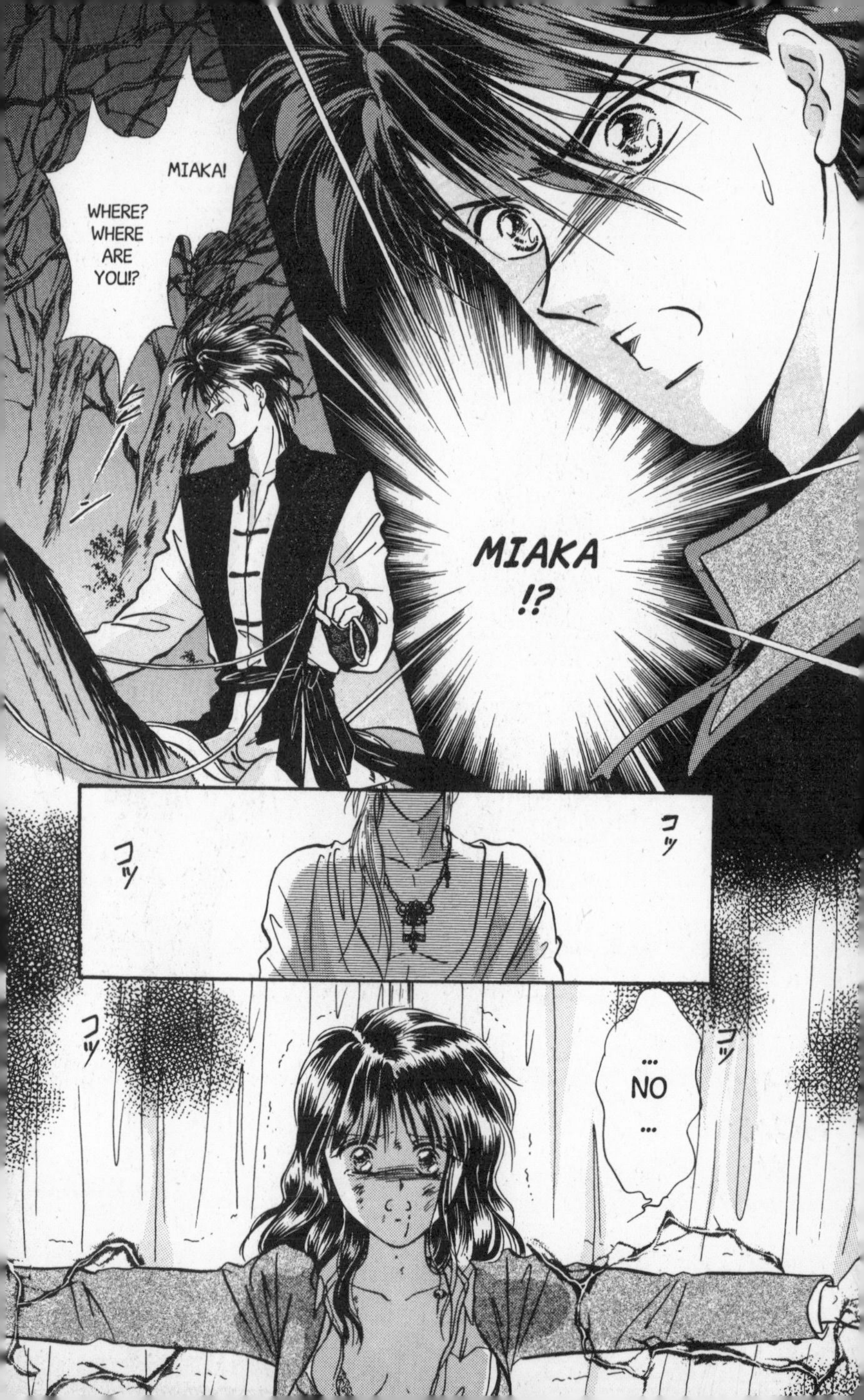
MIAKA !?
MIAKA!
WHERE? WHERE ARE YOU!?
コッ
コッ
コッ
コッ
... NO ...

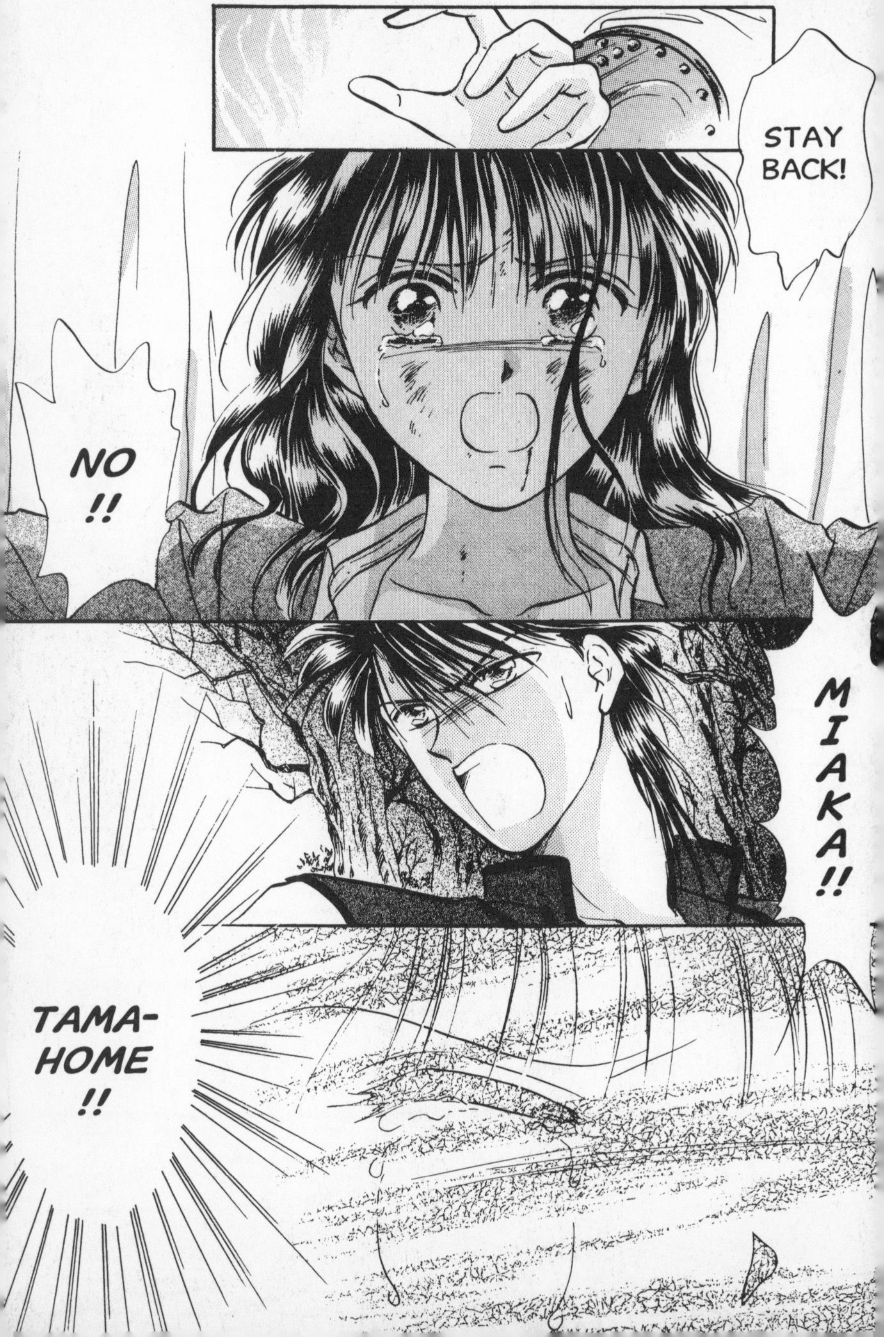
STAY BACK!
NO !!
MIAKA!!
TAMA-HOME !!

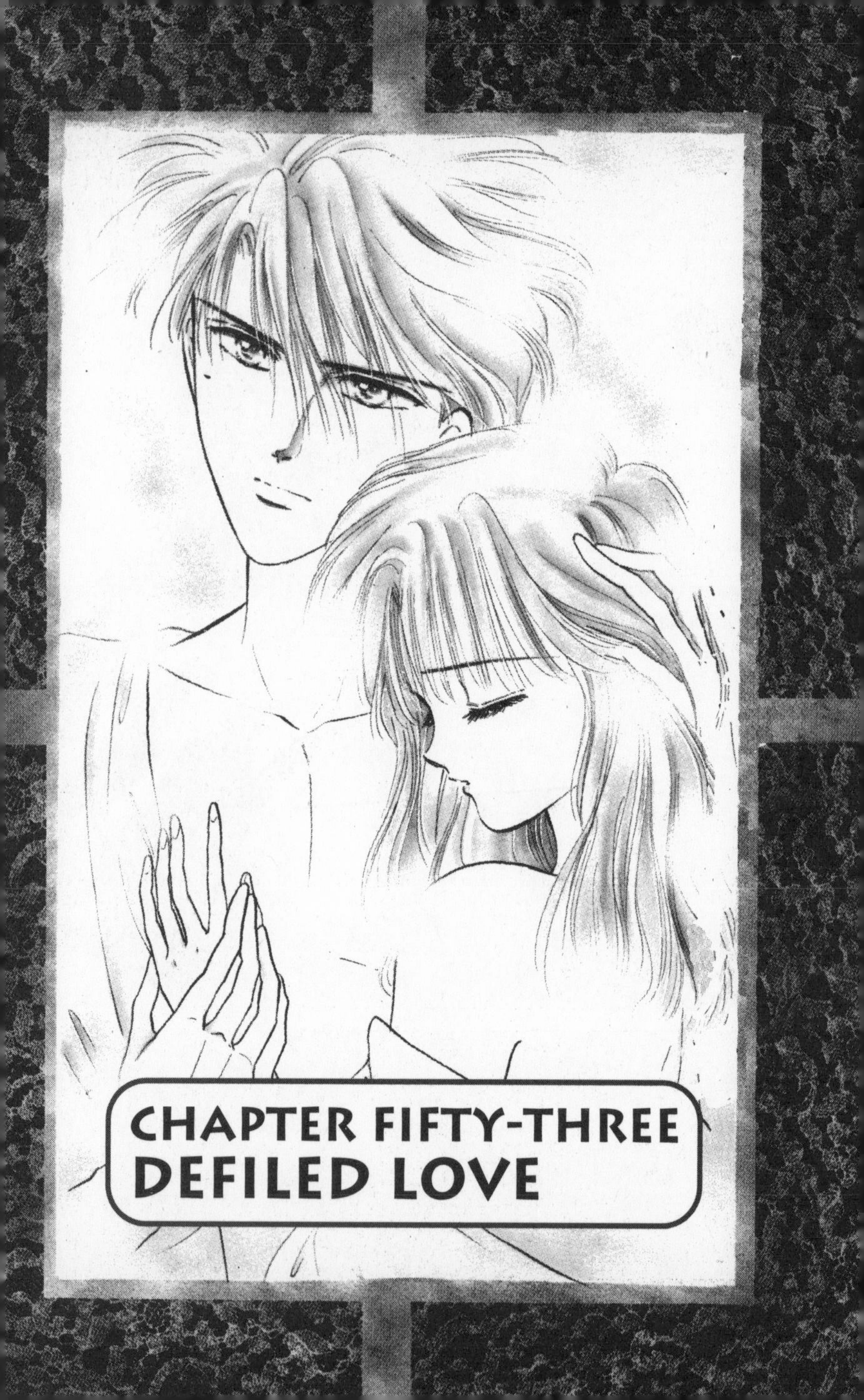
CHAPTER FIFTY-THREE
DEFILED LOVE

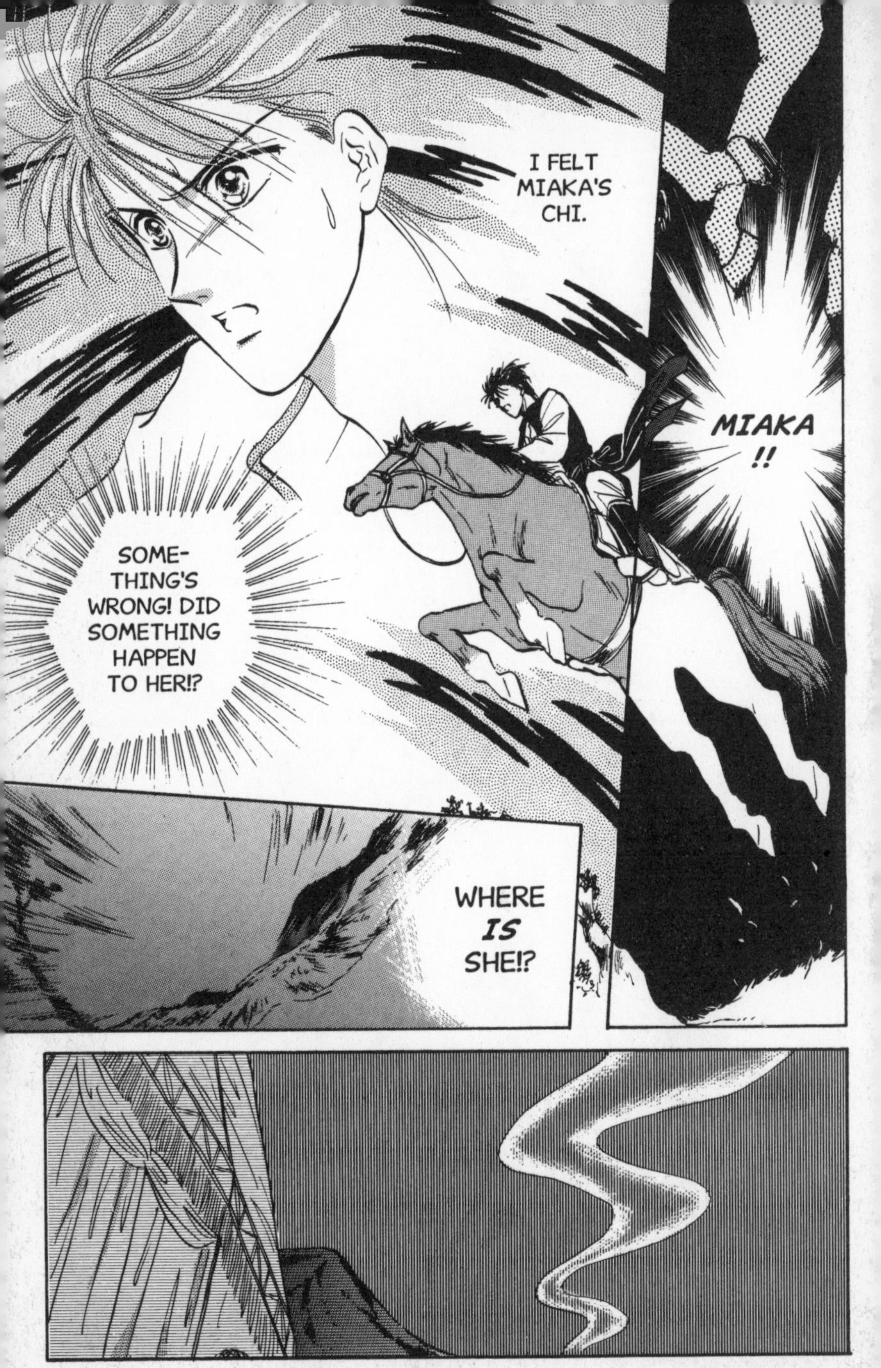
MIAKA!!
I FELT MIAKA'S CHI.
SOME-THING'S WRONG! DID SOMETHING HAPPEN TO HER!?
WHERE *IS* SHE!?

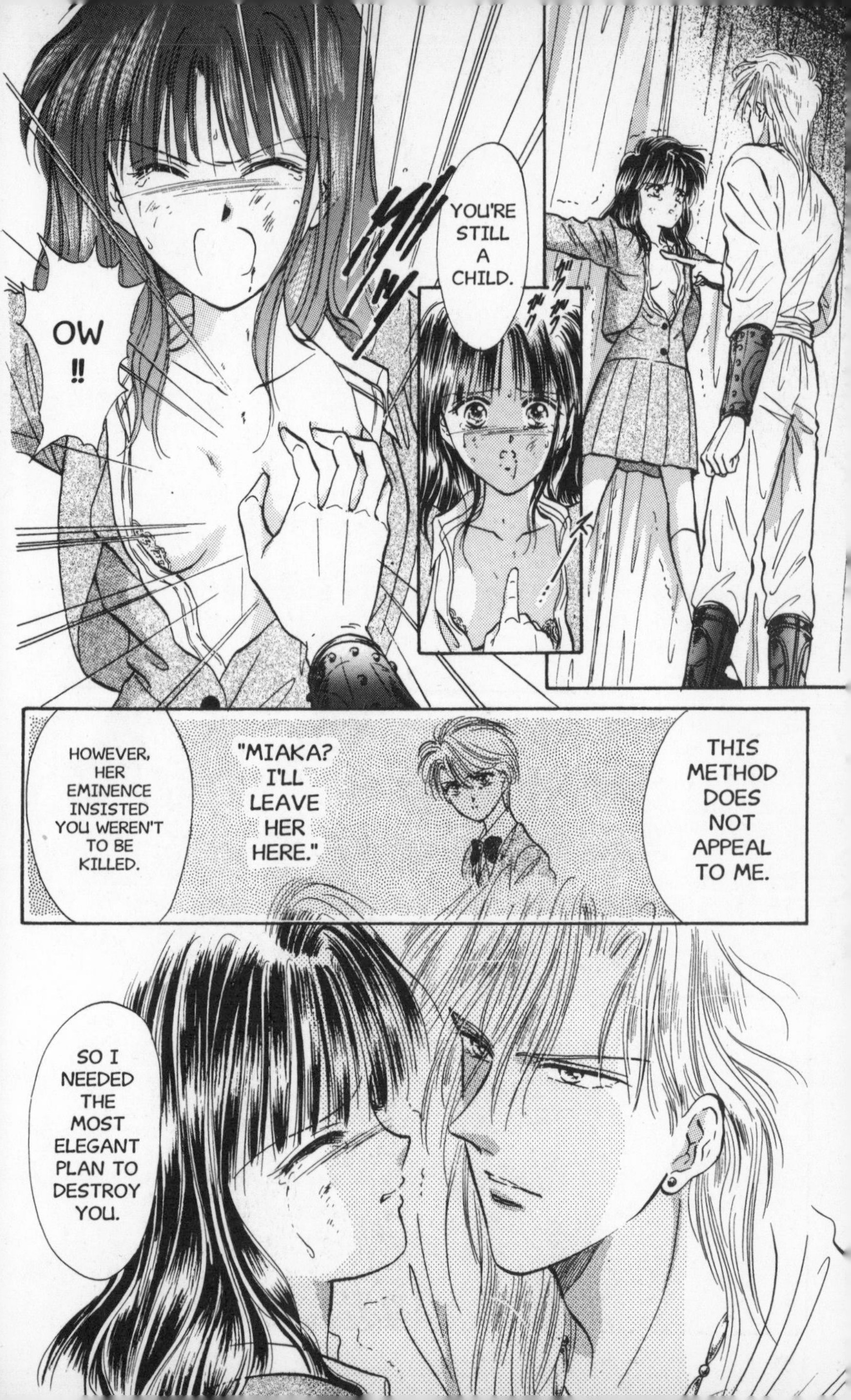
YOU'RE STILL A CHILD.
OW !!
THIS METHOD DOES NOT APPEAL TO ME.
"MIAKA? I'LL LEAVE HER HERE."
HOWEVER, HER EMINENCE INSISTED YOU WEREN'T TO BE KILLED.
SO I NEEDED THE MOST ELEGANT PLAN TO DESTROY YOU.

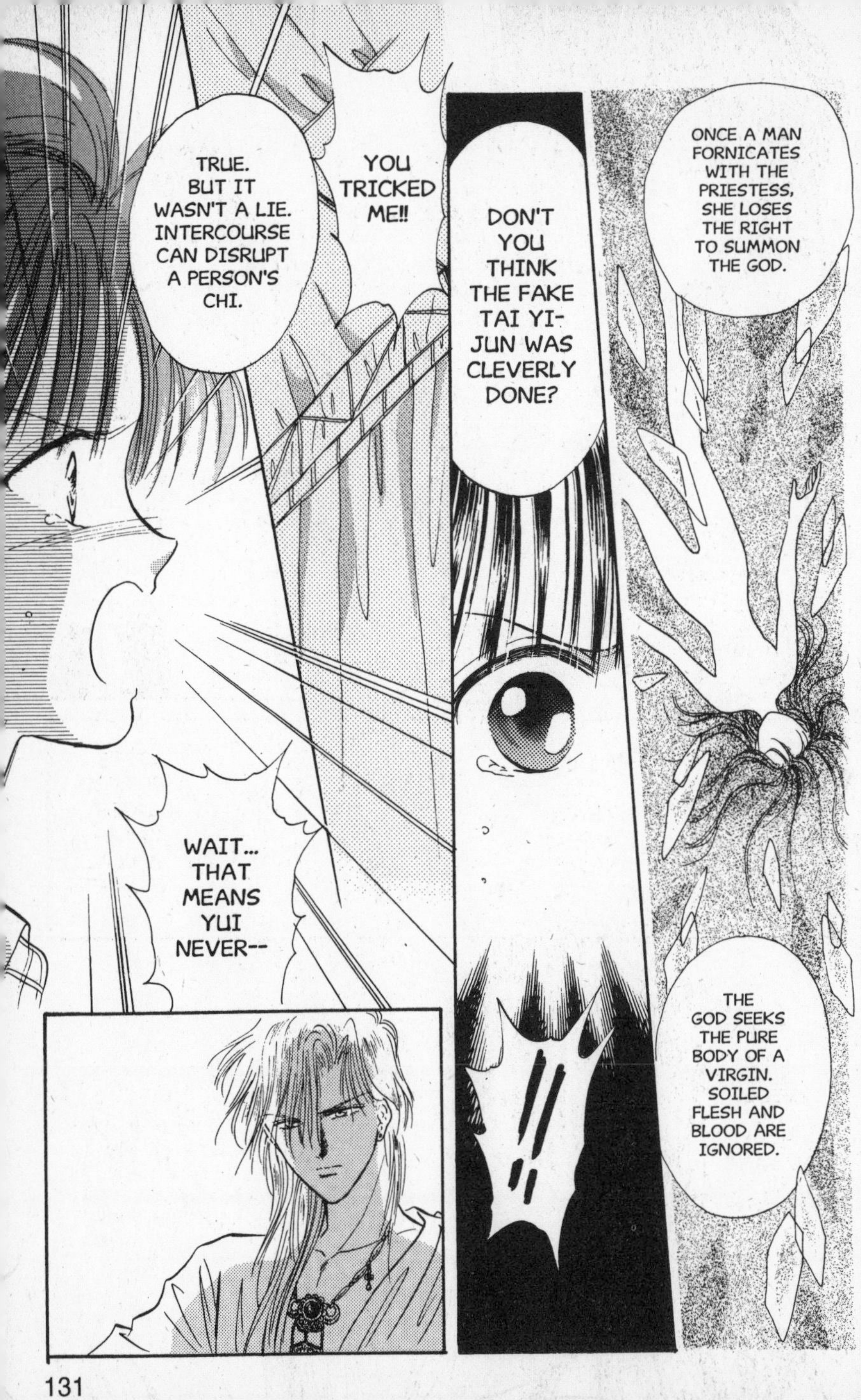
ONCE A MAN FORNICATES WITH THE PRIESTESS, SHE LOSES THE RIGHT TO SUMMON THE GOD.
THE GOD SEEKS THE PURE BODY OF A VIRGIN. SOILED FLESH AND BLOOD ARE IGNORED.
DON'T YOU THINK THE FAKE TAI YI-JUN WAS CLEVERLY DONE?
!!
YOU TRICKED ME!!
TRUE. BUT IT WASN'T A LIE. INTERCOURSE CAN DISRUPT A PERSON'S CHI.
WAIT... THAT MEANS YUI NEVER--

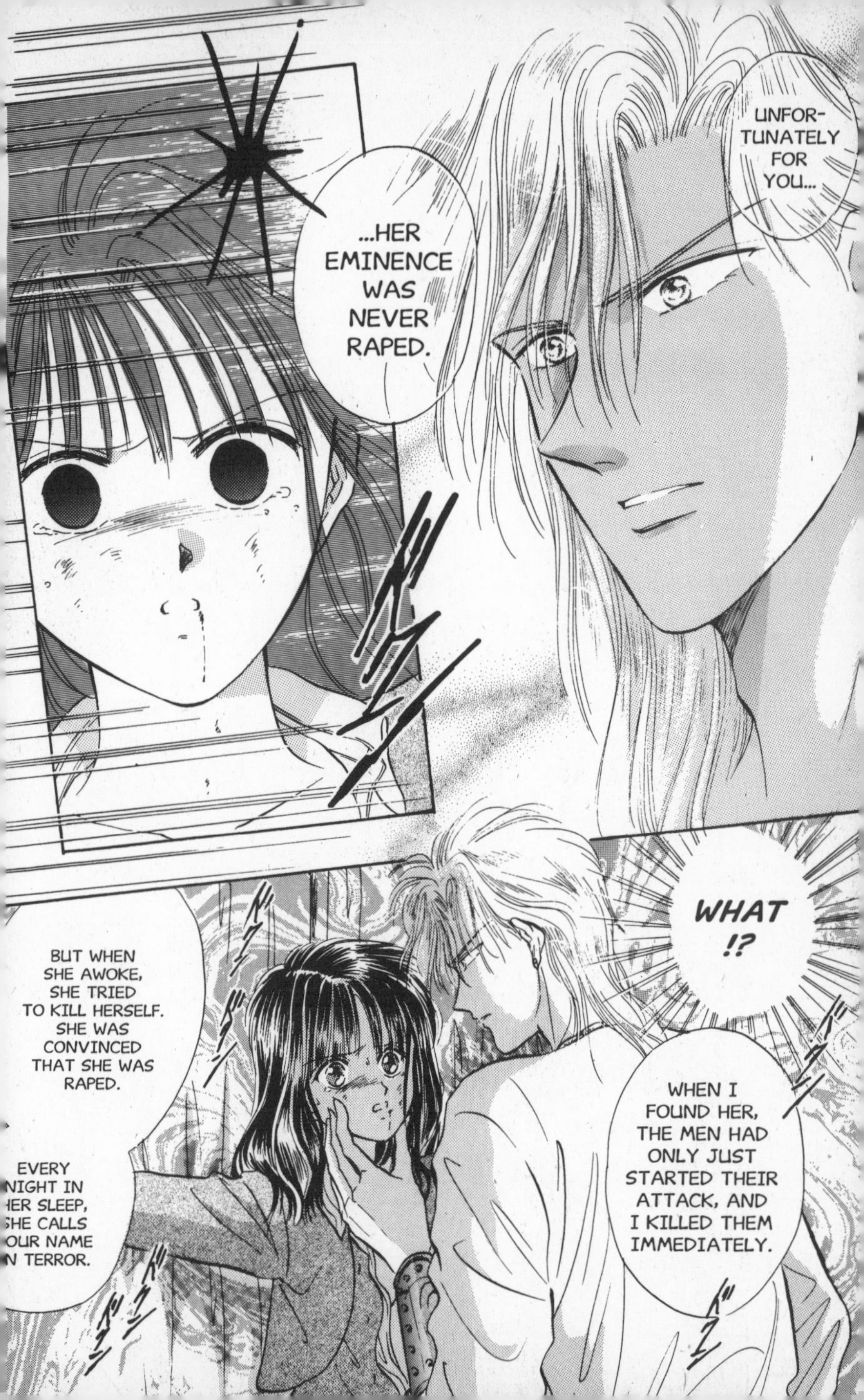

UNFORTUNATELY FOR YOU...
...HER EMINENCE WAS NEVER RAPED.
WHAT!?
WHEN I FOUND HER, THE MEN HAD ONLY JUST STARTED THEIR ATTACK, AND I KILLED THEM IMMEDIATELY.
BUT WHEN SHE AWOKE, SHE TRIED TO KILL HERSELF. SHE WAS CONVINCED THAT SHE WAS RAPED.
EVERY NIGHT IN HER SLEEP, SHE CALLS OUR NAME N TERROR.

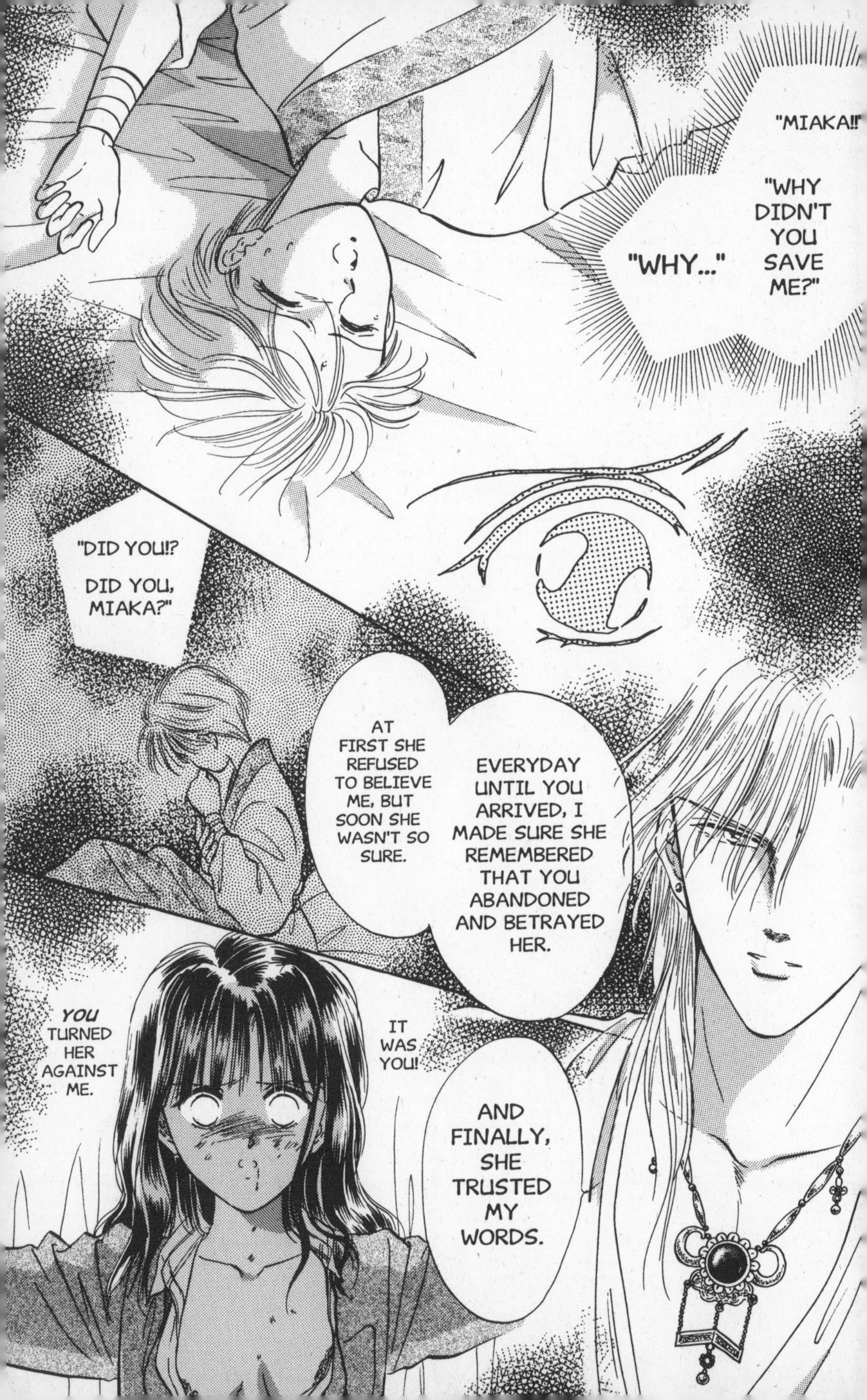
"MIAKA!!"
"WHY DIDN'T YOU SAVE ME?"
"WHY..."
"DID YOU!?
DID YOU, MIAKA?"
EVERYDAY UNTIL YOU ARRIVED, I MADE SURE SHE REMEMBERED THAT YOU ABANDONED AND BETRAYED HER.
AT FIRST SHE REFUSED TO BELIEVE ME, BUT SOON SHE WASN'T SO SURE.
AND FINALLY, SHE TRUSTED MY WORDS.
IT WAS YOU!
YOU TURNED HER AGAINST ME.

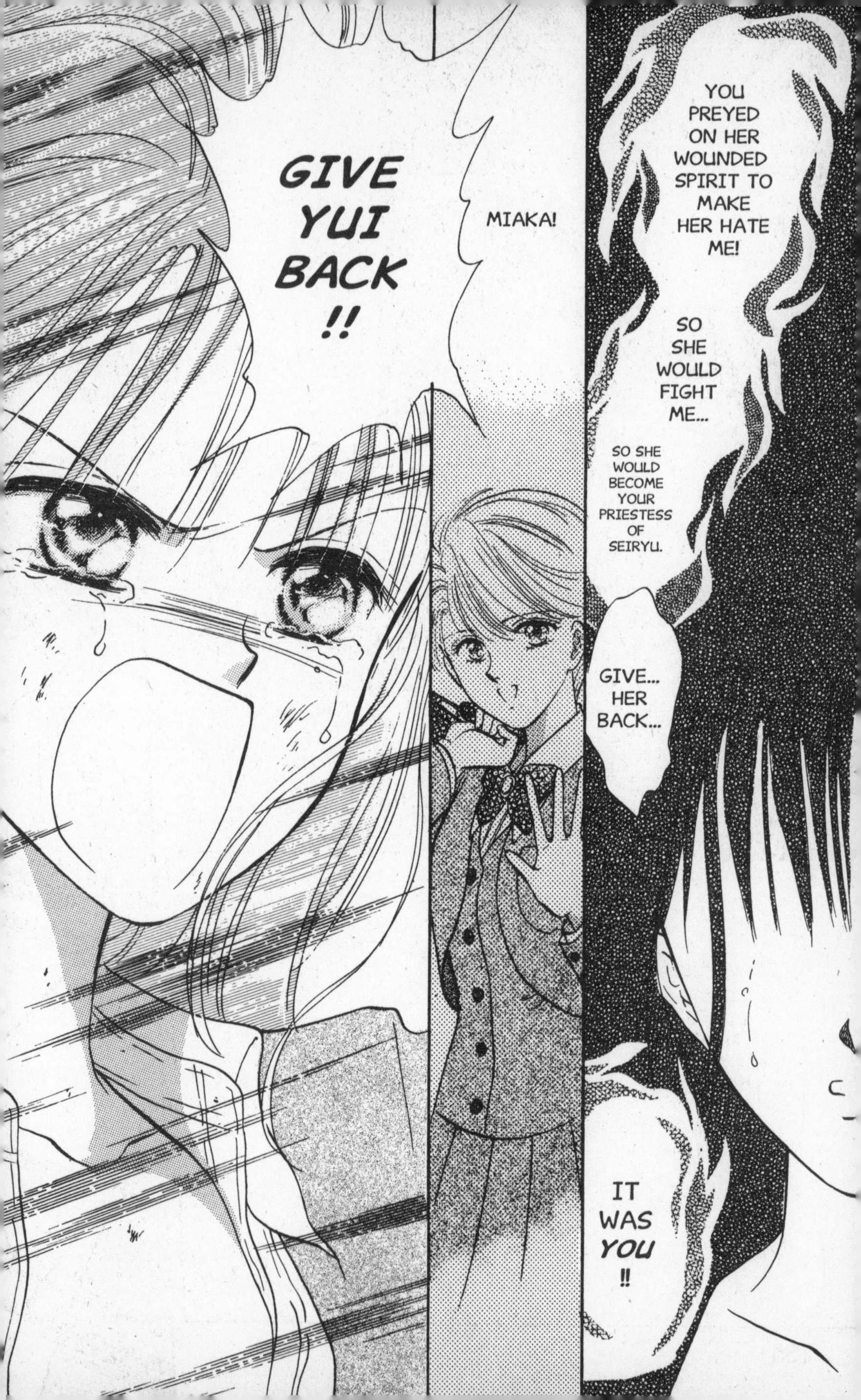
YOU PREYED ON HER WOUNDED SPIRIT TO MAKE HER HATE ME!
SO SHE WOULD FIGHT ME...
SO SHE WOULD BECOME YOUR PRIESTESS OF SEIRYU.
GIVE... HER BACK...
IT WAS *YOU* !!
MIAKA!
GIVE YUI BACK !!

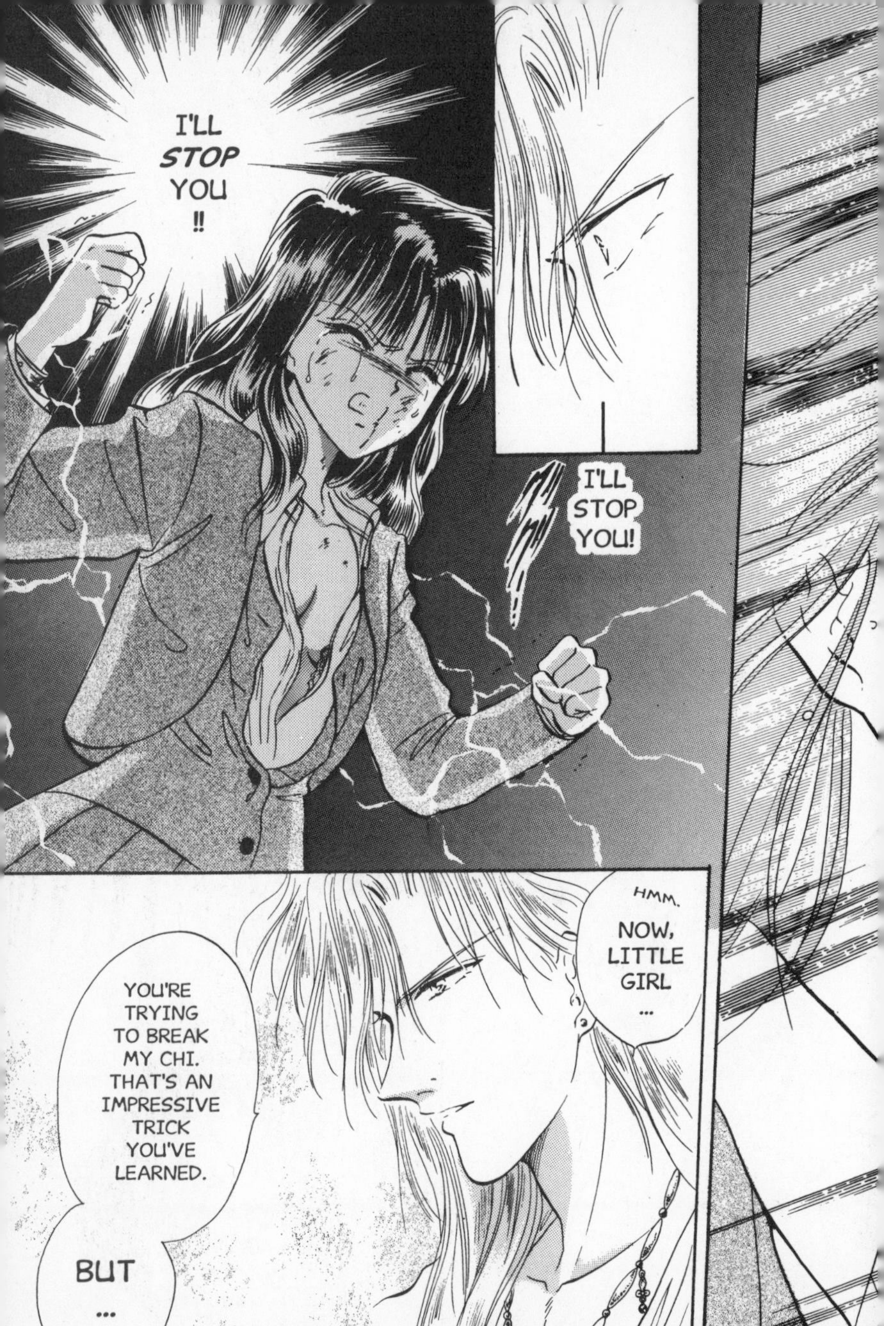
I'LL STOP YOU!
I'LL *STOP* YOU !!
HMM.
NOW, LITTLE GIRL ...
YOU'RE TRYING TO BREAK MY CHI. THAT'S AN IMPRESSIVE TRICK YOU'VE LEARNED.
BUT ...

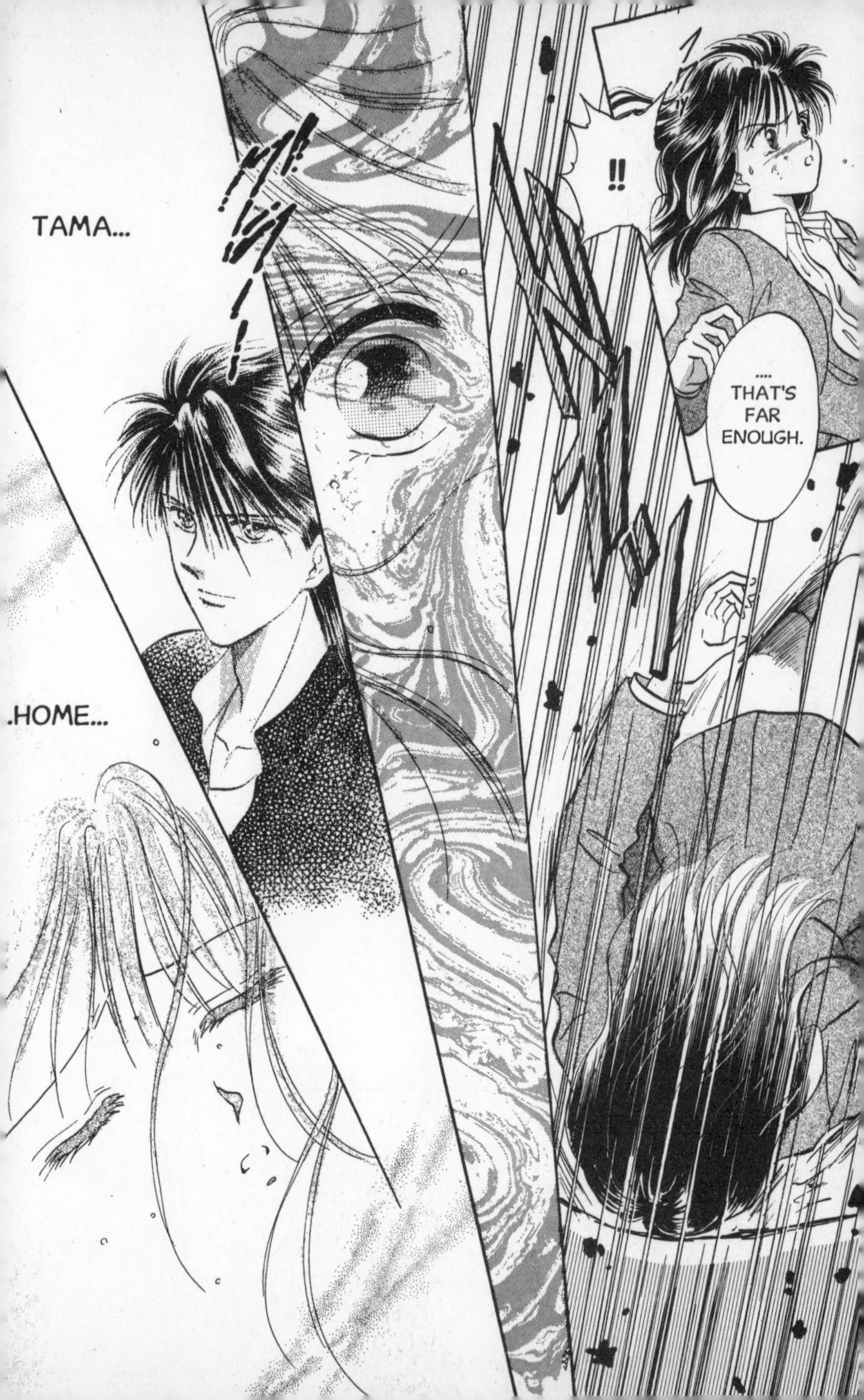
!!
.... THAT'S FAR ENOUGH.
TAMA...
.HOME...

My stomach hurt late into the night. I just collapsed onto my bed, but little did I expect that I'd go through another ordeal right there!
A little before my China vacation, there was a horrible incident where some old people traveling in Xian were killed! The next morning when I was about to leave was the first time that I realized that I'd left the key in the hotel-room door all night! Scary! I heard someone knocking on my door for a while in the night, and I was scared! I thought, "Oh, no!! Should I call on my editor?" But when the person went away, I felt relieved. In the morning, I realized that the person was just knocking because of the key that I left in the door. Of course the key was gone by morning. If the stranger had meant me any harm, he would have come in. "Fushigi Yûgi" might have ended abruptly with a message, "Due to the sudden death of Yû Watase..." Luckily my room was at the end of the hall, and because of the columns, my door wasn't visible from down the hall. Besides, my editor was staying right next door.

In any case, after a good night's rest, I felt fine (Yeah, and I'm the one who, in spite of my tummy-aches, insisted on going to see and taking pictures of the Shanghai Acrobat Troupe).

A girl got into this pose.

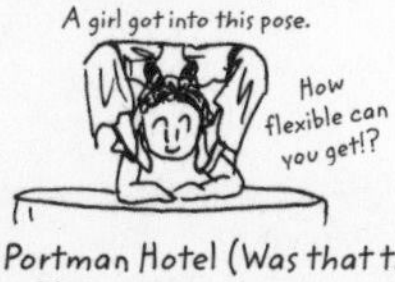
How flexible can you get!?

The Portman Hotel (Was that the name?) in Shanghai was a super luxurious, gigantic, five-star hotel. The front desk clerk was incredibly handsome, really tall, and styling (I wanted someone to take a picture of us together!). The bell boys were tall, too. I've never seen such a grand hotel with huge rooms, even in Japan.

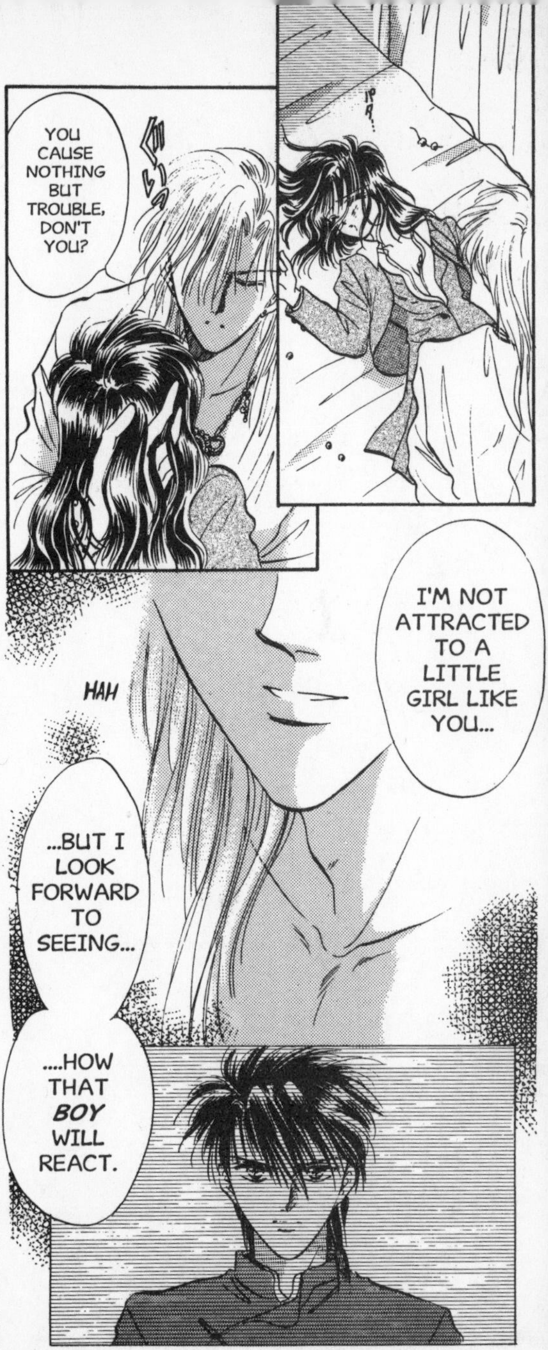
YOU CAUSE NOTHING BUT TROUBLE, DON'T YOU?
I'M NOT ATTRACTED TO A LITTLE GIRL LIKE YOU...
HAH
...BUT I LOOK FORWARD TO SEEING...
....HOW THAT *BOY* WILL REACT.

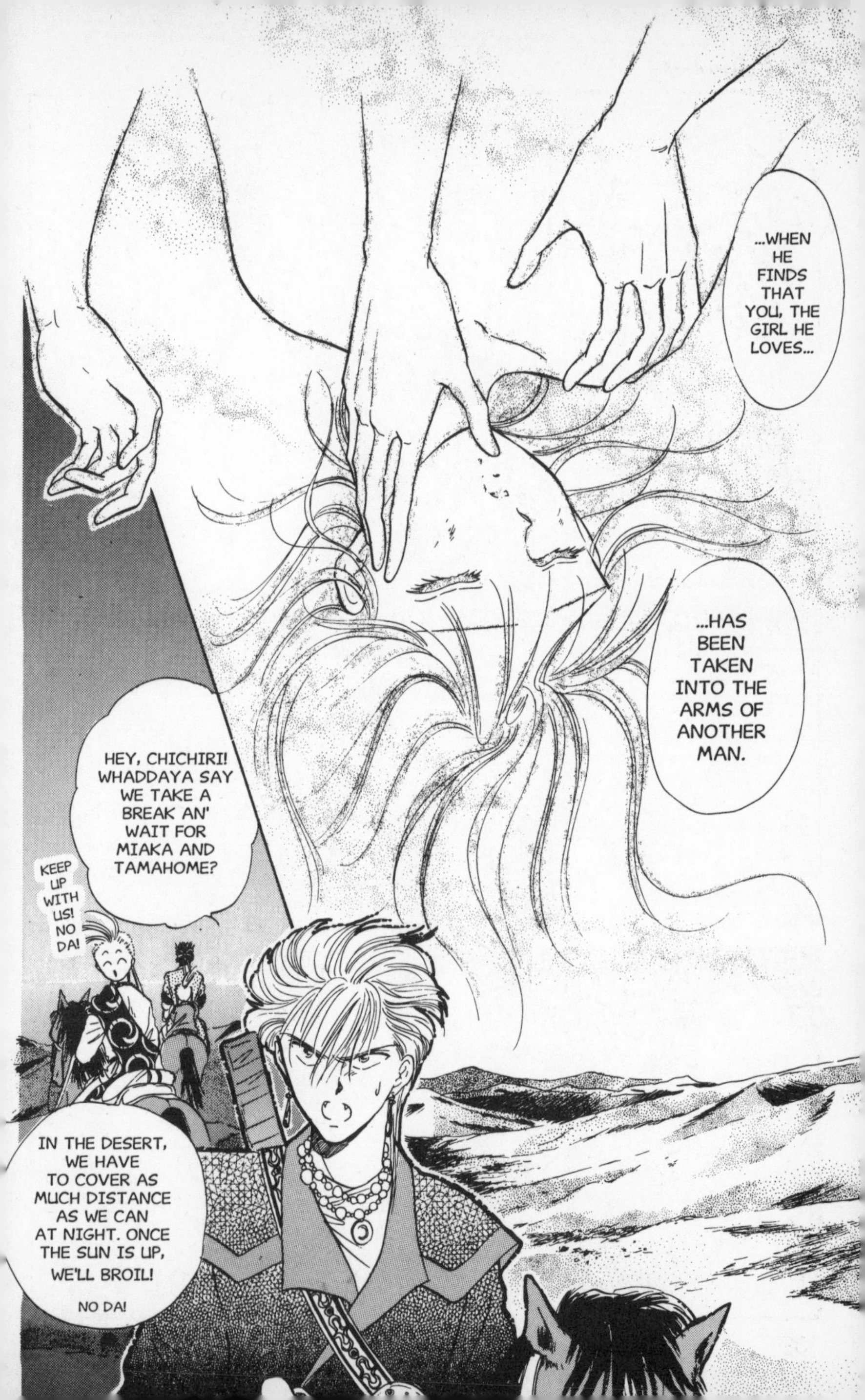
...WHEN HE FINDS THAT YOU, THE GIRL HE LOVES...
...HAS BEEN TAKEN INTO THE ARMS OF ANOTHER MAN.
HEY, CHICHIRI! WHADDAYA SAY WE TAKE A BREAK AN' WAIT FOR MIAKA AND TAMAHOME?
KEEP UP WITH US! NO DA!
IN THE DESERT, WE HAVE TO COVER AS MUCH DISTANCE AS WE CAN AT NIGHT. ONCE THE SUN IS UP, WE'LL BROIL!
NO DA!

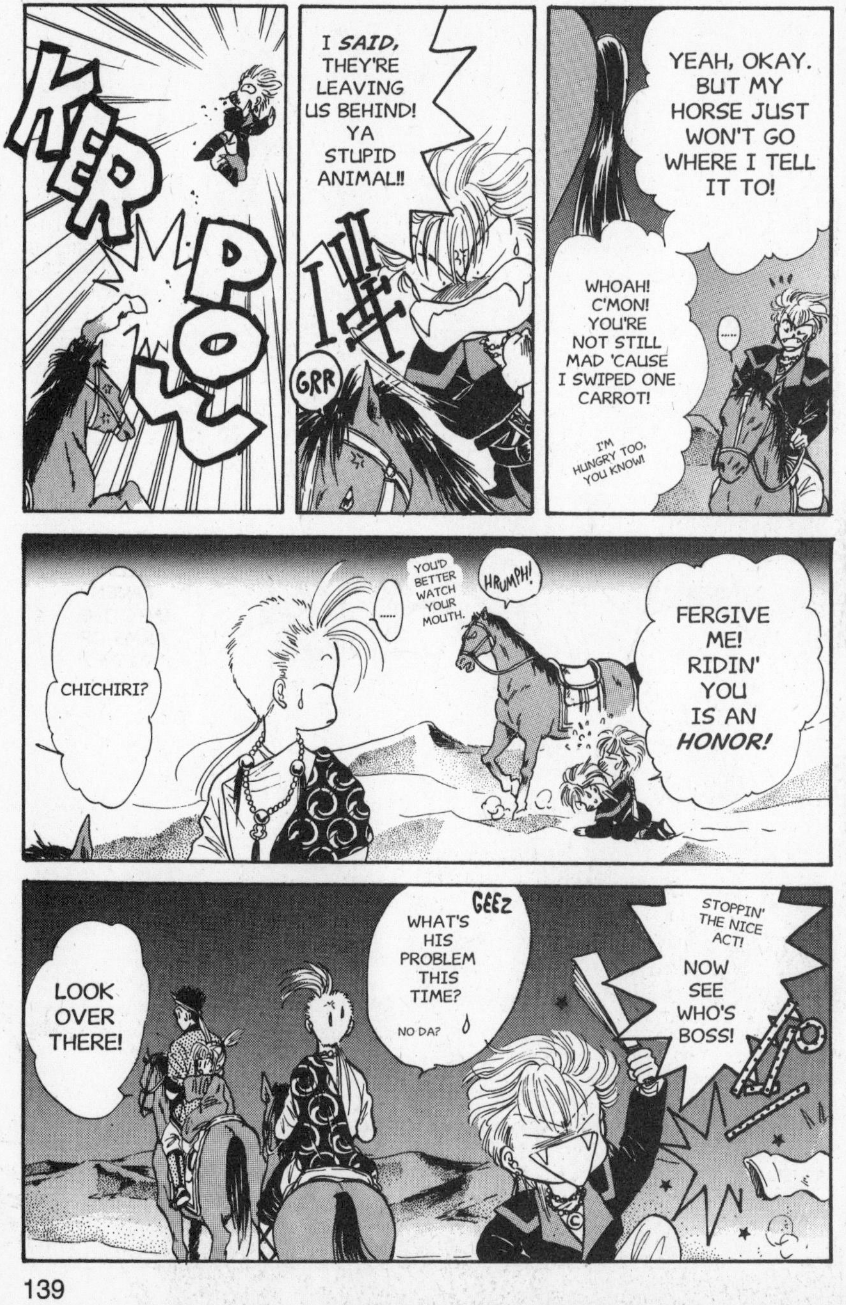
YEAH, OKAY. BUT MY HORSE JUST WON'T GO WHERE I TELL IT TO!
......
WHOAH! C'MON! YOU'RE NOT STILL MAD 'CAUSE I SWIPED ONE CARROT!
I'M HUNGRY TOO, YOU KNOW!
I SAID, THEY'RE LEAVING US BEHIND! YA STUPID ANIMAL!!
GRR
KER POW
FERGIVE ME! RIDIN' YOU IS AN HONOR!
HRUMPH!
YOU'D BETTER WATCH YOUR MOUTH.
......
CHICHIRI?
STOPPIN' THE NICE ACT!
NOW SEE WHO'S BOSS!
GEEZ
WHAT'S HIS PROBLEM THIS TIME?
NO DA?
LOOK OVER THERE!

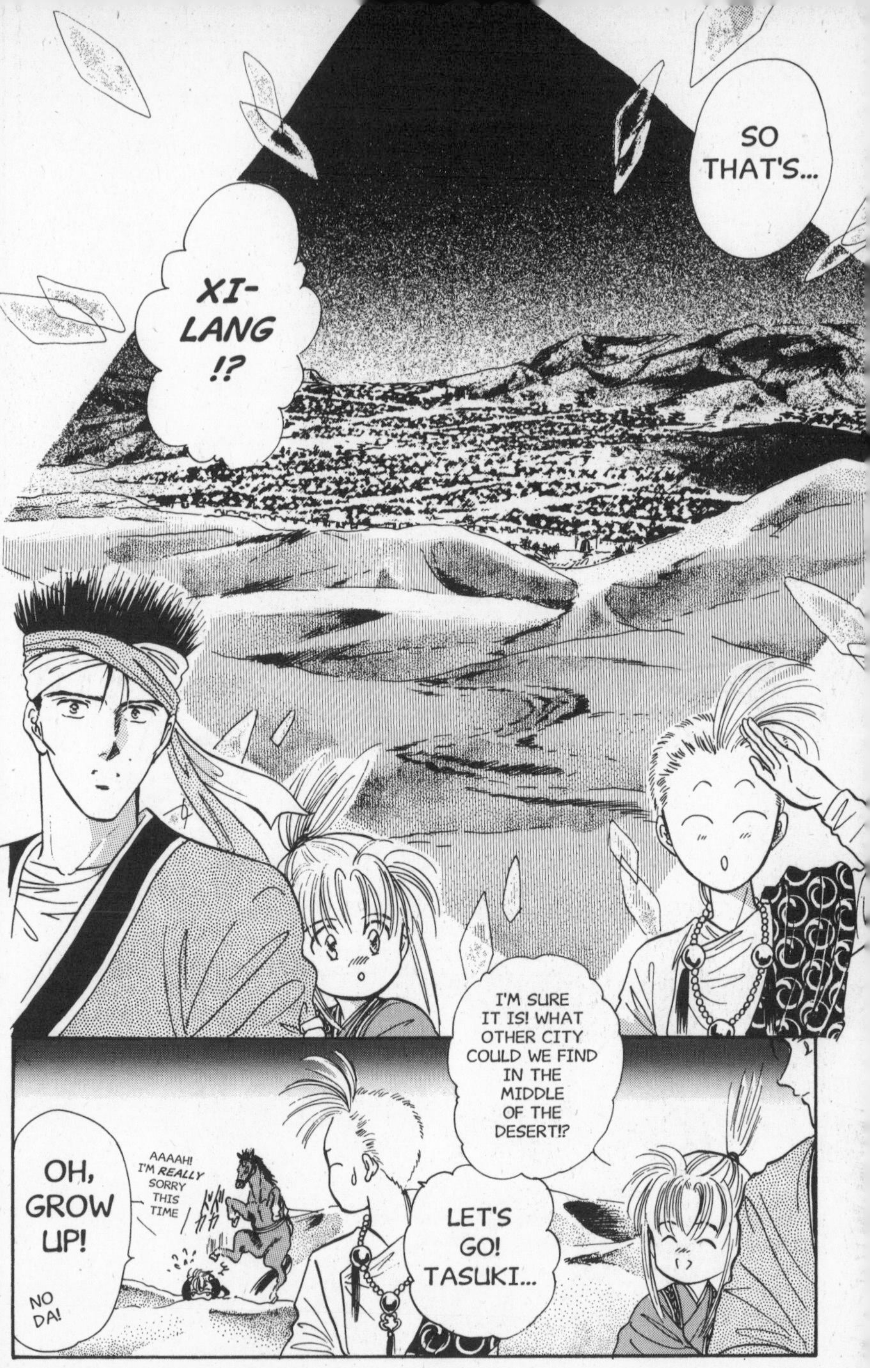
SO THAT'S...
XI-LANG !?
I'M SURE IT IS! WHAT OTHER CITY COULD WE FIND IN THE MIDDLE OF THE DESERT!?
LET'S GO! TASUKI...
AAAAH! I'M *REALLY* SORRY THIS TIME
OH, GROW UP!
NO DA!

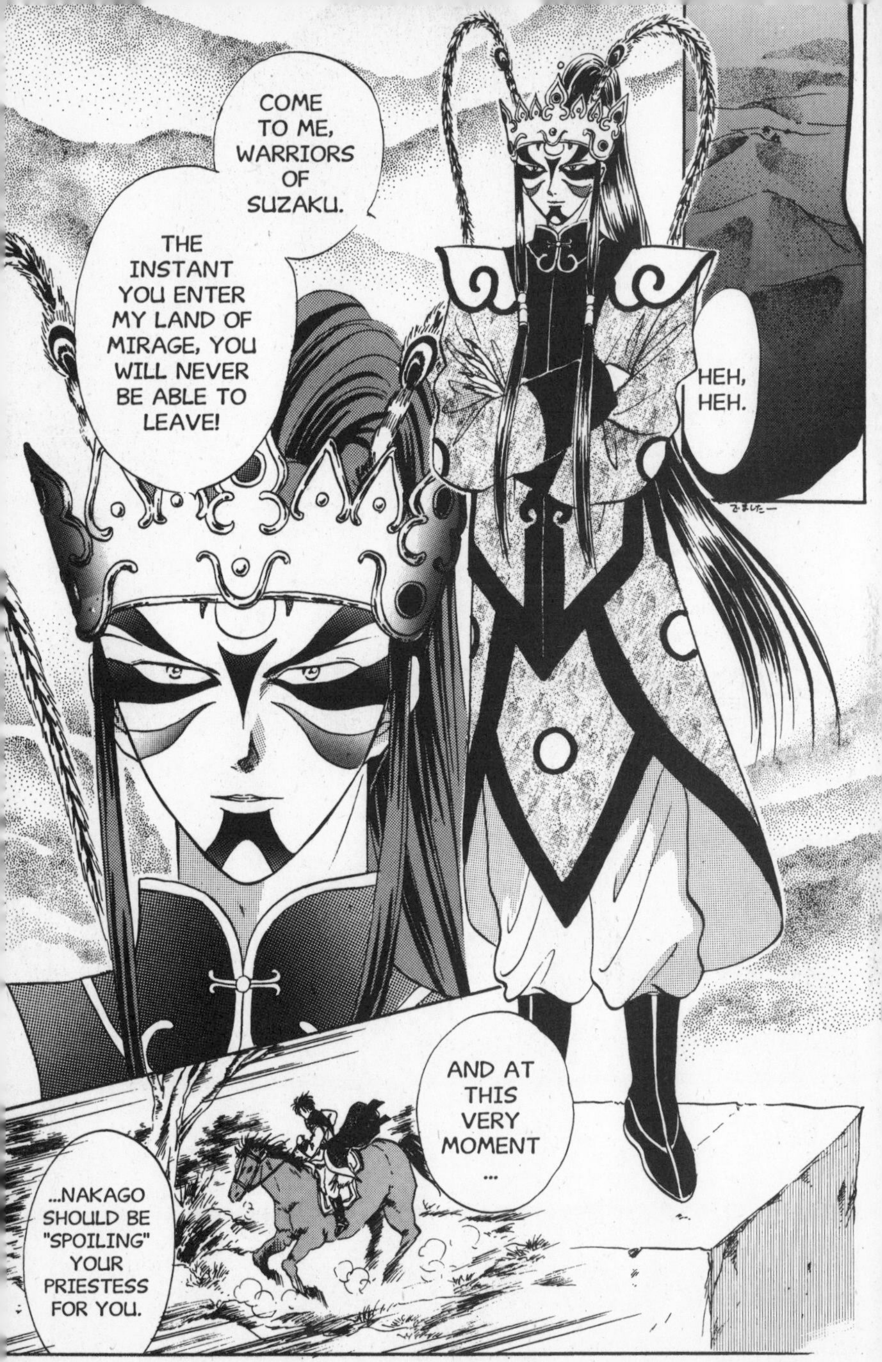
COME TO ME, WARRIORS OF SUZAKU.
THE INSTANT YOU ENTER MY LAND OF MIRAGE, YOU WILL NEVER BE ABLE TO LEAVE!
HEH, HEH.
AND AT THIS VERY MOMENT ...
...NAKAGO SHOULD BE "SPOILING" YOUR PRIESTESS FOR YOU.

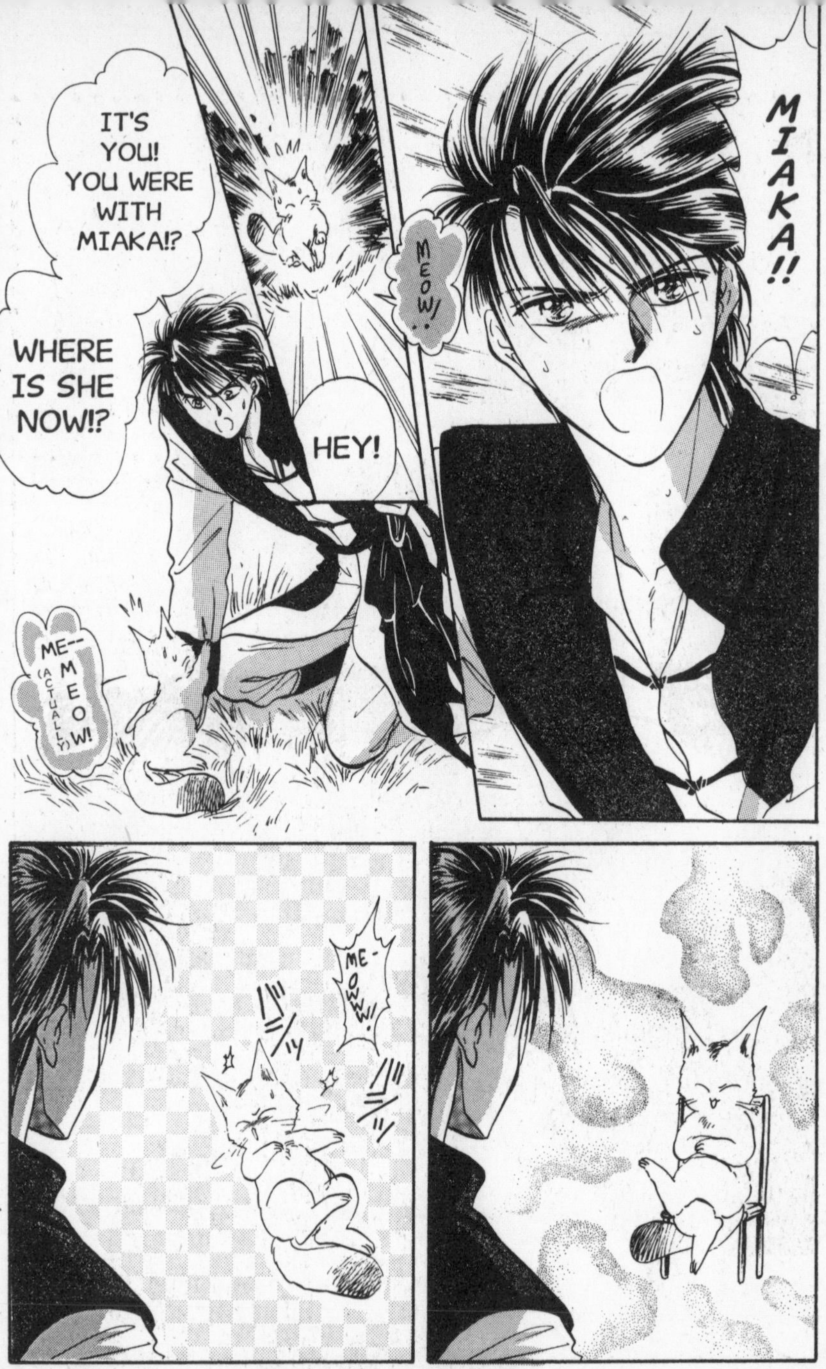
MIAKA!!
MEOW!..
HEY!
IT'S YOU! YOU WERE WITH MIAKA!?
WHERE IS SHE NOW!?
ME-- MEOW! (ACTUALLY)
ME-OWWW!

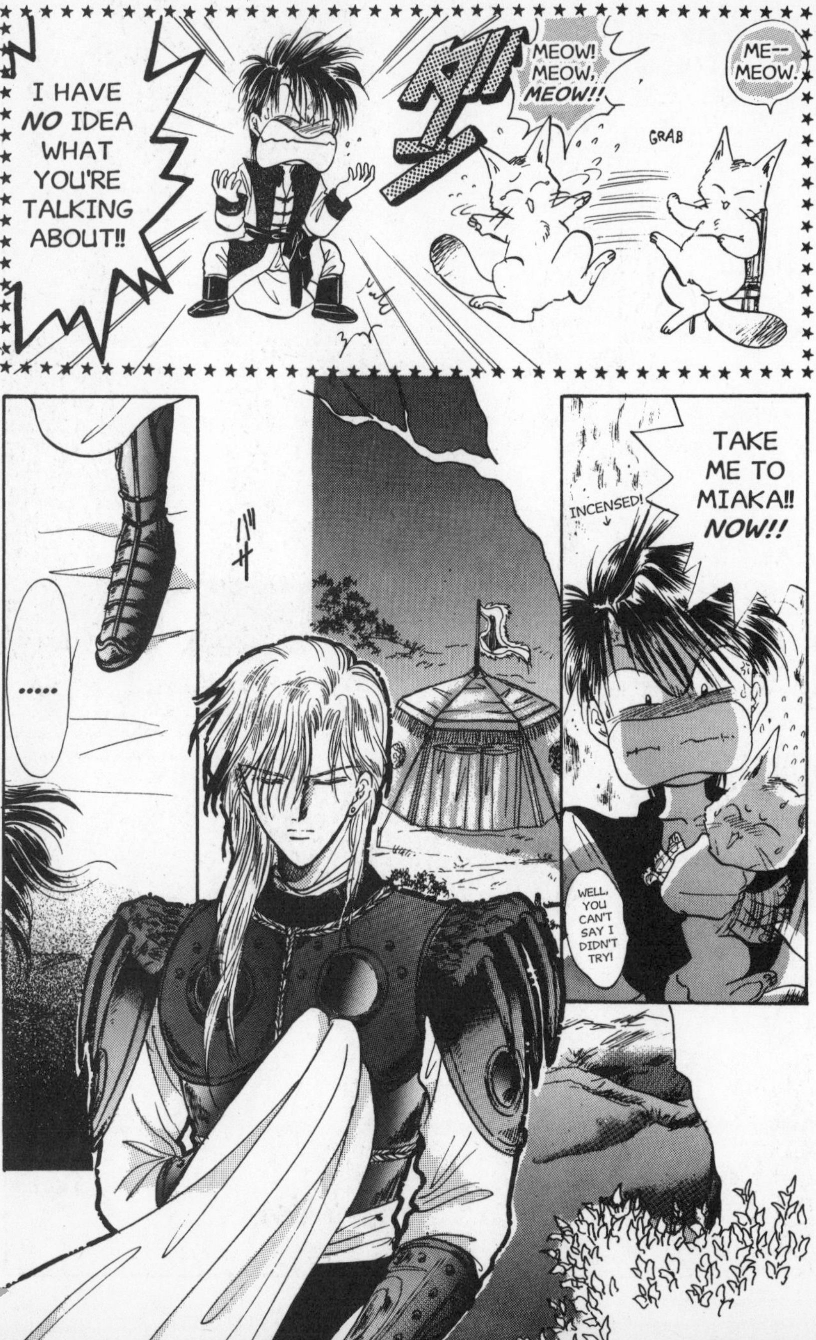
ME--
MEOW.
GRAB
MEOW!
MEOW,
MEOW!!
I HAVE NO IDEA WHAT YOU'RE TALKING ABOUT!!
TAKE ME TO MIAKA!! NOW!!
INCENSED!
WELL, YOU CAN'T SAY I DIDN'T TRY!
バサ
......

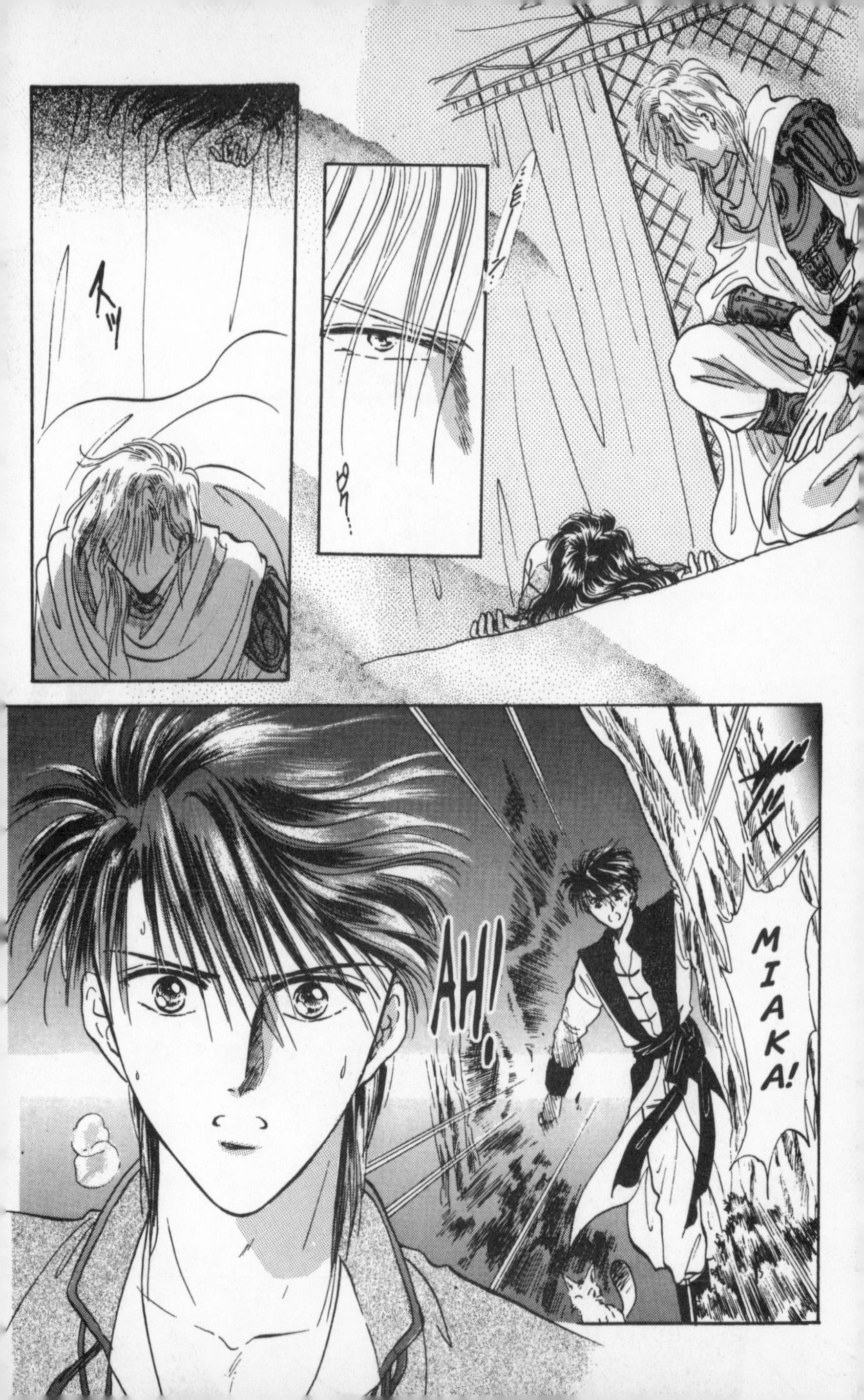
MIAKA!
AH!

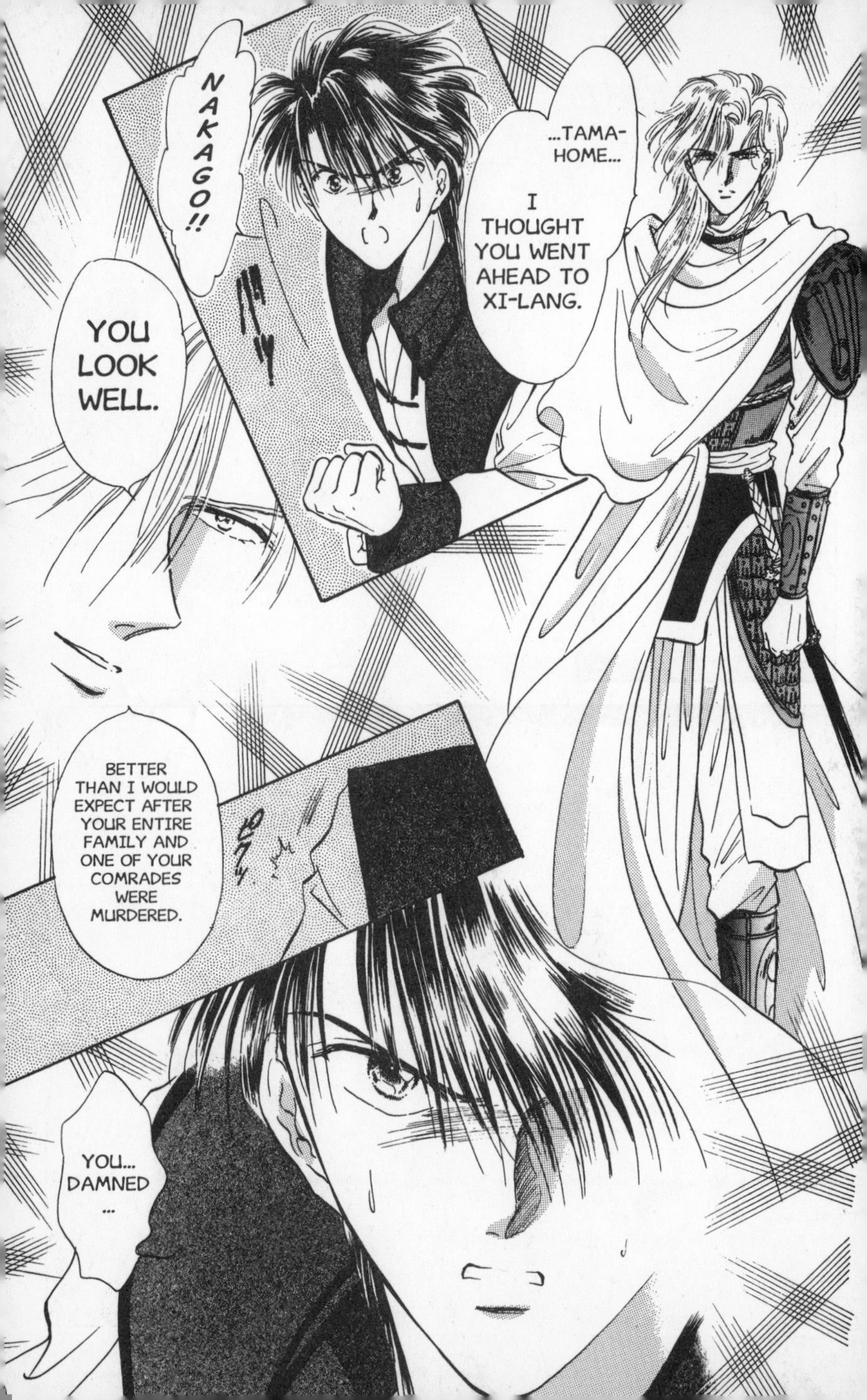
...TAMA-HOME...
I THOUGHT YOU WENT AHEAD TO XI-LANG.
NAKAGO!!
YOU LOOK WELL.
BETTER THAN I WOULD EXPECT AFTER YOUR ENTIRE FAMILY AND ONE OF YOUR COMRADES WERE MURDERED.
YOU... DAMNED ...

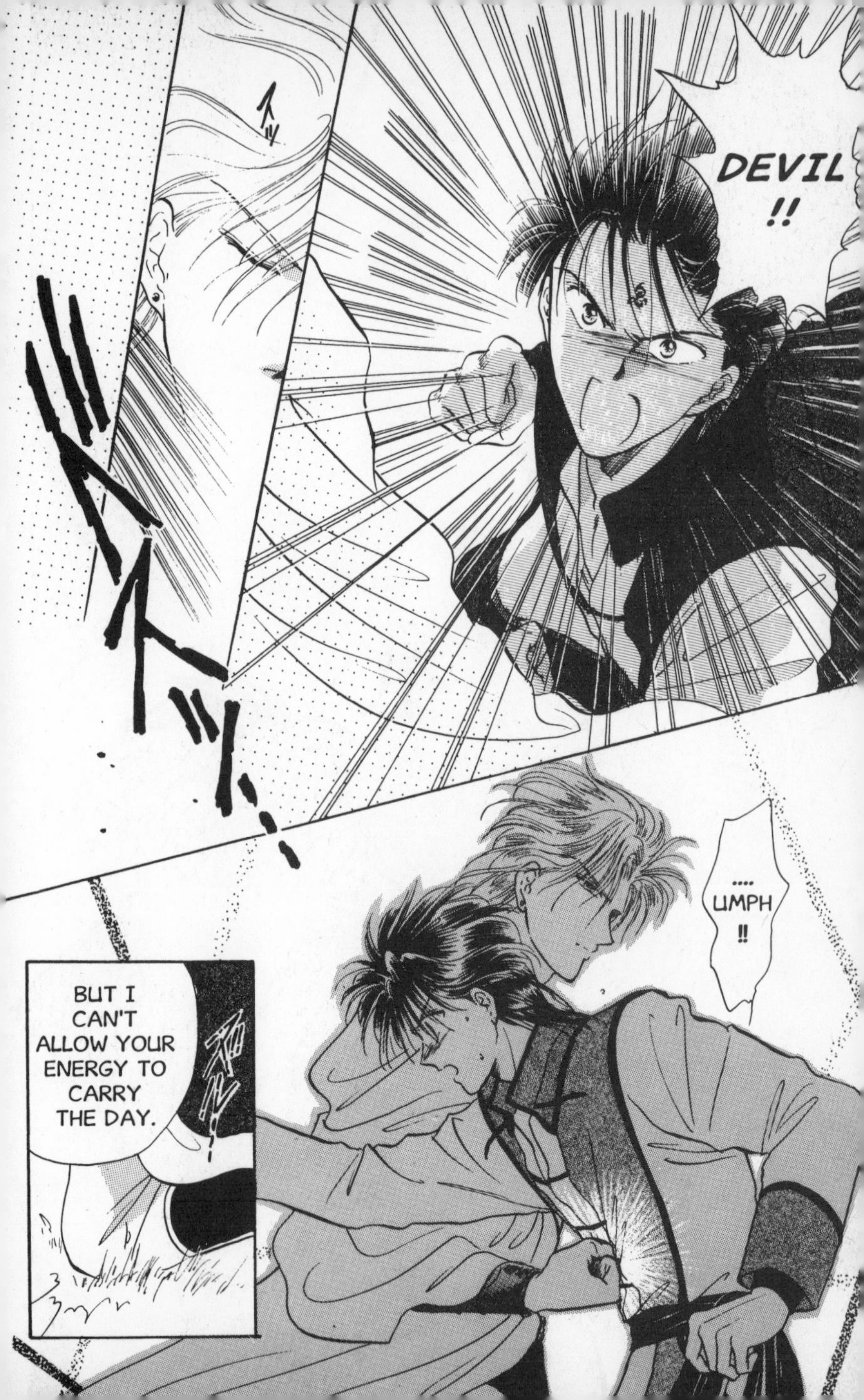
DEVIL !!
.... UMPH !!
BUT I CAN'T ALLOW YOUR ENERGY TO CARRY THE DAY.

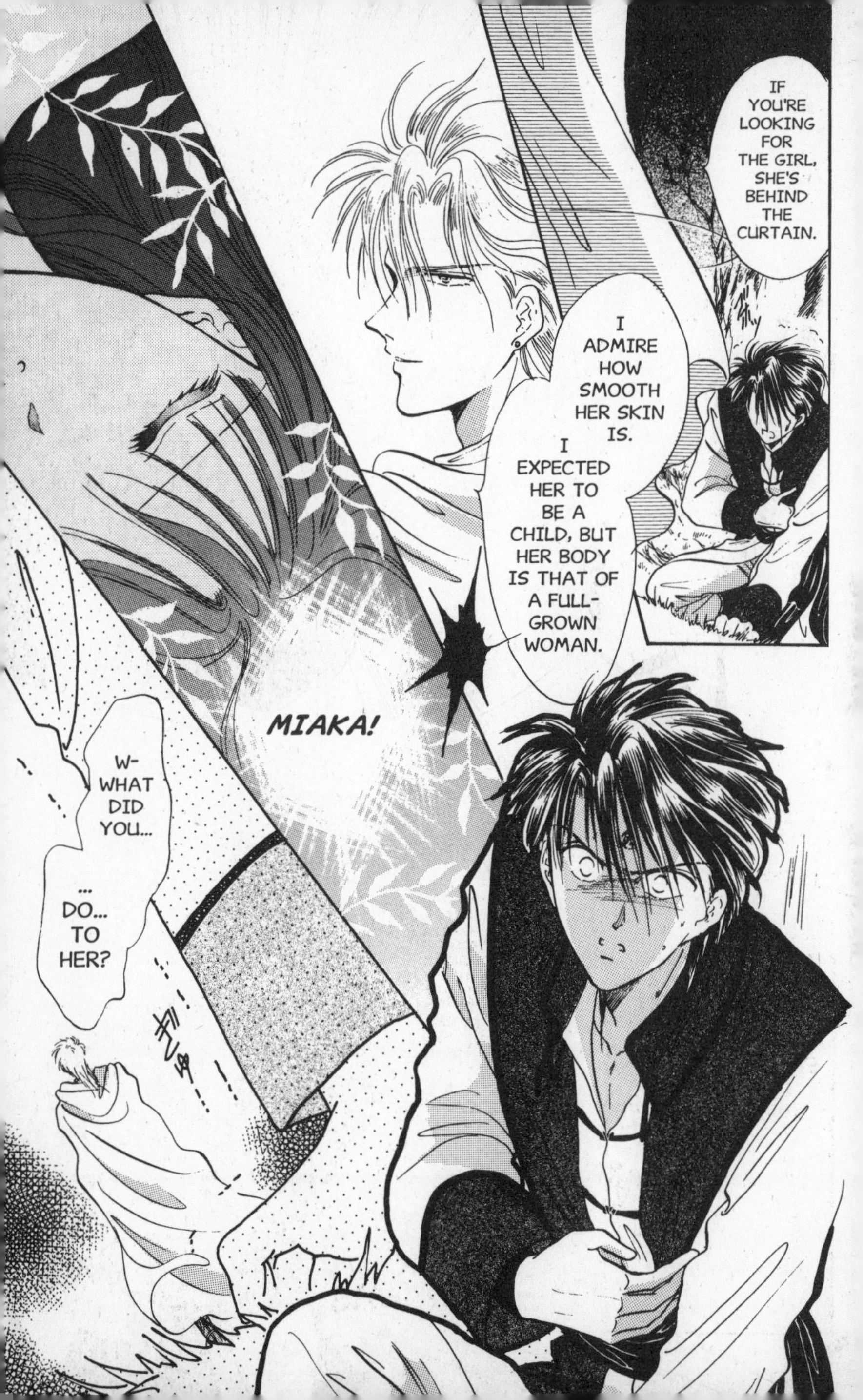
IF YOU'RE LOOKING FOR THE GIRL, SHE'S BEHIND THE CURTAIN.
I ADMIRE HOW SMOOTH HER SKIN IS.
I EXPECTED HER TO BE A CHILD, BUT HER BODY IS THAT OF A FULL-GROWN WOMAN.
MIAKA!
W-WHAT DID YOU...
...DO... TO HER?

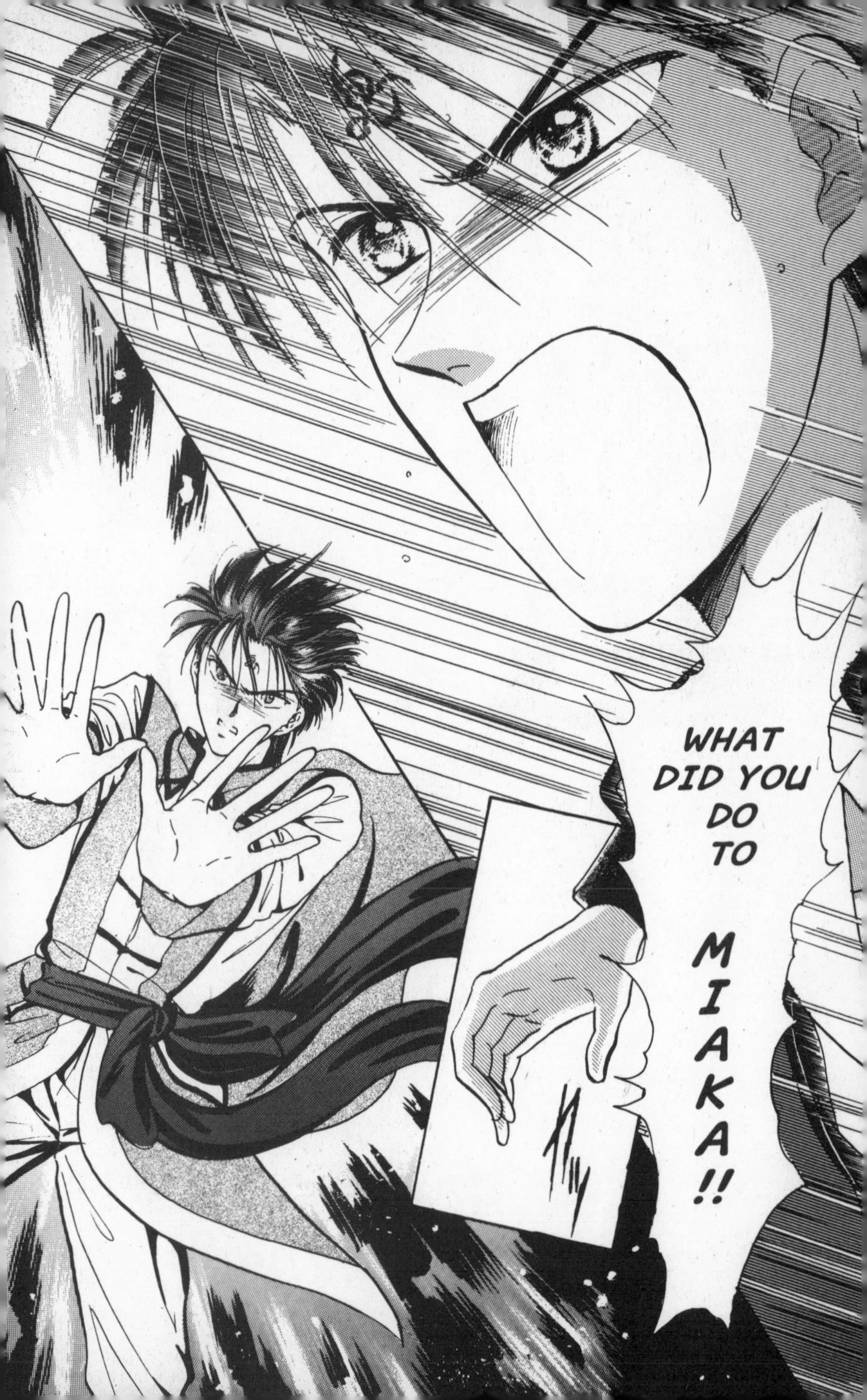
WHAT DID YOU DO TO MIAKA!!

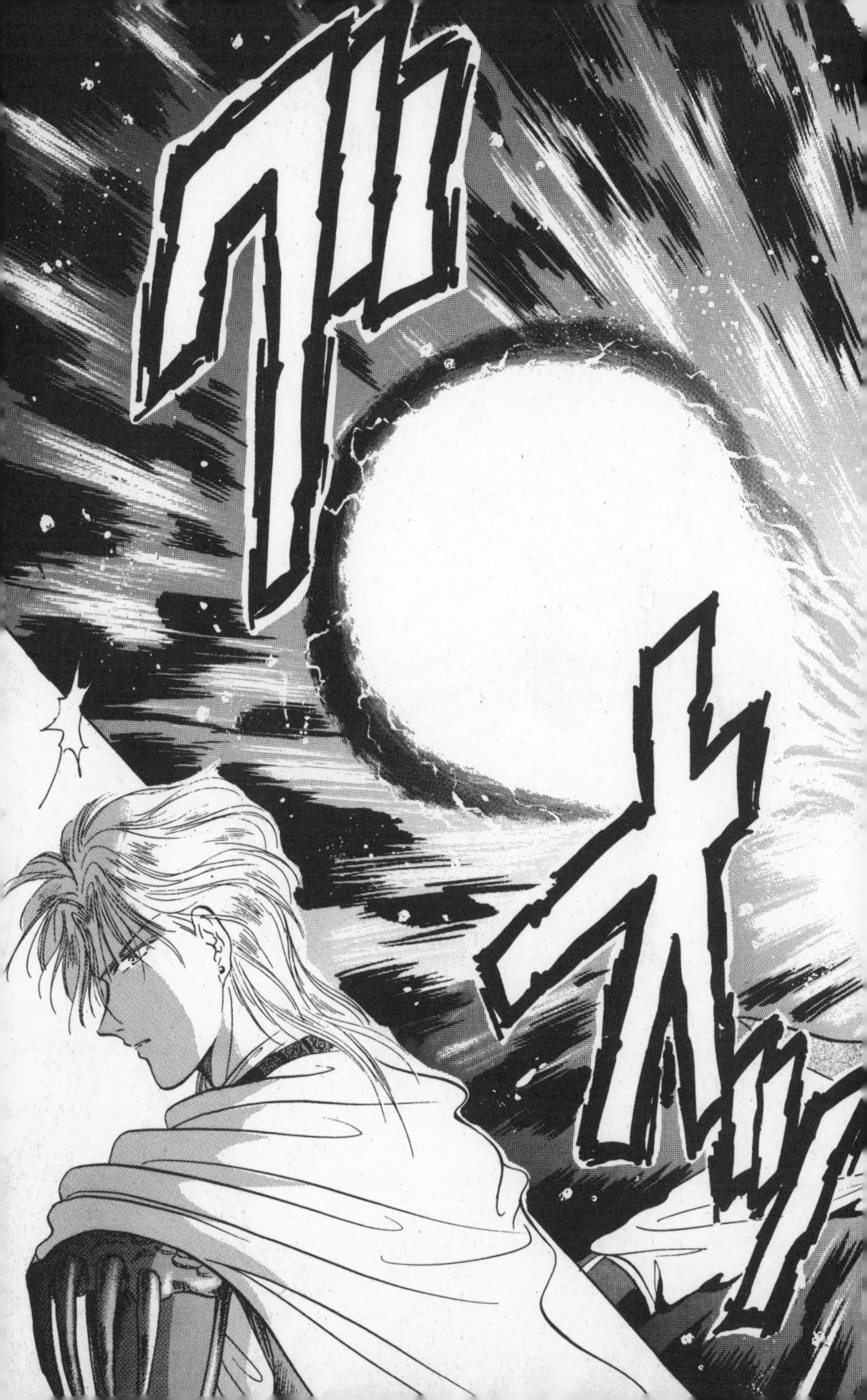

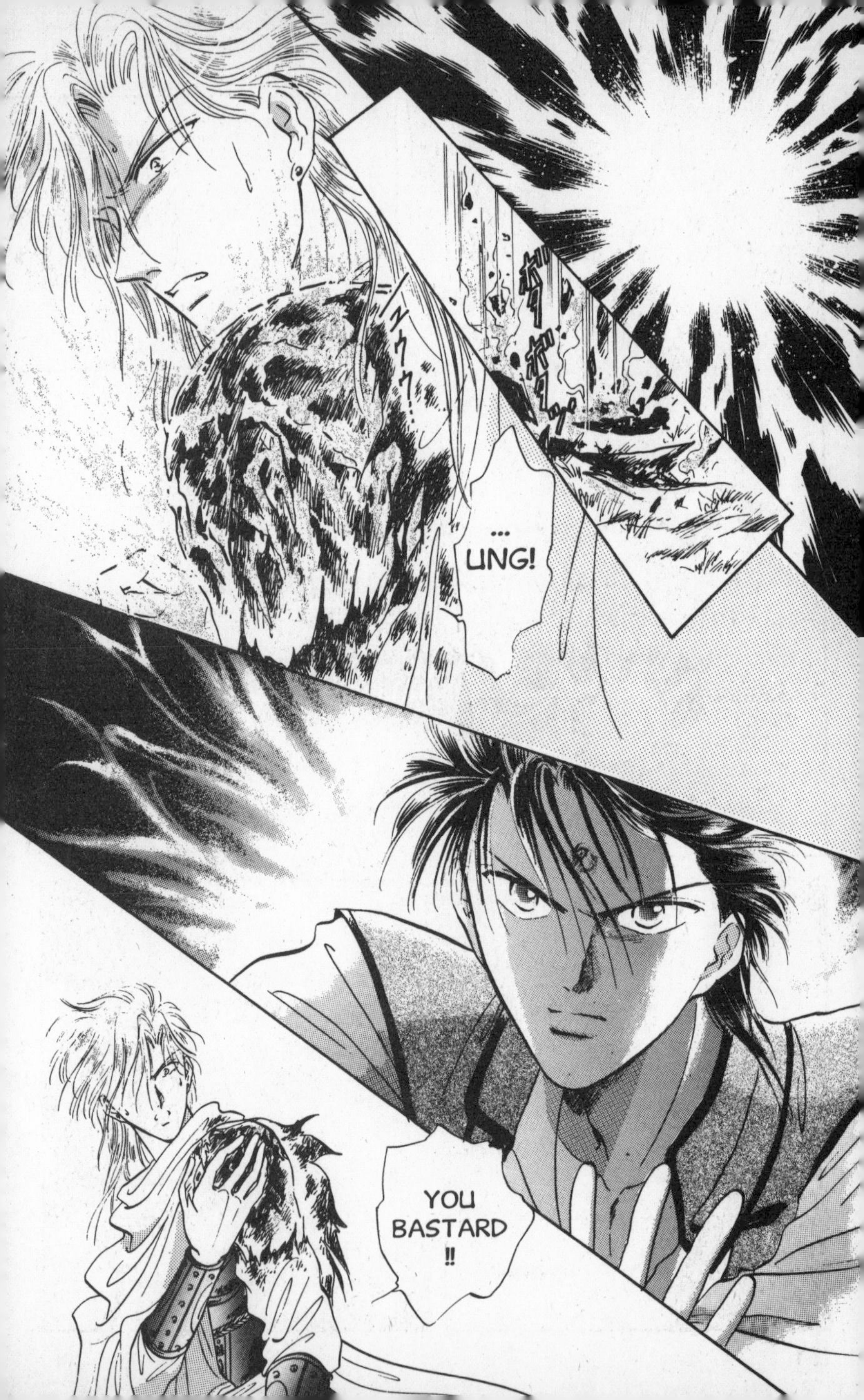
...UNG!
YOU BASTARD!!

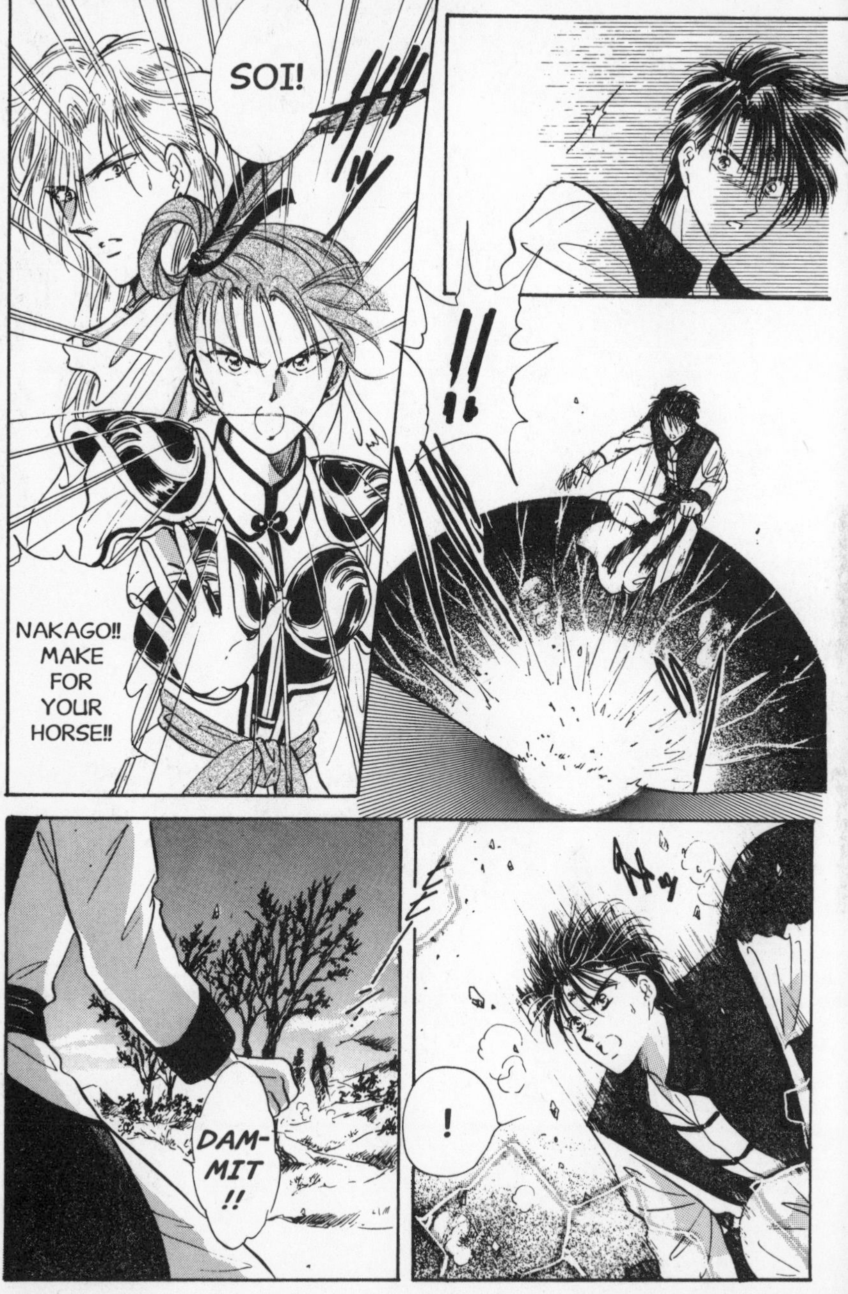
!!
SOI!
NAKAGO!! MAKE FOR YOUR HORSE!!
!
DAM-MIT !!

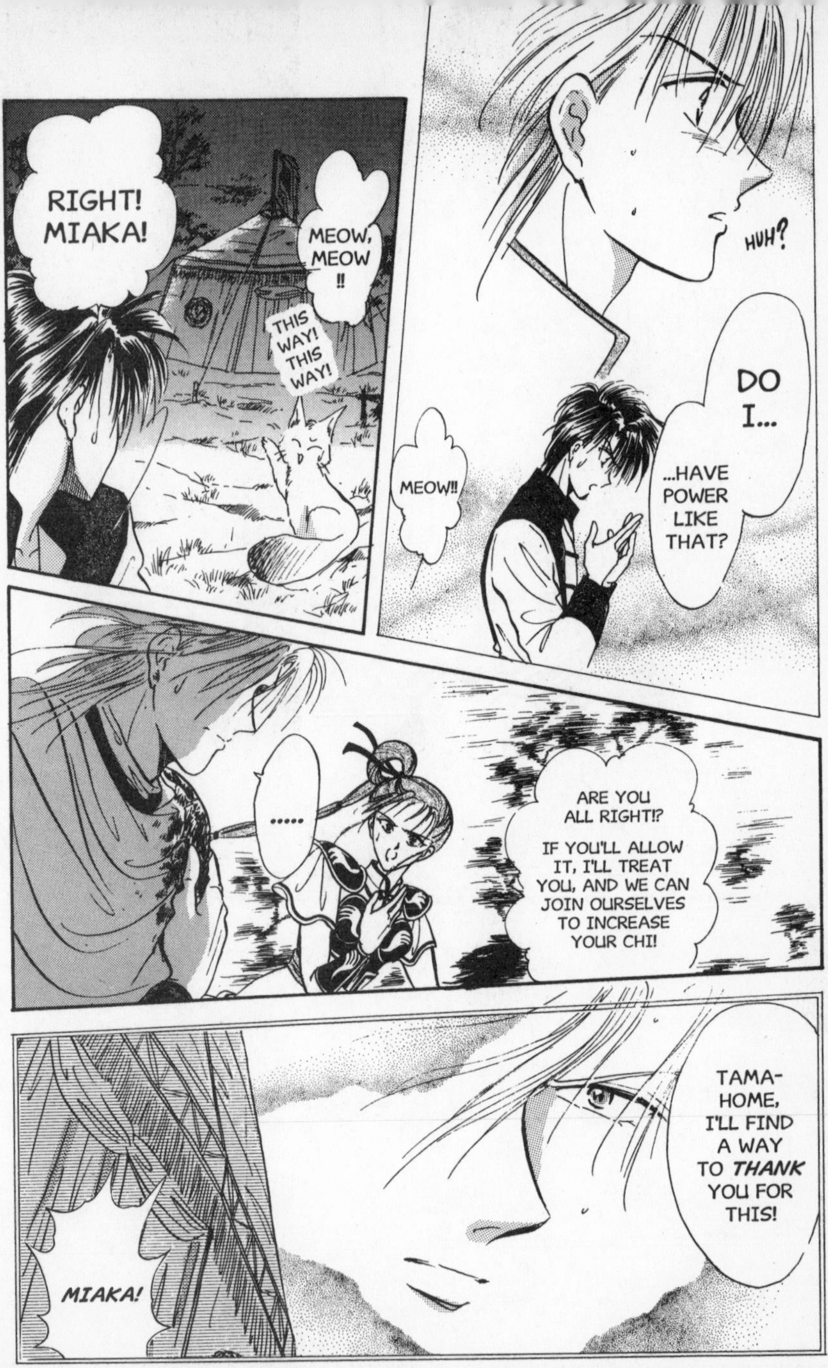
HUH?
DO I...
...HAVE POWER LIKE THAT?
MEOW!!
MEOW, MEOW!!
RIGHT! MIAKA!
THIS WAY! THIS WAY!
ARE YOU ALL RIGHT!?
IF YOU'LL ALLOW IT, I'LL TREAT YOU, AND WE CAN JOIN OURSELVES TO INCREASE YOUR CHI!
.....
TAMA-HOME, I'LL FIND A WAY TO *THANK* YOU FOR THIS!
MIAKA!

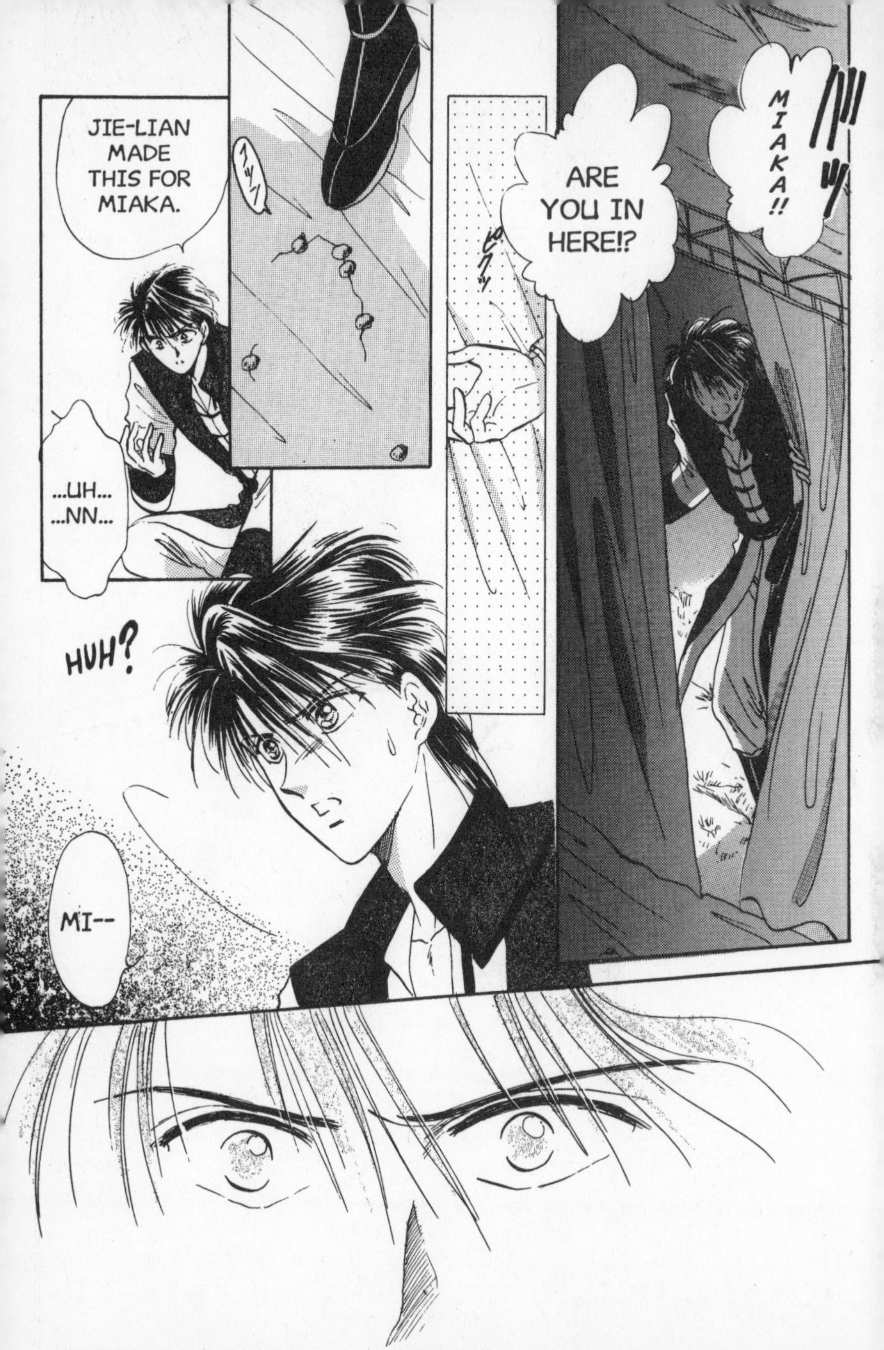
MIAKA!!
ARE YOU IN HERE!?
JIE-LIAN MADE THIS FOR MIAKA.
...UH... ...NN...
HUH?
MI--

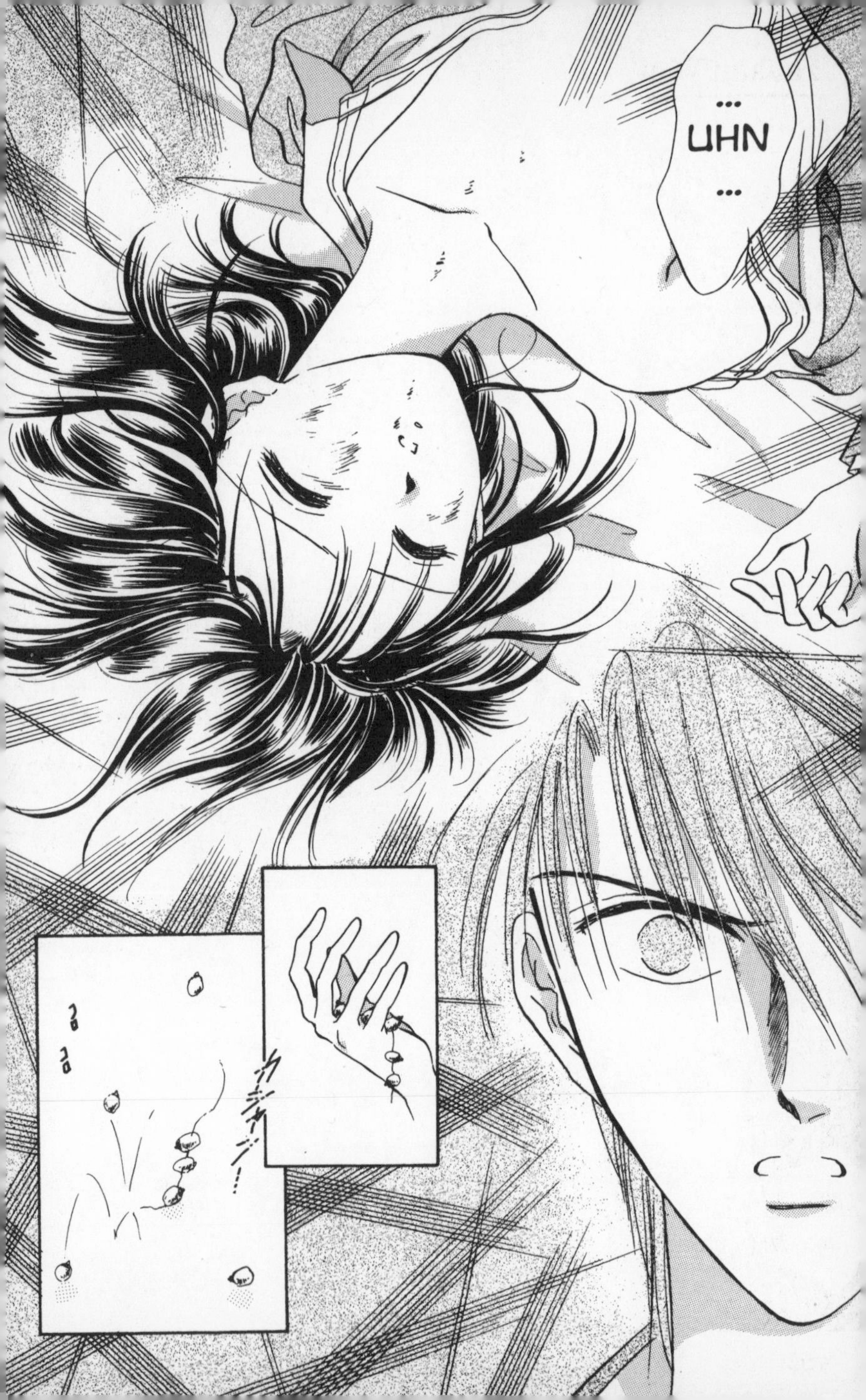
...UHN...

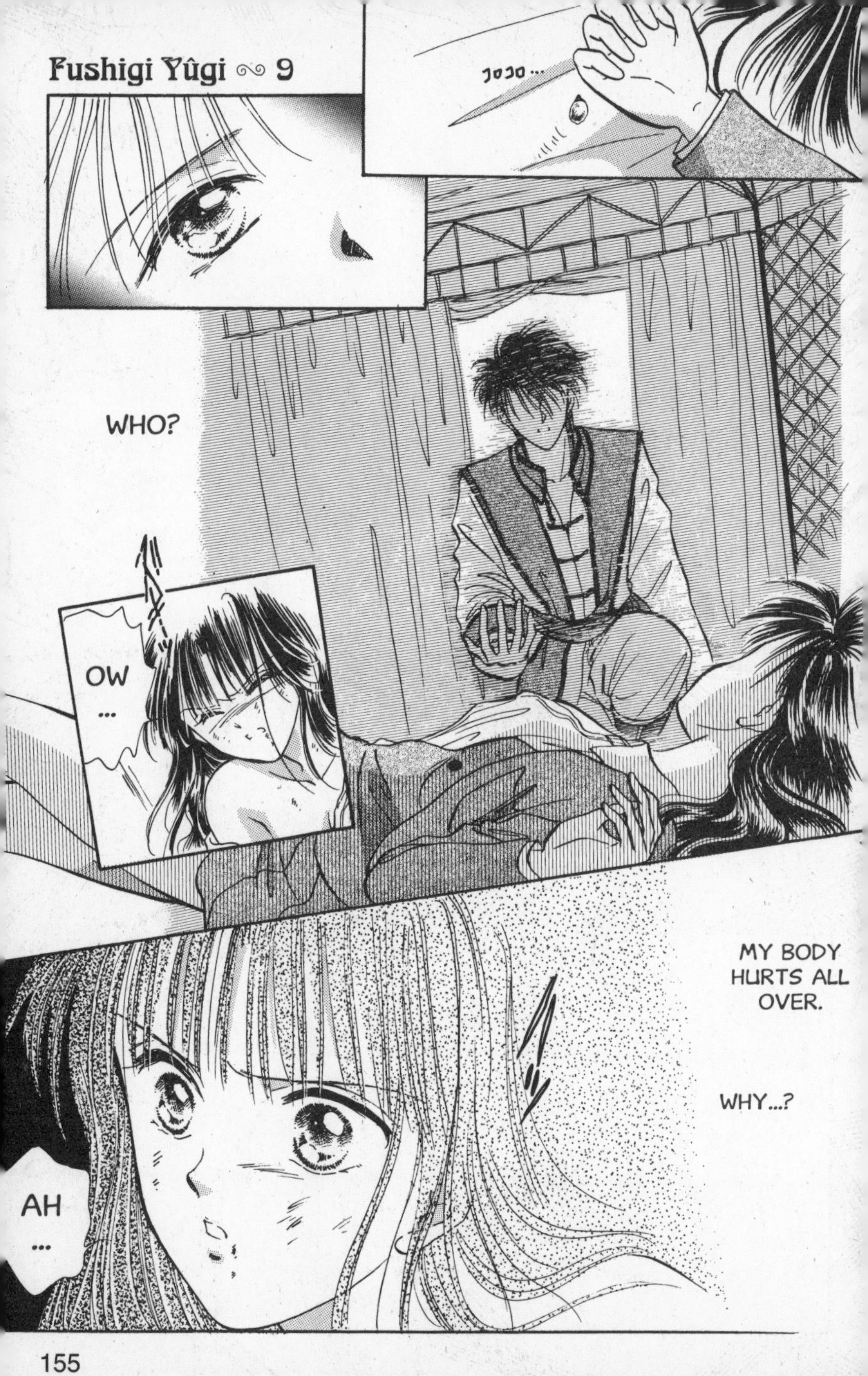
JOJO...
WHO?
OW ...
MY BODY HURTS ALL OVER.
WHY...?
AH ...

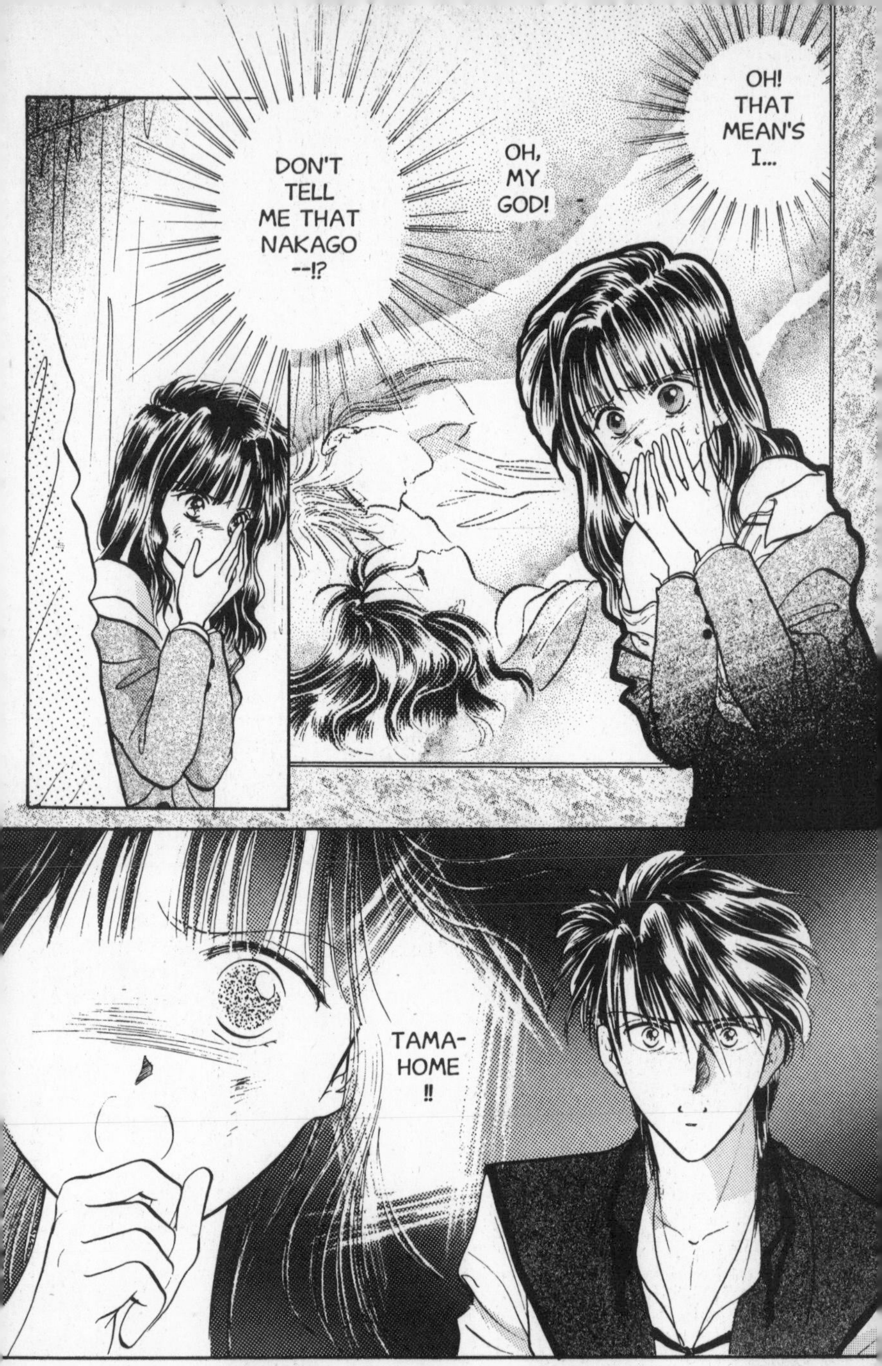
OH! THAT MEAN'S I...
OH, MY GOD!
DON'T TELL ME THAT NAKAGO --!?
TAMA-HOME !!

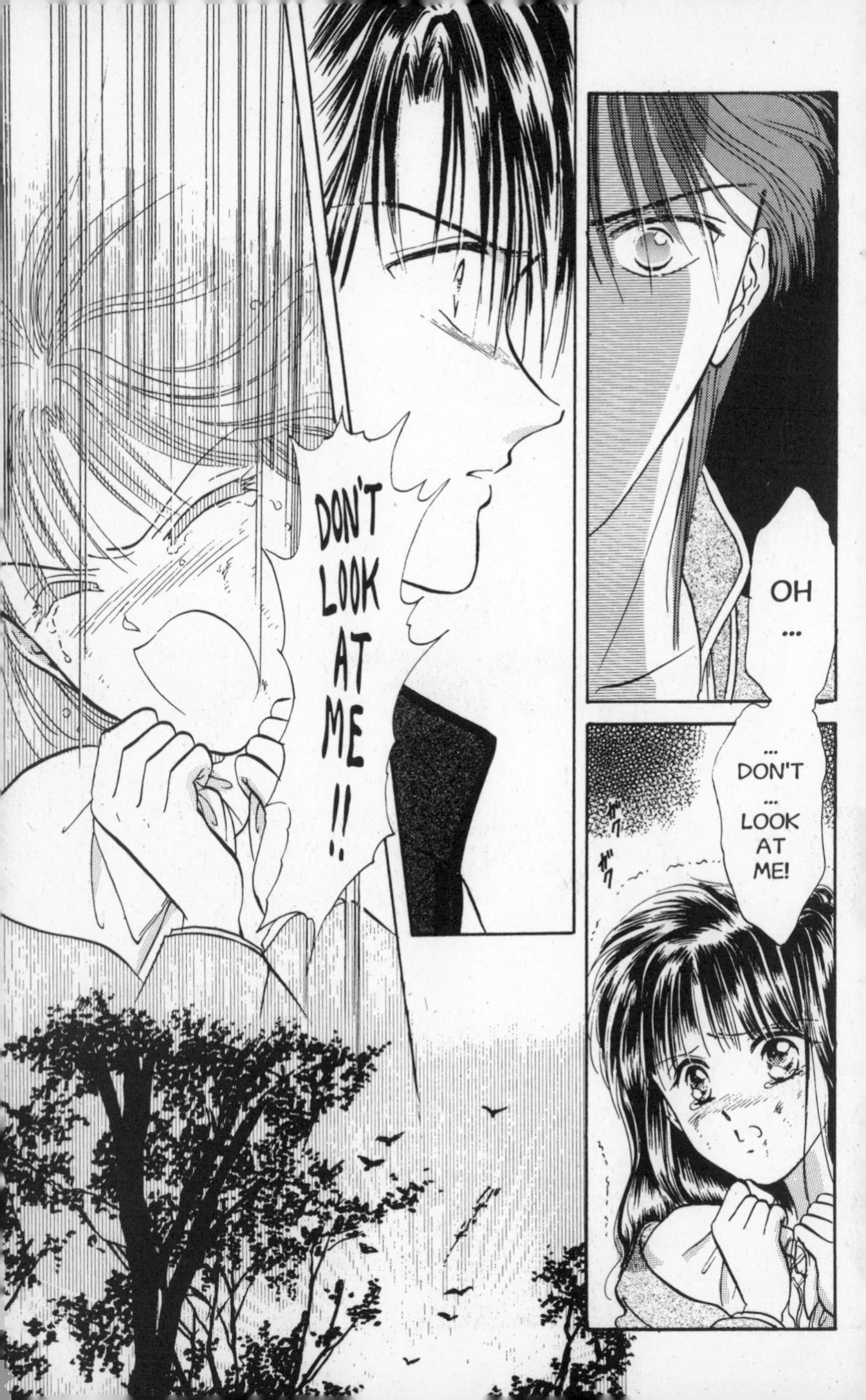
OH ...
... DON'T ... LOOK AT ME!
DON'T LOOK AT ME!!

THE SECRETS OF FUSHIGI YUGI: SPECIAL EDITION!!

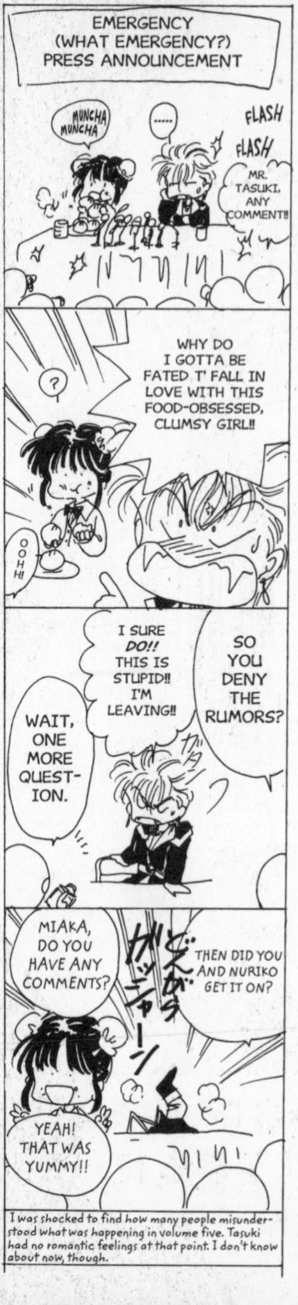
EMERGENCY (WHAT EMERGENCY?) PRESS ANNOUNCEMENT
FLASH
FLASH
MR. TASUKI, ANY COMMENT!!
......
MUNCHA MUNCHA
WHY DO I GOTTA BE FATED T' FALL IN LOVE WITH THIS FOOD-OBSESSED, CLUMSY GIRL!!
?
OOHH!
SO YOU DENY THE RUMORS?
I SURE DO!! THIS IS STUPID!! I'M LEAVING!!
WAIT, ONE MORE QUEST-ION.
THEN DID YOU AND NURIKO GET IT ON?
MIAKA, DO YOU HAVE ANY COMMENTS?
YEAH! THAT WAS YUMMY!!

I was shocked to find how many people misunderstood what was happening in volume five. Tasuki had no romantic feelings at that point. I don't know about now, though.

THE SECRETS OF FUSHIGI YŪGI II

Last time I tried writing in a complicated style, which made me incomprehensible!! So this time, I'll be plain and simple! All the fans said so! I'm such an idiot!

Q1 What the heck is the Diedu (Kodoku)!?
In volume 5, the Diedu made all the Tamahome fans cry... It's not really a spell to "control the minds of others," but a "death curse." Nakago mentioned using the Diedu once, and I thought that in actuality, he would use a different drug... but that was getting too complicated, so I made the Diedu the drug he used in the end. I decided they would just be the exact same thing. The Diedu can be made by taking a poisonous insect... Umm... no point in going into details (as if I really knew), so I'll stop here.
Also, the musk incense that made Tamahome dizzy was taken from the musk deer. Usually, that scent wouldn't have any such effect, so he actually became dizzy because:
1) It actually wasn't musk deer incense.
2) Tamahome came from such a poor background, that the ultra-high-class perfume made him woozy.
3) The author picked it out on a whim and can't make a good excuse for it. You have to choose one of the three.

Q2: Is there really a "bedding technique"?
In fact, there is! Never underestimate China! The "bedding technique" is a special way of having sex where the female is the chi of shadow and the male is the chi of light. By absorbing the woman's shadow chi, the man's light chi is nourished, resulting in long life!! The man takes in his partner's chi to restore his health. (Oh, come on!!)
(But, when you think of the deeper implications you'll want to scream, "That's impossible!!") But it's not that weird. The reason why Nakago takes Soi to bed is to restore his chi. There's something very meaningful about this.

Q3:
How does Tasuki manage to keep his hair like that?
Never underestimate China! I've had some readers who say, "Come on! This is a story out of the ancient past, right?" But Japan's culture in the ancient past was pretty much stolen from China and other countries. I mean when the Three Kingdoms flourished, Japan was still stuck in the Yayoi era (I think). Am I wrong?
They've had hair oils for thousands o'years, don'cha know! (What kind of accent is that?)
When they used to bundle hair for Chinese women, that was meant to last for days, so they must've used serious hair gel (?). That's why they used small blocks of wood or small pillows for their necks when they went to bed. I think they did that in Japan's Edo period as well.
So maybe Tasuki had a supply of oil for his hairstyle. But who knows, it could be natural.

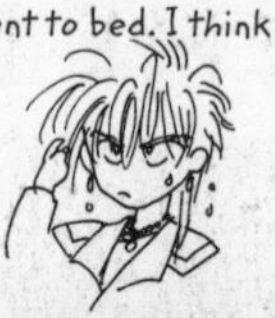

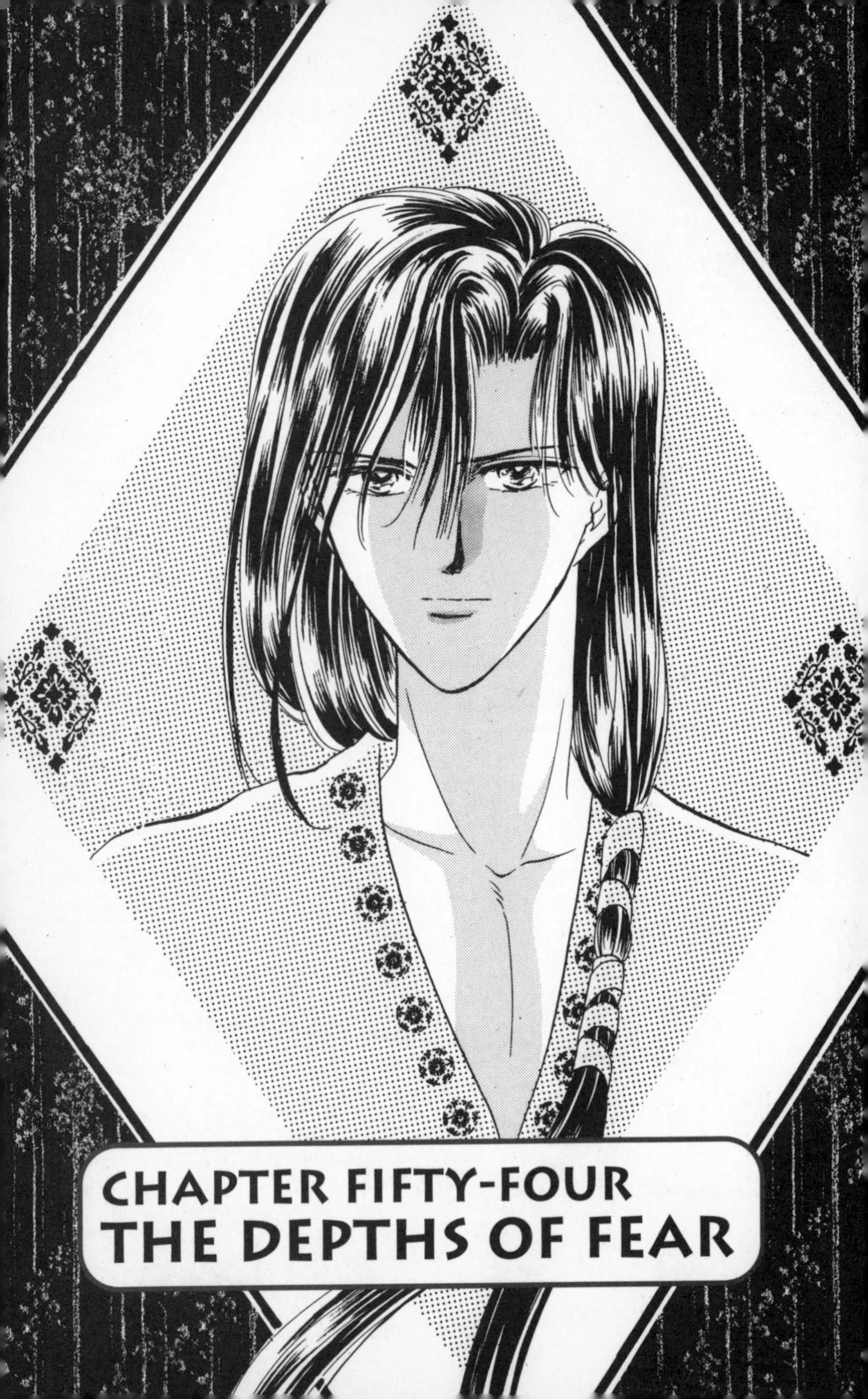
CHAPTER FIFTY-FOUR
THE DEPTHS OF FEAR

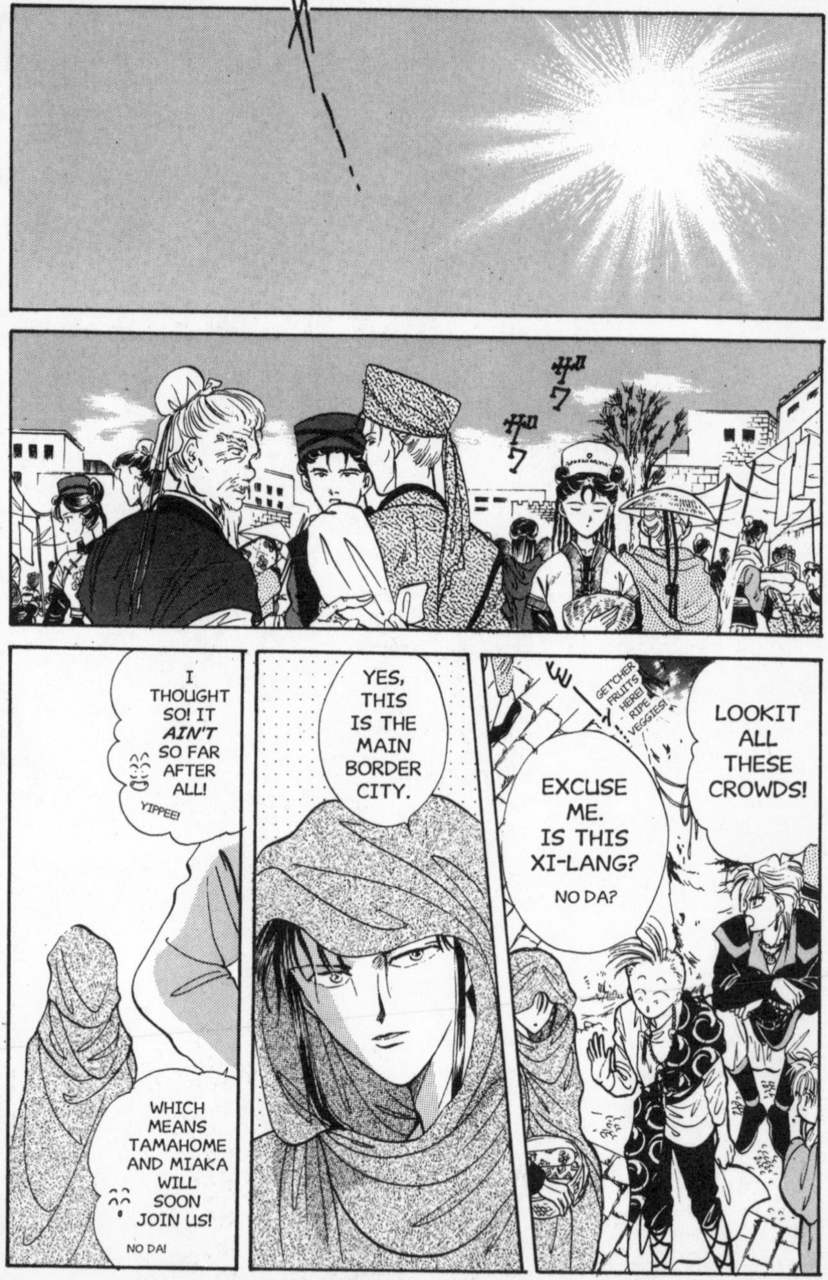
LOOKIT ALL THESE CROWDS!
GET'CHER FRUITS HERE! RIPE VEGGIES!
EXCUSE ME. IS THIS XI-LANG?
NO DA?
YES, THIS IS THE MAIN BORDER CITY.
I THOUGHT SO! IT *AIN'T* SO FAR AFTER ALL!
YIPPEE!
WHICH MEANS TAMAHOME AND MIAKA WILL SOON JOIN US!
NO DA!

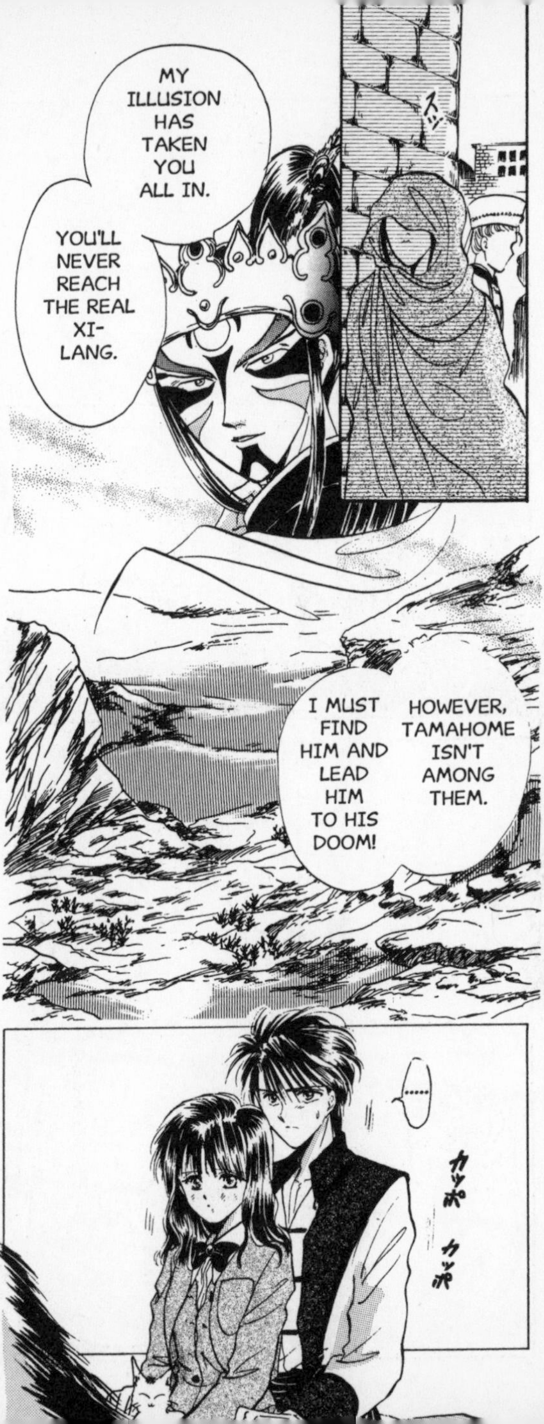
スッ
MY ILLUSION HAS TAKEN YOU ALL IN.
YOU'LL NEVER REACH THE REAL XI-LANG.
HOWEVER, TAMAHOME ISN'T AMONG THEM.
I MUST FIND HIM AND LEAD HIM TO HIS DOOM!
......
カッポ
カッポ

The flights were all on time (Apparently it's common in China to be delayed for hours, so we must've lucked out). Aside from my tummyache, this visit wasn't nearly as hard on me as a previous trip to India was. It was really nice. I definitely want to go again. It's too bad they don't have a manga culture on the mainland though!

After I got back, I began working on Fushigi and realized, "Oh, I should have visited the Silk Road!" I don't know China's western region very well.

I have to say *Fushigi* is getting pretty heavy, but on the other hand, it did turn out that Yui wasn't raped. From chapter 16 until now, the only ones who knew this were me, my editor, my assistants, and a few friends. Nakago's becoming an important character. Someone stop him! He's out of my control! What'll he do next?

I have a backlog of questions from you readers, so here are some of my replies. I'll start with some of the more popular requests. We have the go-ahead to make CD Book II. We haven't decided the contents yet, but that's good news!

A book of illustrations. ◊ It will be coming out...maybe not until early next year. I don't actually know, but it will come out! Also, most of you fans are requesting that *Fushigi* be made into an anime series. I have heard plans.

Please write to Nippon Victor. Ha ha!

To tell the truth, I don't have any influence over the production of anime series, CDs, posters, and other merchandise. It's all up to the editorial department and other production companies. Also, any requests for graphic novels should be directed to my publisher Shogakukan, not me. I'm not a distribution company -- I just draw manga. That's all. And I'm giving it my best!

I guess I'll leave it off here. See you next time!

'94 3/14

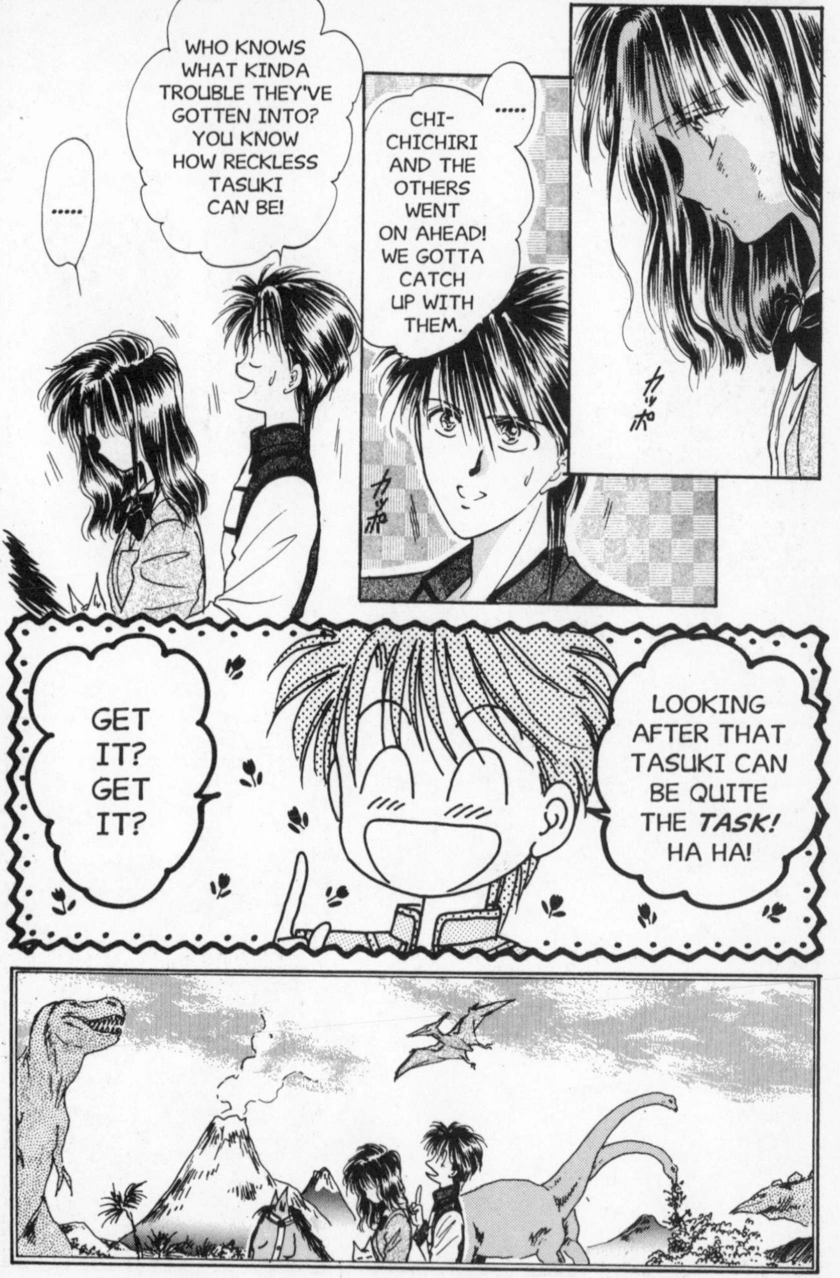
カッポ
.....
CHI-CHICHIRI AND THE OTHERS WENT ON AHEAD! WE GOTTA CATCH UP WITH THEM.
カッポ
WHO KNOWS WHAT KINDA TROUBLE THEY'VE GOTTEN INTO? YOU KNOW HOW RECKLESS TASUKI CAN BE!
.....
LOOKING AFTER THAT TASUKI CAN BE QUITE THE ***TASK!*** HA HA!
GET IT? GET IT?

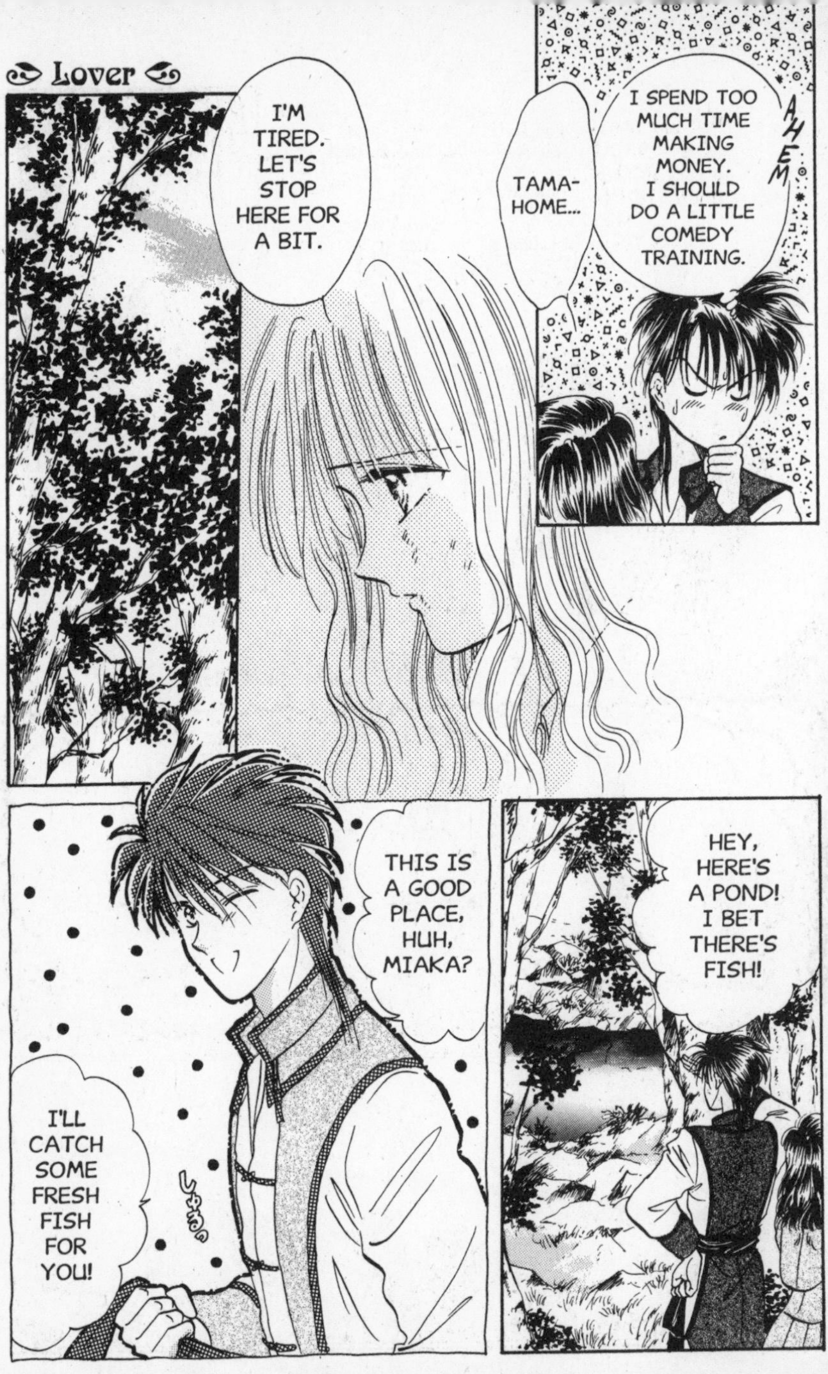
I SPEND TOO MUCH TIME MAKING MONEY. I SHOULD DO A LITTLE COMEDY TRAINING.
AHEM
TAMA-HOME...
I'M TIRED. LET'S STOP HERE FOR A BIT.
HEY, HERE'S A POND! I BET THERE'S FISH!
THIS IS A GOOD PLACE, HUH, MIAKA?
I'LL CATCH SOME FRESH FISH FOR YOU!

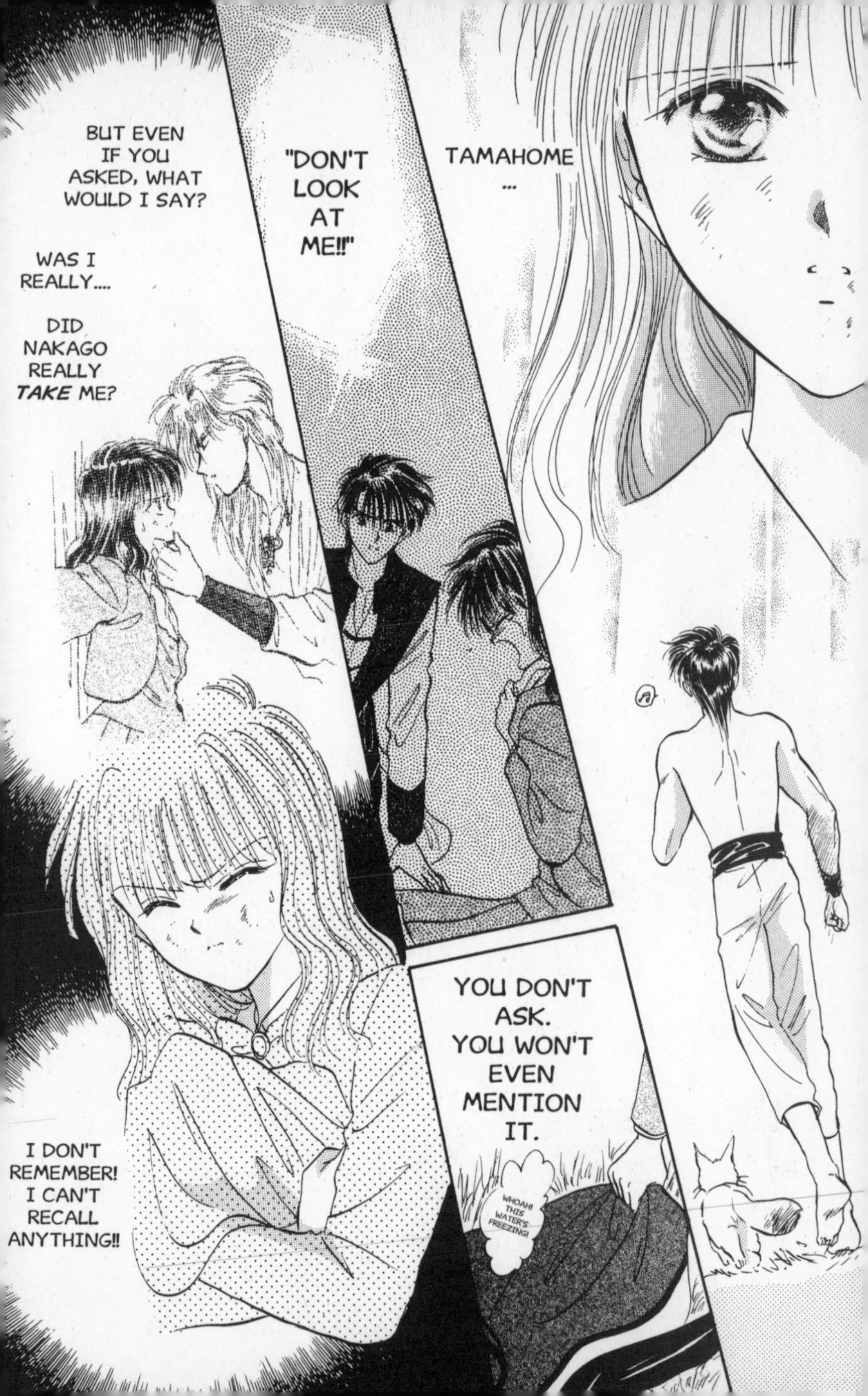
TAMAHOME ...
WHOAH! THIS WATER'S FREEZING!
YOU DON'T ASK. YOU WON'T EVEN MENTION IT.
"DON'T LOOK AT ME!!"
BUT EVEN IF YOU ASKED, WHAT WOULD I SAY?
WAS I REALLY....
DID NAKAGO REALLY *TAKE* ME?
I DON'T REMEMBER! I CAN'T RECALL ANYTHING!!

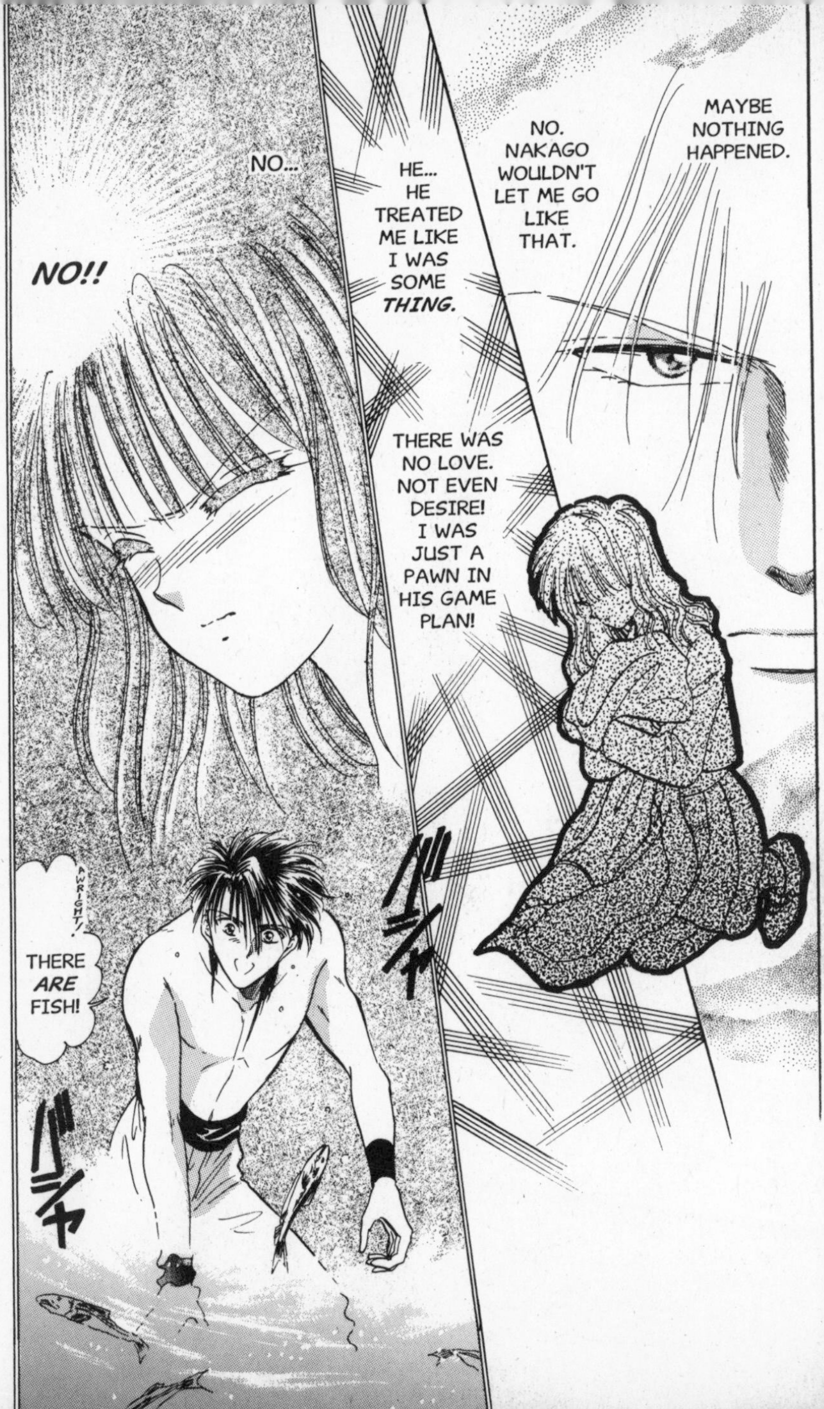
MAYBE NOTHING HAPPENED.
NO. NAKAGO WOULDN'T LET ME GO LIKE THAT.
HE... HE TREATED ME LIKE I WAS SOME *THING.*
THERE WAS NO LOVE. NOT EVEN DESIRE! I WAS JUST A PAWN IN HIS GAME PLAN!
NO...
NO!!
AWRIGHT!
THERE *ARE* FISH!

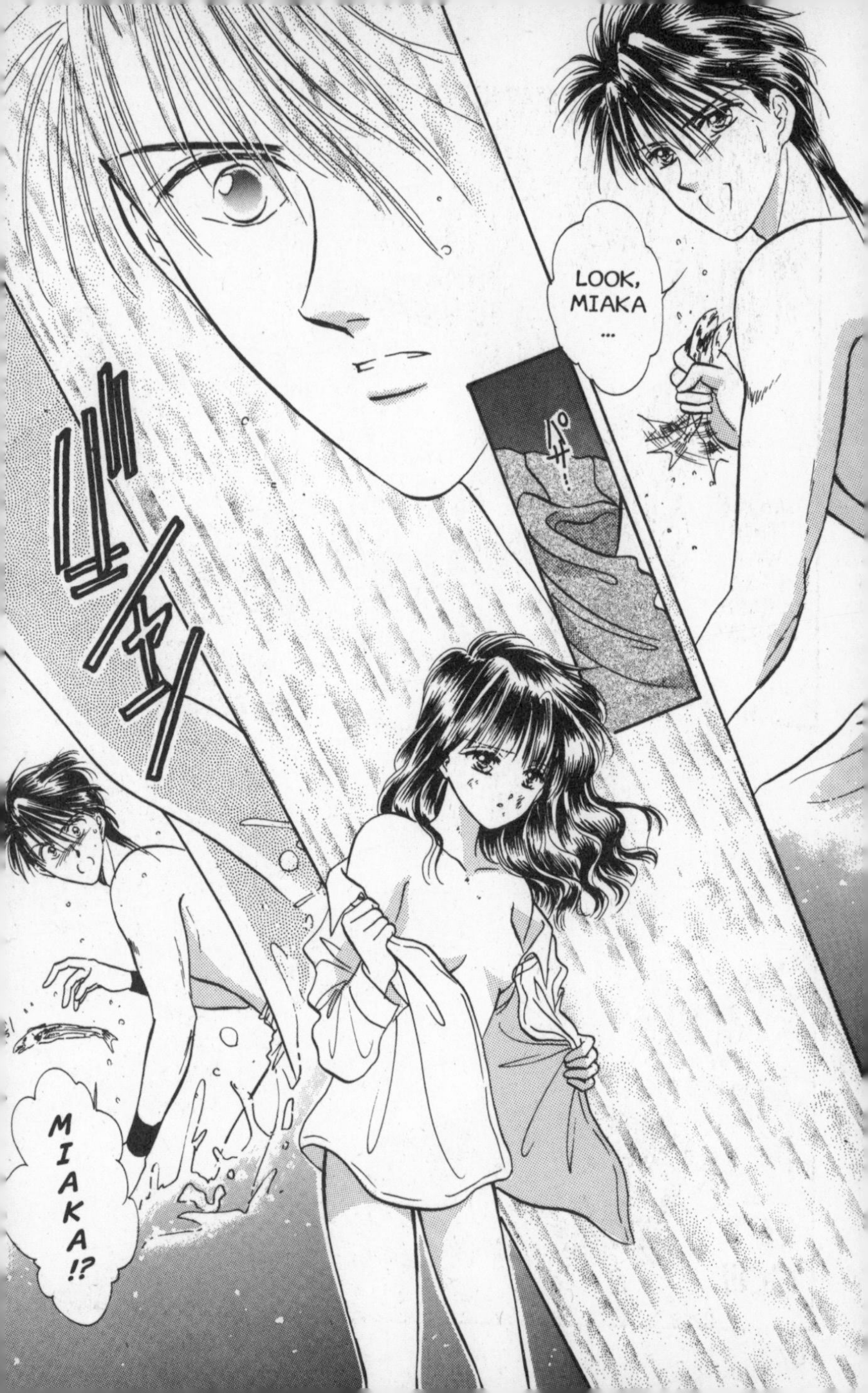
LOOK, MIAKA ...
MIAKA!?

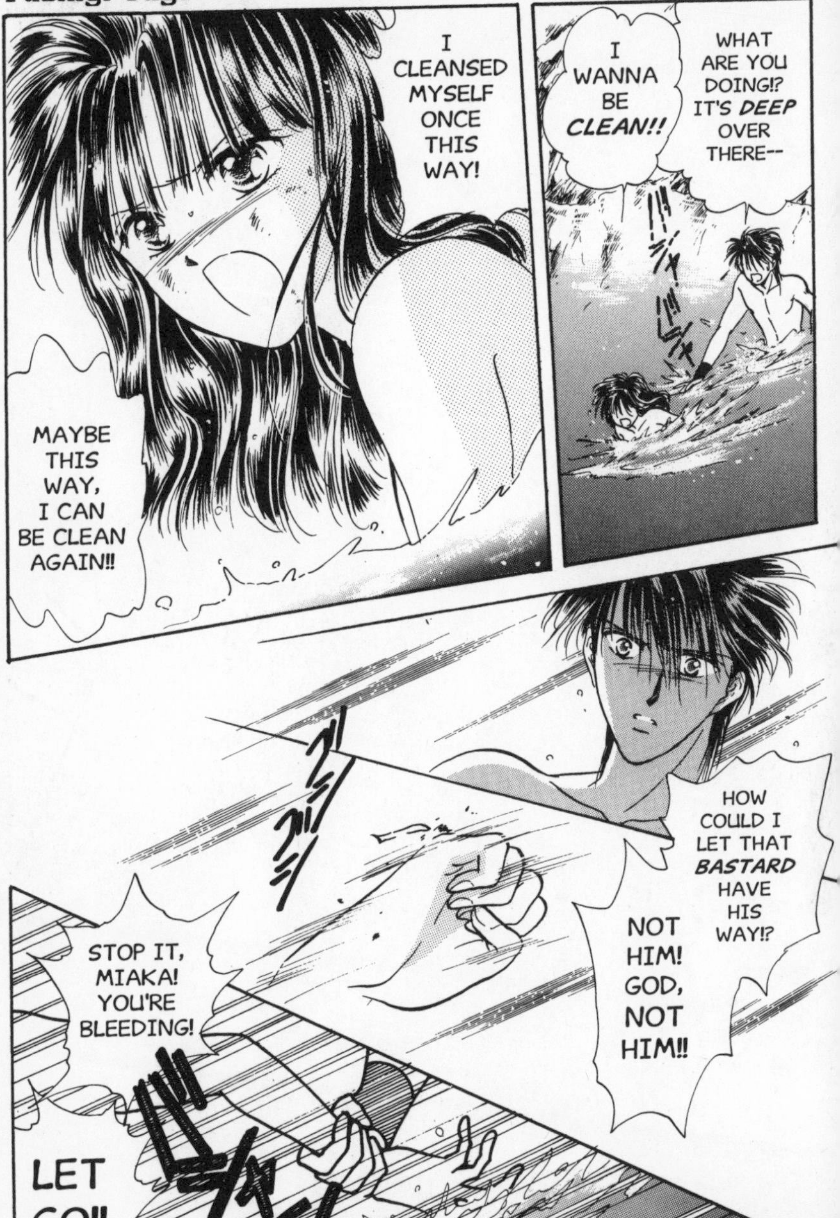
WHAT ARE YOU DOING!? IT'S *DEEP* OVER THERE--
I WANNA BE *CLEAN!!*
I CLEANSED MYSELF ONCE THIS WAY!
MAYBE THIS WAY, I CAN BE CLEAN AGAIN!!
HOW COULD I LET THAT *BASTARD* HAVE HIS WAY!?
NOT HIM! GOD, NOT HIM!!
STOP IT, MIAKA! YOU'RE BLEEDING!
LET GO!!

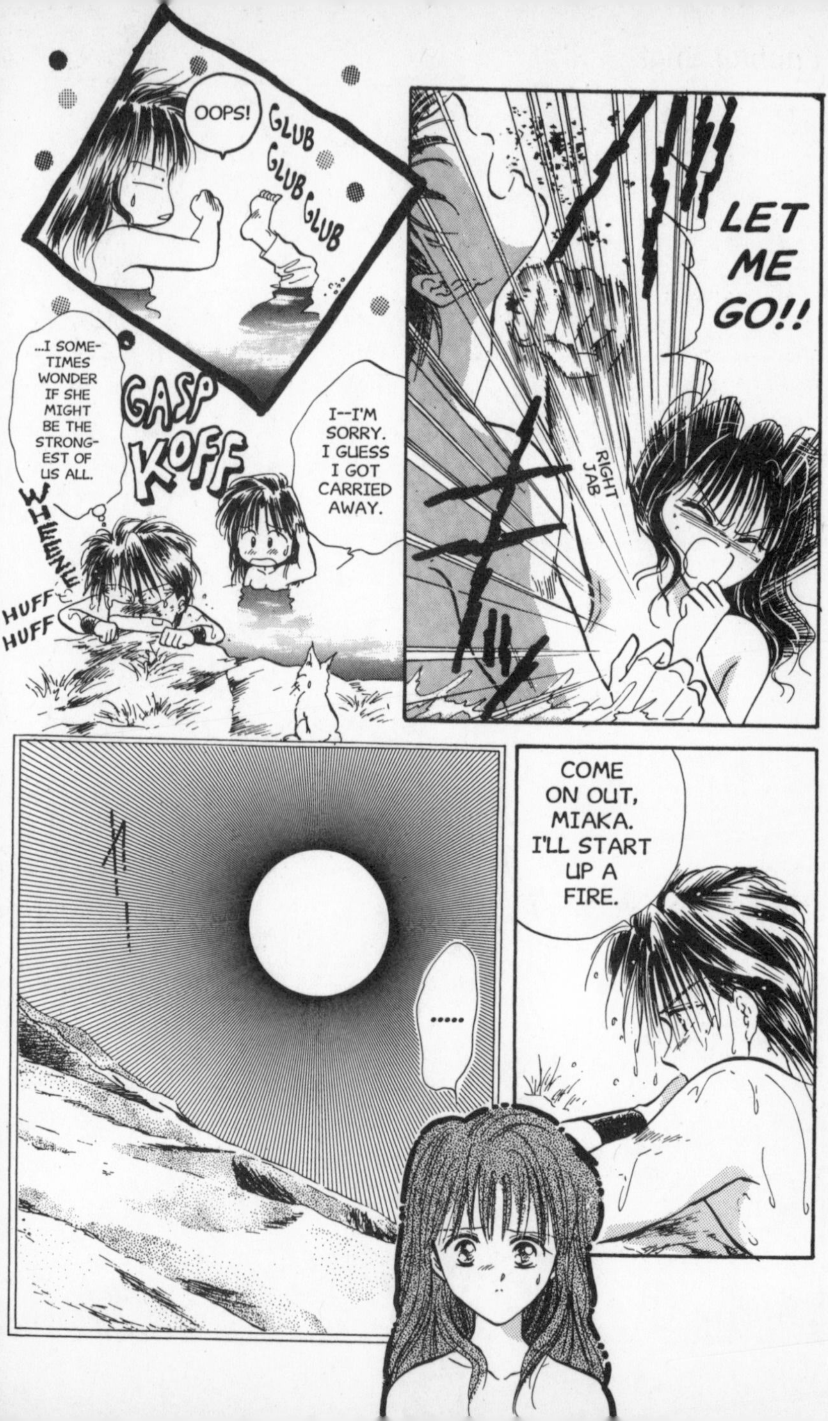
LET ME GO!!
RIGHT JAB
OOPS!
GLUB GLUB GLUB GLUB
I--I'M SORRY. I GUESS I GOT CARRIED AWAY.
GASP KOFF
...I SOMETIMES WONDER IF SHE MIGHT BE THE STRONGEST OF US ALL.
WHEEZE
HUFF HUFF
COME ON OUT, MIAKA. I'LL START UP A FIRE.
......

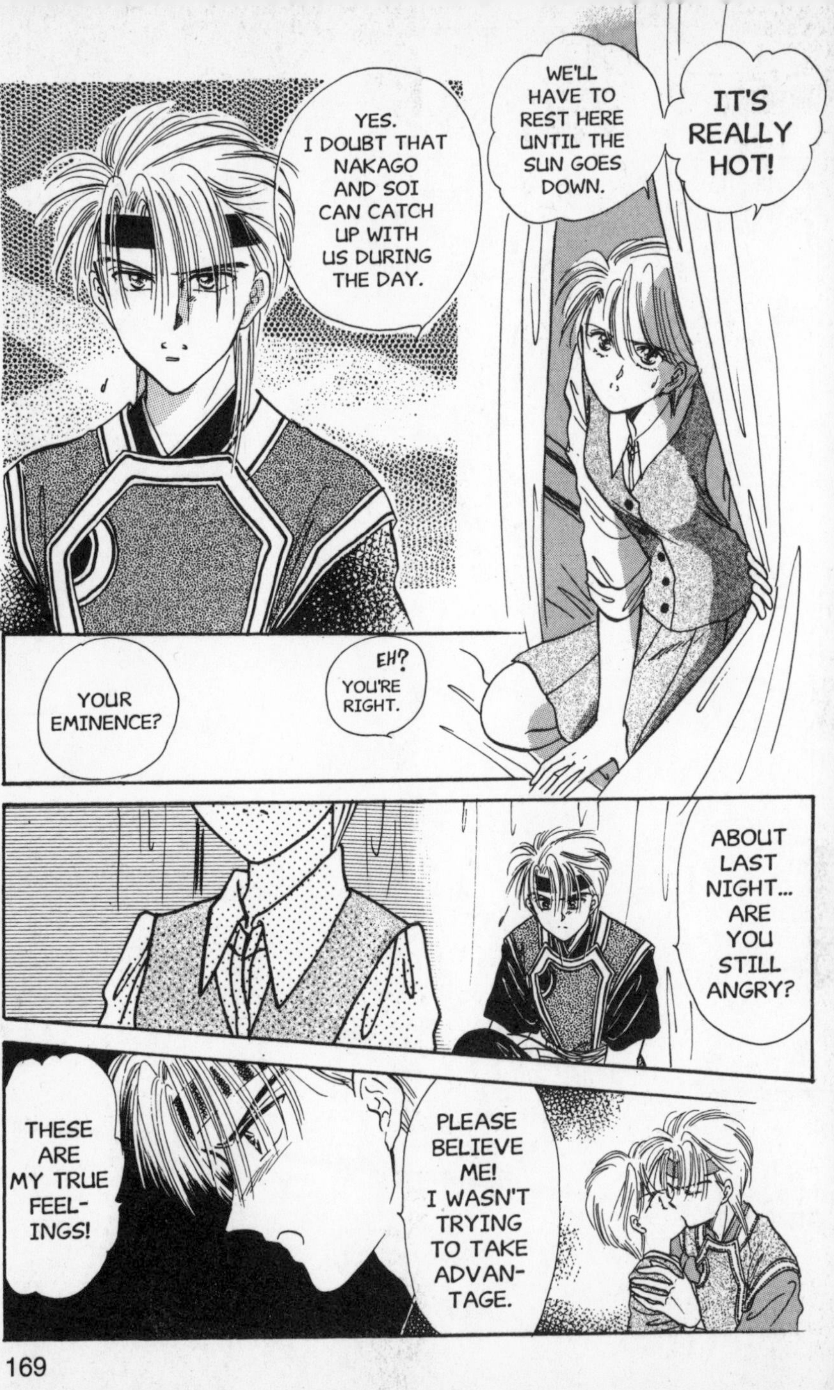
IT'S REALLY HOT!
WE'LL HAVE TO REST HERE UNTIL THE SUN GOES DOWN.
YES. I DOUBT THAT NAKAGO AND SOI CAN CATCH UP WITH US DURING THE DAY.
EH? YOU'RE RIGHT.
YOUR EMINENCE?
ABOUT LAST NIGHT... ARE YOU STILL ANGRY?
PLEASE BELIEVE ME! I WASN'T TRYING TO TAKE ADVANTAGE.
THESE ARE MY TRUE FEEL- INGS!

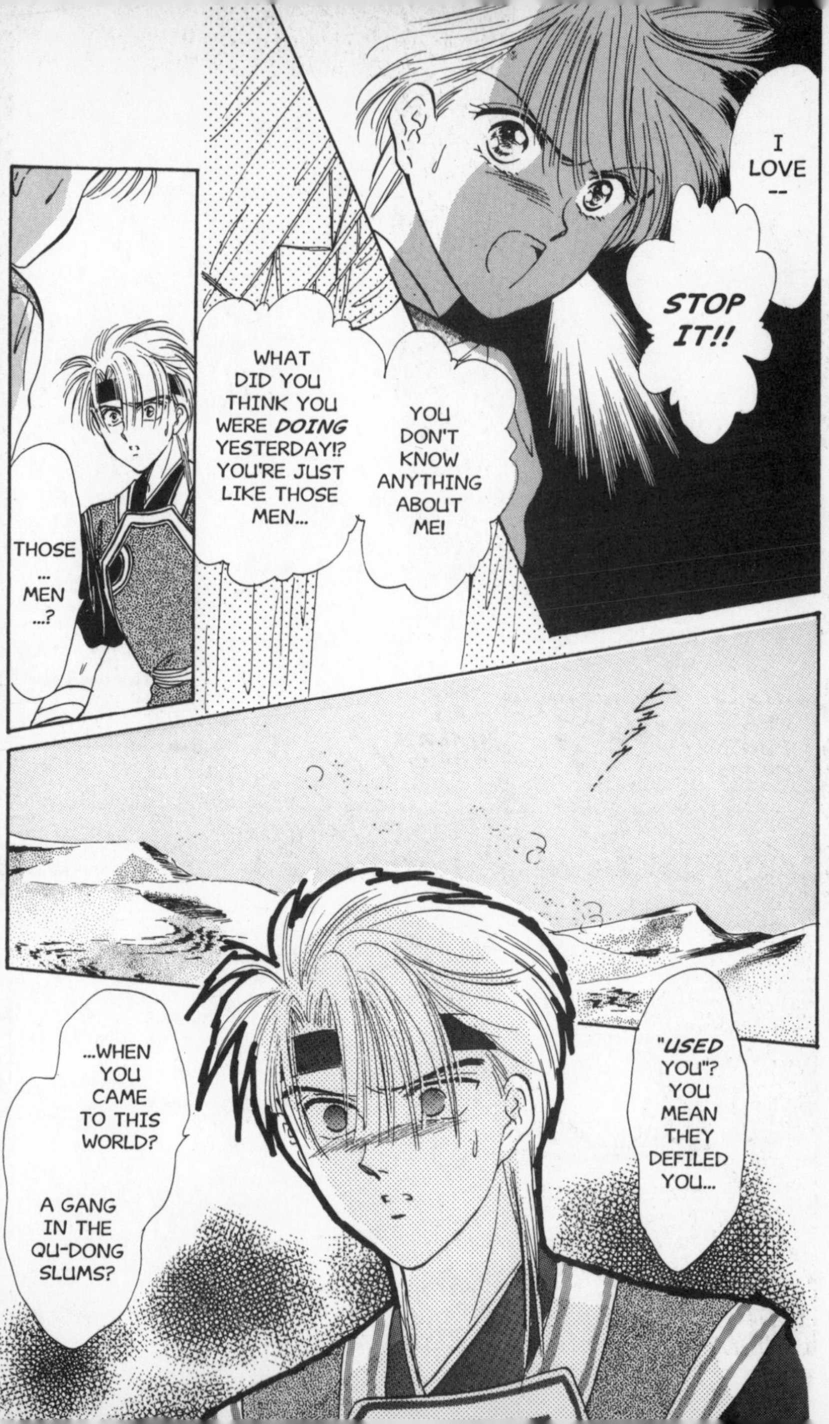
I LOVE --
STOP IT!!
YOU DON'T KNOW ANYTHING ABOUT ME!
WHAT DID YOU THINK YOU WERE *DOING* YESTERDAY!? YOU'RE JUST LIKE THOSE MEN...
THOSE ... MEN ...?
"*USED* YOU"? YOU MEAN THEY DEFILED YOU...
...WHEN YOU CAME TO THIS WORLD?
A GANG IN THE QU-DONG SLUMS?

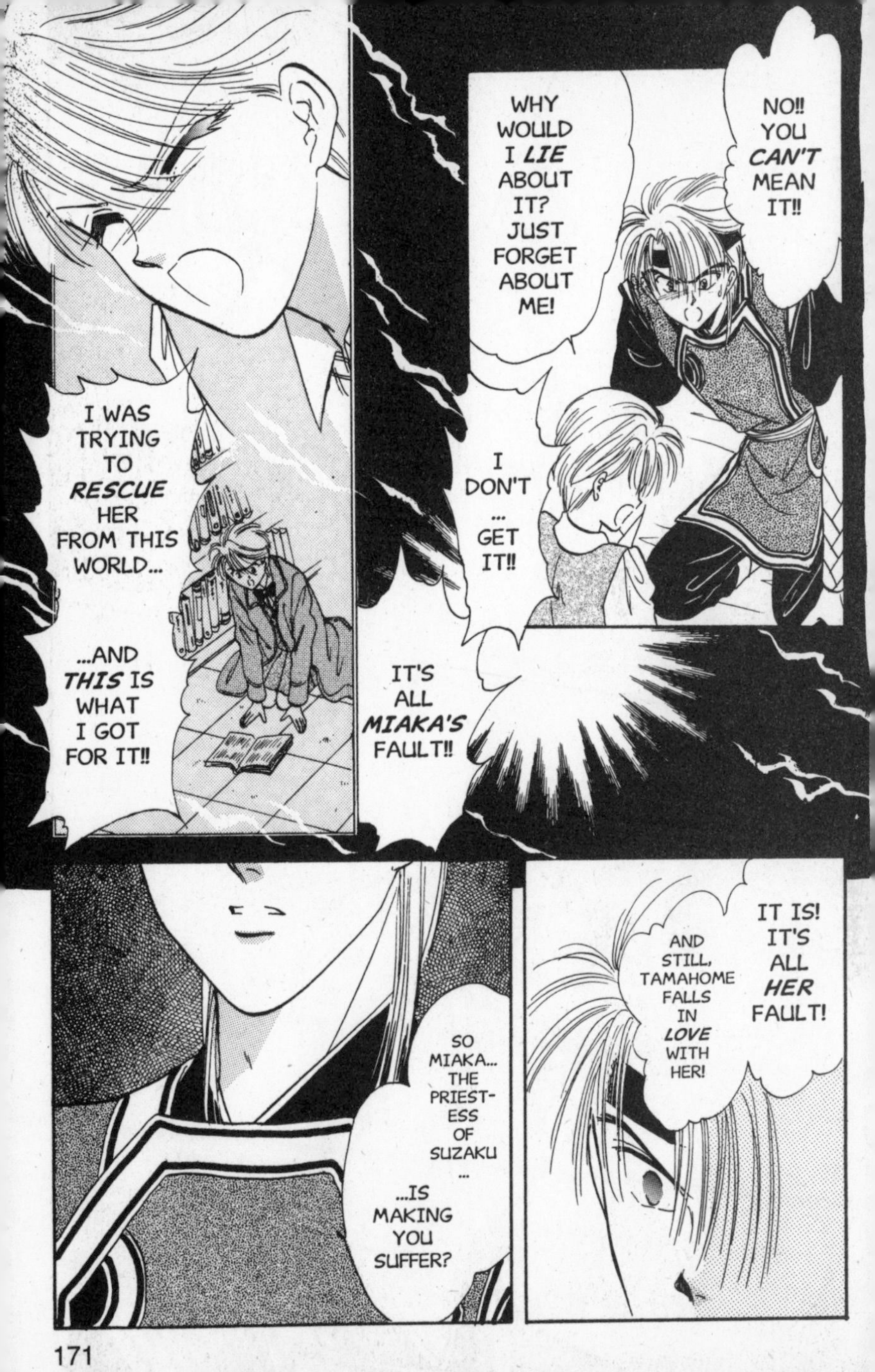
NO!! YOU CAN'T MEAN IT!!
WHY WOULD I LIE ABOUT IT? JUST FORGET ABOUT ME!
I DON'T ... GET IT!!
I WAS TRYING TO RESCUE HER FROM THIS WORLD...
...AND THIS IS WHAT I GOT FOR IT!!
IT'S ALL MIAKA'S FAULT!!
IT IS! IT'S ALL HER FAULT!
AND STILL, TAMAHOME FALLS IN LOVE WITH HER!
SO MIAKA... THE PRIEST-ESS OF SUZAKU ...
...IS MAKING YOU SUFFER?

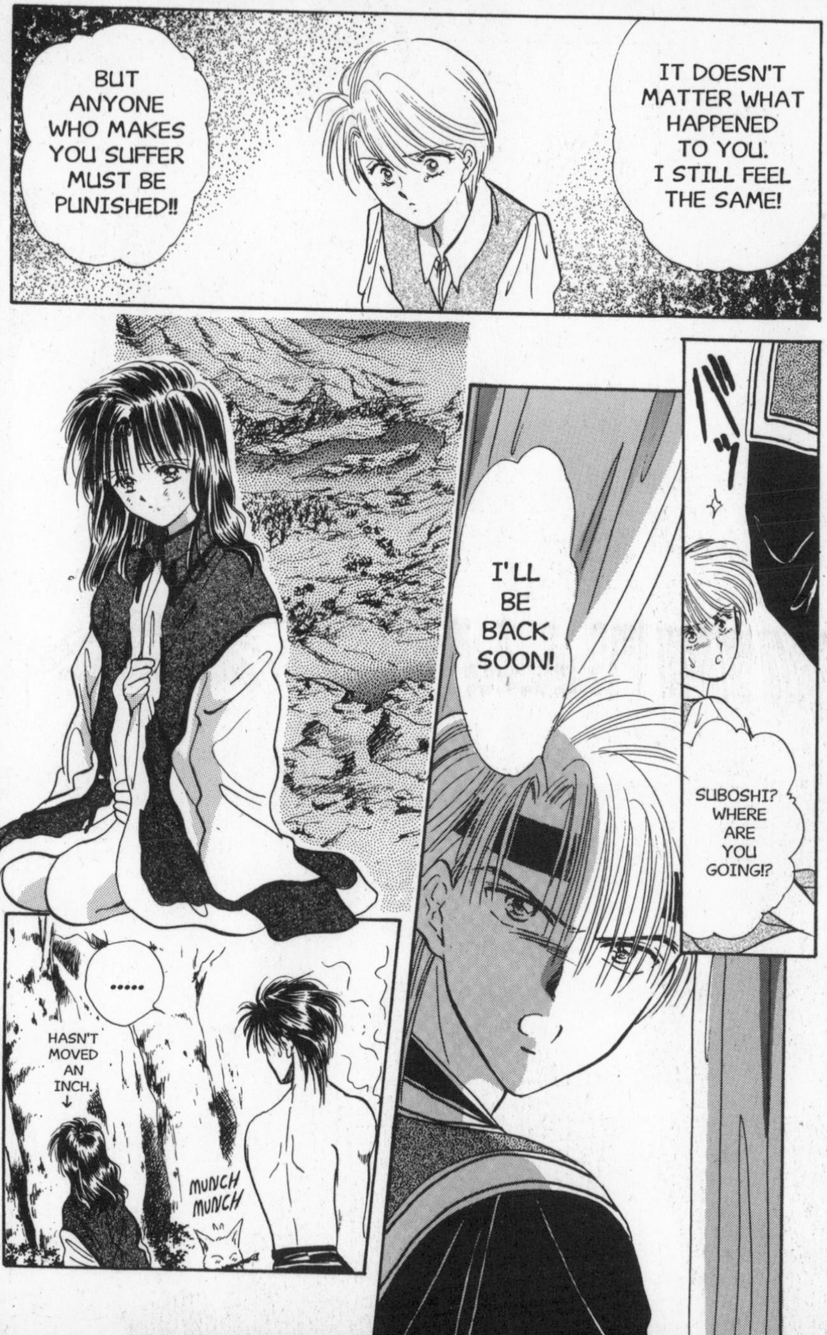
IT DOESN'T MATTER WHAT HAPPENED TO YOU. I STILL FEEL THE SAME!
BUT ANYONE WHO MAKES YOU SUFFER MUST BE PUNISHED!!
SUBOSHI? WHERE ARE YOU GOING!?
I'LL BE BACK SOON!
.....
HASN'T MOVED AN INCH.
MUNCH MUNCH

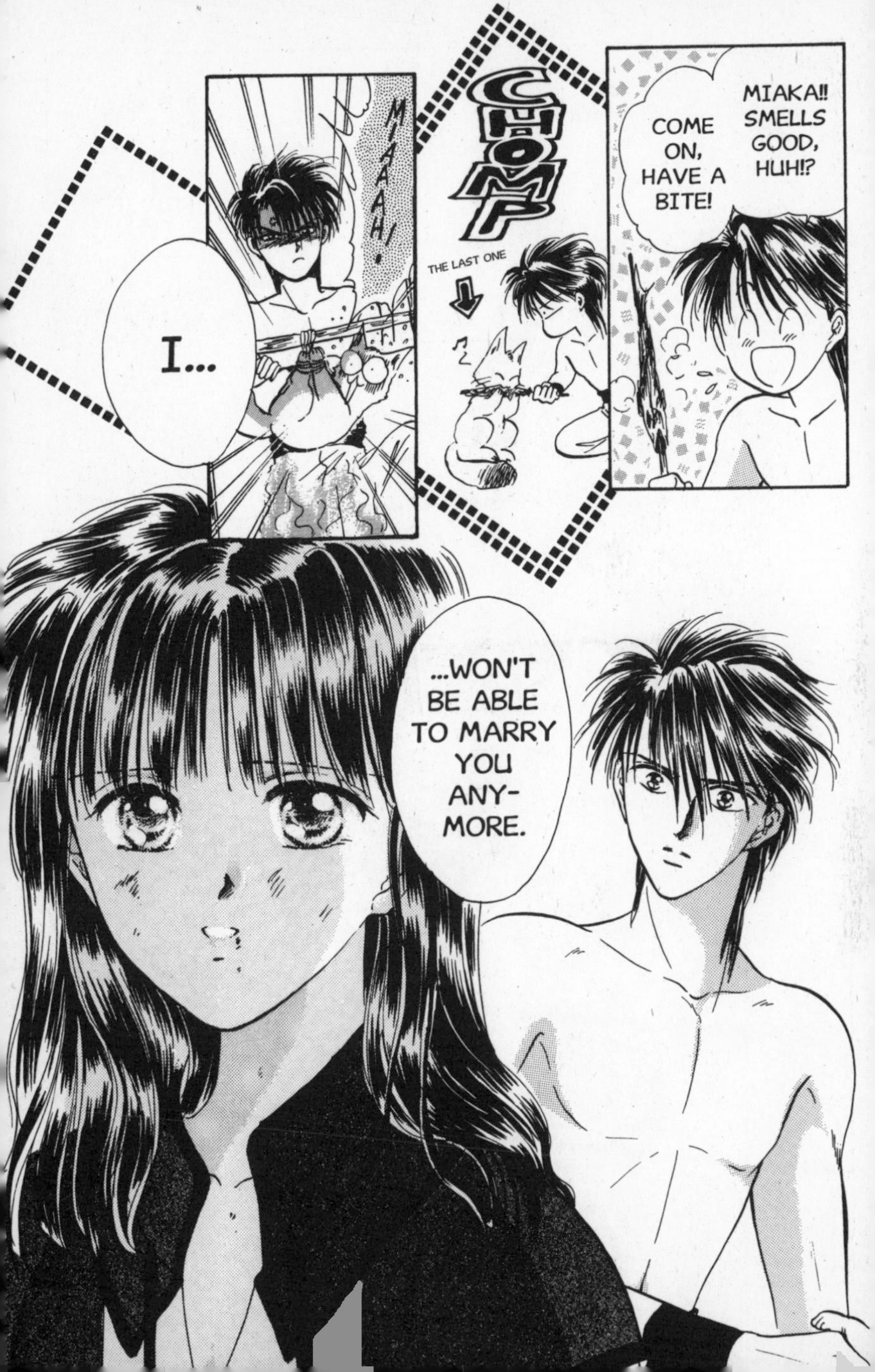
MIAKA!! SMELLS GOOD, HUH!?
COME ON, HAVE A BITE!
CHOMP
THE LAST ONE
MIAAAH!
I...
...WON'T BE ABLE TO MARRY YOU ANY-MORE.

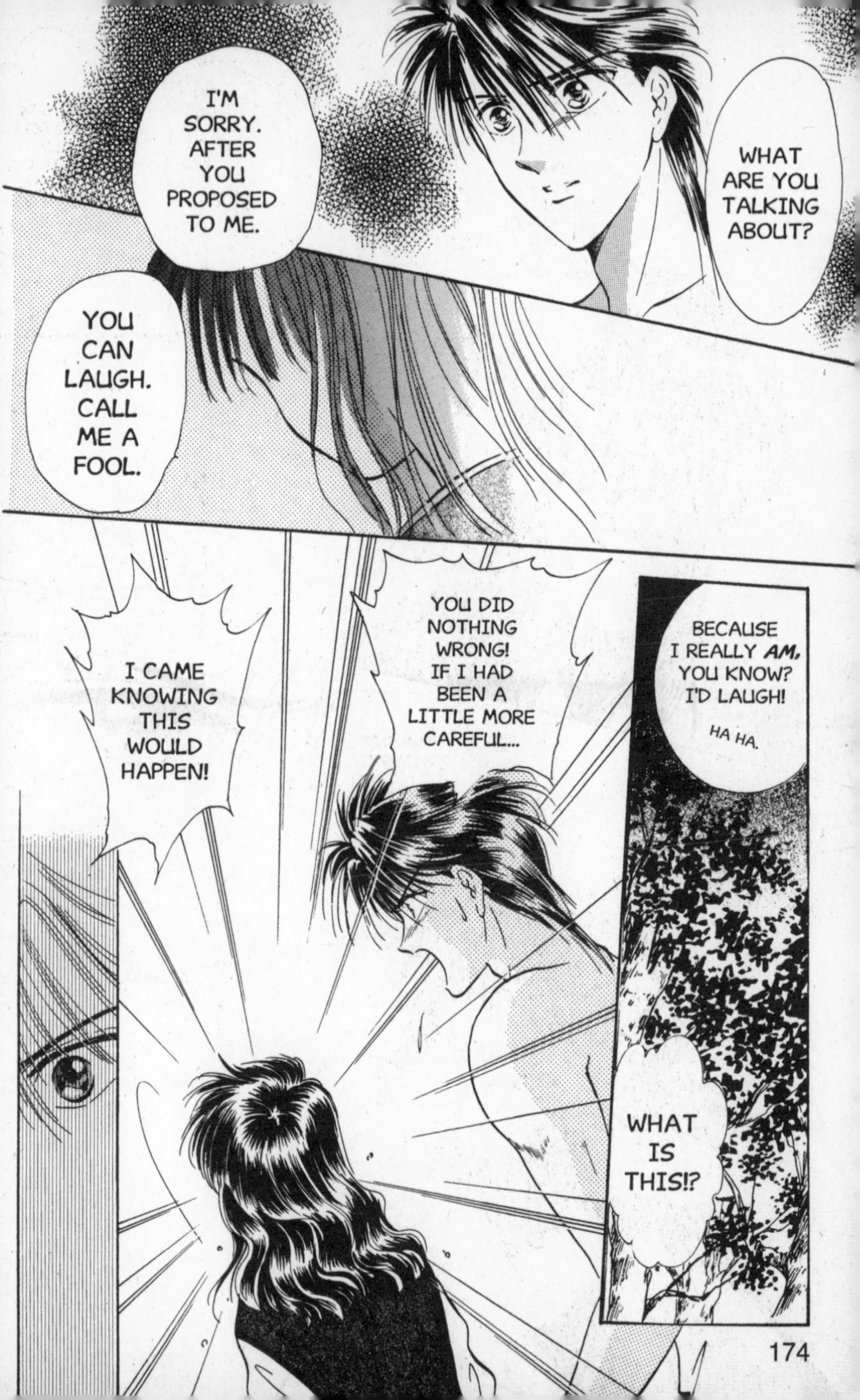
WHAT ARE YOU TALKING ABOUT?
I'M SORRY. AFTER YOU PROPOSED TO ME.
YOU CAN LAUGH. CALL ME A FOOL.
BECAUSE I REALLY *AM,* YOU KNOW? I'D LAUGH!
HA HA.
YOU DID NOTHING WRONG! IF I HAD BEEN A LITTLE MORE CAREFUL...
I CAME KNOWING THIS WOULD HAPPEN!
WHAT IS THIS!?

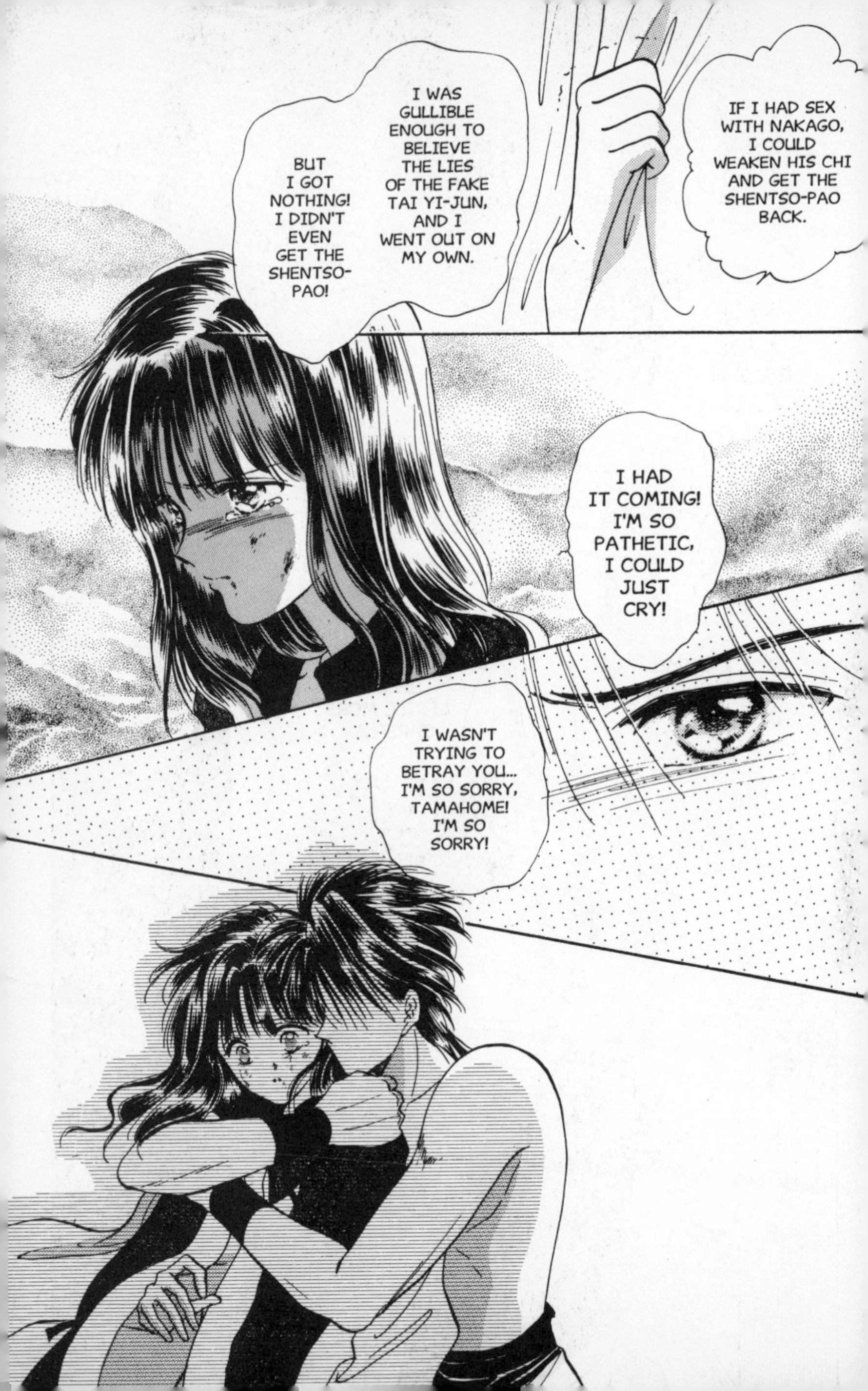
IF I HAD SEX WITH NAKAGO, I COULD WEAKEN HIS CHI AND GET THE SHENTSO-PAO BACK.
I WAS GULLIBLE ENOUGH TO BELIEVE THE LIES OF THE FAKE TAI YI-JUN, AND I WENT OUT ON MY OWN.
BUT I GOT NOTHING! I DIDN'T EVEN GET THE SHENTSO-PAO!
I HAD IT COMING! I'M SO PATHETIC, I COULD JUST CRY!
I WASN'T TRYING TO BETRAY YOU... I'M SO SORRY, TAMAHOME! I'M SO SORRY!

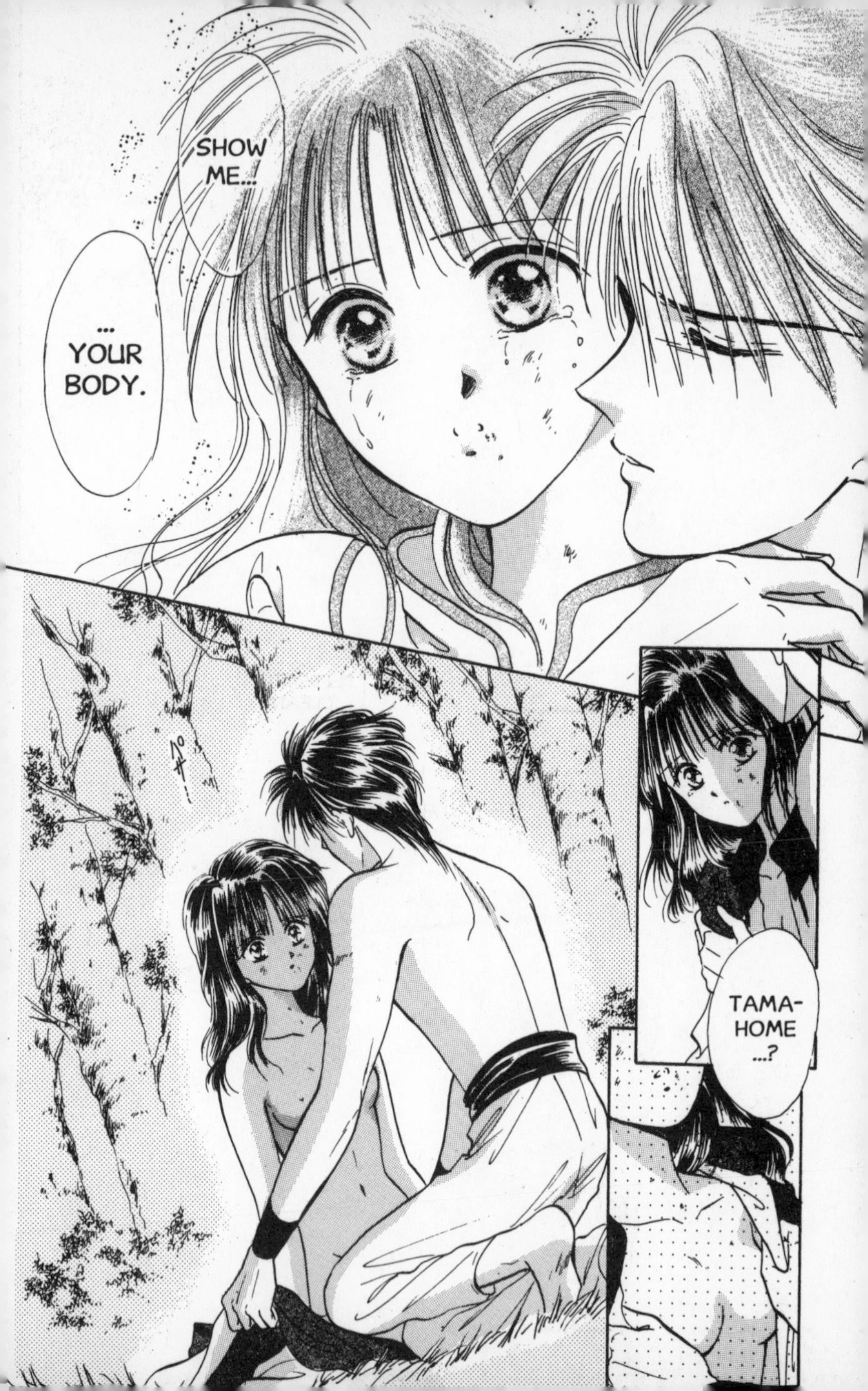
SHOW ME...
... YOUR BODY.
TAMA-HOME ...?
パサ

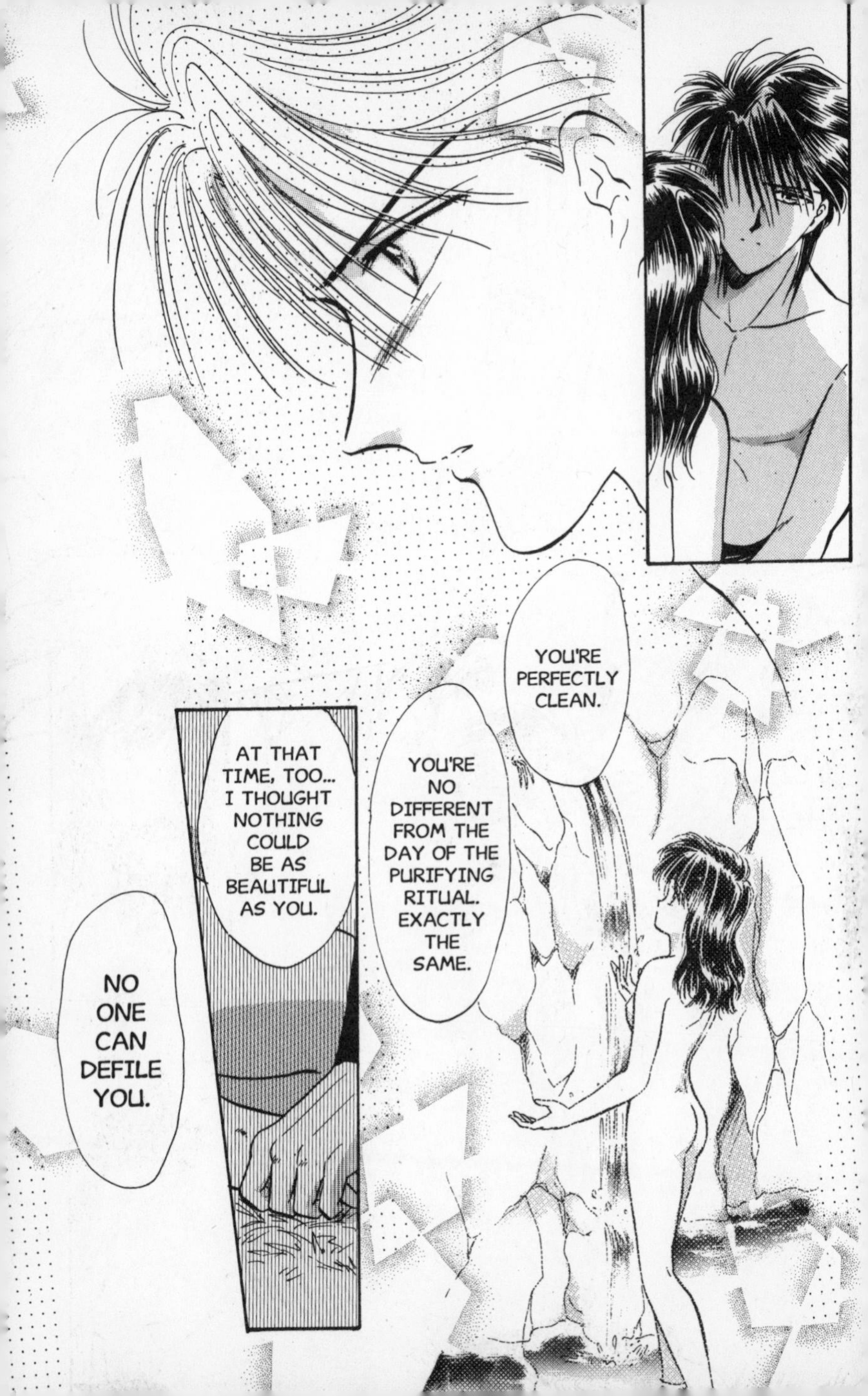
YOU'RE PERFECTLY CLEAN.
YOU'RE NO DIFFERENT FROM THE DAY OF THE PURIFYING RITUAL. EXACTLY THE SAME.
AT THAT TIME, TOO... I THOUGHT NOTHING COULD BE AS BEAUTIFUL AS YOU.
NO ONE CAN DEFILE YOU.

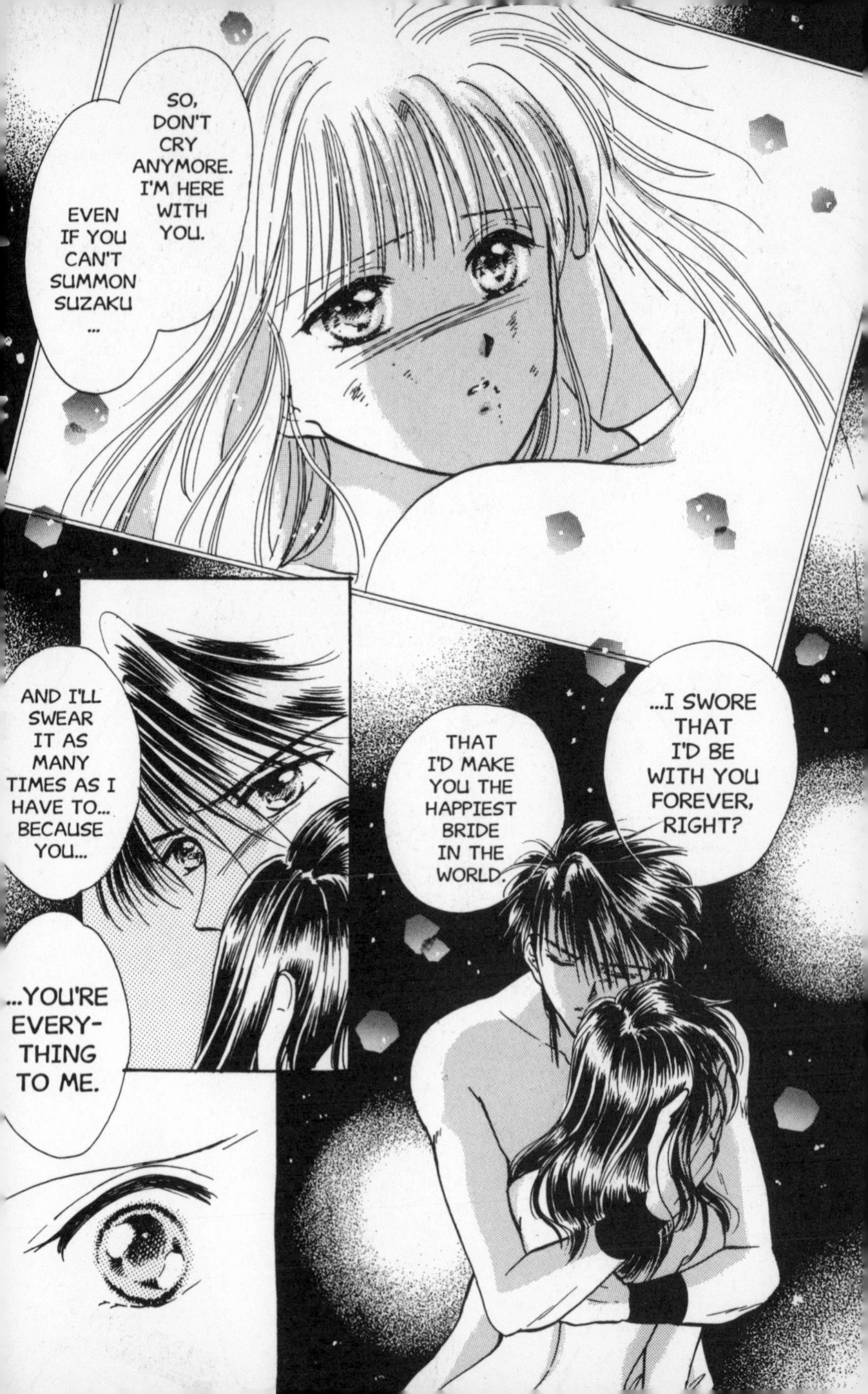
SO, DON'T CRY ANYMORE. I'M HERE WITH YOU.
EVEN IF YOU CAN'T SUMMON SUZAKU ...
...I SWORE THAT I'D BE WITH YOU FOREVER, RIGHT?
THAT I'D MAKE YOU THE HAPPIEST BRIDE IN THE WORLD.
AND I'LL SWEAR IT AS MANY TIMES AS I HAVE TO... BECAUSE YOU...
...YOU'RE EVERY-THING TO ME.

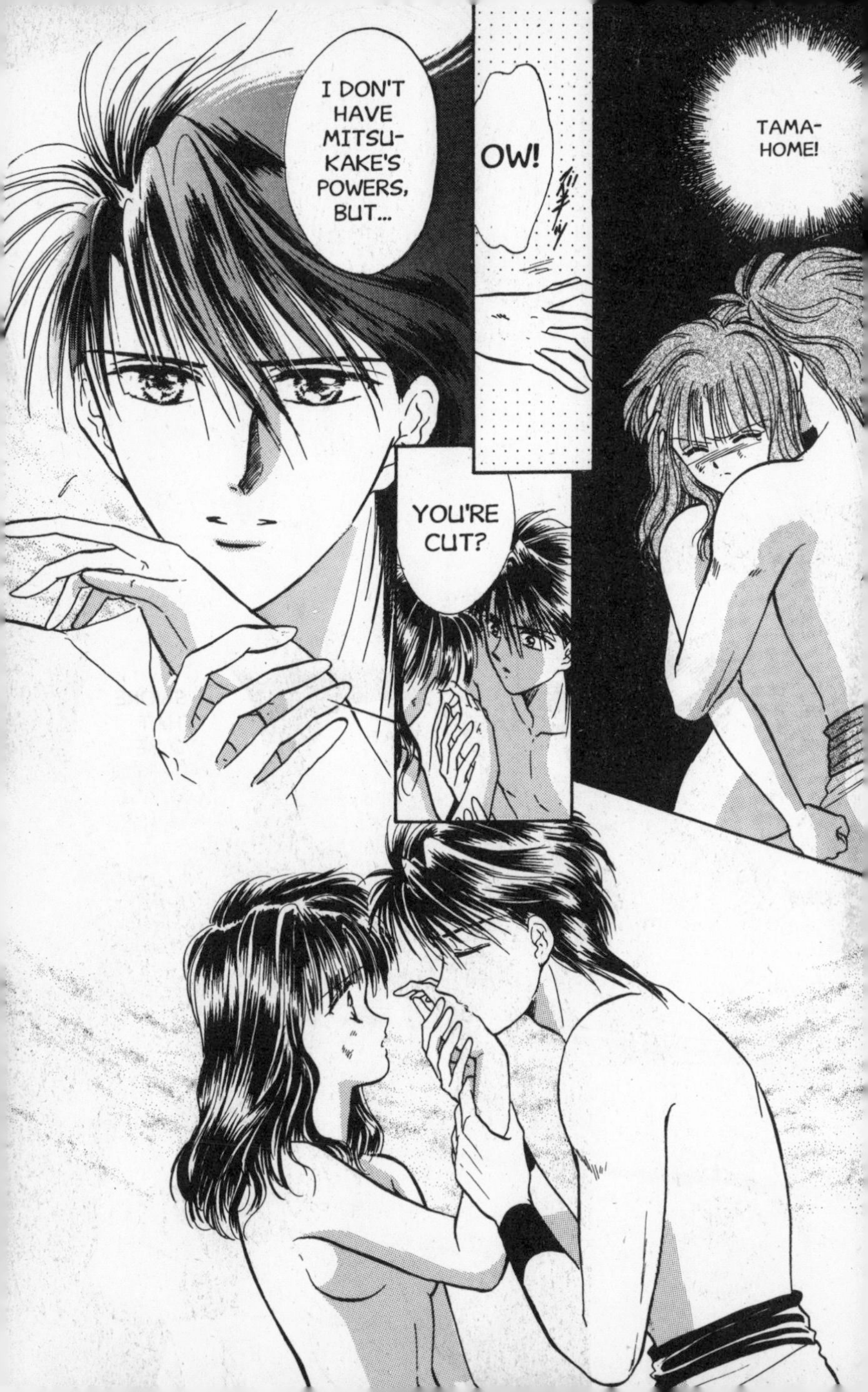

TAMA-HOME!
OW!
YOU'RE CUT?
I DON'T HAVE MITSU-KAKE'S POWERS, BUT...

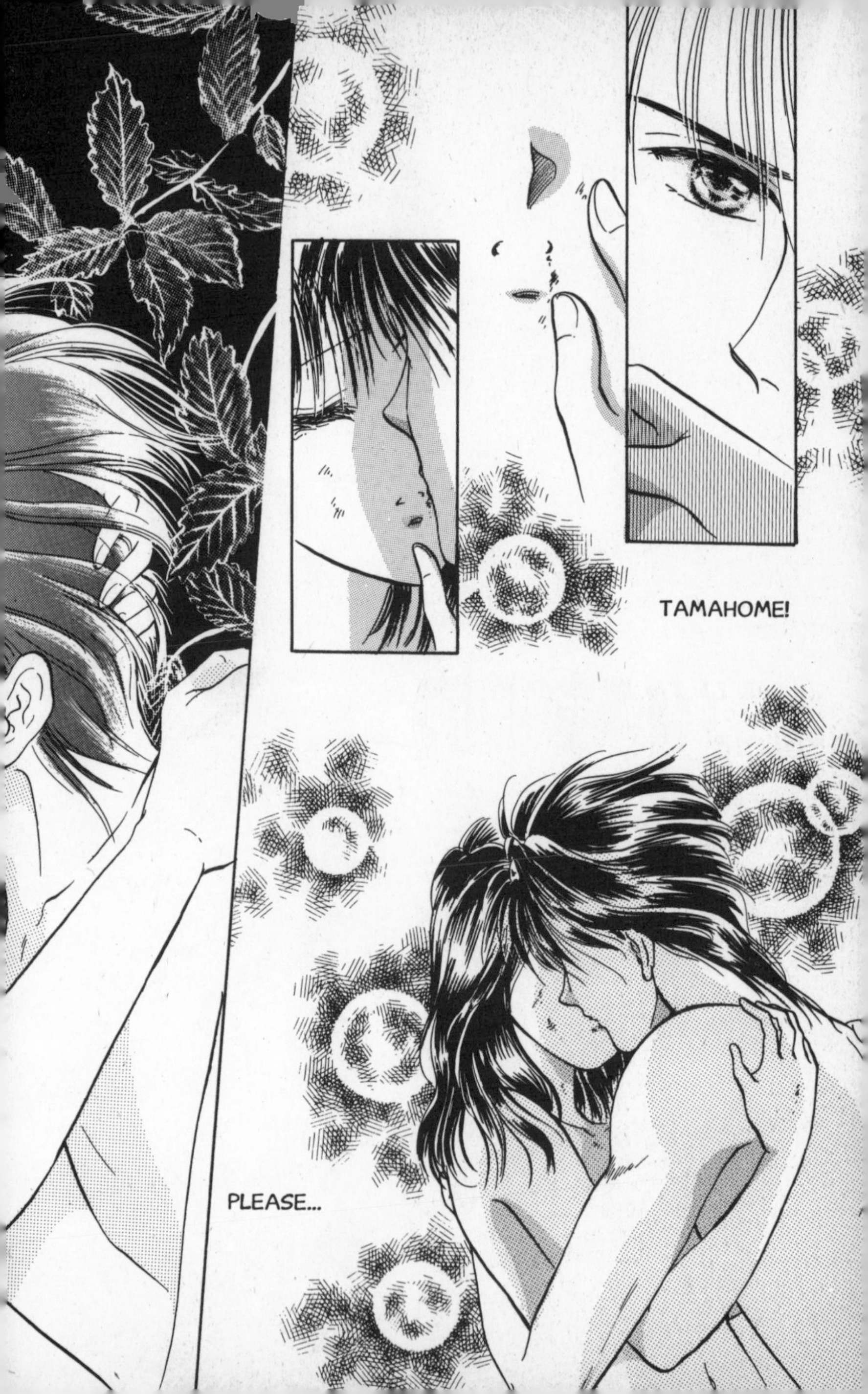
TAMAHOME!
PLEASE...

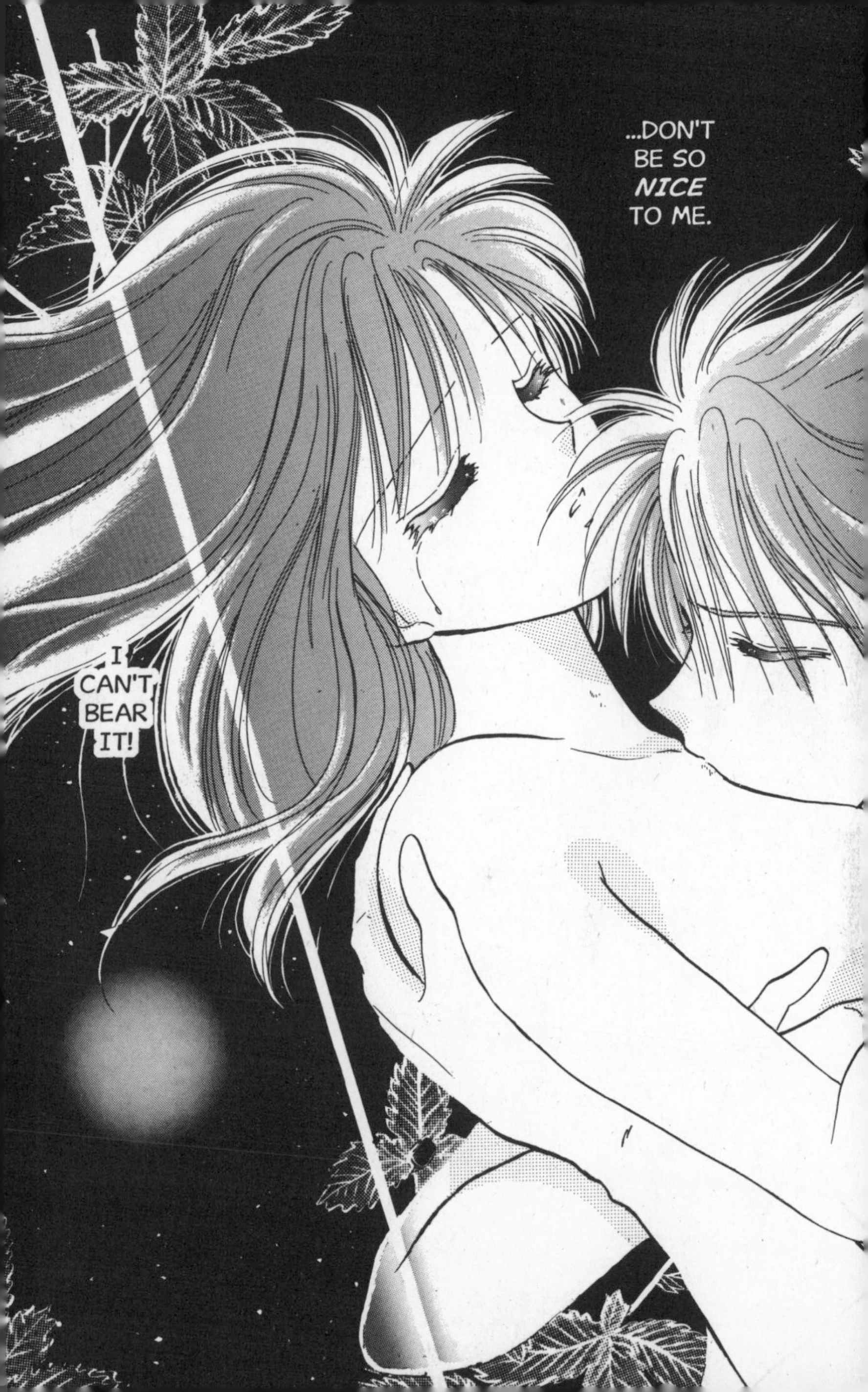
...DON'T BE SO NICE TO ME.
I CAN'T BEAR IT!

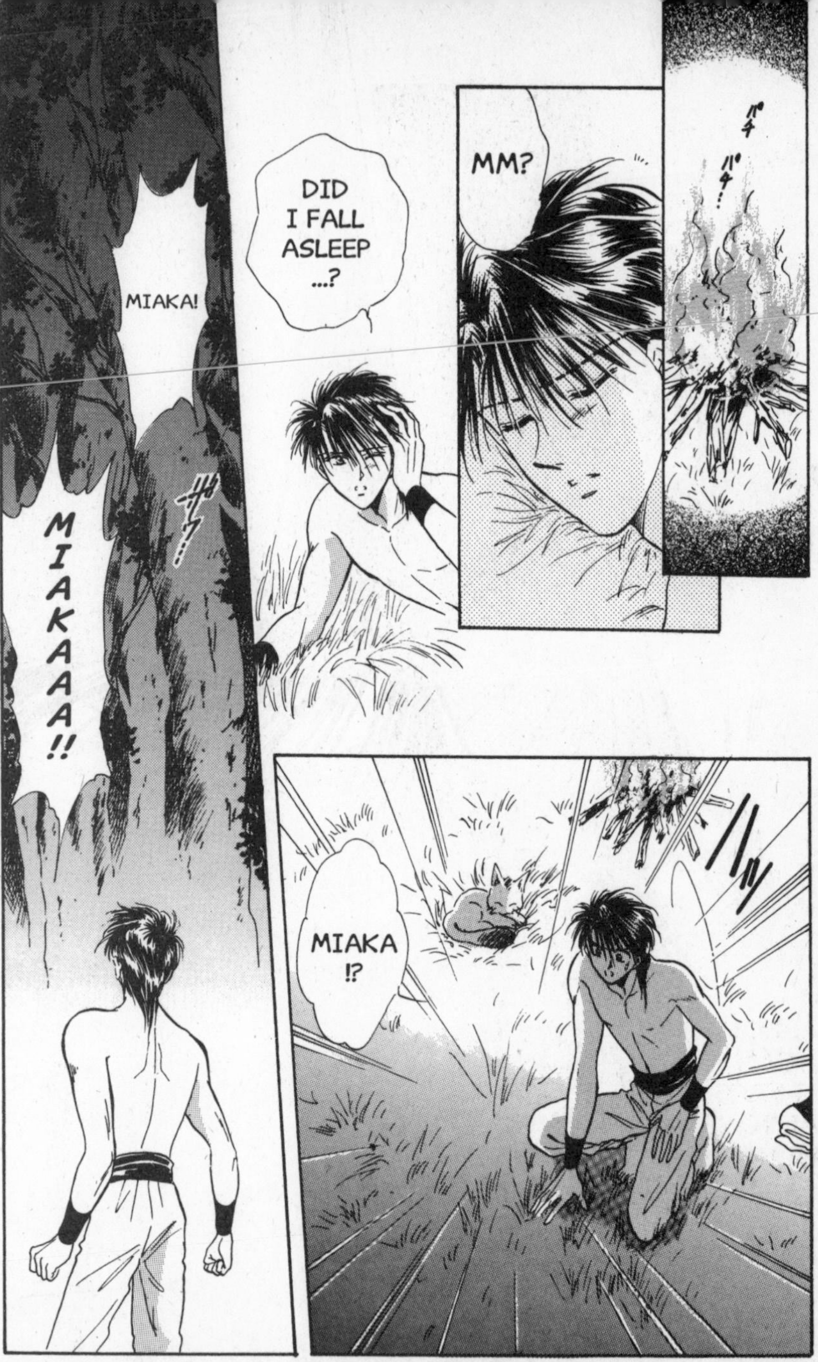
パチ
パチ…
MM?
DID I FALL ASLEEP ...?
MIAKA !?
MIAKA!
ザッ…
MIAKAAAA!!

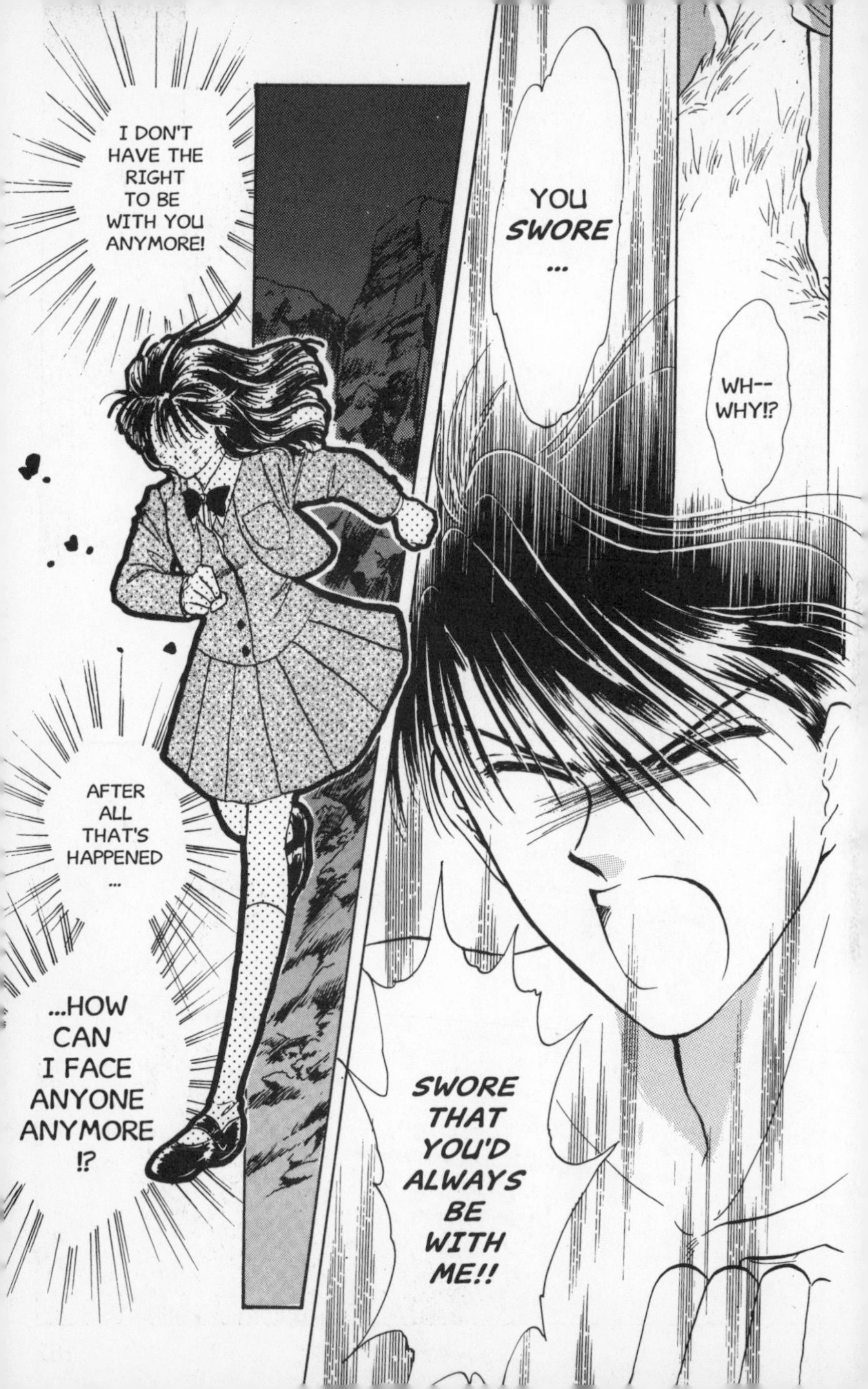
WH-- WHY!?
YOU *SWORE* ...
SWORE THAT YOU'D ALWAYS BE WITH ME!!
I DON'T HAVE THE RIGHT TO BE WITH YOU ANYMORE!
AFTER ALL THAT'S HAPPENED ...
...HOW CAN I FACE ANYONE ANYMORE !?

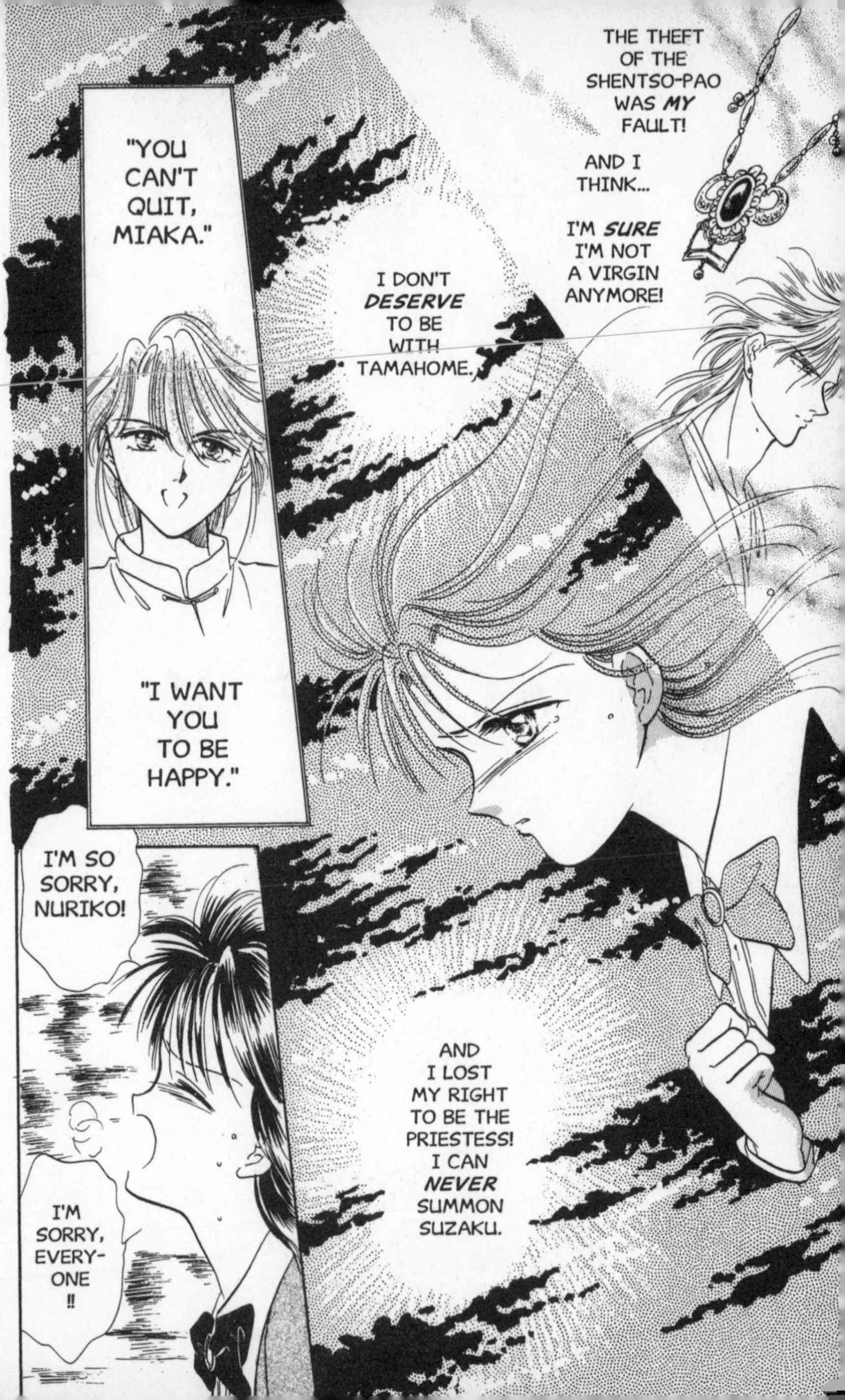
THE THEFT OF THE SHENTSO-PAO WAS *MY* FAULT!
AND I THINK...
I'M *SURE* I'M NOT A VIRGIN ANYMORE!
I DON'T *DESERVE* TO BE WITH TAMAHOME.
AND I LOST MY RIGHT TO BE THE PRIESTESS! I CAN *NEVER* SUMMON SUZAKU.
"YOU CAN'T QUIT, MIAKA."
"I WANT YOU TO BE HAPPY."
I'M SO SORRY, NURIKO!
I'M SORRY, EVERY-ONE!!

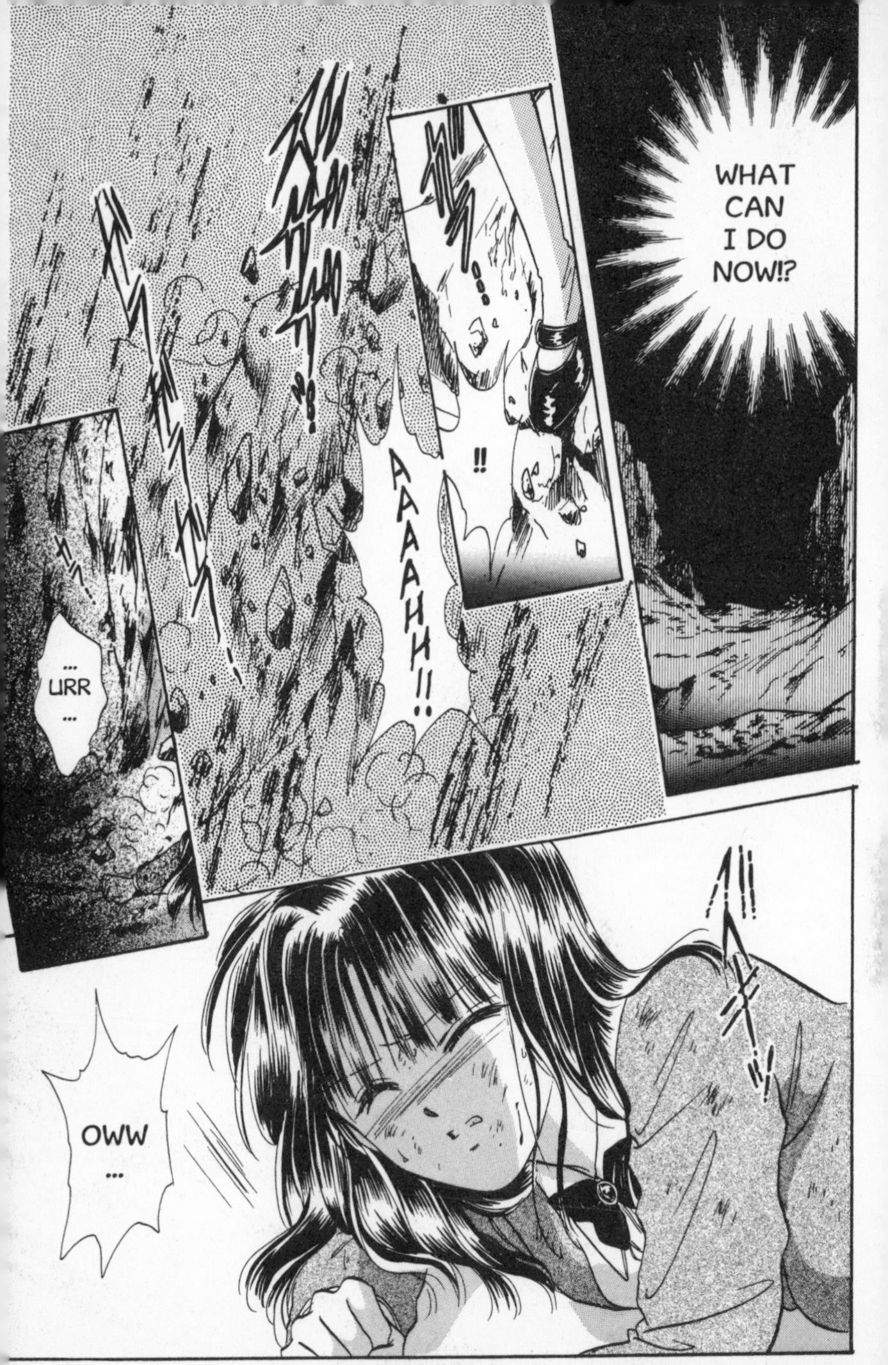
WHAT CAN I DO NOW!?
!!
AAAAHH!!
... URR ...
OWW ...

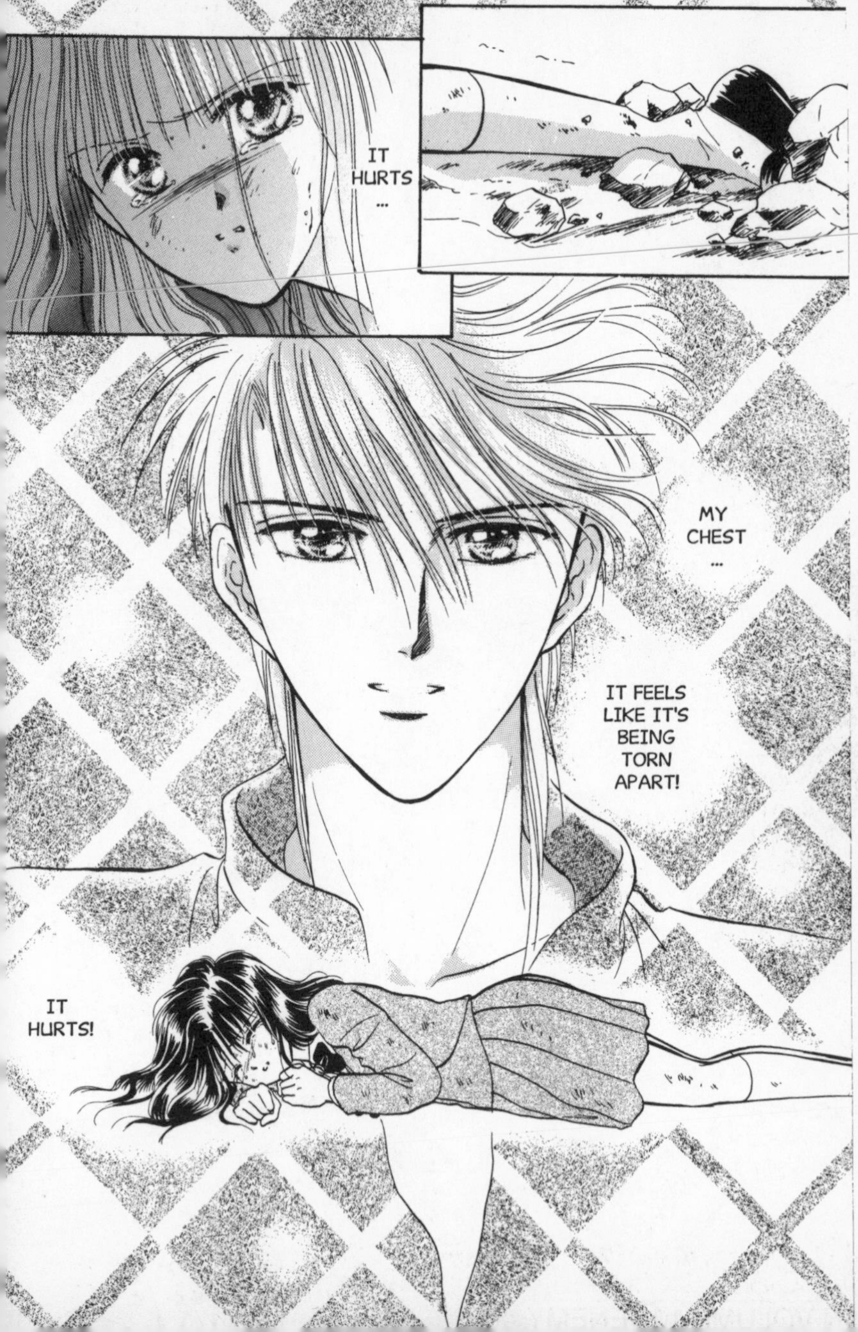
IT HURTS ...
MY CHEST ...
IT FEELS LIKE IT'S BEING TORN APART!
IT HURTS!

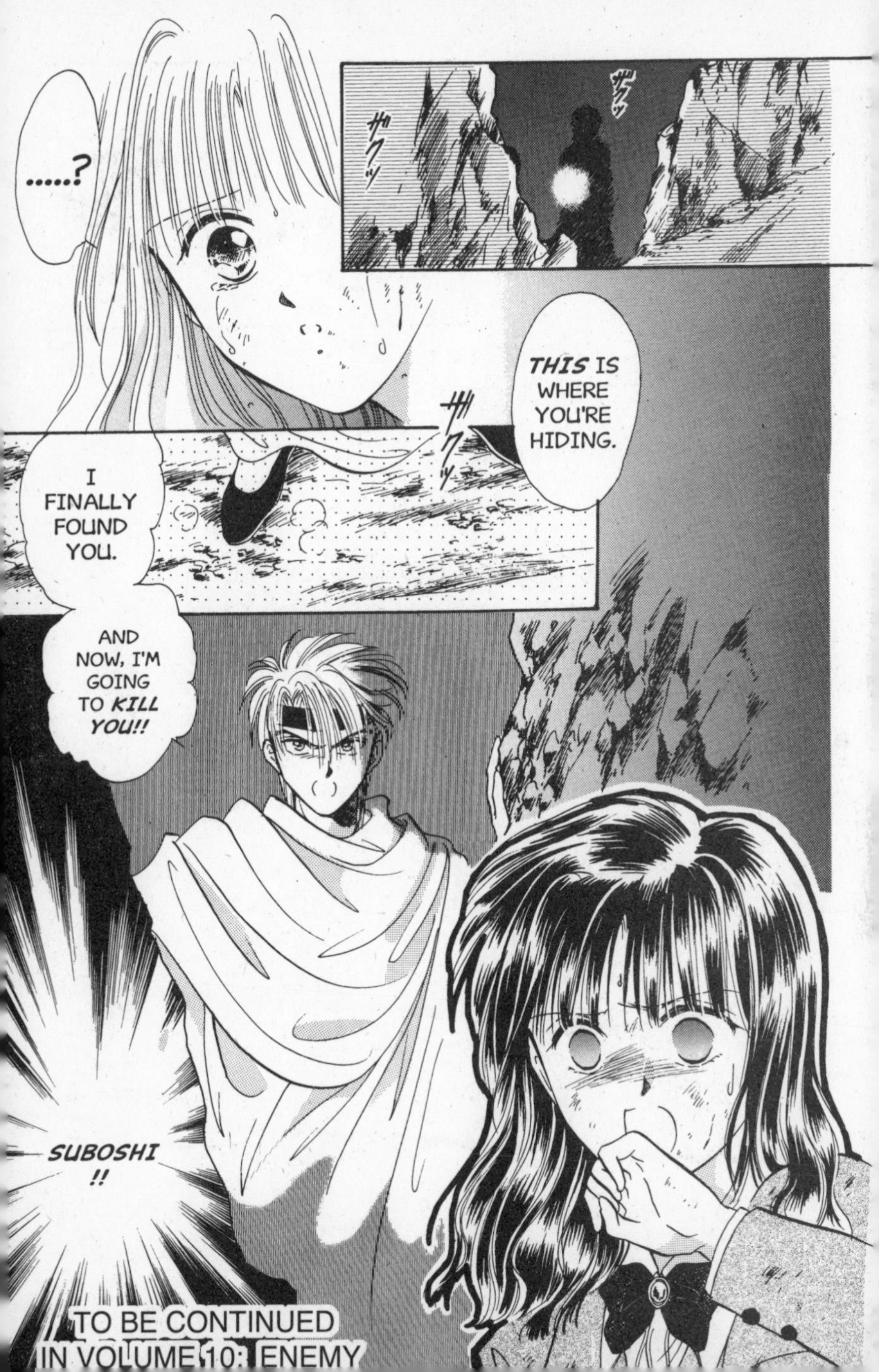

ザッ
ザクッ
......?
THIS IS WHERE YOU'RE HIDING.
ザクッ
I FINALLY FOUND YOU.
AND NOW, I'M GOING TO KILL YOU!!
SUBOSHI!!
TO BE CONTINUED IN VOLUME 10: ENEMY

ABOUT THE AUTHOR

Yuu Watase was born on March 5 in a town near Osaka,
Japan, and she was raised there before moving to Tokyo to
follow her dream of creating manga. In the decade since
her debut short story, *PAJAMA DE OJAMA* ("An Intrusion
in Pajamas"), she has produced more than 50 compiled
volumes of short stories and continuing series. Her latest
series, *ZETTAI KARESHI* ("He'll Be My Boyfriend"), is cur-
rently running in the anthology magazine SHÔJO COMIC.
Watase's long-running horror/romance story *CERES:
CELESTIAL LEGEND* and her most recent completed series,
ALICE 19TH, are now available in North America published
by VIZ. She loves science fiction, fantasy and comedy.

The Fushigi Yûgi Guide to Sound Effects

Most of the sound effects in *FUSHIGI YÛGI* are the way Yuu Watase created them, in their original Japanese.

We created this glossary for a page-by-page, panel-by-panel explanation of the action and background noises. By using this guide, you may even learn some Japanese.

The glossary lists page and panel number. For example, page 1, panel 3, would be listed as 1.3.

30.2	FX:	HA [gasp]
30.3	FX:	BA [arrows shooting]
31.3	FX:	HA [gasp]

CHAPTER FIFTY: ICE GUARDIANS

35.1	FX:	POU [glow]
35.2	FX:	POU [glow]
36.3	FX:	SU [taking out arrows]
36.4	FX:	BABABA [arrows flying]
37.1	FX:	SUTO [duck]
37.2	FX:	HYOOOOO [wind blowing]
37.3	FX:	SU [raising hand]
37.4	FX:	DA [dashing forward]
37.5	FX:	KA [light flashing]
38.1	FX:	BA [whoosh]
38.2	FX:	GA GA [grab grab]
38.4	FX:	PIKI PIKI PIKI [icing over]
39.2	FX:	JU [sizzle]
39.5	FX:	GYU [grasp]
40.2	FX:	DOKUN [ba-dump]
41.1	FX:	KAAA [energy blast charging up]
41.3	FX:	DA [dashing forward]
41.4	FX:	BYU [vwoosh]
41.5	FX:	GOO [blast]
42.1	FX:	BA [fling]
42.3	FX:	BO [vwoosh]
42.5	FX:	GYUUUU [spinning, squeezing]
43.1	FX:	CHUIIN [spinning, cutting into clothes]
43.3	FX:	BAKI [crush]
43.4	FX:	SUU [fluid, circular motion]

CHAPTER FORTY-NINE: VALLEY OF TEARS

6.3	FX:	KYU [crunch]
7.1	FX:	BYOOOOOO [wind blowing]
7.2	FX:	PIKU [jolt]
8.5	FX:	SU [slipping off mask]
10.1	FX:	BYUUUU [wind blowing]
12.1	FX:	BA [fwoosh]
13.2	FX:	SHAN [ching]
14.3	FX:	PASHA [splash]
14.4	FX:	PASHA [splash]
14.5	FX:	SU [quietly raising hand]
15.2	FX:	SU [wounds disappearing]
16.5	FX:	ZA [crunch]
18.3	FX:	GASHI [grab]
19.1	FX:	ZA [stopping suddenly]
22.3	FX:	HYUUU [wind blowing]
22.4	FX:	ZAKU ZAKU [dig dig]
24.5	FX:	ZAKU [dig]
24.7	FX:	ZAKU [dig]
25.3	FX:	ZA [shovel]
28.2	FX:	GII [creak]
29.1	FX:	BATAAN [slam]
29.2	FX:	GASHAN [crash]
	FX:	DOTA [thud]
29.4	FX:	BO [whoosh]

62.2	FX:	KAAAA [glow]
63.1	FX:	KAAAA [glow]
63.2	FX:	GUGU [grip]
63.3	FX:	PAKI [ice breaking]
63.4	FX:	PAKI PAKI PAKI [ice cracking]
63.5	FX:	PISHI PISHI [ice breaking off]
64.1	FX:	PAAAAAN [burst]
65.4	FX:	SU [motioning silently]
65.5	FX:	GALA [crumble]
66.4	FX:	MUGYU [squeeze]
68.5	FX:	KATSUUUN KATSUUUN [clomp clomp]
69.5	FX:	GIII [creak]
	FX:	DOKI DOKI DOKI DOKI [ba-dump ba-dump ba-dump ba-dump]

CHAPTER FIFTY-ONE:
A HAZARDOUS BARGAIN

72.2	FX:	BYUUUU [wind blowing]
72.4	FX:	PIKU [twitch]
73.1	FX:	GIII [creak]
73.4	FX:	DOKI DOKI DOKI [ba-dump ba-dump ba-dump]
74.1	FX:	KACHI KOCHI [body tensing up]
75.1	FX:	JALA [chink]
78.1	FX:	PIKU [ping]
79.5	FX:	GALA GALA [crumble crumble]
80.4	FX:	SUTA SUTA [stomp stomp]
82.3	FX:	GII [creak]
82.4	FX:	BATAAAN [slam]
83.3	FX:	GII [creak]
83.5	FX:	HA [gasp]
84.1	FX:	BA [shake]
84.2	FX:	TSU [trickle]
85.3	FX:	BA [vroom]

44.1	FX:	DON [burst of flame]
44.4	FX:	SU [passing through]
45.1	FX:	SU [passing through]
45.3	FX:	GOOOO [roaring flames]
45.4	FX:	NIYA [sneer]
45.5	FX:	JYU [water sizzling and evaporating]
48.3	FX:	DOKI DOKI DOKI DOKI [ba-dump ba-dump ba-dump ba-dump]
49.1	FX:	SU [motioning quietly]
51.2	FX:	BA [arrows whizzing by]
52.2-4	FX:	DOKUN DOKUN DOKUN DOKUN DOKUN DOKUN DOKUN DOKUN DOKUN DOKUN [ba-dump ba-dump ba-dump ba-dump ba-dump ba-dump ba-dump ba-dump ba-dump ba-dump]
55.4	FX:	GALI GALI GALI [scratch scratch scratch]
56.1	FX:	BA [tearing off clothes]
56.2	FX:	SULU [slipping off clothes]
	FX:	BASA BASA [clothes falling to floor]
56.3	FX:	GACHI GACHI [shiver shiver]
56.4	FX:	HYUUU [wind blowing]
56.5	FX:	ZOKU [shudder]
57.1	FX:	KACHI KACHI KACHI KACHI [ice forming]
57.2	FX:	BIKUN [jolt]
58.1	FX:	KACHI KACHI KACHI [ice forming]
58.5	FX:	DON DON DON DON [bam bam bam bam]
59.2	FX:	GACHI GACHI GACHI [shiver shiver shiver]
59.4	FX:	PIKI PIKI PIKI [shake shake shake]
60.1	FX:	PIKI [being iced over]
60.2	FX:	ZULU [slump]
61.1-4	FX:	DOKUN DOKUN DOKUN DOKUN DOKUN DOKUN DOKUN DOKUN DOKUN [ba-dump ba-dump ba-dump ba-dump ba-dump ba-dump ba-dump ba-dump ba-dump]

112-3.1	FX: KACHAN [clank]
112-3.2-3	FX: DOKUN DOKUN DOKUN DOKUN [ba-dump ba-dump ba-dump ba-dump]
112-3.4	FX: GUI [grab]
112-3.6	FX: GALI [biting lip]
114.1	FX: TSUU [drip]
114.3	FX: KIIIN [kreeeee]
	FX: GU [stopping midstep]
114.4	FX: BASHI [smack]
115.1	FX: GUGU [squash]
115.3	FX: FU [pressure letting up]
115.4	FX: PAN [slap]
118.1	FX: GUI [grab]
118.5	FX: BASHA [splash]
119.2	FX: DAN [push]
121.2	FX: SU [extending hand]
121.4	FX: PAKA [shell opening]
121.5	FX: PAA [glow]
122.4	FX: BASHI [smack]
123.2	FX: JALA [chink]
123.3	FX: DA [dashing off]
123.4	FX: PITA [stop]
123.5	FX: BASHI [force field repelling]
124.1	FX: BALI BALI BALI [crackle crackle crackle]
124.3	FX: SU [raising hand]
125.1	FX: GU [clench]
125.2	FX: BI [rip]
126.2	FX: HIHIIIN [neigh]
126.3	FX: KOTSU KOTSU [clomp clomp]
126.4	FX: KOTSU KOTSU [clomp clomp]

CHAPTER FIFTY-THREE: DEFILED LOVE

130.2	FX: GAKU GAKU GAKU [tremble tremble tremble]
	FX: SUUU [stroke]
130.3	FX: GU [grab]
132.2	FX: DOKUN [ba-dump]

86.2	FX: SU [disappearing into the mist]
86.3	FX: ZAZA [rustle]
86.4	FX: DOSA [thud]
86.5	FX: FU [disappearing into the mist]
	FX: GYU [clench]
87.3	FX: ZAWA [leaves rustling]
88.3	FX: PITA [stopping in place]
89.1	FX: ZA [zoom]
90.5	FX: SHUUU [attack energy dissipating]
91.1	FX: SHUUU [attack energy dissipating]
94.1	FX: ...DOKUN DOKUN DOKUN DOKUN DOKUN DOKUN [ba-dump ba-dump ba-dump ba-dump ba-dump ba-dump]
95.2	FX: BIKU [jolt]
96.1	FX: DOKUN DOKUN [ba-dump ba-dump]
96.3	FX: SU [standing up quickly]

CHAPTER FIFTY-TWO: MIRAGE OF HELL

101.1	FX: ZA [crunch]
102.5	FX: FU [disappearing]
103.6	FX: BASA [clothes dropping]
106.1	FX: KAPO KAPO [clop clop]
106.2	FX: KAPO KAPO [clop clop]
106.3	FX: GUI [yank]
106.4	FX: HIHIIIN [neigh]
107.2	FX: GASA [rustle]
108.4	FX: SHAKA SHAKA SHAKA SHAKA [shuffle shuffle shuffle shuffle]
108.5	FX: PITA [stopping in place]
108.6	FX: KASHA [klink]
109.2	FX: SOU [sneak]
109.3	FX: SU [step]
111.6	FX: PITA [stop]

132.3 FX: DOKUN DOKUN DOKUN DOKUN DOKUN DOKUN [ba-dump ba-dump ba-dump ba-dump ba-dump ba-dump]

135.3 FX: GUGU [groan]

136.1 FX: FUWA [float]
136.2 FX: DOKA [thud]
136.3 FX: GULA [faint]

137.1 FX: PATA [ka-tunk]
137.2 FX: GUI [grab]

139.2 FX: BAKI [bam]
139.5 FX: PAN [whack]

140.2 FX: DOKA DOKA [kick kick]

142.5 FX: BASHI BASHI [smack smack]

143.1 FX: DAN [bam]
143.4 FX: BASA [whish]

144.2 FX: HIHIIN [neigh]
FX: PIKU [ping]
144.3 FX: SU [silently rising]
144.4 FX: ZA [crunch]

145.2 FX: BA [clench]
145.4 FX: PIKU [twitch]

146.2 FX: SU [swoosh]
146.3 FX: DOSU [punch]
146.5 FX: ZULU [slip]

147.4 FX: GYU [tremble]

148-9.2 FX: KA [flash]
148-9.3 FX: GUO [blast]

150.2 FX: BOTA BOTA [thud thud]
150.3 FX: SHUUU [sizzle]

151.2 FX: BA [bam]
151.3 FX: ZA [whoosh]
151.4 FX: SUTO [landing lightly]
151.5 FX: HIHIIN [neigh]

153.1 FX: BA [pushing curtains]
153.2 FX: PIKU [twitch]
153.3 nut: KOTSUN [kick]

154.4 FX: KASHAN [clank]
FX: KOLO KOLO [roll roll]

155.1 FX: KOLO KOLO [roll roll]
155.4 FX: ZUKI [ouch]

157.2 FX: GAKU GAKU [tremble tremble]
157.4 FX: BASA BASA [flap flap]

CHAPTER FIFTY-FOUR: THE DEPTHS OF FEAR

160.1 FX: KA [scorching heat]
160.2 FX: ZAWA ZAWA [chatter chatter]
160.3 FX: HIHIIN [neigh]

161.1 FX: SU [swoosh]
161.4 FX: KAPO KAPO [clop clop]

162.1 FX: KAPO [clop]
162.2 FX: KAPO [clop]

163.5 FX: SHULU [clench]

165.3 FX: BASHA BASHA [splash splash]

166.2 FX: PASA [clothing falling to the floor]
166.4 FX: BASHAN [splash]

167.1 FX: BASHA BASHA [splash splash]
167.4 FX: GOSHI GOSHI [rub rub]
167.5 FX: BASHAN [splash]

168.5 FX: KA [scorching heat]

170.4 FX: HYUUU [wind blowing]

172.2 FX: BA [whoosh]

179.2 FX: ZUKI [pang]

182.1 FX: PACHI PACHI [crackle crackle]
182.5 FX: ZAWA [rustle]

185.2 FX: GALA [crumble]
185.3 FX: ZUZAZA [slide]
FX: GALA GALA GALA [crumble crumble crumble]
185.4 FX: KALA [stumble]
185.5 FX: ZUKI [pang]

187.1 FX: ZAKU ZAKU [crunch crunch]
187.3 FX: ZAKU [crunch]

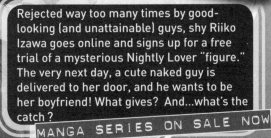

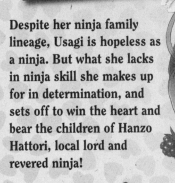

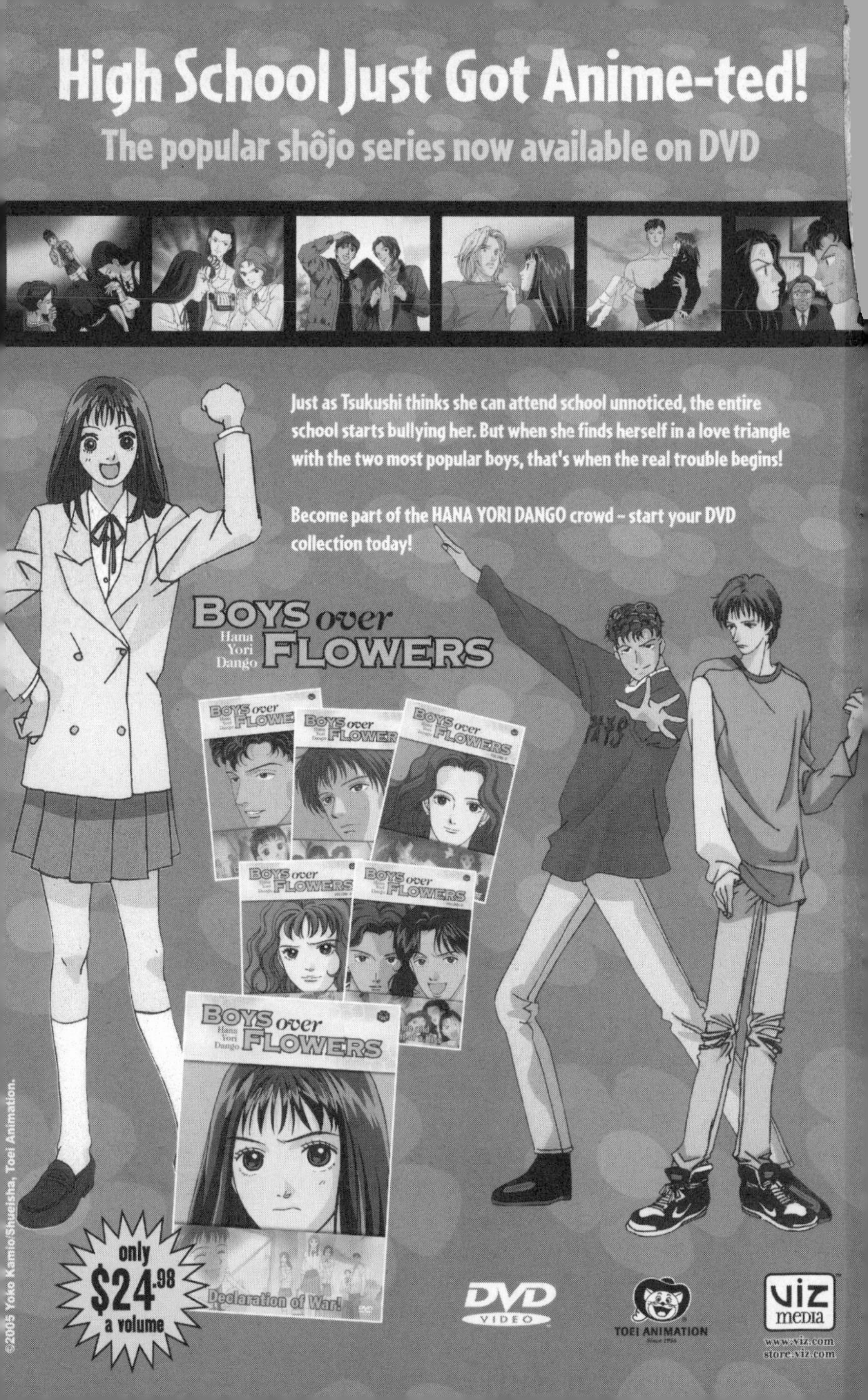
High School Just Got Anime-ted!
The popular shôjo series now available on DVD
Just as Tsukushi thinks she can attend school unnoticed, the entire school starts bullying her. But when she finds herself in a love triangle with the two most popular boys, that's when the real trouble begins!
Become part of the HANA YORI DANGO crowd – start your DVD collection today!
BOYS over FLOWERS
Hana Yori Dango
only $24.98 a volume
Declaration of War!
DVD VIDEO
TOEI ANIMATION
viz media
www.viz.com
store.viz.com
©2005 Yoko Kamio/Shueisha, Toei Animation.

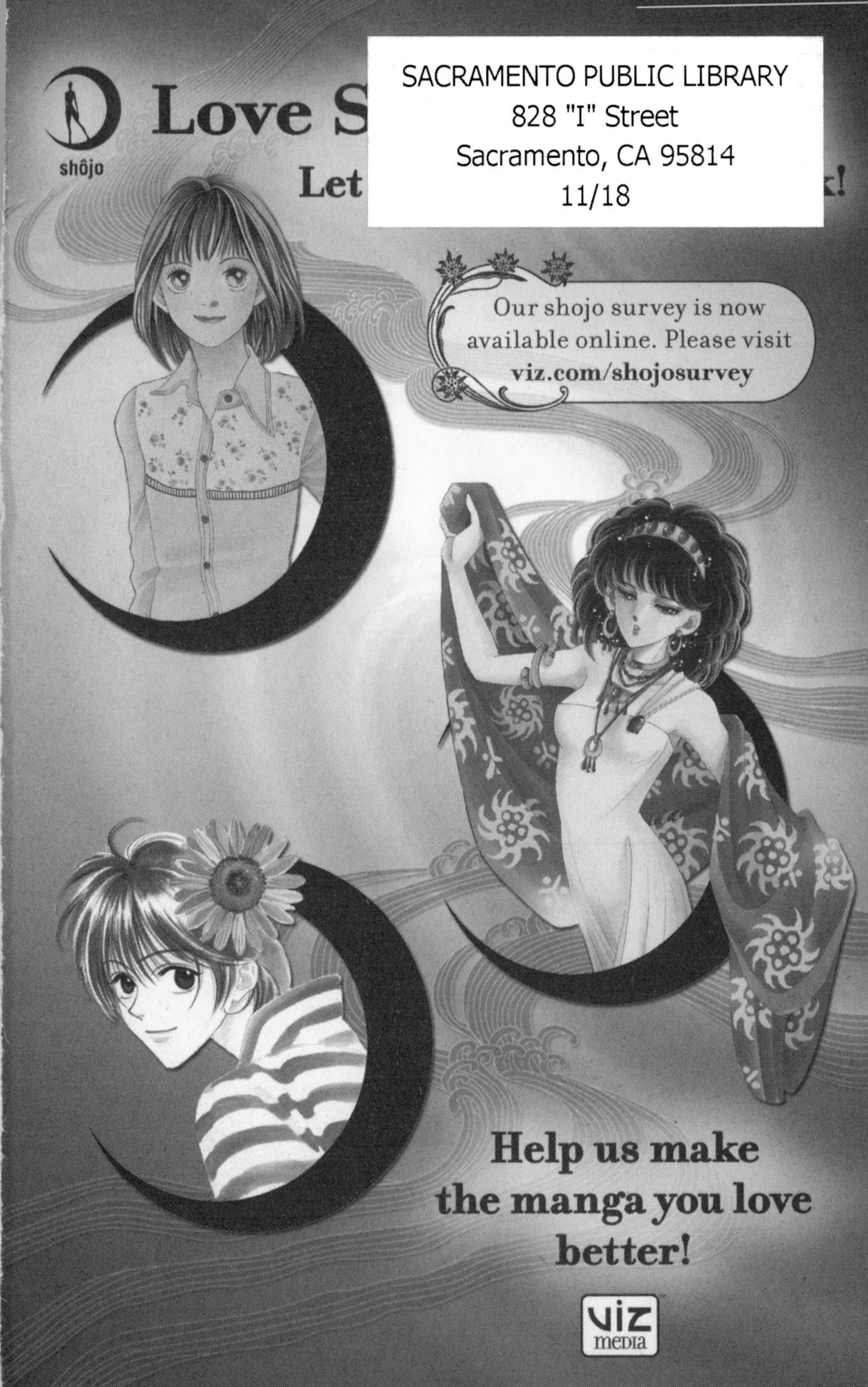
shôjo
Love S
Let
k!
Our shojo survey is now available online. Please visit viz.com/shojosurvey
Help us make the manga you love better!
VIZ MEDIA